E. Thiessen

C0-AZW-170

PSYCHOLOGY AND ETHICAL DEVELOPMENT

by R. S. Peters
Authority, Responsibility and Education
Ethics and Education

PSYCHOLOGY AND ETHICAL DEVELOPMENT

A collection of articles on psychological theories
ethical development and human understanding

R. S. PETERS

Professor of the Philosophy of Education
University of London Institute of Education

London
GEORGE ALLEN & UNWIN LTD
Ruskin House   Museum Street

First published in 1974

This book is copyright under the Berne Convention. All rights are reserved. Apart from any fair dealing for the purpose of private study, research, criticism or review, as permitted under the Copyright Act, 1956, no part of this publication may be reproduced, stored in a retrieval system, or transmitted, in any form or by any means, electronic, electrical, chemical, mechanical, optical, photocopying, recording or otherwise, without the prior permission of the copyright owner. Enquiries should be addressed to the publishers.

© George Allen & Unwin 1974

ISBN   0 04 150049 0 hardback
        0 04 150050 4 paperback

Printed in Great Britain
in 10 point Times Roman type by
Alden & Mowbray Ltd
at the Alden Press, Oxford

'But the effect of her being on those around her was incalculably diffusive; for the growing good of the world is partly dependent on unhistoric acts; and that things are not so ill with you and me as they might have been, is half owing to the number who lived faithfully a hidden life, and rest in unvisited tombs.'

George Eliot, *Middlemarch*. Concluding sentence

CONTENTS

CONTENTS 11

Part Four: BIOGRAPHICAL BACKGROUND

PREFACE

This collection is put together basically out of self-defence. I often receive requests for non-existent offprints of articles. I also receive requests to reprint articles in other people's collections. So, in a breathing space provided by what, in more leisurely times, used to be called the Long Vacation, I decided to assemble some articles in a collection of my own.

These articles are therefore selected both because they seem to be the ones most in demand and so that in themselves they form some kind of organic whole. I have omitted (a) the work which I have done in ethics and social philosophy, most of which can be found in *Ethics and Education* (London: Allen & Unwin, 1966), (b) more popular talks put together in *Authority, Responsibility and Education* (London: Allen & Unwin, 1959, revised and enlarged edition, 1973), and (c) those covered by my *The Concept of Motivation* (London: Routledge & Kegan Paul, 1958), and by my book on *Hobbes* (Harmondsworth: Penguin, 1956, reprinted with minor revisions in the Peregrine edition in 1967).

Every academic is indebted to his teachers and colleagues, though some academics acknowledge this more explicitly than others. In my early career in 'pure' philosophy I was most indebted to Sir Karl Popper and to Alec Mace. In the gestation period of my Ph.D. thesis on 'The Logic of Psychological Enquiries' I was in despair about philosophy, bogged down in W. E. Johnson's *Logic* and in interminable seminars about sense-data (referred to affectionately as 'the little animals' by Sir Alfred Ayer, at whose feet I also sat) and other minds (that marathon series of articles in *Mind* by John Wisdom). John Passmore breezed aggressively into this atmosphere of solipsistic frustration and settled himself in Mace's and Ayer's seminars. I got to know him quite well and was heartened by the breadth of his interest in and knowledge about psychological and social issues and impressed by the calibre of his scholarship. He said to me very early on during his visit: 'These sense-data are a scholastic legacy of Descartes. Go over to the London School of Economics and try another point of view from Karl Popper.' I did – and the heavens cleared again. All my old excitement for philosophy returned. Popper was a magnificent lecturer and the power and range of his intellect was exhilarating. I also attended Sir Karl's post-graduate seminar for three years and learnt from him more than I can say. Popper's stature as a philosopher has only recently been widely appreciated since the publication of Bryan Magee's book. Mercifully Sir Karl is still alive to enjoy this recognition. I was one of many who attended and who were greatly influenced by him without becoming one of his disciples. In acknowledgment, therefore, of this indebtedness to him I thought it appropriate to start off this collection with one of my earliest articles, on 'Observationalism in Psychology'. This article, which was a précis of part of my Ph.D. thesis, was a critique of current trends in scientific psychology from the standpoint of Sir Karl Popper's philosophy of science.

Alec Mace taught me most of the psychology which I did not learn the hard way by reading it up for myself. He also supervised my Ph.D. thesis. I then worked for fifteen years, first as a lecturer and then as a reader in the departments of philosophy and psychology at Birkbeck College, University of London – that marvellous institution for those who come to discover as mature students the subjects which really interest them. Alec Mace was Professor of Psychology during that period and did much, both by his humane approach to psychology as a science and by his democratic form of administration, to establish it as one of the best in the country. I was, needless to say, enormously influenced by his views on explanation in psychology and on motivation. The fact that, to a large extent, I was critical both of his flirtation with Behaviourism and of his homeostatic theory of motivation, and wrote my *The Concept of Motivation* in part as an exercise in 'killing the father', is in no way inconsistent with my indebtedness to him. Mace, in spite of my persistent badgering, never managed to revise his Tarner lectures on teleological causation to a degree which, in his view made them fit for publication. He therefore never quite achieved the fame in philosophy which some of his work deserved. This was a great pity; for his lectures would have provided an interesting and more psychologically informed complement to Gilbert Ryle's *The Concept of Mind*, which influenced us all so much in the post-war period. Marjorie Mace's collection of his writings, which has recently been published, was long overdue. In acknowledgement of my indebtedness to Alec Mace, I include in this collection my contribution to the 'festschrift' on his retirement entitled *C. A. Mace: A Symposium*, which was edited by his secretary, Vida Carver.

When I moved over into the field of philosophy of education I found very little which was particularly helpful in the literature save the perceptive writings of Louis Arnaud Reid, my predecessor in the chair at the University of London Institute of Education. The exceptions were the work of Israel Scheffler, who had stimulated my interest in the field by getting me invited to Harvard in 1961, and the work of Michael Oakeshott. In *Social Principles and the Democratic State* (London: Allen & Unwin, 1959), which I published after five years' work with Stanley Benn, we were critical in a measured sort of way of Oakeshott's traditionalism in political theory. I found, however, that his writings on education were stimulating and suggestive, as is clear from my inaugural lecture at the University of London Institute on 'Education as Initiation'. I felt strongly that, even though I disagreed with many of Oakeshott's characteristic theses, he was an eminently educated man who really knew what education was about. I therefore have included in this collection my contribution to the 'festschrift' presented on his retirement from the chair of politics at the London School of Economics, which was compiled under the title of *Politics and Experience* (Cambridge: C.U.P., 1968) by two of his former students, Preston King and B. C. Parekh.

Amongst my contemporaries those who have helped me most by their friendship, discussion and critical comments, have been Ruth Saw, then head of the Department of Philosophy at Birkbeck College and later Professor of Aesthetics, David Hamlyn (now Professor of Philosophy at Birkbeck College) and A. Phillips Griffiths (now Professor of Philosophy at the University of Warwick), who were colleagues of mine for about ten years at Birkbeck College. In the same category come Israel Scheffler, with whom I worked as Visiting Professor at the Harvard Graduate School of Education, and Paul Hirst, who was for many years in my department at the University of London Institute, and with whom I collaborated to produce *The Logic of Education* (London: Routledge & Kegan Paul, 1970), and who is now Professor of Education at Cambridge University. In the same category, too, are, of course, Stanley Benn, now Professorial Fellow at the Australian University, John Passmore, the Professor of Philosophy at ANU, and Geoffrey Mortimore, whom I got to know during my period there as Visiting Fellow in 1969.

Recently, in 1972, during my visit to the University of Canterbury at Christchurch, New Zealand, I was privileged to work with Ivan Snook, who is doing so much to develop philosophy of education in New Zealand, and to enjoy both his friendship and critical company and that of Geoffrey Nuthall and Philip Lawrence who, in my view, are two of the best psychologists whom I have encountered in the field of educational theory. I found a constant source of stimulation in interdisciplinary explorations, between Ivan Snook and myself on the one hand and the two psychologists on the other, without tiresome demarcation disputes about what were psychological and what were philosophical issues.

Finally my abiding interest in problems on the borderline between philosophy and psychology has been continually advanced by Ted Mischel, who is Professor of Philosophy at the State University of New York at Binghampton. He has worked tactfully and indefatigably over the past six years in organising what Max Black recently referred to, somewhat facetiously, as the 'Binghampton Circle'. This consists of a group of American and English philosophers and psychologists who meet every other year in the U.S. to discuss such borderline issues. Ted Mischel has edited three volumes which record the details of our deliberations to date. They are *Human Action* (New York: Academic Press, 1969), *Cognitive Development and Epistemology* (New York: Academic Press, 1971) and *Understanding Other Persons* (Oxford: Basil Blackwell, 1974). Three of the articles in this collection have appeared in these volumes.

The contents of the collection tell more or less their own story. The first section on 'Psychological Theories and Rational Psychology' represents expositions and critiques of those psychological theories which have interested me most, both in general and in their application to education. These are the theories of the Behaviourists, of Freud, and of Piaget. The pieces on Behaviourism are generally critical. The article on 'Freud's Theory', on the other hand, is a dead-pan exposition which I was asked to produce for a centenary volume on Freud. My brief was to expound his leading ideas in logical rather than in historical sequence, which is the more usual form of exposition. My more critical comments on Freud, though of a constructive character because of my admiration for his Copernican revolution in psychological theory, are contained in Chapter Three of *The Concept of Motivation*. My leanings in psychological theory, as will be gleaned from reading many of the articles in this collection, are towards a judicious blend of Piagetian and Freudian theory which, in my view, are complementary to each other.

At the end of Part One there is an article which explores the general relationship between psychology and teaching. There are also two reviews of books by psychologists who have achieved notoriety by applying their theories to education. These are selected explicitly because they represent opposed positions in both psychological and educational theory. On the one hand there is B. F. Skinner's directive, instruction-based approach, supported by extrinsic incentives; on the other hand there is Carl R. Rogers's client- or student-centred, facilitating of learning approach, which stresses intrinsic motivation and good personal relationships. These are two outstanding examples of the traditional and progressive approaches to education, based on opposed psychological theories, against which my own views both on psychology and on educational theory are to be defined. I am also reprinting Carl Rogers's letter in reply to my review.

The second section on 'Ethical Development' records, in historical sequence, a series of attempts to become clearer about moral development which has always interested me in both a theoretical and practical way. Again the papers deal largely with borderline theories between ethics and developmental psychology.

The third section on 'Education and Human Understanding' represents some more speculative and less analytic musings on problems to do with understanding other people and the role of the humanities in general. The first piece on 'Personal Understanding and Personal Relationships' is relatively straightforward – an attempt to provide a new look at problems of understanding others by a combination of the psychology of Verstehen, work previously done by myself on personal relationships, and the application of the Piaget–Kohlberg stage theory to a new sphere.

The second piece on 'Subjectivity and Standards' is written in a less analytic style for a philosophically non-specialist audience consisting of university teachers such as Lionel Knights, Barbara Hardy, Denys Harding, Ben Morris, Marjorie Reeves and John Coulson, who were gathered together by Roy Niblett to discuss problems to do with the role of the humanities in the universities. It attempts to set the role of the humanities against a wider background of religion, ethics and metaphysics. This represents a return to preoccupations with religion which first started me off on systematic philosophy.

It is customary, nowadays, for collections to include biographical material. So this is covered in Part Four. For the basic background I have, with his kind permission, reprinted Peter Hobson's biographical Commentary which he compiled for a collection of his own (P. Hobson (Ed.), *Theories of Education: Studies of Significant Innovation in Western Educational Thought*. New York: Wiley, 1974).

My own contributions to this section are two hitherto unpublished broadcast talks. The first is a piece that I did about George Orwell, who was our holiday tutor and who had a marked influence on us when we were boys. I include this because I am often asked for

off-prints and it probably reveals as much about me as about George
Orwell.

The second is the first broadcast talk which I ever gave – a contribution to a series entitled 'I Was Twenty Then' produced by
Mrs B. C. Horton of the B.B.C. The idea was to put on four talks by
people who were twenty in 1925, 1930, 1935 and 1940, in which they
reminisced about how the world looked to them at that age. Mine
was the last in the series. I was recommended for this role, I believe,
by someone in the Workers' Educational Association, in whose cause
I was very active at that time. I owe a great deal, both for this talk
and for the transfer of her training to later talks, to Mrs Horton. The
collection is entitled *Psychology and Ethical Development*. This piece
records a stage of my own.

My motive for including these more personal pieces at the end of
an academic collection of this sort is not purely one of vanity. It is
also done, like the production of this collection generally, out of
self-defence. It has become fashionable for 'sociologists of knowledge' to give a social diagnosis of the views of those who not only
write books, but whose books are read by others than specialists in
their particular field. I have always been mildly hostile to this practice; for I have always taken very seriously Popper's maxim for
discussion that one should ignore the man and listen to the argument.
But when this type of exercise is perpetrated with scant regard to
what a person actually says, and to plain facts about his personality
and life, as has been done with one or two such attacks on my works,
it has become something rather different from a brilliant and amusing
sortie in academic gossip, such as Ernest Gellner's *Word and Things*
(Harmondsworth: Penguin, 1968). It is for this reason, amongst
others, that I have seen fit to end this collection with these personal
pieces. At least others who may indulge in such sociological speculation will not then have the excuse that there is no published material
out of which such a case can be constructed.

There are other criticisms of a more responsible sort of the analytic
mode of philosophising, which I have taken as a form of encouragement in deciding to publish this collection. The outstanding example
of this type of criticism is that of Abraham Edel, an anthropologist
of repute as well as a philosopher, who, in my opinion, wrote the
most perceptive critical review of *Ethics and Education* which I have
come across (*Studies in Philosophy and Education*, Vol. VI, No. 1,
Winter 1968). In this some of his remarks are worth quoting
because they cover the philosophical method often followed in this
collection:

'Professor Peters leads off in a fashion that is familiar these days, with a genuflection to the revolution in philosophy. . . . This is, of course, sheer ritual, like an old-line Behaviourist's preliminary invocation to the protons and electrons before going on to forget about them, or an old-line Soviet philosopher's initial bow to dialectics. . . . The shibboleths of the analytic movement prevent Professor Peters from facing his own philosophical outlook directly. But it is not this alone. Two other factors seem to be relevant. One is that on the whole British education in the older universities has been remarkably good in developing an intellectual outlook: Peters thus takes the view of what is worth-while for granted, and submits it to little analysis, seeing the task as extending it to larger groups rather than as reconstructing it. The second factor is the pluralistic historicism that is inherent in the whole British analytic movement – language as a long-time growth with many ramifications so that it cannot be reduced to formalistic principles. (The aversion of the common-law mentality to the rationalism of a Napoleonic code is the obvious model.) Now such historicism invariably sees its opponents as grandiose philosophers, and itself as common sense. . . . It creates a conceptual order with subtlety. Perhaps it came from a sensitive attention to the terms and their use. But I rather suspect that it was enriched by Professor Peters's own immersion in psychology and especially his concern with the varieties of models in that discipline, with the role of cognitive elements in the emotions, with the relation of purpose and intellect, and a whole host of relevant issues. At any rate, when he moves on to the second chapter, he begins to think more directly in terms of models, such as the moulding model or the growth model. He looks to the underlying psychological accounts of the development of the mind, rejects atomistic empiricism, and calls attention to the social character of the development of mind, referring even to Hegel's notion of 'objective mind' and Marx's stress on the social determinants of individual consciousness. Perhaps eventually the great-grandchildren of the revolution will come to realise that questions which once took an onotological grab and then an epistemological garb and at times a pragmatic garb are not to be avoided just because they now take a linguistic garb.'

In my reply to Edel's review which constitutes, in part, an apologia for the type of method which so many adopt in tackling a philosophical problem, I said:

'When I read Professor Edel's sympathetic account of my book I was reminded of the way in which I was greeted recently by an old philosophical friend of mine who had moved over into social science in a neighbouring institution. Instead of asking how I was, he asked me how my symptoms were. I was a bit puzzled by this strange form of salutation and asked for elucidation. He said: "Oh, I mean your concepts – the ones that are troubling you at the moment." I was at a loss to know quite what to reply to such a salutation in rather the same way as I am at a loss to know quite what to reply to Professor Edel's diagnosis of my philosophical condition.

'I belong to the perhaps old-fashioned school of thought that maintains that arguments matter, that one should listen carefully to what people say and consider what grounds they produce for the positions which they adopt. In philosophy generally, too, I hold, and make clear in my book, that conceptual analysis (whatever that may be) is only a part of philosophy and that those who concentrate on it should constantly ask themselves whether anything of importance depends upon the distinctions that are being made. I also make the point, especially in relation to the concepts of "education", "respect", and "punishment" that ultimately nothing depends on the analysis which we give. Supposing, for instance, we conclude that "punishment" is applicable only to cases where pain is inflicted on those who have committed offences. The question still remains whether there should be punishment both in so far as this involves the infliction of pain and in so far as this must be inflicted on the guilty. Arguments have to be produced on both counts for punishing people, even granted that this is what "punishment" implies. . . . Indeed I would regard an appeal to existing usage as a way of settling substantive issues as the most subtle form of the naturalistic fallacy. Similarly in the main ethical sections of the book I appeal to transcendental arguments but make clear that this is not a linguistic type of argument; it appeals to presuppositions that lie behind the development of differentiated forms of thought that are enshrined in public discourse. Was Kant a linguistic philosopher in Professor Edel's understanding of that stereotype?

'I can only ask him to read my book a bit more carefully and to abandon his rather undiscriminating attitude to "the analytical movement", for he misrepresents my actual position about the role of conceptual analysis in philosophy. In so far as he correctly appreciates that the main philosophical problems in ethics are problems of justification rather than of analysis he dubs this approach as "one of the types that has emerged in the later phases of the analytical revolution". This is surely arrant nonsense unless the "analytical revolution" is to be traced back to Socrates. For what moral philosopher worth his salt has not been concerned with this problem? Professor Edel's approach reminds me of that of many modern philosophers infected by sociology and moral relativism. When confronted by crucial questions of justification they shift the discussion to the customs of the Azande! This is parallel to some modern approaches to the philosophy of religion. Awkward questions about the truth of religious beliefs are side-tracked by combining a study of comparative religion with an analysis of the role of religious belief in a way of life. Indeed if one asks questions about the truth of such beliefs one is sometimes made to feel a very crude fellow indeed. I have always thought that, both in morals and in religion, the questions that matter most relate to the grounds of belief. In both these spheres I remain unrepentantly a crude fellow.

'. . . Professor Edel will be interested and relieved to learn that I am now at the beginning of a complementary book to *Ethics and Education* which is to be called something like *Education and the Concept of Man*. In this notions such as "development", "mental health", and "self-realisation" will be examined, as well as more mundane matters to do with motivation, emotion and habits. I have a strong suspicion, however, that, if Professor Edel ever reviews that book, he will suggest that what merits it may possess derive from my long-standing interest in psychology rather than from my adherence to the tenets of the British analytical movement, whatever they may be! But perhaps Professor Edel might note that philosophers in this tradition, such as Hobbes, Locke, Hume, Mill and Russell, were also acutely interested in problems connected with psychology and politics, to which they too were no doubt introduced in their "British education in the older universities". Indeed in British education generally it is regarded as a bad thing to study philosophy on its own; it usually forms part of some kind of joint degree course.'

In this volume I try to draw together the fruits of labours on psychology and developmental theories, which, together with the study of ethics and social philosophy, are the main determinants of my intellectual point of view and of my philosophy of education. The articles bear witness to what Professor Edel calls my 'immersion in psychology'. My hope is that a philosophical approach to psychology has done something to throw light on the questions which have absorbed me more than any others, namely those to do with how a man should live and with the explanation of human behaviour.

University of London Institute of Education
August 1973

ACKNOWLEDGEMENTS

These articles are reprinted with acknowledgement to the editors and publishers of the books and journals concerned. The details of their source are given in small print in the Table of Contents.

ACKNOWLEDGMENTS

Part One

PSYCHOLOGICAL THEORIES
AND
RATIONAL PSYCHOLOGY

1

OBSERVATIONALISM IN PSYCHOLOGY

INTRODUCTION

It now seems to be quite widely accepted that philosophical theories
have a second-order character in that they are either descriptions
of or recommendations about the procedures of first-order activities
like scientific research and moral behaviour. Often, so it seems to
me, these procedural reviews have had an effect on the procedures of
scientists and moralists. Philosophers, whether wittingly or unwittingly, have contributed to creating or changing rules of procedure in their endeavours to understand them. Most people,
with the examples of Kantians and Utilitarians in mind, would
concede this point with regard to morality, but they might feel that
it was rather far-fetched with regard to science. Surely, they might
argue, scientists pay scant attention to the methodologists; they just
get on with their job of testing hypotheses without worrying much
about what the methodologists say. Now this may be a tenable point
of view with regard to a lot of workers in the advanced physical
sciences, but there is evidence to suggest that the practice of many
social scientists and psychologists is or has been strongly influenced
by certain philosophical assumptions about method. Professor
Popper, for instance, in his 'Open Society', tries to reveal and combat
the influence of 'historicism' on social science. He also attacks frequently what he calls 'observationalism' or 'inductivism'. In this
article I want to support his general attack on 'observationalism' by
suggesting that this philosophical description of scientific method
has in fact exerted an influence on the development of a particular
science, psychology – an influence which has not been altogether
fruitful.

1   WHAT IS OBSERVATIONALISM?

The view, which Professor Popper refers to as 'observationalism', started with Aristotle and became influential after Francis Bacon in the writings of those philosphers of science who tried to provide an alternative to the Cartesian account of the acquisition of knowledge. They tended to share Descartes' rationalism in thinking that there is an infallible method for acquiring certain or highly probable knowledge but differed radically in their account of the required recipe. They put a salutary stress on observation as opposed to deduction from axioms and substituted for Descartes' simple natures, sensory atoms collected by simply looking at Nature. They maintained not only that scientific laws were descriptions of invariable sequences of these sensory atoms but that things also, including ourselves and others, were clusters of such sense-data built up, as a matter of psychological fact, by correlating such atomic sense-data. This psychological description and the psychology which developed from it, though later abandoned by sense-datum theorists, was a way of reinforcing the view of scientific method which succeeded that of Descartes. Locke and Hume created a psychology dictated largely by their epistemological preoccupation. Locke's passive mind, for instance, was a way of assuring us that we could not make mistakes about the simple ideas which provided a solid foundation for knowledge. His preoccupation with the certainty of knowledge influenced his quest for its 'original'. Hume's isolated and incorrigible impressions served a similar epistemological function. Locke and Hume established a tradition both of psychology and philosophy and the psychological tradition was strongly influenced by their philosophical views about the correct way of obtaining knowledge.

The inductive account of scientific method, which is an alternative way of stating observationalism, postulated the careful and meticulous collection of data by 'pupils of Nature', the cautious generalisation which must not go beyond the data, and the 'interpretation' which emerged when a judicious man like Francis Bacon surveyed the tables of classified data. This picture of the scientist in action, combined with the Kantian aphorism that a discipline is as scientific as it contains mathematics, led to the tacit acceptance of the view that the scientist proceeds by observing events in Nature, measuring them, noticing correlations or laws between the sets of measurements, and finally relating laws under theories.

There emerged, therefore, two connected presuppositions about science which had a considerable effect on psychology. In the first place it was assumed that a science is to be distinguished by the special kind of 'data' or 'subject-matter' from which it starts. In the second place it was assumed that a science must start from impeccable 'data', e.g. measurements – if theories were to emerge at the end. Let us briefly assess these two presuppositions before illustrating their effect on psychology.

Few would deny that emphasis on 'data' and on 'subject-matter', in so far as it was a way of stressing the observational basis of science, was a salutary antidote to Cartesianism because it brought out, if in rather a misleading way, that scientific hypotheses are *tested* by observation. The objection to Locke, Bacon and Hume is that they maintained that the scientist must *start from* observations. This tended to make people neglect the important of hypotheses in science. Instead, in psychology, for instance, there were endless arguments about what the 'subject-matter' of psychology was. No doubt there is a quite harmless and usual sense of 'subject-matter' in which, on any account of scientific enquiry, petrologists, ornithologists and astronomers can be said to have a 'subject-matter' of their own. Some scientists single out certain classes of objects and ask questions about rocks rather than rooks or stars. But this rough and ready distinction in terms of objects of interest is not much help in the sciences of man which are all concerned in one way or another with the behaviour of human organisms. For practical and didactic purposes the sciences of man can be sorted out by reference to the sort of questions asked about man and the types of procedures used in answering such questions. This facilitates the organisation of university departments, enables examination syllabuses to be drawn up, and ensures that rabbits are not laid out on the benches of the chemistry laboratory or microscopes in the geography room. But nothing of *theoretical* importance depends upon such divisions. The social scientist or psychologist who does research as well as teaching is a student of problems, not of subject-matters. Some of his problems cut across all usual clear-cut distinctions of 'subject-matter'. Neuro-physiologists, for instance, are now making discoveries about the pre-frontal lobes which are exceedingly relevant to the kind of problems with which Freud was confronted – the aetiology of changes in social dispositions. A working scientist cannot rule out possible answers to questions because they are not on the syllabus. If, therefore, we find psychologists seriously perturbed about what their 'subject-matter' is we may reasonably suspect them of being haunted by the old Baconian picture of the scientist who must start from certain specific and clear-cut data.

Again, on any view of scientific activity, a prominent place must be found for the part played by measurement, the main function of which is to facilitate the testing of hypotheses. Quantitative techniques enable scientists to answer more exactly questions unearthed by cruder qualitative methods. But there is no need to bring this out in the observationalist manner by saying that the scientist *starts from* measurements or 'operations'. This methodological rule was certainly not observed by people like Freud and McDougall who made greater contributions to the advance of psychological theory than any of those who became preoccupied with obtaining quantitative 'data'. As Köhler says: 'If we wish to imitate the physical sciences we must not imitate them in their contemporary, most developed form. We must imitate them in their historical youth, when their state of development was. comparable to our own at the present time . . . let us imitate the physical sciences, but intelligently.'[1] Some psychologists, for instance Clark Hull, being wise to the proper function of measurement in the development of explanatory theory, have constructed systems of measurement alongside the development of testable hypotheses.[2] But this has not been the case with all psychologists who have become preoccupied with measurement. Is it not plausible to suggest that much of this premature quantification was a consequence of observationalist presuppositions?

In this article I shall endeavour to substantiate my case about the influence of observationalism on the practice and methodological discussions of psychologists by citing some historical examples. The case of measurement in psychology might provide detailed evidence; but it would need a separate article for adequate treatment. Similarly a separate article would be needed for the case of the 'understanding' psychologists who thought that psychology must be a branch of history rather than science because of the peculiar and unique 'data' from which we must start in studying human beings, or for that of some Gestalt psychologists who stressed the importance of starting from 'direct experience' (e.g. Köhler) or 'the behavioural environment' (e.g. Koffka). I intend, however, to confine myself to the controversy between Behaviourists and Introspectionists and to the development of the operationist school in psychology, these two examples being clear illustrations of the influence of observationalism.

In a thesis of this kind there is a great danger of appearing to claim too much. I do not want to deny for a moment that there were other reasons for the development of these 'schools' of psychology which others, like Woodworth,[3] have brought out. But I do not think that any of those who have treated comparatively the different 'schools' of psychology have drawn attention to the common, and in my view mistaken, methodological assumptions without which the almost fanatical fission of psychology into 'schools' need never have arisen. 'Schools' of psychology do not reflect simply different interests or rival hypotheses. If this were the case they would be a healthy symptom. They reflect, as well, rival recipes about how to do psychology. How weary we get of that introductory chapter to psychology books which maintains either that the enquiry to follow is perfectly scientific or that the enquiry to follow is the only useful sort of psychological enquiry. This assumption that there is a magic method for advancing a science is itself a philosophical prejudice dating back to Descartes and Bacon. The effect on psychology of the particular recipe, that scientists must start from the right sort of data, I shall now proceed to illustrate.

2 OBSERVATIONALISM IN PSYCHOLOGY

(a) The Behaviourist–Introspectionist Controversy

One of the most violent disputes about method in psychology was the dispute at the beginning of this century about psychological data. There were heated disagreements between 'schools' of psychology who maintained that other people's enquiries were vitiated by the use of data which were scientifically suspect. Lashley, for instance, relegated introspection 'to a subordinate place as an example of the pathology of scientific method'.[4] Underlying these disputes about data was the observationalist assumption that scientists must *start from* data. It therefore became a major dispute of policy as to which data were to be so favoured. 'We are agreed, I suppose', said Titchener, 'that scientific method may be summed up in the single word "observation"; the only way to work in science is to observe those phenomena which form the subject-matter of science.'[5] And Watson said: 'You will find, then, the Behaviourist working like any other scientist. His sole object is to gather facts about behaviour – verify his data – subject them both to logic and mathematics (the tool of every scientist).'[6] Do not both these statements imply an observationalist view of science? Could not Behaviourists be regarded as deriving their name from their determination to *start from* overt behaviour or visual data instead of from introspective data? Is not their assumption that the scientist must decide what data he must start from before he can begin his enquiries? Is he, for instance, to start from 'tangible and approachable' rats in mazes or from images and 'raw feels' or the 'direct experience' of Kohler?

The Behaviourists accepted what has often been called the Book of Nature view of science just as the Introspectionists did. They were opposed to introspection because, in their view, the Introspectionists were laboriously perusing blank pages of the Book and mistaking their own finger prints for Nature's secrets. The plight of the Introspectionists was due, in the opinion of the Behaviourists, to their having inherited from philosophy a dud subject-matter. 'Today', says Watson, 'the Behaviourist can safely throw out a real challenge to the subjective psychologists – Show us that you have a possible method, indeed that you have a legitimate subject-matter!'[7] Hunter, too, echoes this refrain: 'Psychology, unlike the other sciences, has not found it possible to continue with the subject-matter bequeathed it by philosophy.'[8]

What, then, was the remedy proposed by the Behaviourists? Watson can be construed as saying that we must, with the example of the abortive discussions about 'imageless thought' in mind, be most meticulous about the data which we feed into the machine of logic and mathematics, like napkins in a washing-machine. Otherwise the machine may grind importantly and 'imageless thoughts', which no one can spot properly, may emerge at the other end like soap-bubbles. The same disastrous results could not possibly be obtained if palpable data like rats and terrified babies were fed in at the start. Similarly Hunter's long-winded homilies on the superiority of his new 'anthroponomy' to the old psychology is simply riddled with pointless discussions about subject-matter. The Book of Nature view comes out clearly in such passages as these:

'Anthroponomy thus takes its place among the sciences which study specific objects in the environment. Here also belong such disciplines as botany which studies plants, geology which specialises upon the inorganic structure of the earth, and physiology, where the functional activities of the various structures of the body become the subject-matter for investigation.'[9]

His objection to the Introspectionists is that in studying 'consciousness' they were just cataloguing the environment of man –'such things as roses, books, configurations and meolodies almost exactly as did the philosophers Berkeley and Hume'.[10] But though he is shrewd enough to remark 'I think that one great reason for the continued, although apparently waning, popularity of psychology lies in the belief that psychologists are conducting Cook's tours of experience',[11] he never questions the basic presupposition which he shared with the Introspectionists that scientists start from 'data' or a specific 'subject-matter'. His concern is rather to define an alternative subject-matter for anthroponomy – man rather than man's environment. Thus there was no radical criticism of the sort of dicta in which Titchener specialised like

'All science is talk, but not all talk is science. . . . Science is orderly and methodical talk, talk that gives a complete and exhaustive account of the subject, talk in which no details are left out which can help us to explain the things talked about. . . . The science of mind must give a complete account and an orderly, well-arranged account of its subject, keeping the facts steadily in view and never running off into mere speculation.'[12]

Professor Mace, in a yet unpublished article,[13] shows in detail how Titchener mistook philosophical analysis for science. Did not the Behaviourists, in their turn, mistake methodological sermons for science?

In view of the similarity of their methodological assumptions it is not surprising that the systems of the early Behaviourists, when 'behaviour' had been substituted for 'consciousness' bore a marked similarity to that of the Introspectionists.[14] Wundt started from consciousness as his subject-matter, Watson from behaviour. By the method of experimental observation and analysis Wundt arrived at sensations and Watson at reflexes. These were bound together by principles of synthesis, in Wundt's case the laws of association, in Watson's case the laws of conditioning. In both cases we find the search for simples deriving from Descartes and Locke and a more detailed rendering of Hume's 'gentle force'.

The Behaviouristic recipe, as one might expect, produced no startling results. Objective methods had been practised for a long time by working psychologists before the Behaviourists presented them as a key to Nature's secrets. In the psychophysical methods, the experiments done on memory and learning, and the conditioned response experiments of the Russians these methods had been used with success. As early as 1905 McDougall had defined psychology as 'the positive science of the conduct of living creatures' and rejected the usual definition of 'the science of mind' because he insisted on objective methods as well as introspection in the study of behaviour.[15] Even when we turn to a later Behaviourist like Tolman we find, in the main, a translation of existing assumptions into a rather cumbersome behaviouristic jargon. It is true that Tolman, in his *Purposive Behaviour in Animals and Men*, performed a valuable tidying up operation on McDougall by distinguishing between those 'drives' which have obvious initiating physiological conditions and terminating states of physiological quiescence and those which have not, by dealing in detail with the cognitive demands of the organism, by eliminating McDougall's introspectable quale as the criterion for distinguishing different instincts, and so on. Also, in making explicit the methodological device of the 'intervening variable' (drive, habit, demand, etc.) he turned out a lot of metaphysical lumber from the 'hormic' psychology. But it is difficult to find in Tolman a hypothesis which cannot also be found in the work of McDougall, Spearman, the Gestalt psychologists, and previous theories of learning. What is new is his appallingly cumbersome terminology which is dictated by his methodological recipe. Even Freudian assumptions appear in a chapter on 'Personality Mechanisms' decked out in Behaviourist trappings. The reader's job is mainly one of translation and he is often left to reflect that all this could be said without recourse to such pretentious jargon. In Tolman we find a philosophical *re*-description of what others assumed; we do not find many new explanations. Research seems almost a mere excuse for linguistic ingenuity.

Let it not be thought, however, that the Introspectionists and Behaviourists did not try to practise what they preached. There are cases where scientists indulge in a lot of methodological talk which is contradicted by their practice, e.g. anthropologists who claim to collect data about primitive tribes without making any assumptions about them. Certainly Titchener and the Introspectionists cannot be accused of this kind of inconsistency. They really took their methodology seriously and tried to study experiences as 'existences' without 'meanings' which were the concern of the logician. They literally tried to isolate pure 'sense-data'– a heroic undertaking. Their attempt to compile an inventory of the mind was a result of taking Locke's injunction to pursue 'the plain historical method' seriously. The sterility of traditional introspection derived not so much from the fact that they introspected (or gave retrospective reports on their own doings and feelings), but from the fact that they did this in order to compile an inventory rather than to test fruitful hypotheses. Observation was really regarded as 'the Alpha and the Omega of science'.[16]

Similarly, the Behaviourists avidly turned their gaze upon rats and

have more or less feasted their eyes upon them ever since. This concentration on animals renders most of what they say about human
beings programmatic. They are not, however, at all modest in issuing
promissory notes about the future. Hull, in his recent *Principles of
Behaviour*, is quite in keeping with the optimism of Behaviourists
generally when he forecasts a 'true behaviouristic science' concerning
individual and social behaviour, skills and their acquisition, problem-
solving and reasoning, social and ritual symbolism, economic and
familial behaviour, individual adaptive efficiency (intelligence),
formal educative processes, psychogenic disorders, social control
and delinquency, character and personality, culture and acculturation, magic and religious practices, custom, law and jurisprudence.'[17]
And all this without committing the grievous scientific sin of using a
subject's reports on his own doings and feelings as evidence! Such a
science may emerge. The proof of any scientific pudding lies in the
eating, not in the recipe for making the pudding. And that is precisely
my criticism of the Behaviourists – that they produced a recipe rather
than a new theory. Historically speaking Behaviourism was the
nemesis of Introspectionism. 'All limited methodologies have their
day. . . . There is a final epoch of endless wrangling over minor
questions.'[18] Psychology became, with the Introspectionists, more or
less identified with a technique of observation and the minor question
was hotly debated as to which kind of observation was to be endowed
with a halo. Hull's claim is that Behaviourism alone can save us from
the belles-lettres of the 'so-called social sciences'. Behaviourists did
not produce a plethora of fertile hypotheses. They did not claim that
their theories were better tested than other theories in the field or
that more facts could be deduced from them. As a matter of fact their
concentration on rats, dogs, cats and apes prevented them from
producing many hypotheses in which other psychologists and social
scientists were much interested. Their main principle of explanation
was as old as Hume. Their claim was rather than it was only by
pursuing a certain method, by starting from the 'behavioural data'
that scientifically fruitful theories could be obtained. Mind became,
as Pratt picturesquely puts it,[19] a 'verbal ghost' but the ghosts of
Descartes and Bacon materialised in the laryngeal motions of Watson
and his followers.

Now, though I have maintained that, historically speaking, Behaviourism was presented as a rationalist recipe for arriving at
scientifically respectable hypotheses by starting from impeccable
'behavioural data', I do not want to deny either that there were
other reasons for the emergence of this 'school' of psychology or

that their attack on introspection raises some interesting methodological cal issues which can be stated in a way which makes them independent of observationalism. If we reject not only observationalism but also the Cartesian view that there is an inner realm of the mental to be observed by special techniques, the question raised by the Behaviourists becomes the practical question of the reliance to be placed on a subject's own retrospective reports of his doings and feelings in testing hypotheses about human behaviour.[20] Though we might maintain that, in principle, there is little difference between my own reports on my feelings and doings and other people's reports on them, in practice, surely, I occupy rather a privileged position. Doctors would find their work rather laborious if they dispensed with symptoms as evidence and relied only on signs. Patients often make mistakes about themselves and sometimes have special motives for cooking the evidence; but we are not always inaccurate about our own doings and feelings any more than we are always in the position of the hypochondriac or malingerer. In trying to test, for example, a Freudian hypothesis about forgetting it would seem, *prima facie*, to be an unnecessary self-denying ordinance to refuse to accept as evidence the report of a subject to the effect that he had a name 'on the tip of his tongue' because he was reporting on his own tongue rather than on someone else's. Behaviourists have, in the main, confined their experiments to organisms which are incapable of giving retrospective reports on their own doings and feelings which might be used as evidence in testing hypotheses about them. So the use of introspective evidence has not presented itself as a practical problem in research. Whether Behaviourism, which I interpret as a self-denying ordinance imposed upon the testing of psychological hypotheses, is a wise or practicable prescription in testing more complicated hypotheses about human behaviour involving speech, sympathy and social conventions, is a question which falls outside the scope of this article. I have been concerned to suggest only that, historically speaking, the practice and methodological discussions of both Introspectionists and Behaviourists were much influenced by observationalism. I hope that my reference to explicit methodological dicta, to explicit preoccupation with subject matter, to similarity in principles of explanation, and to the influence of methodology on actual practice has been sufficient to substantiate this suggestion. Others have sufficiently dealt with different aspects of this long-standing controversy;[21] I only claim to have drawn attention to one aspect of it which, because it involves a widespread assumption about scientific method, has tended to have been overlooked.

(b)   *Operationism in Psychology*

One of the more recent offshoots of observationalism in psychology is the operationist movement. It is difficult to be clear quite what operationism is because it is not always very clearly stated. Certainly all operationists are rationalistic in the sense that they maintain that unless scientists define their terms operationally they will not uncover Nature's secrets. But what does it mean to define a term 'operationally'? It could mean that hypotheses must be expressed in terms which render them testable by observation. This would be the view about the language of science which is parallel to the salutary part of the observationalist doctrine – that scientific hypotheses must be tested by observation. But, if my interpretation of operationist literature is correct, operationism is misleading in exactly the same way as observationalism is misleading. And this is because operationism is an offshoot of observationalism. Just as it is salutary to say that observation is decisive in testing hypotheses but misleading to say that scientists 'start from' observations, so also is it salutary to say that scientific terms are meaningful because there are concrete operations by means of which it can be determined whether or not a term is applicable or whether or not what is asserted in a sentence containing scientific terms is true or false, but misleading to say that scientists define terms by means of 'operations' or that terms 'stand for' operations. There is thus a wider and a narrower interpretation of 'operationism'. The wider doctrine is accepted by all scientists who make careful attempts to test hypotheses; the narrower doctrine is accepted only by those who assume an observationalist view of scientific method. I shall thus be concerned in this article only with the narrower sense of operationism.

This movement in psychology was a reflection of the movement in physics epitomised in Bridgman's book *The Logic of Modern Physics*. There were a number of articles in the *Psychological Review* terminating in a symposium on 'Operationism in Psychology' in 1945 as well as a book called *The Logic of Modern Psychology* written by Professor Pratt from an avowedly observationalist stand-point. The operationists tried to apply Bridgman's remark that 'The proper definition of a concept is not in terms of properties but in terms of actual operations'[22] to psychology. I will quote two typical expressions of the view by psychologists: 'Operationism may be defined as the practice of talking about (1) one's observations, (2) the manipulational and calculational procedures involved in making them, (3) the logical and mathematical steps which intervene between earlier and later statements, and (4) nothing else.'[23] This expression has at least the virtue of being clear. The same, however, cannot be said for my other example: 'Operational definition makes explicit recognition of the fact that a concept, or a proposition, has empirical meaning only if it stands for definite concrete operations capable of execution by normal human beings.' And: 'A term or proposition has meaning (denotes something) if, and only if, the criteria of its applicability or truth consists of concrete operations which can be performed.'[24] In this latter example we note a shift or wobble. In Stevens's first formulation a concept or proposition has meaning only if it 'stands for' definite concrete operations; in the second formulation it has meaning only if 'the criteria of its applicability or truth' consist in concrete operations. This is like saying that the word 'horse' stands for my looking, touching and smelling operation when confronted with (a horse?) and then going on to say that the word 'horse' can only have application if I can look at, touch, or smell a horse. In the first formulation it is clear that the word 'horse' stands only for my discriminatory operations (which is a bizarre kind of phenomenalism); in the second formulation the more non-committal rule is laid down that I may only use the word 'horse' if there are concrete operations by means of which I can decide whether the word is applicable. No mention is made in the second formulation of 'standing for' and the question of definition in terms of observed properties is left open. It could thus be interpreted as a statement only of the wider sense of 'operationism'.

Operationists claimed to give an account of what scientists in fact do, of how they in fact define their terms. Concepts, they said, find their meaning in specific laboratory experiments; their meaning must be reconstructed from the context of the scientific activities in which they in fact occur. Stevens makes this explicit when he identifies the much talked of 'operations' with 'discriminatory responses'.

It may well be the case that this sort of analysis is plausible with an example like 'length', where obviously the question 'What is the *real* length of *x*?' needs the answer 'Measuring is something we do to things'. But this hard-headed kind of reply does not necessitate the conclusion that a simple property like extension is defined only in terms of or 'stands for' discriminatory operations. The difficulty we encounter with the operationists, especially in psychology, is that they make no effort to sort out the different sorts of terms used by scientists which belong to different levels of abstraction. The only member of the 1945 symposium who does this is Herbert Feigl and he is not an operationist in the narrow sense at all. He distinguishes 'qualitative', 'semi-quantitative', 'fully-quantitative', 'causal-genetic' and 'theoretical' terms. The extreme operationists, however, make no similar attempt to distinguish these different levels, and as they talk airily about 'properties' as well as about high-level constructs like 'force' we must presume that their doctrine is meant to apply to every sort of scientific term – even those that are 'ostensively defined'.

Surely, too, if the operationists were serious in maintaining that they were giving an empirical account of how scientific terms have meaning, they would produce case-histories of people like Newton, Harvey and Galileo. In fact this sort of confirmation is not produced. In view of this it is plausible to suggest that their view, far from being an empirical description, was a way of talking necessitated by phenomenalism and observationalism. Do not the operationist extremists assume that scientists *start* with specific operations like 'discriminatory responses', measuring operations, manipulations of material and so on? General terms in science emerge from the correlation of similar operations, and laws and theories from the correlation of measurings. Would not this implicit assumption account for Skinner's insistence that terms stand for nothing more than observations, the manipulational and calculational procedures involved in making them, and the logical and mathematical steps which intervene between earlier and later statements? Scientific laws and theories are presumed to emerge from logical and mathematical operations on the 'data' which are observations and measurements.

L. J. Russell, in his review of Bridgman's book,[25] showed that the general theory of operationism is unable, in its narrower sense, to give an account either of error or generality. If 'heat' stands for particular operations involved in measuring (heat?) there is no sense in talking of better ways of measuring (heat) or of being mistaken in such measurements. For 'heat' stands only for the particular operations involved in measuring and nothing else. Similarly a synapse discovered by different techniques would be a different thing and the meaning of 'synapse' would necessarily change not only with changes in the examining devices but also on every occasion on which it was examined afresh by anyone. There is no way of accounting for the generality of terms if it is assumed that we start with 'sheer particulars' or that terms are tied down to specific operations. Observation and measurement, as well as other manipulational and calculational operations, presuppose not only things with observable properties to deal with, but also a wealth of previous theory and general assumptions about them. The assumptions which we already have determine the questions we ask, the observations which we make, and the operations which we perform. We never 'start from' such operations. We can and do use different operations to measure length, for instance, because of our existing qualitative knowledge about extended bodies, and it is because of our existing knowledge that we know that it does not matter which end of a cricket pitch we start from if we want to measure it and that we can perform the operation indifferently with a piece of stick, with a piece of tape, or with an iron bar. Our existing assumptions assure us of the equivalence of these operations. But on a strict operationist view the length of a cricket pitch is defined only in terms of measuring operations and the equivalence of the results is inexplicable, as we never measure the same thing, the properties being defined by means of operations. In actual fact we trust a given measurement more if we have another way of making it that acts as a confirmation. This shows the amount of existing knowledge which is presupposed by measurement. We trust measurement with a tape-measure if it is confirmed by triangulation method just as we are satisfied that we have seen a dog in the twilight if we also hear it bark.

There are many other objections to operationism in general which other methodologists, more competent than I, have put forward; these all hold good *a fortiori* of operationism in psychology. There is, however, another point that needs to be made with reference to the application of this doctrine to psychological concepts. My acquaintance with operationist literature is not very extensive, but I have been surprised at the dearth of examples which operationists give to illustrate their thesis. We would expect a list of typical psychological terms ranging from 'super-ego', 'infantile sexuality' and 'Oedipus complex' to terms like 'instinct', 'drive', 'habit', 'field', 'conditioned response', and so on. Instead, we get not only very few examples but constant citation of the term 'experience' and the term 'intelligence'. 'Intelligence is what the intelligence tests test'[26] is a good slogan. But surely care should be taken in erecting a general theory of psychological terms on such a shaky foundation.

It may well be that the slogan 'Intelligence is what the intelligence tests test' seems plausible because many testers who constructed battery tests and so on were not quite sure what they were testing, rather than because this approach to the problem of scientific definition was an adequate one. Would it be equally plausible to suggest that kleptomania is (what) the psychiatrists diagnose and the courts pronounce judgement on and nothing more?

The other usual illustration is that of the term 'experience' which is another notorious skeleton in the psychologist's cupboard.[27] Stevens points out that experience is, for the purpose of science, to 'react discriminatively'. Similarly Professor Mace, who is not an operationist in the narrower sense of the term, is wont to define words like 'consciousness' and 'experience' in terms of 'differential reactions'.[28] In cases like these the operationist thesis is convincing for the simple reason that scientifically useful definitions are being sought for words that may be construed as describing varous types of human operations. Talk about consciousness and experience, which has long metaphysical associations, is replaced by talk about discriminatory and differential reactions. As what we are trying to define are regarded as being themselves reactions or operations of organisms it is not surprising that operational definitions (in a literal sense) can be given. To say that A 'experiences' x is to say that A 'reacts discriminatively' to x. But if the narrower sense of operationism is adopted, to say that A 'experiences' x is to say that B 'makes a discriminatory response to' (A making a discriminatory response to x) where B is a scientific observer. Biologists, using terms about rats, would always look for the meaning of the terms they used in describing the behaviour of the rats in their own reactions to the behaviour of the rats. This, though flattering to the rats, would be a very bizarre procedure.

Perhaps I can clarify my interpretation of operationists by quoting against them another avowedly empirical account of 'meaning'. Charles Morris, in his *Signs, Language and Behaviour* claims to be giving an empirical account of sign behaviour. He distinguishes between the interpreter, the interpretant, the denotatum and the significatum of a sign.

'Any organism for which something is a sign will be called an interpreter. The disposition in an organism to respond, because of the sign, by response sequences of some behaviour-family will be called an interpretant. Anything which would permit the completion of the response sequences to which the interpreter is disposed because of a sign will be called the denotatum of a sign. A sign will be said to denote a denotatum. Those conditions which are such that whatever fulfils them is a denotatum will be called a significatum of the sign. A sign will be said to signify a significatum; the phrase "to have signification" may be taken as synonomous with "to signify".'[29]

The phrase 'stands for' which is so common in operationist literature, seems to be *in ordinary usage* the equivalent of Morris's 'signify' and/or 'denote'. Morris claims that

'A merit of the present usage of 'signify" is that it does not make the signaficatum of every term such as "spiral nebulae" or "atom" include biological events, though it recognises that there are no signs which signify without dispositions to respond (that is without interpretants). And since with this usage a sign does not denote its significatum, the temptation is avoided to make the significatum into a special kind of thing – a temptation which seems to underlie the Platonic doctrine of ideas and various philosophical doctrines of "subsistence".'[30]

Would it not be possible to interpret the operationist view as an over 'tough-minded' resolution of conundrums like: 'What is the *real* length of x?' In their determination to avoid 'essences' and metaphysics generally they seemed to by-pass Morris's 'denotation' and 'signification' and to anchor their signs to earth by equating the 'meaning' of a sign or what a sign 'stands for' with actual responses or with dispositions to make responses of certain behaviour-families – i.e. with the 'interpretants' of a sign. Thus, though they dispensed with Platonic heavens, their remedy was so drastic that they must be for ever running round the earth in circles – always defining words in terms of their own responses. But, as Morris points out:

'The interpretant, as a disposition to respond caused by a sign, answers to the behavioural side of the behaviour-environment complex; the significatum, as the set of terminal conditions under which the response-sequences to which the organism is disposed can be completed, connects with the environment side of the complex. Each, therefore, involves the other.'[31]

That a word should have interpretants, as James so often stressed, is a necessary condition of its having 'meaning'; but it is not a sufficient condition. We cannot escape reference to properties by speaking only of the observations, and manipulational operations of investigators.

I hope that I have by now succeeded in showing that operationism will not do as an empirical description of how scientific terms have meaning, that in general it fails to distinguish between the ways scientific terms at different levels have meaning, that in psychology it derived a certain amount of plausibility from the selection of a few words which are not fair samples of the terminology of working psychologists, and that, though a healthy reaction against metaphysical conundrums, the doctrine in its narrow form is full of absurdities. My suggestion is that the extreme form of the doctrine could only have won the small measure of acceptance which it did win because of the observationalist assumptions of its proponents and of those whom they managed to seduce by their slogans. Operationism, in its narrow form, is a cross between a recipe for scientists and a threat to metaphysicians. Metaphysicians may have trembled but few working scientists have ever attempted to put into practice such a fantastic recipe.

CONCLUSION

In maintaining that observationalist assumptions formed the basis of the Behaviourist–Introspectionist controversy and of operationism in psychology, I have, no doubt, over-simplified many of the issues in order to grind a particular axe about psychology. I do think, however, that my suggestion does provide one explanation of the dearth of fertile hypotheses in a great deal of psychological work. Of course, I emphatically do not want to suggest either that all psychologists have been influenced by observationalism or that this influence has been altogether bad. It is quite obvious, for instance, that Freud was little influenced by observationalism. His interests were technological rather than methodological and technological pressure meant that he *had* to think up hypotheses to explain and cure his patients. Many, however, might maintain that a mild dose of operationism would have done him good in that he might have been led to express some of his hypotheses in a more precise way so that we could know what could count against them. Others, however, might counter that a methodological super-ego would have tended to cramp his style and would have dried up his fertility. They would say that in the early stages of a science we must have bulldozers to clear a passage-way through a jungle as well as under-labourers to convert the passage way into a public thorough-fare. Operationists stop people from talking nonsense; but if there were too many of them in the vanguard of scientific advance, the pioneers might never talk at all. A balance must somewhere be struck between metaphysics and scholasticism. Today in psychology there are many who see the key to progress in impeccable data, in operational definition, in postulational techniques and the construction of mathematico-deductive systems; yet all this is of no avail without a lot of bright ideas. Too much preoccupation with method often districts people from the necessity of fertile hypotheses. Of course I would not deny that careful and patient experimentation often produces results. Maybe the brilliant hypotheis is often produced by the man who is patient enough to try a thousand others first. My point is that 'collection of data' in itself will not lead to progress in a science. The collectors must at least have some questions which they wish to answer and must suggest alternative answers which they can then compare with observation. But there are simply no rules for producing such answers or hypotheses. Some men may get them under drugs, others lying in a bath, others while methodically working in a laboratory using postulational techniques. There must, of course, be some kind of familiarity with tradition and with what is already assumed in order for scientifically interesting questions to arise. Questions never arise *in vacuo*. But given a question, there is no recipe for answering it in a theoretically powerful manner. I have attacked observationalism not because I do not regard it as vitally important that hypotheses should be tested (with the corollary that they must be expressed precisely enough to permit this) but because I see in observationalism a kind of rationalist recipe which tended to stifle the imagination and to prevent interesting questions being asked. 'Some of the major disasters of mankind have been produced by the narrowness of men with a good methodology. To set limits to speculation is treason to the future.'[32]

REFERENCES

1. Kohler, W., *Gestalt Psychology*, pp. 31–3.
2. See Hull, C., *Principles of Behaviour*.
3. See Woodworth, R., *Contemporary Schools of Psychology* (rev. edn 1949).
4. Quoted by Pratt, C., *The Logic of Modern Psychology*, p. 49.
5. Titchener, E. B., *Lectures on the Elementary Psychology of Feeling and Attention*, p. 175.
6. Watson, J. B., *Behaviourism*, p. 7.
7. Ibid., p. 17.
8. Hunter, W. S., 'The Psychological Study of Behaviour', *Psychological Review* (1932), p. 7.
9. Hunter, W. S., 'Psychology and Anthroponomy' in C. Murchison, *Psychologies of 1925*, p. 97.
10. Hunter, W. S., 'Anthroponomy and Psychology', in C. Murchison, *Psychologies of 1930*, p. 282.
11. Hunter, W. S., 'Psychology and Anthroponomy', in C. Murchison op. cit., p. 87.
12. Titchener, E. B., *A Primer of Psychology*, p. 2.
13. 'Introspection and Analysis.' Now published in Mace, Marjorie, *C. A. Mace Selected Papers* (London, Methuen, 1973) pp. 254–266.
14. For this point I am indebted to Pratt, op. cit., pp. 6–12.
15. In his *Physiological Psychology*.
16. Pratt, op. cit., p. 32.
17. See Hull, C., op. cit., pp. 399–401.
18. Whitehead, A. N., *The Function of Reason*, p. 14.

19. Pratt, op. cit., p. 26.
20. Some might say that the use of retrospective reports is quite consistent with Behaviourism as we are then dealing with 'verbal behaviour'. (See, e.g., Professor Mace, 'Some Implications of Analytical Behaviourism', *P.A.S.*, 1948.) But this is to use the word 'behaviour' so widely that it loses its sting and ceases to do any work. The point is surely that no other organisms use language to *describe* their own doings and feelings and the use of the word 'behaviour' in an omnibus way makes us tend to ignore some of the important differences between rats and men.
21. See, for instance, Dewey, J. 'Conduct and Experience' in C. Murchison *Psychologies of 1930*; Woodworth, op. cit.; the famous 'Battle of Behaviourism' between Watson and McDougall and the more familiar philosophical commentators like Broad, Russell, Pratt, and Mace.
22. Bridgman, P., *The Logic of Modern Physics*, p. 6.
23. Skinner, B. F. 'The Operational Analysis of Psychological Terms', *Psychological Review* (1945), p. 270.
24. Stevens, S. 'The Operational Definition of Psychological Concepts', *Psychological Review* (1935), pp. 517–18.
25. Mind, 1928.
26. Pratt, op. cit., p. 79.
27. See Stevens, op. cit., pp. 520–3 and Pratt, C., 'Operationism in Psychology', *Psychological Review* (1945), pp. 262–4.
28. Mace, C. A. 'Some Implications of Analytical Behaviourism', *P.A.S.* (1948), Presidential Address, p. 8.
29. Morris, C. *Signs, Language and Behaviour*, p. 17.
30. Morris, op. cit., p. 19.
31. Ibid., p. 18.
32. Whitehead op. cit., pp. 8, 30.

2

BEHAVIOURISM*

INTRODUCTION

It is sometimes said that La Mettrie, or Hobbes, or even Aristotle was the first Behaviourist. But such claims ignore the cardinal point that Behaviourism was essentially a methodological movement in psychology which can only be understood in the historical context of the early twentieth century. Its basic tenet, proclaimed by John B. Watson, its founder, was that psychology could only become a science if it based itself on the sort of objective observations and measurements that were made by natural scientists and biologists. This claim had point because it was made at a time when intro-spective psychology had run itself into the ground with abortive controversies about imageless thoughts and when, by contrast, the study of animal behaviour, which had received great impetus from Darwin's theories, was advancing rapidly. The time, therefore, was ripe for Watson's polemical suggestion that the only way to advance the scientific study of human beings was to adopt the same sorts of observational techniques that had proved so successful with the study of animals. This was the kernel of Behaviourism and, in-cidentally, about the only doctrine which was common to all those who later called themselves Behaviourists.

Connected with this claim about the appropriate data of science was a view about the proper function of science. Watson held that the function of science was not so much to explain events but to predict and control them. Behaviourism, therefore, had close affinities with certain aspects of American pragmatism as represented by John Dewey, Charles Peirce and William James, and fitted in well with the general American tendency to believe that the obvious way to

* 'Behaviourism' is reprinted with the permission of Charles Scribner's Sons from *Dictionary of the History of Ideas*, Vol. 1. Copyright © 1973 Charles Scribner's Sons.

improve the condition of man was to manipulate the external environment which was regarded as the main determining influence on his behaviour.

What, then, has led people to claim that previous figures in the history of psychology, such as Hobbes and Aristotle, might be termed Behaviourists? Partly, perhaps, the fact that many others before Watson had approached the study of man *objectively*, but without, in fact, relying much on introspective reports; for there were previous thinkers who had proceeded more or less in this way without erecting it into a methodological doctrine. More important, however, was the fact that there were other doctrines espoused by Watson which fitted well with his methodological directives, and previous thinkers had advanced these doctrines.

Watson, like many other Behaviourists, held a tacit or an implicit metaphysical doctrine about the sort of entities that there are in the world. He was a *materialist* who believed, for instance, that thought was identical with movements in the brain and larynx. Connected with his materialism was his view about the sort of concepts that were appropriate in developing a science of psychology. Like Hobbes before him and Hull after him be believed that the concepts should be *mechanical* in character. This belief was shared by many later conceptual Behaviourists who were not prepared to take up any position on metaphysical issues which, they claimed, lay outside the province of science. Finally Watson was an *associationist* in his theory. He believed that simple reflex arcs were linked together in behaviour by principles of association. In this respect his theory was quite unoriginal: for he merely transferred to the sphere of simple bodily movements a theory which had previously been put forward to account for the links between simple ideas. He stressed the importance of peripheral connections between stimuli and minimised the role of central processes. He thus founded what has come to be called the S-R (stimulus-response) theory of learning.

When, therefore, assertions are made about the more remote historical origins of Behaviourism these usually relate not so much to the methodological doctrine, which was central to it as a movement in psychology, as to other aspects of Watson's thought, which not all Behaviourists shared – to his materialism and to his use of mechanical concepts and of associationist principles. There was also the less self-conscious use of objective methods by many before who studied human behaviour.

This brief analysis of what was distinctive of Behaviourism suggests a convenient method of treating it as a phenomenon in the history of ideas. A few key figures in the history of psychology will first be introduced to substantiate the position here defended that only in rather contingent respects could they be regarded as precursors of Behaviourism. This will pave the way for the exposition of the more closely connected antecedents of Behaviourism as a movement in the history of psychology.

1 THE INTELLECTUAL ANCESTRY OF BEHAVIOURISM

Aristotle

Many things in the history of thought have been traced back to Aristotle with varying degrees of appositeness, but there is almost nothing apposite in tracing back Behaviourism to him. To credit him, for instance, with taking up a position on the central methodological issue of the use of publicly observable data, as distinct from introspective evidence, in studying human beings would display a gross lack of historical perspective; for the distinction between the private world of the individual's own consciousness and the public word, which all could observe, was alien to the Greeks. Indeed there is a sense in which the Greeks had no concept of consciousness in that they did not link together phenomena such as pain, dreams, remembering, action and reasoning as exemplifying different modes of individual consciousness. The concept of consciousness was largely a product of individualism, of the various movements such as Stoicism, Epicureanism and Christianity, which supplied types of conceptual schemes that were very different from those which were appropriate to the shared life of the city-states. The co-ordinating concept of individual consciousness was not made explicit until it found expression in the systems of Saint Augustine and Descartes. The use of introspection as a technique for investigating consciousness went along with such systems of thought, and Behaviourism can only be understood as a reaction against such a technique. It would, therefore, be absurd to search for hints of the central doctrine of Behaviourism in a thinker such as Aristotle, whose way of thinking about human life antedated the conceptual schemes which permitted such questions to be raised.

What can be said about Aristotle is that, being a marine biologist by training, he was the first to approach the study of human beings in an objective and systematic way. He developed a classificatory system which included plants, animals and man as belonging to the same genus of living things. He sent his research workers all over the known world to provide him with facts, not only about the different species of living things but also about the different types of customs and systems of government under which men lived. This was all recorded and fed into the classificatory system that he developed at the Lyceum.

When, however, we turn to Aristotle's *Metaphysics* and *De Anima*, and study the conceptual scheme which he thought appropriate for describing and explaining human behaviour, we find not just that his doctrine of form and matter was incompatible with the materialism espoused by many behaviourists but that, in his psychology, he was an explicit critic of the mechanists of his day.

Aristotle held that a living thing is a 'body with a soul', 'soul' designating the self-originated tendency of living things to persist towards an end. This tendency can be exhibited at the nutritive and reproductive level as in plants, at the level of sensation and movement as in animals, and at the rational level as in man. Aristotle accused mechanists such as Democritus and Empedocles of the all-pervading mistake of concluding from the fact that the soul is the cause of movement, that it is itself moved. He maintained that the soul moves the body 'by means of purpose of some sort, that is thought'. Thinking is not a sort of motion any more than desire or sensation are. His predecessors had misunderstood the sort of concept that 'soul' was. In so far as it is a capacity, how could it be moved? A capacity is not the sort of thing that can be moved. In so far as it is an exercise of a capacity, such as thinking, it is manifest in a process that cannot adequately be described as a change in motion. Aristotle deployed many ingenious arguments to substantiate this criticism of mechanical theories, many of which are similar to those which can oe found in the work of modern philosophers such as Ryle.

There are thus almost no grounds for linking Aristotle with Behaviourism either in respect of its central doctrine or in respect of its more peripheral ones. If Aristotle is to be linked with any school in twentieth-century psychology the obvious one would be that of the 'hormic' (purposive) psychology championed by William McDougall. For here too we find behaviour studied objectively, an exaltation of purpose as the most important explanatory concept, and a vehement attack on the mechanists of his day, namely J. B. Watson and the reflexologists. Indeed McDougall's indebtedness to Aristotle is explicitly acknowledged at many points.

Hobbes
There would be more plausibility in attempting to trace Behaviourism

back to Hobbes than to Aristotle. To start with, Hobbes was one of the great thinkers of individualism and wrote at a time when the private world of the individual was both recognised and valued – and threatened by tendencies towards absolutism. Hobbes himself regarded man's capacity to form 'phantasms' or images as one of his most miraculous powers. 'Of all the phenomena or appearances which are near to us, the most admirable', he says, 'is apparition itself, φαίνεσθαι; namely, that some natural bodies have in themselves the pattern almost of all things, and others of none at all' (Hobbes, *De Corpore*, p. 389). It was man's mysterious power to register within himself what was going on around him and to store up his impressions for use on further occasions that awakened Hobbes's passionate curiosity. How could this mysterious power be explained? This was the problem that lay at the heart of Hobbes's psychology and theory of nature.

Thus Hobbes's starting point in psychology reveals both the conceptual possibility of Behaviourism for him and also the absurdity of thinking that, in the most important respect, Hobbes was in fact a Behaviourist; for no Behaviourist could regard the problem of imagery as the most important phenomenon for a psychologist to explain. It is also difficult to see how much could be done about explaining it without constant recourse to introspection.

On the central question of the appropriate data for a science of human behaviour Hobbes was, as a matter of fact, absolutely explicit. In his Introduction to *Leviathan* he wrote:

'But let one man read another by his actions never so perfectly, it serves him only with his acquaintance, which are but few. He that is to govern a whole nation, must read in himself, not this or that particular man; but mankind: which though it be hard to do, harder than to learn any language or science; yet when I shall have set down my own reading orderly, and perspicuously, the pains left another, will be only to consider, if he also find not the same in himself. For this kind of doctrine admitteth no other demonstration'.

Hobbes not only extolled introspection as the appropriate method for investigating mankind; he also pointed to the unreliability of inferences made on the basis of the observation of others. Since Hobbes accepted the use of introspective evidence, why has his linkage to Behaviourism seemed so plausible to so many? There are, first of all, some underlying assumptions which are common to the views of Hobbes and modern Behaviourists, and these are so deeply embedded in modern thought that we tend to take them for granted. The first is the assumption that there is some reliable method for advancing knowledge. Hobbes was one of the many 'new men' of the post-Renaissance period who believed that knowledge of nature was available to anyone who was prepared to master the appropriate method. He thought that Copernicus and Galileo had revealed the method for investigating the natural world, that Harvey had applied this to the study of the body, and that he, Hobbes, was showing how this method, the resoluto-compositive method of Galileo, could be applied to psychology and politics.

Hobbes's early contact with Francis Bacon, for whom he had worked for a period as a kind of literary secretary, had also convinced him that knowledge meant power. Hobbes's psychology and politics were constructed with a very practical end in view – the preservation of peace, and he thought that there was no hope for England, in the throes of civil war, unless those who had some influence on the course of events, could be persuaded to accept the logic of his demonstrations concerning man and civil society. This practical concern underlying his theorising, which was later to be applauded by Marxists, was another underlying link between Hobbes and the Behaviourists.

A much more explicit link between Hobbes and the Behaviourists was his materialism, and his attempt to extrapolate the concepts and laws of Galileo's mechanics to the human sphere. 'For seeing life is but motion of limbs . . . what is the heart but a spring; and the nerves but so many strings; and the joints but so many wheels, giving motion to the whole body, such as was intended by the artificer' (Hobbes, *Leviathan*, Introduction). Desires and aversions are motions towards and away from objects. Thinking is but motion in some internal substance in the head and feeling is movement about the heart. Imagery, which he found so wonderful, was to be viewed as a kind of meeting place of motions. The phenomena of perception and imagination could be deduced from the law of inertia. In order to make such deductions Hobbes postulated infinitely small motions, which he called 'endeavours', in the medium between the object of sense and the brain, and he had recourse to them also to explain how movements coming from outside bodies are passed on through the body so that they eventually lead to the gross movements observable in desire and aversion.

Within Behaviourism it is customary, following Tolman, to distinguish between molecular and molar theories of behaviour. A **molecular** theory, such as that of Clark Hull, is one which starts from postulates at the physiological level and attempt to deduce the movements involved at the molar level, e.g. the gross movements of the body, from them. Hobbes anticipated such molecular theories to an astonishing extent by his 'endeavours'. But such anticipation had nothing to do with Behaviourism in a strict sense. It was rather the consequence of applying the hypothetico-deductive procedure of Galileo, together with his mechanical concepts and laws, to the realm of human behaviour. Hull combined this Galilean approach to psychology with the restriction of data to what could be publicly observed, which was the central feature of Behaviourism. Thomas Hobbes, therefore, can properly be regarded as the father of mechanistic theories in psychology rather than of Behaviourism; for not all Behaviourists were mechanists, and Hobbes himself relied on introspection in the psychological sphere.

Descartes
It would be more absurd to regard Descartes as a Behaviourist than Hobbes; for he was notorious for the dualism of mind and matter which he postulated. But, as a matter of fact, both his dualism and his assumptions about scientific method did much to create the climate of opinion which made Behaviourism possible, if not almost inevitable.

Descartes held that there are two sorts of substances in the world, mental and physical. If the behaviour of these substances was to be scientifically studied, assumptions about them had to be made explicit and exhaustively analysed until clear and distinct ideas were arrived at, which were simple in the sense that no further analysis of them was possible. In the case of ideas about material objects, for instance, the scientist eventually arrived at the simple ideas of extension, figure and motion. If certain of these simple ideas were combined, relationships could be grasped between them which served as postulates for a deductive system, as in geometry. Thus the understanding of bodies and of minds respectively rested upon clear and distinct ideas which had no features in common. Descartes' problem about the relationship between mind and body derived from the fact that, though in our confused everyday experience we are aware of interaction, as when our limbs move because of our intentions, no clear and distinct idea can be formed of the manner of this union. Such perspicuous ideas are only forthcoming in the spheres of the mental and the physical when they are proceeding independently of each other – as in logical reasoning on the one hand or in reflex movements on the other.

Descartes' dualism and his assumptions about scientific method thus gave rise to two traditions of enquiry which came to be pursued more or less independently of each other. On the one hand the human body, which was regarded as functioning mechanically right up to the level of instinctive behaviour and simple habits, becomes a fit subject for objective study. Harvey had made a splendid advance in this field with his mechanical theory of the circulation of the blood. On the other hand, the mind, by which Descartes meant mainly the higher thought processes and the will, could only be studied introspectively. The consequence of Descartes' dualism was, therefore, the school of mechanistic biology and reflexology on the one hand and the introspective school of psychology on the other, which reached its culmination about 250 years later in the laborious experimental work of Wundt and Titchener.

It was against the assumptions of the introspective school that Watson revolted – their assumptions about both introspective method and the 'stuff' of consciousness which he claimed they were trying to study by this method. And when he revolted he fell back on the other tradition stemming from Descartes: mechanistic biology and reflexology. All he did was to attempt to extend its domain to the level of thought and action which had previously been regarded as 'mental' and hence to be studied by introspective methods. And when Watson theorised about behaviour he was unwittingly Cartesian in his approach. He thought that the complex phenomena of behaviour could be explained by analysis into clear and distinct units of behaviour – simple reflexes.

Reflexology
Descartes' dualism involved the assumption that the behaviour of the body, below the level of willed action, could be explained mechanically. He had, however, a crude idea of how the body works. He thought of it as a statue or machine made of earth and was much impressed by the feats which mechanical manikins could be made to perform in the gardens of the aristocracy by arranging water-pipes within them. They could be made to move their limbs and even to produce sounds like words. He thus pictured the nervous system as a piece of intricate plumbing. The nerves were thought of as tubes along which 'animal spirits', which occupied an indeterminate status between the mental and the physical, flowed continuously. Changes in the motion of these spirits cause them to open certain pores in the brain. When this happens the motion of the animal spirits is changed and they are 'reflected' into the muscles which move the body. For

he thought that many movements of the body are not brought about by conscious intention, but by an *undulatio reflexa*, or a movement of rebound in the animal spirits at the meeting of the sensory and motor channels at the pineal gland, where the mind could also influence the body by means of images. The automatic reactions of the body, which were not under voluntary control, were thus called reflexes.

Little was done to refine this conception until 1811 when Charles Bell published a paper entitled 'An Idea of a New Anatomy of the Brain', which he communicated to the Royal Society in 1821, and in which he claimed that the nerves, which are connected with the spinal centres by anterior roots, are employed in conveying motor impulses from the brain outward, and that the sensory nerves are connected with the posterior roots of the spinal cord. This was confirmed by Magendie in 1822. In 1833 Marshall Hall demonstrated clearly the existence of reflex action which proceeded independently of conscious volition, and in the latter part of the nineteenth century the antics of animals deprived of their higher brain structure were a commonplace. In 1851 Claude Bernard pioneered physiological work on the influence of specific nerves on the blood vessels and the consequent changes throughout the sympathetic system, thus helping to understand the connection between the brain and the viscera and other changes involved in emotional and motivational states. Evolutionary theory, especially that of Herbert Spencer, led Hughlings Jackson to postulate different levels of evolution in the nervous system from the less to the more organised, from the automatic to the voluntary.

From the point of view of the history of Behaviourism the crucial step forward was taken by Pavlov, whose particular interest was in the digestive system. In 1897 he published a book on *The Work of the Digestive Glands*, in which he noted that there are certain irregularities and interruptions in the work of these glands, which he attributed to psychic causes, e.g. that sometimes the glands would start to work before food was given to a dog, when the dog saw the man who usually fed it. In 1902 he embarked on a long series of experiments to study such phenomena. He concentrated on salivation, rather than on gastric secretion, because it was more accessible to experimental analysis. A dog was strapped in a test frame, with elaborate experimental controls, and a bell (conditioned stimulus) was repeatedly sounded before food (unconditioned stimulus) was placed in the mouth to produce salivation (unconditioned response), until eventually the sound of the bell brought about salivation (conditioned response) before the presentation of the food. Pavlov also found that the conditioned stimulus becomes generalised, in that the dog comes to respond to a wide range of stimuli. He found, too, that dogs could be taught to discriminate between stimuli by rewarding responses to one stimulus, such as a circle, but not to another, such as an ellipse. If the difference between the stimuli was gradually reduced a point would be reached where the dogs behaviour evinced all the symptoms of acute neurosis. The concept of 'reinforcement' was invented to refer to this process in which the conditioned stimulus is presented in close juxtaposition to the unconditioned stimulus. Many have commented on the similarity between this concept and that of Thorndike's 'reward', central to his law of effect. But the two concepts emerged from very different theoretical backgrounds and their differences are as important as their similarities.

Pavlov was unrepentantly a physiologist and he linked his experimental findings with a theory about irradiation and processes of excitation and inhibition in the brain. He expressed contempt for psychology and refused to take sides in psychological controversies. Nevertheless his influence has been nugatory in physiological theory but vast in psychology, because the Behaviourists later seized upon his findings. His contemporary, Bekhterev, on the other hand, who also popularised the conditioned reflex, was more catholic in his interests. In 1907 he published his *Objective Psychology* in which he proclaimed that the future of psychology depended upon objective, external observation. He envisaged excluding introspective data and mentalistic concepts and basing psychology on physical and physiological findings. In this respect Bekhterev harped back to La Mettrie and the materialistic tradition in psychology. In his conditioning experiments he did not confine himself to reactions such as salivation but met with some success in conditioning motor responses as well. He also took an interest in speech, as also did Pavlov towards the end of his life.

Watson embarked upon his Behaviouristic programme in ignorance of the physiological studies of Pavlov and Bekhterev, but he gradually incorporated them into his theory when he became familiar with them through translation. Thus Watson's reflexes functioned in his theory as the direct descendants of Descartes' 'simple natures' in the bodily sphere. The links between them, however, namely the principles of association, and the assumptions about how generalisations could be arrived at about such links, came from another source – the empiricist tradition. A brief exposition of the leading ideas of this tradition will complete the account of Behaviourism's intellectual ancestry.

The Empiricist Tradition

The other aspect of Descartes' thought, the interest in the contents of consciousness, was developed by both rationalists and empiricists alike. The empiricists, like the rationalists, were really preoccupied with problems of knowledge. As John Locke put it, they were concerned with the 'original, extent, and certainty' of human knowledge. They held, however, that knowledge was based on experience, not in the unexceptionable sense that however we come to obtain beliefs about the world, their truth or falsity must be tested by comparing them with what can be observed, but in the much more dubious sense that our ideas about the world *originate* in our own individual sense-experience. Therefore, questions about the extent and certainty of knowledge tended to resolve themselves into speculations about how ideas originated; for followers of what was called 'the way of Ideas' held that genuine ideas must be tracked back to impressions of sense. The result was that philosophical questions about the meaning of terms and about the grounds of knowledge were systematically confused with questions in genetic psychology about their origin. It was not until the nineteenth century, when F. H. Bradley proclaimed in his *Principles of Logic* that: 'In England we have lived too long in the psychological attitude' that this confusion, which persisted from Locke to James Mill and Alexander Bain, began to be systematically exposed.

The net result of this confusion was that the work of the empiricists contained both a philosophical theory about the grounds and acquisition of knowledge and a psychological theory about the working of the mind. The philosophical theory came straight from Francis Bacon. To obtain knowledge, it was held, a start had to be made with simple uninterpreted data, or impressions of sense. There must be no premature hypotheses or 'anticipations of Nature'. Generalisations had to be made which reflected regularities in the data. Bacon elaborated tables of copresence, coabsence, and covariation of instances to ensure that these generalisations were well founded. These were later elaborated by Mill in his celebrated methods of experimental enquiry. It was of cardinal importance in this process of 'induction' that generalisations should not go beyond the data and that no recourse should be made to unobservables. Laws expressed correlations between what could be observed.

The psychological theory which developed *pari passu* with this philosophical theory about the grounds and acquisition of knowledge had two main features. First, it maintained that the experience, thought, and consequent action of the individual is caused from without. The environment causes simple ideas (Locke) or impressions

(Hume) to arise in the individual. The individual's body was also regarded as part of the external world which gives rise to impressions of reflection – e.g. of pleasure and pain – which enter the mind through different types of receptor. (This was later on called 'the inner environment' by Behaviourists.) Secondly, it was held that the ideas arising from these two environmental sources become linked together by principles of association such as contiguity and resemblance. Action is inititated by an idea that has become linked with pleasure or pain. Thus food, for instance, gives rise to an idea in the mind, which has become linked to the idea of eating, which in its turn has been linked with the idea of pleasure. This brings about the action of eating the food. This account of the initiation of action can be found in Hobbes, though he did not give much prominence to the association of ideas in his account of thinking. He stressed the importance of plans deriving from desire.

The history of empiricism is largely the history of the elaboration and sophistication of these basic ideas. In the philosophical and methodological sphere there were three main derivative doctrines. First, the notion of 'data' was gradually sophisticated into modern theories of sense-data, which can be found in the work of philosophers such as G. E. Moore, Bertrand Russell, and A. J. Ayer. In the scientific sphere Kant did much to popularise the idea that the domain of science was coextensive with the domain of the measurable. It became important, therefore, for scientists to obtain data which were as precise and pure as possible by devising various forms of measurement. In psychology the nineteenth-century concentration on psychophysics, stemming largely from the work of Weber and Fechner, bore witness to this search for measurable data – the notorious just noticeable differences.

Secondly, a theory of meaning developed which has come to be known as 'logical empiricism'. This maintained that only those terms are strictly meaningful that can be cashed by reference to what can be observed. The language of morals and of poetry is, strictly speaking, meaningless (or has merely 'emotive meaning') because it cannot be tied down in this way to observables. Scientific terms have either to be 'operationally defined' or related indirectly to observation by a process of 'logical construction'. In the early twentieth century P. W. Bridgman's book *The Logic of Modern Physics* (1927) popularised this view of scentific terms. Its leading ideas were applied to psychology by C. C. Pratt in *The Logic of Modern Psychology* (1939) and exerted a considerable influence on B. F. Skinner, a leader of modern Behaviourism.

The third development was the attempt to formulate precisely the methods for arriving at well-founded generalisations and to get clearer about the theory of probability which was presupposed. The works of J. S. Mill, W. E. Johnson, and J. M. Keynes were classics in this tradition.

The psychological theory which was favoured by most of the empiricists was given an ambitious start by David Hume who pictured himself as the Newton of the sciences of man. Simple impressions were regarded as mental atoms and the principles of association were postulated as performing, in the mental sphere, the same function of uniting them together as was performed by the principle of gravitational attraction in the physical sphere. David Hartley developed an even more ambitious version of this type of theory; for he held that the psychological principles of association paralleled the mode of operation of physiological disturbances in the substance of the nerves, spinal marrow, and brain, which he called 'vibrations'. It was left to James Mill, however, to free associationism from Newtonian pretensions and physiological speculation and to attempt to formulate soberly and prosaically the basic principles in terms of which ideas were thought to be connected. Most of the subsequent work in the nineteenth century of the British associationist school consisted in criticism, refinements, and simplifications of Mill's edifice.

In France, largely through the infectious cynicism of Voltaire, British empiricism came to exert an influence that was more mundane, and less theoretical. It encouraged thinkers to observe more carefully and more objectively how men in fact behaved. Diderot's *Lettre sur les aveugles* and *Lettre sur les sourds et muets* were classics of their kind – concrete case studies of individual lives. Similarly Condillac approached Locke's problems in a more concrete, if more imaginative way, by creating the fiction of a statue endowed only with the faculty of smell. And Cabanis, a vehement critic of Condillac, began his psychophysiological writings in 1795 with an attempt to answer the concrete, if depressing, question of whether the victims of the guillotine suffer any pains after decapitation. His theory, which attacked Condillac's starting point of imagining a being capable of sensation in isolation from the structure of the organism as a whole, was diametrically opposed to the atomism of the associationist tradition. But it was a theory based on actual observations of men from childhood to maturity. Similarly, La Mettrie, who elaborated Hobbes's thesis that man is a superior type of machine, developed his theory not as an imaginative extrapolation from Galilean mechanics but partly as a result of his medical studies under Hermann Boerhave, and partly from direct observation of his own experiences during a fever. And in the nineteenth century Taine, who represented very much the antimetaphysical, positivistic school in France, scrambled together, in his *De l'intelligence* (1870; trans. as *On the Intelligence*, 1871), reports from asylums, physiological facts, and references to Mill's *Logic*!

It would be tempting to suppose that this interest in the concrete behaviour of men, and the attempt to study it objectively, which was so characteristic of French empiricism, was one of the formative influences in the development of Behaviourism. There is, however, little plausibility in this suggestion. For the rise of Behaviourism is to be explained partly as a methodological reaction to introspective psychology and partly as a consequence of the success which was being attained in the study of animals. Almost the last thing which the Behaviourists actually came to study was the concrete behaviour of men. Let us now pass, therefore, to the immediate origins of Behaviourism.

2 THE IMMEDIATE ORIGINS OF WATSON'S BEHAVIOURISM

J. B. Watson was by no means the first to see the importance for psychology of the objective study of behaviour. William McDougall, in his *Physiological Psychology* in 1905, had defined psychology as 'the positive science of the conduct of living creatures' and had resisted the tendency to describe it as the science of experience or of consciousness. In 1908, in his *Introduction to Social Psychology*, he explicitly introduced the term 'behavior' claiming that psychology was 'the positive science of conduct or behavior'. He maintained that psychology must not regard introspective description of the stream of consciousness as its whole task. This had to be supplemented by comparative and physiological psychology relying largely on objective methods, the observation of man and animals under all possible conditions of health and disease. Similarly, in 1911, W. B. Pillsbury, a pupil of Titchener, published his *Essentials of Psychology* in which he claimed that psychology should be defined as 'the science of human behaviour'. But neither McDougall nor Pillsbury put forward a puritanical or restrictive position. They were merely arguing that the objective study of animals and of physiology had a lot to contribute to psychology. It was therefore unwarranted to give a definition of psychology which excluded their findings from the outset.

What was distinctive about Watson's view of psychology was what it excluded rather than what it included; for McDougall himself was a devotee both of physiology and of animal studies. Watson was determined to rule out introspection as a legitimate method of obtaining data and to banish 'consciousness' and other mentalistic terms from the conceptual scheme of his new science. What led him to this methodological puritanism?

Animal Psychology

From the time of Darwin's *Origin of Species* (1859) and *Expression of the Emotions in Man and Animals* (1872) there had been a growing interest in the behaviour of animals, birds, and insects in order to test his hypothesis of the continuity between animals and man. In 1872, for instance, Spalding had studied swallows in order to determine whether they learnt to fly by imitation or whether they had an inborn tendency to do so. Between 1879 and 1904 Fabre had made a long series of observations on insects to determine how much of their behaviour was due to instinct. The thesis that intelligence is continuous between animals and men was examined by Romanes, Lloyd Morgan, and Loeb on the basis of observations of animal behaviour. But the decisive step, from the point of view of the rise of Behaviourism, was taken when in 1896 E. L. Thorndike introduced cats, dogs, chickens, and monkeys into the laboratory and carried out experiments on them in order to determine how they learn. From the gradual, though irregular, improvements in the learning curves Thorndike inferred that the animals could not learn by 'insight' or by reasoning. Imitation was ruled out by experimental controls. 'Trial and error' seemed the only possibility left. The animals, he suggested, went through a variety of responses. Gradually the unsuccessful responses were eliminated and the successful ones were stamped in.

Thorndike believed that there were two basic laws which explained this process. The law of exercise maintained that connections were strengthened by use and weakened by disuse; the law of effect maintained that connections, which were rewarded and thus led to satisfaction, were strengthened. This was not a particularly original theory, as the principles employed were a commonplace in the associationist tradition. What was original was his application of such principles to the connections between stimulus and response and the experimental evidence from his laboratory which he provided to support his view.

Watson, significantly, started his academic career in philosophy, but switched to psychology during his period of graduate study at the University of Chicago, and devoted himself to animal psychology. In

1908 he became professor of psychology at Johns Hopkins University and in 1912 he launched his polemic in some public lectures which were eventually published in 1914 in his book entitled *Behavior*. The vehemence of his attack was to be explained partly by his resentment of the grudging and slightly condescending attitude of most orthodox psychologists of the day towards animal studies. Instead of putting a reasoned case, as did McDougall and Pillsbury, for the importance of animal studies and physiology for psychology, Watson pointed a derisive finger at the state of introspective psychology. 'Today', proclaimed Watson in his *Behaviourism*, 'the Behaviorist can safely throw out a real challenge to the subjective psychologists – Show us that you have a possible method, indeed that you have a legitimate subject-matter'. This jibe was occasioned by the 'imageless thought' controversy amongst introspectionists and other examples of divergent results obtained in different laboratories by well-trained introspectionists. Watson confidently asserted that psychology could only become a science, instead of a debating society, if the methods were used which had proved so successful in animal laboratories.

Inductivism

The second positive starting point of Behaviourism was the view about scientific method which Watson shared with the introspectionists whom he attacked. Wundt and Titchener, the giants of the introspective school, had been vehement in their ambition to base psychology on properly controlled experiments. The general appeal to look into oneself in order to decide upon psychological questions, which one can find, for instance, in the controversies between Locke, Berkeley, and Hume, was not good enough. Introspective observers had to be carefully trained. Moreover, Titchener argued that they had to be trained to distinguish pure experience as 'existences' from the 'meaning' which it has for men in their ordinary lives. Unless this could be done psychology would never arrive at any pure data on which a science of mind could be created.

This presupposed a certain view of scientific method, dating back to Bacon, which is often called 'inductivism' or 'observationalism' as by Popper. The leading idea of this conception can be summed up in Titchener's own words: 'We are agreed, I suppose, that scientific method may be summed up in the single word 'observation'; the only way to work in science is to observe those phenomena which form the subject-matter of science' (see supra p. 31). Watson himself had basically the same conception of scientific method. To quote his *Behavourism* again: 'You will find, then, the Behaviorist working like any other scientist. His sole object is to gather facts about behavior – verify his data – subject them both to logic and mathematics (the tool of every scientist)'. Watson's basic objection to introspectionism was that it was an attempt to form a science on very unreliable data about which experimenters could reach no agreement, and which purported to reveal facts about a nonexistent subject matter, namely consciousness. If psychologists were to start from data provided by rats in mazes they would at least have a chance of developing a science on the basis of publicly observable data.

When it came to making generalisations Watson again showed his inductivist allegiance; for the Baconian view was that generalisations should never go beyond the data. They should simply record correlations between observables. Thus Watson was as uninterested in physiological speculation about intervening processes as he was hostile to any recourse to unobservable mental entities or processes to explain what could be observed. One should, of course, quantify the data if possible and operate mathematically on it. But this was merely a way of arriving at correlations.

Associationism
The correlations which Watson discerned were again part and parcel of the introspectionist tradition, namely, the laws of association. He did not reject the postulate of instincts, but accorded them less and less importance in comparison with the influence of the environment via learning. In his theory of learning he rejected Thorndike's law of effect because the concept of 'satisfaction' was mentalistic. He relied on the law of exercise under which Thorndike had subsumed the old principles of association such as frequency and recency. He also minimised the importance of the brain and of central processes in learning. All behaviour, he believed, was sensori-motor, consisting of S-R units. It was initiated by the stimulation of a sense organ and terminated in a muscular or glandular response.

Thorndike produced conclusive evidence to demonstrate the inadequacy of the law of exercise as a sufficient explanation of learning, but Watson kept his head above water by incorporating into his theory the postulate of the conditioned response which Pavlov had first put forward in 1902. This, together with the concept of reinforcement, gave a more acceptable account of the type of strengthening of connections which Thorndike had covered by his mentalistic law of effect. But it was only gradually that the work of Pavlov and of Bekhterev, who put forward a similar theory of associated reflexes at about the same time, became known in America. It seems as if Watson was familiar with the Russian work from about 1914 onwards but he only gradually grasped its importance for his theory. By 1924 he had come to entertain the view that the conditioned response might afford the key to all habit formation. Other Behaviourists, however, took over the conditioned response with alacrity. Indeed, in a modified form, it kept their theory going for about a quarter of a century as will later be explained.

If Watson had stuck rigidly to what could be externally observed he would have severely restricted his 'subject-matter'. However, he claimed that thinking could also be studied because it consisted in implicit speech reactions or in subvocal talking. The implicit behaviour, which constitutes thinking, becomes substituted for overt manipulation. The child begins by learning to name things that he is doing while he is doing them, speech being a series of conditioned responses. He then learns to do this inaudibly and as a substitute for doing them. Thinking is therefore surrogate behaviour.

Watson also contrived to include emotions within his subject matter by claiming that they consisted in implicit visceral reactions. He espoused the James–Lange theory, while disregarding the introspective feelings which James claimed to be consequent on the visceral changes. In his actual studies of emotion, however, he rather ignored their visceral source and concentrated on their overt manifestations. He singled out three emotions – rage, fear, and love – as being innately determined, and suggested that all others are acquired by conditioning. He achieved some fame, or notoriety, by showing how small children can be conditioned to develop aversions to harmless animals like rabbits and white rats, if their appearance is associated with a noxious stimulus such as a loud noise.

Thus on the slender basis of the conditioning of reactions such as salivation and simple movements, of a bizarre and quite dubious theory of thinking, and of a few interesting experiments in conditioning children's emotional reactions, Watson made optimistic claims for what could be achieved in education and social life generally by a process of systematic and benevolent conditioning. His doctrine fitted well with the thinking of a nation one of whose basic problems was to create American citizens out of a multitude of immigrants of diverse origins, and who, in their approach to life combined a pragmatic outlook with a high level of technical skill, and a friendly extroverted disposition with an optimistic attitude towards the future.

3 THE DIFFERENT TYPES OF BEHAVIOURISM

It has been argued that Behaviourism was basically a methodological movement in psychology which laid down restrictions on the data on which a science could be properly based. In the case of its founder, J. B. Watson, this central doctrine was supported by an inductivist view of scientific method flanked by the metaphysical doctrine of materialism and by the associationism of a peripheralist, or S–R, type as a psychological theory. Few of the later Behaviourists shared all these assumptions. In commenting, therefore, on the main features of their theories special attention will be paid to their adherence to or departure from these other tenets of Watson which have come to be loosely associated with Behaviourism.

Early Materialists
Some of Watson's more immediate contemporaries had more in common with his bold, metaphysical brashness, than his later followers. Albert P. Weiss, for instance, published a book entitled *A Theoretical Basis of Human Behavior* in 1925 in which he banned consciousness and introspection from psychology and claimed that all behaviour could be interpreted in terms of physiochemical processes. Nevertheless he argued that what is distinctive of a human being is that his environment is social. Psychology is therefore a biosocial science which is particularly concerned with the impact of the social environment on a biological organism. Weiss was particularly interested in child development and learning, but he never seriously tackled the conceptual problems facing his reductionism, of how features of the social environment, such as commands, promises, and moral exhortation can be analysed in purely physical terms.

Another early Behaviourist, who showed equal *naïveté* about the environment, was W. S. Hunter. He held that consciousness or experience for the psychologist is merely a name which he applies to what other people call 'the environment'. This suggestion epitomises the epistemological innocence of most of the early Behaviourists, against which Koffka reacted so strongly. Hunter, however, distinguished himself in other ways. He thought that the new look in psychology deserved a new name and attempted, without any success, to substitute 'anthroponomy' for 'psychology'. He also was the first to use the temporal maze for the study of motor learning.

A more ingenious and interesting theorist of early Behaviourism was E. B. Holt. He was one of the first to try to deal with Freudian phenomena within a Behaviouristic framework and his *The Freudian*

Wish and its Place in Ethics (1915) is a classic in this tough-minded tradition, which was later to include O. H. Mowrer, J. Dollard, and N. E. Miller. Holt also developed Watson's idea that thinking is subvocal talking and theorised about the connections between language and conditioning. He thus anticipated later much more ambitious, if abortive, attempts to exhibit language as a system of conditioned responses.

Karl S. Lashley was a pupil of Watson's who made distinguished contributions to the physiology of the nervous system. This, however, did not prevent him from making pronouncements about the subject-matter of psychology and about its methods, for instance, that introspection is 'an example of the pathology of scientific method'. His physiological findings, however, as expressed in his *Brain Mechanisms and Intelligence* (1929), did not support other doctrines of Watson. His postulates of equipotentiality – that one part of the cortex is potentially the same as another in its capacity for learning, and of mass action – that learning is a function of the total mass of tissue, favoured a centralist theory of learning rather than Watson's peripheralist theory. He became very critical of S–R theories which postulated a simple connection between stimulus and response and which ignored the role of intervening cortical processes. The simple switching function accorded by Watson to the brain, which he inherited from Descartes, was denied.

Lashley, however, never departed from Watson's materialistic standpoint. Like Weiss and Hunter he believed that ultimately behaviour could be describable in the concepts of mechanics and chemistry. It is also significant that all these early Behaviourists shared an inductivist view of scientific method. They thought of the different sciences as having different subject-matters and as consisting of generalisations about them derived from reliable data drawn from these subject-matters. In this respect they shared not only Watson's methodological recipes but also the view of scientific method from which these recipes arose.

E. C. Tolman

One of the most influential and forceful converts to Behaviourism was E. C. Tolman; for he was calling himself a 'purposive Behaviorist' as early as 1920, though his definitive work entitled *Purposive Behavior in Animals and Man* did not appear until 1932. He aligned himself with the Behaviourists because he accepted their central methodological doctrine about the sort of evidence on which a scientific psychology should be based. He did not indulge, like

Watson and Weiss, in metaphysical assertions about the sorts of entities which there are in the world; he admitted that, at a common-sense level, men introspect and manage well enough with mentalistic terms. What he doubted, however, was the adequacy of this terminology for scientific purposes. 'Raw feels' are scientifically useless, and mentalistic terms can be translated into the language of observable behaviour. Tolman, in other words, was a conceptual Behaviourist rather than a materialist, as well as being a Behaviourist in his explicitly stated methodology.

In the conceptual sphere Tolman made at least three contributions, two of which were of permanent importance. First, he called himself a purposive behaviourist because he maintained that the concept of purpose was irreducible. As has been mentioned (pp. 51–2), he distinguished between the *molecular* and the *molar* level of behaviour, whose unity as segments of behaviour is provided by the ends towards which movements persist and in the attainment of which they are docile. He accused Watson of not distinguishing clearly between the molecular and the molar levels of analysis and maintained, against Hull, that behaviour at the molar level is an 'emergent' which has descriptive and defining properties of its own. Descriptions of it cannot be reduced to or deduced from analyses at the molecular level.

Secondly, Tolman made rather bizarre attempts to translate mentalistic terms, which had application at the molar level, into a Behaviouristic type of terminology. 'Consciousness' became 'the performance of a "sampling" or "running-back-and-forth" behaviour.' He even suggested that Freudian personality mechanisms can be translated into this type of terminology.

Thirdly, Tolman introduced into psychological theory the notion of intervening variables. Terms like 'instinct' had previously been used, e.g. by McDougall, not simply to postulate that certain purposive behaviour patterns were unlearned; they also had a metaphysical dimension to them – a suggestion of Aristotelian entelechies, of dynamic mental atoms activating behaviour. Tolman argued that it was perfectly legitimate for a Behaviourist to use a term like 'drive' which did not denote an unobservable entity, but which was a shorthand symbol for stating a correlation between antecedent conditions, e.g. food-deprivation, and variations in behaviour, e.g. eating.

This conceptual clarification helped to set psychology free to theorise without fear of metaphysics. It led on to the use of hypothetical constructs, which did commit theorists to postulates about unobservables usually of a physiological sort. Tolman thus contributed to ridding psychology of the inductivist myth, shared by the early Behaviourists, that scientists must never go beyond what is observed. In fact, however, the postulation of unobservables to explain the observed has been one of the most potent sources of scientific advance.

In the details of his psychological theory Tolman was eclectic. He stressed the importance of both demand variables and cognitive variables in behaviour, and attempted to state more precisely assumptions of the sort which McDougall had incorporated in his theory of instincts, i.e. of innate dispositions to pay attention to and behave in specific ways towards objects of a certain class.

In his account of the demand variables, Tolman distinguished first-order drives, which are linked with specific antecedent physiological conditions and consequent states of physiological quiescence (e.g. food-hunger, sex-hunger) from second-order drives (e.g. curiosity, constructiveness) which are not so obviously linked. This distinction, which was later to become that between biological and acquired drives, was important in the history of Behaviourism. On the cognitive side Tolman postulated 'means-end readinesses' for 'means-objects' which are innate but docile relative to the success of the organism in attaining its goal. Also in his account of 'behavior supports' he tried to escape the sensory atomism of stimulus-response psychology. He also developed the concept of the 'sign-Gestalt expectation' to incorporate the findings of Gestalt psychology into his assumptions about the organism's perceptual field.

Although Tolman emphasised the importance of innate appetites and aversions in behaviour he was equally emphatic on the importance of learning, in which he stressed the role of cognitive variables. He argued, also, that the evidence of latent learning was inconsistent with Thorndike's law of effect. In trial and error learning a refinement of sign-Gestalts takes place. A kind of cognitive map develops of the different possibilities as the various alternatives are explored.

Motivational variables are, of course, important in learning in that they determine which aspects of a situation will be emphasised. But learning depends primarily on the expectancy of achievement and on confirmations of the expectancy. In learning animals and men make predictions and the maps which they use to do this are refined more and more as experience confirms or falsifies them. As Tolman developed his theory he became more and more interested in and convinced of the importance of cognitive variables. It is therefore understandable that Behaviourists became increasingly embarrassed by Tolman's claim that he was one of them.

C. L. Hull

Behaviourism was basically old philosophy masquerading as a new scientific theory. In the 1930s philosophers began to be extremely critical of the old inductivist view of scientific method, which most of those in the empirical tradition had accepted, though Whewell in the nineteenth century had been an acute critic of this view. The role of hypothesis and deduction in science, which had been so prominent in the work of Galileo, was emphasised. Psychology began to be influenced by this change of emphasis in the philosophical climate. It was suggested, notably by Kurt Lewin and by Clark Hull, that psychology was in a state of disarray, split into warring factions, because it had not yet entered its Galilean phase. Lewin, a Gestalt psychologist, wrote a detailed methodological polemic to this effect in his chapter on 'Aristotelian and Galilean Modes of Explanation' in his *A Dynamic Theory of Personality* (1935). He envisaged the use of the resoluto-compositive method of Galileo to erect a field theory in psychology employing postulates taken from dynamics.

Clark Hull, unlike other prominent Behaviourists, was not trained in an animal laboratory. He had established a reputation for himself as an ingenious and talented designer of experiments in concept formation, hypnosis, and suggestibility. He next turned to Pavlov's laws of conditioning, and Hull's love for mathematics led him to set up a hypothetico-deductive model of learning. He became more and more ambitious and revived Hobbes's dream of a mechanical system in which the laws of human behaviour could be deduced from postulates about 'colourless movements' at the physiological level. He accepted Tolman's distinction between molecular and molar Behaviourism, but differed from Tolman in thinking that behaviour at the molar level could ultimately be explained in terms of movements at the molecular level. In 1943 he set out his ambitious programme in his *Principles of Behavior*, and in 1951 he published a revised and more formalised version of his system in his *Essentials of Behavior*.

There was little original in the actual content of Hull's system save the appearance of exactitude created by his technical constructs and mathematical form of expression. Hull started from the biological postulate of self-preservation and maintained that the organism is in a state of need when there is a deviation from optimum conditions for survival, e.g. lack of food, water, air. These needs are reduced by adaptive actions. The pattern of actions which lead to a reduction of a need becomes reinforced – as in Thorndike's law of effect. A stimulus which leads to a need-reducing action may become associated with another stimulus in accordance with principles of conditioning, though Hull believed that there is no conditioning without need-reduction.

Hull acknowledged the importance of what Tolman had called 'intervening variables' in theory construction, and also took over his concept of 'drive'. He regarded needs as producing primary animal drives, which enabled him to correlate observable antecedent conditions – e.g. of food deprivation with the energy expended in behaviour, e.g. in eating. He classified drives on the Darwinian principle of whether they tended towards survival of the individual organism or of the species. Whereas, however, Tolman only postulated such drives in order to explain the activation of behaviour patterns, Hull postulated them to explain their acquisition as well, and their consolidation into habits. Tolman, as has already been explained, was critical of the law of effect. Hull, on the other hand, tried to provide a mechanical theory to explain its operation. He also rejected Tolman's emphasis on cognitive variables and claimed that they could be derived from his fundamental postulate of stimulus-response association. Like Watson he was basically a peripheralist and an associationist in his orientation. He merely attempted to formulate these assumptions more precisely as part of a mechanical system.

Hull said that his book had been written

'on the assumption that all behavior, individual and social, moral and immoral, normal and psychopathic, is generated from the same primary laws; and that the differences in the objective behavioral manifestations are due to the differing conditions under which habits are set up and function' (*Principles of Behavior*, Preface, p. v).

This was programmatic. In fact his definitions and postulates were not well rooted in physiological findings, and precise deductions to level of motor behaviour were never made – if indeed they ever could be made. Unobservables, such as drive-stimuli, drive-receptors, etc., which were meant to fill in the mechanical picture of the workings of needs and drives, functioned more as hypothetical constructs relating to entities whose existence was shadowy and whose interrelations were highly obscure. The main value of his work was to formulate assumptions about animal learning at the motor level in a precise enough way to be refutable. And most of his assumptions were in fact refuted, e.g. by Hebb, Young, Harlow, and others. His system, however, became popular. Needs and acquired drives proliferated which lacked even the pretence of being anchored to physiological moorings. Drive-reduction became a classic example of twentieth-century metaphysics.

E. R. Guthrie

Hull had been content to state empirical laws at the molar level in terms of actions such as 'biting the floor-bars' and 'leaping the barrier' on the assumption that laws at this level of description could eventually be deduced from physiological postulates. E. R. Guthrie, on the other hand, a contemporary of Hull, eschewed physiological speculation and attempted to reduce behaviour at the molar level to movements such as muscle contractions and glandular secretions, between which correlations could be stated. He claimed that all such correlations were derivable from the old associationist law of contiguity, namely that stimuli acting at the time of a response tend on their recurrence to evoke that response. He was an S–R theorist par excellence.

Guthrie was one of the few Behaviourists to stress the difference between acts and movements. An act, he claimed quite rightly, is a movement, or a series of movements, that brings about an end and acts are classified in terms of the ends which they bring about. Learning, he argued, deals with movements, not with acts. Thorndike's law of effect concerns acts, not movements. It does not therefore deal with the basic laws of learning which state correlations between movements – e.g. between the stimulation of a sense organ and a muscular contraction. In a famous series of experiments which he did with Horton in 1946 Guthrie placed a cat in a box, release from which was obtained by touching a pole in the middle of the floor. It was demonstrated that the cat tended to repeat the posture in which it first touched the pole and obtained release. This experiment at least showed that contiguity is an important principle of learning; it did not establish that it is the only principle and later experiments (e.g. by Seward) showed that improvement in learning was brought about by providing an additional reward. Whether Guthrie's experiment showed anything about the wider issue of the importance of movements in learning as distinct from acts is quite another question. It is significant that Guthrie had to go to extreme lengths in constructing a situation where no intelligence was required to escape from the box, in order to make his reduction look in the least plausible. Nevertheless Guthrie was an important figure in the history of Behaviourism because he at least saw the importance of the distinction between movements and acts, and because he saw it as an obstacle in the path of any reductionist programme.

B. F. Skinner

Skinner is the last survivor of the great men of the Behaviourist era, but in many ways he is the most old-fashioned of all of them in his methodology; for in Skinner we encounter the pure strain of the inductivist doctrine of scientific method. Skinner believes that a scientist must start from empirical data and gradually move towards making inductive generalisations or laws. Then, at some later stage, he may be in a position to formulate a theory which unites the laws. He must therefore be very careful to start from reliable public data. Skinner admits that men have 'inner lives' which are of importance to them as well as to novelists, as Skinner himself portrayed in his novel *Walden Two*. But data drawn from this source can never form a reliable basis for a science. Skinner's polemics against other psychologists, such as Freudians, who based generalisations on data drawn from this inner realm, have been as forceful as Watson's polemics against the introspectionists.

Skinner has also accepted the inductivist warning that a scientist must never go beyond the observable in order to explain the observed. He has had no more use for physiological speculation about what goes on inside the organism than he has had for mentalistic constructs. He accords a limited importance to Tolman's intervening variables such as 'drive' provided that it is clearly understood that such terms are shorthand symbols for designating the operations by which the rate of responses can be measured. To speak of hunger as a drive, for instance, is to pick out of the effects of operations such as deprivation on the probability of eating behaviour.

Another significant feature of Skinner's approach is his operationism, which has recently been fashionable as a theory about the language of science. (See p. 57 above and supra pp. 37–43.) To Skinner this meant 'the practice of talking about (1) one's observations, (2) the manipulative and calculational procedures involved in making them, (3) the logical and mathematical steps which intervene between earlier and later statements, and (4) nothing else'. This doctrine maintained that a term like 'length' or 'hunger' refers not to a characteristic of an object or to a state of an organism but to the experimenter's operations of observing, manipulating, and measuring it. It was an offshoot of positivism and of the verificationist theory of meaning which came to the fore during the period between the two World Wars.

This theory of meaning has now been abandoned by most philosophers. But it lives on in the methodology of Skinner and some other Behaviourists, where it has the added appeal of being in line with the emphasis on control and manipulation of the environment which was so characteristic of Behaviourism in the Watsonian tradition. Behaviourism was in many respects an offshoot of American pragmatism. The experimenter has not got to trouble his head with theoretical questions about why organisms behave as they do, especially if reference might be made to recondite inner causes in order to answer them. It is sufficient to see what forms of behaviour develop if one environmental variable is manipulated rather than another. This will lead to predictions which will eventually enable the experimenter to 'shape' behaviour.

Skinner claims that he has no 'theory' of behaviour but only notes correlations. But this, of course, is either naïve or a matter of stipulation about the use of the term 'theory'. In fact his work has presupposed a biological theory of a Darwinian type in which conditioned reflexes are postulated as having survival value. In formulating the laws in accordance with which these 'reflexes' are built up Skinner in fact revived many of the established principles of associationist theory.

In formulating these laws Skinner made an important distinction between 'respondent' and 'operant' behaviour. This was facilitated by his introduction of the Skinner box, which enabled him to study instrumental conditioning in a much more controlled way than had been possible in Thorndike's puzzle box. In a respondent reaction there is a known stimulus, such as the ticking of the metronome, with which a reaction such as salivation can be correlated as in classical conditioning. In an operant response, however, such as lever pressing, there are no known stimuli with which the response can be correlated in this way. There may, of course, be some form of internal stimulation, but such speculations were ruled out by Skinner's operationist approach. So operant responses must be regarded as functions of experimental conditions such as food schedules which can be manipulated by the experimenter. As behaviour consists largely of such operant responses, which are instrumental in obtaining a variety of goals, Skinner thought that the study of conditioned operants and their extinction must provide the basic laws which would enable behaviour to be predicted and controlled. One day a theory might be devised to unify these laws; but the scientist must proceed to such 'interpretations' in a Baconian manner. He must not 'anticipate' Nature by premature theorising – especially if this involves speculations like those of Hull about the internal workings of the organism. Thus Skinner rejected the peripheralist approach of Watson but has remained agnostic about the central processes which mediate between stimuli and responses. Operant conditioning has been, in fact, another way of reformulating Thorndike's Law of Effect, in nonmentalistic terminology.

Like Watson, Skinner has not been averse to extending his conceptual scheme to cover other aspects of behaviour. For instance in his *Science and Human Behavior* in 1953 Skinner made pronouncements about emotions, the names of which serve to classify behaviour with respect to various circumstances which affect its probability. In spite, too, of his hardheaded positivistic approach in his *Verbal Behavior* (1957), he outlined an ambitious scheme for including language within the Behaviouristic framework. This work, however, was just about as programmatic as Hull's *Principles of Behavior*, and has been severely criticised by philosophers and linguists alike

In recent times Skinner has been very much preoccupied with providing a technology of teaching in which skills and sequences of material are carefully broken down and the path of learning systematically shaped by positive reinforcement. However, his concept of 'reinforcement', which has always been criticised for its obscurity and circularity, has undergone such changes that his recipes for teaching amount to little more than injunctions that material should be logically analysed and students should be taken through it step by step in a way which minimises the repetition of mistakes, and which supplies constant rewards for success. This type of procedure, as Skinner himself has admitted, could be devised without much reference to his elaborate laws of operant behaviour.

4 SUMMARY AND EVALUATION

It has been argued throughout this article that Behaviourism, as an historical phenomenon, has been a loosely knit collection of doctrines and theories woven round a central prescription about the proper method to use in developing a science of psychology. Behaviourism, first of all, has often been associated with the *metaphysical* doctrine of materialism. Nowadays there is less reluctance to discuss metaphysical problems than there was in the heyday of Behaviourism and of 'the revolution in philosophy'. Materialism has been revived, though it has few adherents amongst philosphers except in Australia. One of its problems has been to state coherently what could be meant by saying that mental and bodily processes are identical.

It would be difficult to maintain that, in the sphere of *scientific theory*, Behaviourism has advanced the understanding of behaviour in any major respect. The theory which was most widely employed was that of associationism which was as old as Hobbes, Hume, and Hartley. The Behaviourists merely transferred this theory from the realm of ideas to the realm of movements. What occupied them most was disputes amongst themselves within this type of theoretical framework. There were two major issues which divided them. The first related to the importance of reward or reinforcement in setting up S–R connections. The second issue concerned the relative importance of central as distinct from peripheral processes. It was not really surprising that the Behaviourists in fact contributed little in the way of theory to the understanding of behaviour; for basically most of them were not interested in explaining behaviour or even learning for that matter. They were interested in conditioning. Even at the animal level it is extremely doubtful whether rats, dogs, cats, and monkeys in fact learn much by conditioning in a normal environment. Ethological studies certainly cast grave doubt on the omnipresence of this type of learning. It is probable that this type of learning is an artifact of the situations in which animals have been confined. The extrapolation of this type of learning to the human level, where the pattern of life is determined largely by social rules and purposes, was largely programmatic. However, Behaviourists showed that associationist principles might well apply to the learning of simple reactions and motor habits. Little more could in fact be claimed for their contribution to psychological theory.

Many of the defects in Behaviouristic theorising, especially their programmatic extrapolations to the human level, derived from their lack of clarity about such *concepts* as stimulus, reinforcement, and response. Underlying these particular confusions were fundamental confusions about the concept of behaviour itself, due to their aversion to assuming the existence of consciousness. Guthrie was most sensitive to this difficulty. He made the distinction between acts and movements and tried to arrange an experiment which dealt only with movements; for he realised only too well that descriptions of behaviour at the molar level are in terms of acts and not in terms of mere movements. And we identify their acts by reference to what human beings have in mind when they make certain movements. For example, an act involving the same movements of the arm is identified as either signalling to a friend or fanning the face.

Skinner, in his distinction between operants and respondents, actually hit upon a distinction which is crucial for getting clearer about the concept of action. Respondent reactions like salivations and eye-blinks, which can be dealt with reasonably well by classical conditioning theory, are indeed reactions which can be correlated with stimuli. But they are not, strictly speaking, actions; they are events that happen to us. When, however, we pass to Skinner's operants, to things done as instrumental to an end, we are entering the sphere of action proper. Such actions, at the human level at any rate, cannot either be described or explained as mere movements exhibited at the reflex level. For an action is not simply a series of bodily movements; such movements as are necessary to it are done for the sake of something, as Aristotle pointed out in his criticism of the mechanists of the ancient world. They are classed as belonging to an action because of their assumed relevance to an end (*telos*).

Similarly, on the perceptual as distinct from the motor side of behaviour, the importance of consciousness is inescapable. Human beings, and probably animals as well, do not often simply react to stimuli in terms of their purely physical properties, as the Gestalt psychologists pointed out in their distinction between the psychological and physical or geographical properties of the environment. They see things as meaning something; they respond to features of situations which are interpreted in terms of their understanding of them. Skinner, for instance, was grossly misleading when he claimed that what we call emotions are names for classifying behaviour with respect to various circumstances which affect the probability of the behaviour's occurrence; for the circumstances are those which are *interpreted* by the subject in a certain light, e.g. as dangerous in the case of fear, as involving somebody else having something which we want in the case of envy. The relationship between circumstances and the subject is not one of purely physical causality.

In brief, even what the Bchaviourists called 'behaviour' includes a range of phenomena between which there are very important distinctions, let alone other purely mental phenomena such as remembering and dreaming, which may have no overt expressions and which may lead to no overt actions. Many more distinctions than these can be drawn which would complicate the picture even further. But this would not affect the two cardinal points that need to be emphasised: first, that it is impossible to make such distinctions without reference to consciousness and, second, that Behaviourists tend to think that the form of description and explanation applicable at the lowest level of reflex behaviour can be extrapolated to explain the much more complex phenomena at higher levels.

About the *methodological* doctrine that was the kernel of Behaviourism – that psychology should base itself as a science on the type of publicly observable data that biologists use when theorising about animals – the first point to make is that it is an example of the long-standing delusion that success in science depends upon following a particular method. A study of the history of science gives no support for the belief that science has in fact been advanced by following any particular method, if this is interpreted as meaning following a particular procedure for making discoveries or arriving at laws. It is impossible to formulate any method for arriving at hypotheses; all that can be done is to lay down general rules about testing them.

Is there then anything to be said for the Behaviourists' prescription as a procedural rule relating to the testing of hypotheses rather than to their formulation? If they had been concerned solely with animal behaviour their prescription would have been unexceptionable but otiose; for there is no possibility of obtaining introspective reports from animals. In so far, however, as they studied animals partly with the intention of making extrapolations to human behaviour, their prescription seems to be very much a self-denying ordinance, for in science it is advisable to obtain all the evidence available. Also the sort of observations which are appropriate depends upon what is being studied. If it is reactions such as salivation, knee-jerks, and simple motor skills, which were the main field of interest amongst Behaviourists, introspective reports may not be of great significance. If, however, hypotheses about dreams, perception, delusions, remembering, emotional phenomena, or moral development have to be tested, it is very difficult to see how much relevant evidence could be accumulated without recourse to reports by the subject. And it simply will not do to say that the experimenter is then relying on another form of behaviour, namely verbal behaviour. Furthermore, this move by Behaviourists is a form of *conceptual* Behaviourism. The methodological doctrine, which is distinctive of Behaviourism, would evaporate if a subject's reports were readmitted as evidence because they too were regarded as forms of behaviour.

Historically, therefore, Behaviourism was a salutary corrective that was pushed to inordinate extremes. At a time when psychology was largely preoccupied with examining the minutiae of a subject's introspections there was some point in drawing attention to what could be publicly observed. But this injunction unfortunately was not accompanied by any suggestion of new hypotheses that might be tested. If functioned mainly as a new recipe for continuing the old associationist programme. The widespread implementation of this recipe, however, had very important consequences for psychology generally. It enhanced the status of psychology as a science amongst the scientific community. Psychologists could now wear lab-coats like biologists and be admitted to the Faculty of Science. Although Behaviourism was basically a philosophical movement psychologists were now able to part company with philosophers and set up on their own.

Whether this separation has been beneficial in advancing our understanding of human behaviour is another question; for the basic problem in the central spheres of action, motivation and emotion, perception, learning, remembering, etc., is to decide what is a psychological question. In the sphere of learning, for instance, in which Behaviourists evinced most interest, how much depends upon the conceptual and logical relationships involved in what has to be learnt and how much depends on general empirical conditions about which psychologists might reasonably test hypotheses? The work of theorists such as Jerome Bruner and Jean Piaget, who have been concerned with human learning and development in a concrete rather than a programmatic way, raises such problems in an acute form. But it is difficult to see how much progress can be made until issues of this sort are squarely faced. But to face them would involve a revolution in psychology as radical as the methodological movement which Watson himself initiated.

3

FREUD'S THEORY

INTRODUCTION

It is usual for expositions of Freud's theory to take the form of a historical reconstruction. Freud is featured as the Copernicus of psychology and his discoveries are charted against the background of the psychology of his time as he slowly made explicit his revolutionary insights. In such an account prominence would be given to his discovery of unconscious processes, of repression, and of infantile sexuality, following the example of his own Introductory Lectures. But these assumptions were incorporated by Freud in a considerable texture of theory; it may therefore be of value to set the whole theory out as briefly as possible so that it can be seen as a whole and compared with other theories. This is the purpose of this brief exposition.

1 THE PRESERVATION OF EQUILIBRIUM

Human beings, like other organisms, tend to preserve a state of equilibrium. They are enabled to do this by their nervous system which is an apparatus having the function of abolishing stimuli, or of reducing excitation to the lowest possible level, an apparatus which would even, if this were feasible, maintain itself in an altogether unstimulated condition. Our mental life is a function of this apparatus and our experience of pleasure and pain reflects the manner in which this mastering of stimuli takes place.

Stimuli are of two sorts, external and internal (instinctual). The latter act as constant forces and are best described as needs. Flight will not avail against them, and the common distinction between 'outer' and 'inner' is due to this fact. Thus 'by an "instinct" is provisionally to be understood the psychical representative of an endosomatic continuously flowing source of stimulation, as contrasted with a "stimulus" which is set up by single excitations coming from without'. When considered collectively we may refer to these psychical representations as the *id*.

Instincts have

(a) An impetus – their demand on energy.
(b) An aim – the satisfaction obtained by abolishing the source of stimulation.
(c) An object – that in or through which their aim is achieved.
(d) A source – the somatic process from which the stimulus results.

Thus instincts manifest themselves in mental life as emotionally charged ideas or wishes for objects the attainment of which will reduce the needs which initiated behaviour.

These wishes may be *conscious*, *preconscious*, or *unconscious*, the criterion at the purely descriptive level being introspective accessibility. If unconscious they are prevented from becoming conscious by *repression*, which manifests itself, especially during analysis, as *resistance* to attempts to bring them into consciousness.

Instinctual satisfaction is modified by perception of the environment, learning, and the development of speech. Restraint of motor discharge is effected by thought, which is imaginative experimentation, and the uncertain pleasures of the moment are renounced in favour of assured satisfaction later. The *ego* develops as an intermediary between the *id* and the external world, and the *reality principle* comes to supersede the pure *pleasure principle*. But a type of thought activity persists which is solely subservient to the pleasure principle. This is *phantasy*.

Many have thought that the distinction between the *primary processes* under the control of the pure pleasure principle and the *secondary processes* under the control of the reality principle, was one of Freud's most important contributions to psychological theory. He claimed that unconscious mental activity in dreams, phantasy, and in certain types of hysterical and obsessional thought follows the same laws and is of quite a different order from ordinary conscious mental processes. In the primary process there is, for instance, no consciousness of time, of contradiction, or of relation to the real world. *Condensation* of ideas and *displacement*, or the substitution of one object of an instinct for another object, take place freely; thinking is carried on in pictures, not verbally, and is directed only by the striving for discharge. It is also characterised by its own type of *symbolism* in which no distinction is made between emotionally equivalent objects – e.g. penis and snake, the relation of representing, which characterises symbols of conscious thought, being quite foreign to it.

The clearest examples of instincts are the *ego-instincts* – e.g. hunger, thirst, and defecation, which manifestly are ways in which the organism preserves its equilibrium.

Allied to these are the *sex-instincts*, because

(a) They serve to preserve life, albeit that of the species rather than simply of the individual organism.
(b) Their source is in the *erotogenic zones* of the body (mouth, anus, and genitals) and they are originally aroused by self-preservative activities like feeding and excreting.

But their aim is *organ-pleasure* and they later detach themselves from the ego-instincts and act independently. They are incorporated and work together in the final organisation of the sexual function, in the usual sense of 'sexual'.

This original classification of instincts, apart from its Darwinian justification, was adopted as a heuristic tool because, in the early work on the psychoneuroses, the root of the affections was found to lie in the conflict between the claims of sexuality and those of the ego.

(Freud suggested in his later work that in opposition to the *life-instincts* – i.e. the sex and ego instincts – and working against the tendency of the organism to preserve its equilibrium, was the *death-instinct*. According to this later suggestion every organism has also a tendency to destroy itself or to return to the inorganic.)

2 MECHANISMS FOR PRESERVING EQUILIBRIUM

The external world, with its reservoir of stimuli, presents itself as alien and hostile to the developing ego. But the ego also has to defend itself against danger from instinctual wishes whose satisfaction would bring about disaster in the face of the physical or social environment. To deal with such dangers the ego employs certain *mechanisms* or techniques of defence, some of which are only partially successful. The onset of a danger situation is felt as *anxiety*, which represents both the feeling of helplessness in the face of great danger and the expectation that such a danger situation is imminent.

In some of the mechanisms the ego makes use of techniques which also characterise the primary process. In *identification*, for instance, *introjection* is employed; for primary identification involves the putting into the mouth of what is perceived which is one of the child's most primitive ways of dealing with its environment. The mother is both imitated and taken into the mouth, there being little distinction between these two processes at the early stage in which the ego is not differentiated from the external world. In secondary identification, however, the ego loves an external object – e.g. mother or father – which it cannot attain, and guards itself against loss of the loved object by introjecting it or taking it into itself.

Projection, similarly, denotes the earliest type of rejection in spitting out what is painful. But as the ego develops as distinct from the external world, it wards off emotions or excitations which are a threat to it and attributes them to the environment. The offensive impulse is thus projected or perceived in another thing or person instead of being thought of as in the threatened individual.

In *sublimation* the aim or object of an instinct is changed without blocking it, which enables sexual strivings to be satisfied in a desexualised manner. This presupposes that the instinctual wishes are not repressed in such a manner as to produce pathological symptoms.

Repression is the most important of all the mechanisms. This defence consists in letting pass out of consciousness, and preventing from re-entering consciousness, wishes for or thoughts of events which represent possible temptations for disapproved of and punishable instinctual demands. The repressed, though unconscious, continues to exert its influence, and the individual is often beset by anxiety to which no object can be attached. But repression, though only a partially successful defence, prevents what has been repressed from being put to conscious use by the ego in motility. The cost of achieving such limited safety is often very great, especially as energy is used up in keeping the material repressed.

Reaction-formation is another defence against instinctual danger to the ego. It consists in an exaggerated tendency in opposition to the unconscious wish, in which the personality is permanently prepared for the onset of an insistent instinctual danger – e.g. the worshipper of cleanliness who thus struggles against his unconscious demand for dirt. A reaction-formation may ally itself with another drive, the aim of which is opposite to that of the feared instinctual demand.

In *rationalisation* the ego compromises with objectionable instinctual demands by satisfying them under the cloak of socially acceptable reasons.

In *isolation* the ego defends itself by isolating an idea or hiving it off from its emotional significance. Or the idea may be emotionally entertained but separated from motility. Day-dreams of murder illustrate the latter possibility; the gratification of sexual desires by recourse to prostitutes, without any tender feelings towards them, illustrates the former.

Regression consists in dealing with frustration by returning to an earlier period of life when satisfaction was obtained. The period depends on *fixation*. For, in the development of the child, fixation tends to occur if there is too little or too much satisfaction of an instinct. This mechanism is not set in motion by the ego; rather it presupposes a weak ego formation and is set in motion by the instincts which demand a substitute satisfaction. Thus a person who is blocked in adult forms of sexuality may regress to an infantile form of sexuality. To understand what is meant by this and to be clearer about the typical threats to the ego which occur at the different stages of development we must pass to Freud's next set of assumptions.

3   THE DEVELOPMENT OF LIBIDO

Freud was at first interested almost exclusively in the development of the sexual instincts and of *libido* or sexual longing – 'that force by which the sexual instinct is represented in the mind'. This has definite stages.

The baby is subject to erotic sensations and is originally auto-erotic aiming at organ-pleasure from the different erotogenic zones. It is because of this primary *narcissism* that the sex-instincts take longer than the ego-instincts to become subservient to the reality-principle.

At different stages of development interest is centred on and pleasure predominantly obtained from the different erotogenic zones – first the mouth, then the anus, then the genitals. These are what are known as the oral, anal, and phallic stages of development; and fixation may occur at any of them if frustration or gratification is excessive.

Love, which originates in the capacity of the ego to satisfy some of its instincts auto-erotically, is transferred to objects associated with organ-pleasure and expresses the motor striving of the ego after these objects as sources of pleasure. Love for objects is thus originally connected with feeding, care, protection, cuddling, and so on. It may be *anaclitic* if the mother is the object-choice, or *narcissistic* if directed predominantly towards the self.

The development of libido is complicated by Freud's contention that love is always *ambivalent* – i.e. accompanied by hate. The relationship between love and hate is so complicated that we cannot do better than quote from Freud's own summary in his definitive paper on 'Instincts and Their Vicissitudes':

The preliminary stages of love reveal themselves as temporary sexual aims, while the sexual instincts are passing through their complicated development. First amongst these we recognise the phase of incorporating or devouring, a type of love which is compatible with abolition of any separate existence on the part of the object, and which may therefore be designated ambivalent. At the higher stage of pregenital sadistic-anal organisation, the striving after the object appears in the form of an impulsion to mastery, in which injury or annihilation of the object is a matter of indifference. This form and preliminary stage of love is hardly to be distinguished from hate in its behaviour towards the object. Only when the genital organisation is established does love become the antithesis of hate.

The relationship of hate to objects is older than that of love. It is derived from the primal repudiation by the narcissistic ego of the external world whence flows the stream of stimuli. As an expression of the pain-reaction induced by objects, it remains in constant intimate relation with the instincts of self-preservation, so that sexual and ego instincts readily develop an antithesis which repeats that of love and hate. When the sexual function is governed by the ego instinct, as at the stage of the sadistic-anal organisation, they impart the qualities of hate to the instinct's aim as well.

The history of the origin and relations of love makes us understand how it is that love so constantly manifests itself as 'ambivalent', i.e. accompanied by feelings of hate against the same object. This admixture of hate in love is to be traced in part to those preliminary stages of love which have not been wholly outgrown, and in part is based upon reactions of aversion and repudiation on the part of the ego-instincts which, in the frequent conflicts between the interests of the ego and those of love, can claim to be supported by real and actual motives. In both cases, therefore, the admixture of hate may be traced to the source of the self-preservative instincts.

(This view about the relationship between love and hate was later complicated by the introduction of the death-instinct. For Freud postulated that the self-destructiveness of the organism was often turned outwards towards objects in aggression or sadism.)

Masochism is a development of sadism. For instincts undergo what Freud called *vicissitudes* one of which is when an instinct, which is frustrated in relation to an external object, turns round upon the subject. Thus the original sadism directed towards an object in the external world may be turned on the self thereby occasioning pain together with accompanying sexual excitation. Another person may then be sought to inflict this pain, and this constitutes masochism. (The infliction of pain is not part of the original sadistic aim, only the mastery of the object.)

The development of libido reaches a culmination at about the age of four, when interest is centred predominantly on the genitals. This is the famous Oedipus phase. The boy wishes for sexual contact with his mother and develops as a rival of his father. The way in which this situation is resolved depends upon the degree to which masculinity or feminity (identification with the parent of the same sex) is developed in the boy or girl. For Freud postulated a fundamental *bi-sexuality*. In some masculinity and in others feminity will be more pronounced; and this does not always follow the biological make-up of the child. Thus a boy in whom masculinity is predominant will wish for sexual contact with his mother and will be aggressive towards his father and fear castration at his hands, whereas a boy with pronounced feminine tendencies will develop a negative Oedipus complex and will wish for castration. The girl, similarly, may act out different roles. The child, depending on his or her sexual make-up, can take either parent as a love-object or can identify himself or herself with either as an extension of narcissism and thus develop an *ego-ideal*.

The way in which the Oedipus situation is resolved is crucial in the formation of the *super-ego* which is the heir to the Oedipus complex. The beginnings of this occur in primary identification when the child introjects the mother or father together with parental prohibitions. When the ego is distinguished from the external world the loved object is also introjected as a defence against losing it. Thus identification succeeds object-cathexis and the super-ego is formed as a kind of precipitate of past object-choices, the later identifications reinforcing and being superimposed on the earlier ones. As relations with the parents reach a climax at the Oedipus period the final character of the super-ego will depend very much on the type of secondary identification here adopted, which, in its turn, will depend a lot on the balance of masculinity and feminity in the child.

The broad general outcome of the sexual phase governed by the Oedipus complex may, therefore, be taken to be the forming of a precipitate in the ego, consisting of these two identifications in some way combined together. This modification of the ego retains its special position; it stands in contrast to other constituents of the ego in the form of an ego-ideal or super-ego.

In this way parental norms are effective in modifying the behaviour of the child without the parent having to be present to preside over the child's conduct.

But the super-ego is not merely a deposit left by early object-choices; it also represents an energetic reaction-formation against such choices which are likely to be disapproved of and hence dangerous. The ego-ideal therefore stands also inside the child as an obstacle to the realisation of Oedipus wishes of an incestuous kind. The ego is reinforced in carrying out its repressions by erecting, in the form of a reaction-formation, an obstacle within itself to the satisfaction of such objectionable demands.

The establishment of the super-ego brings to an end the Oedipus period and starts the period of latency. This continues until, with the development of sexual organs, genital sexuality proper develops.

4 CAUSAL-GENETIC ASSUMPTIONS

In addition to the above principles, mechanisms, and stages of development we must also assume:

(a) That childhood wishes persist and, even if unconscious, exert a great influence on later behaviour.
(b) That the mechanisms we adopt to solve conflicts inevitable at the stages of development are formative in the development of character.

We can now sketch the sorts of explanations made possible by Freud's theory.

The general postulate of the persistence of unconscious wishes explains by means of the same principles the previously disconnected phenomena of dreams, phantasy thinking, art, unintentional acts like slips of the tongue, lapses of memory, failures in observation and attention, jokes, and thought constructions like those of religion, metaphysics, and Utopian politics.

The theory of infantile sexuality, the development of libido, and the persistence of methods of solving conflicts at the stages of development not only explains character-traits but also links these with

the behaviour of neurotics. Previously disconnected traits are unified
– e.g. orderliness, parsimony, pedantry, conscientiousness in the anal
character. Examples of the way in which the operation of certain
mechanisms rather than others at the stages of development tends to
develop constellations of character-traits are:

the oral character and the link with schizophrenics and manic-
    depressives.
the anal character and the link with obsessionals and megalomaniacs.
the phallic character and the link with anxiety neurotics and hysterics.

The solution of the Oedipus situation along the lines of anaclitic or
narcissistic object choice, together with the way in which identification takes place, is, of course, crucial in relation to the pattern of love
relationships set up and the influence it has on genital sexuality.
Homosexuality, failure of men to love and respect women with whom
they have sexual intercourse, sexual perversions, impotence, frigidity,
and countless other such manifestations of sexual maladjustment are
referred back to their infantile prototypes.

Freud was also bold enough to extend his principles to explain
cultural phenomena. The social bond which links men together in
groups was explained in terms of identification and aim-inhibited
libido. Conscience was explained in terms of introjection, identification, and aggression turned round on the subject. Universal
prohibitions like those on incest, totemic practices, and religious
rituals were all fitted into the above system of explanation.

Examples could be multiplied of the fields to which Freud extended his principles of explanation. He produced a fertile and an
exciting theory in that he not only put forward new explanations for
hitherto unexplained behaviour but also linked together by means
of his theory forms of behaviour which were previously thought of
as disconnected. The attempt of this paper has been merely to present
as coherently as possible the main principles by means of which he
attempted to do this.

4

MOTIVATION, EMOTION AND THE CONCEPTUAL SCHEMES OF COMMON SENSE

INTRODUCTION

In reflecting upon what contribution I might most usefully make to a symposium of philosophers and psychologists on a conceptual framework for human actions, I came to the conclusion that I would attempt a bridging and synoptic one. Presumably the psychologists will approach this topic from the vantage point of the conceptual scheme that they have found to be most fruitful in research. The philosophers, on the other hand, are likely to concern themselves with less heuristic conceptual and methodological matters to do with action, reason, cause and the status of teleological explanations. I thought it might be useful, therefore, to try to relate psychological theories of motivation and emotion, especially those favoured by the psychologists contributing to this symposium (in so far as I am familiar with them), to the conceptual scheme of human actions the 'logical geography' of which philosophers of the analytic school try to map.

This is a vast and ambitious undertaking that would tend to meander from one theory to another unless some connecting thread were provided. I have therefore attempted to provide one by developing a unifying thesis about the indispensability in psychological theory of what I call the conceptual schemes of common sense. This has helped me to get a bit clearer about what has puzzled me profoundly on and off for the past twenty-five years, which is the problem of the relationship between psychological theories and the less specialised knowledge that enables us most of the time to make sense of each other's behaviour and of our own.

1   PSYCHOLOGY, COMMON SENSE AND THE INSTITUTIONAL FRAMEWORK

One of the sources of George Kelly's* dissatisfaction with psychological theories of motivation, which have been in fashion during the last half century, has been that such theorists seem to propound two theories (Bannister, 1966, p. 361). The first deals with the behaviour of the organism, which is characterised as impelled by drives, reacting to stimuli, or at the mercy of unconscious wishes; the second relates to the psychologist himself, who constructs theories and derives and tests hypotheses in the endeavour to understand, predict, and control his environment. Although the first is usually called a scientific theory and the second an account of scientific method, both are thought to have application to human behaviour. Kelly's own theory of 'personal constructs' derived from his attempt to take the second type of account of man seriously. He extrapolated the notion of 'man the scientist' from this type of situation and conceived of human behaviour generally in terms of the attempt to understand, predict, and control the environment. Personal constructs are conceptual templates that enable individuals to anticipate events (Kelly, 1955, Chs 1–3).

The suggestion that psychologists should think seriously about a typically human activity, such as thinking scientifically, as well as atypical animal activities, such as running mazes and pressing levers, is one with which I have great sympathy; for my belief is that much of the work done in this century by psychologists reveals very little about the psychology of animals, let alone of men. But I do not think that Kelly has pursued far enough the implications of his initial insight. Many, of course, would object to the emphasis on control and prediction in his account of the scientist, and many would demur at the extrapolation of this type of human activity rather than some other; but my objection to a possible interpretation of this starting point is much more deep seated. It is that man the scientist might be postulated in isolation from the rules and procedures that are constitutive of this form of activity. Science is one of the most rule-ridden of all human activities. One must listen to what other people say; one must accept nothing as true unless evidence is produced; one must state one's hypotheses as clearly and in as impersonal a way

* The device of launching this paper from the pad provided by Kelly's theory was first adopted when it was thought that Kelly was to be a participant in the colloquium. His untimely death, however, prevented this. Nevertheless it was thought fitting to retain this way of introducing the topic.

as possible; one must not cook the evidence or misrepresent other people's assumptions. Men only come to think 'scientifically' if they have been brought up in this kind of critical tradition, with the overriding value that it places on truth and, as Francis Bacon argued so forcibly in his *Novum Organum*, this way of thinking goes against inveterate tendencies of the human mind.

If, therefore, one pursues the implications of Kelly's starting point, one comes to see not just that scientific thinking is only possible within a certain type of tradition, but that it is only intelligible to us as a form of human activity because we have been initiated into such a tradition. This is how we are placed in relation both to science and to all typically human activities. For most of us, however, most of the time the preoccupations of the scientist are pretty remote, unless notions like 'control' and 'prediction' are extended so that they cease to distinguish scientific from any other typically human activity. This is because much of our time is spent in making different forms of judgement within various human activities rather than in systematically trying to understand them in a more detailed way. On occasions we state our intentions, make promises, and justify our conduct; on other occasions we praise and blame people, we give advice and warnings, select some for jobs and reject others. We listen to music, perhaps; appreciate pictures; watch and participate in games. We make love, money, and cakes. Sometimes we even give people orders. All such activities presuppose distinctive structures of rules and distinctive types of languages. No doubt within these public forms of life we develop our own criteria of importance, our personal constructs, if you like. But these arise as personal emphases out of a public stock, and they are made on situations that are intelligible to us only because we have developed a shared system of concepts and ways of behaviour.

What is called our common sense knowledge consists largely in what we possess when we have learned our way around this complex heritage. It comprises no set or fixed body of beliefs; in content it is, to a large extent, culture bound, depending on the level of differentiation and complexity that a society has attained. It may include deposits of scientific theories that have been incorporated in a popular way into the common stock of assumptions; it may vary from group to group within a society. Its main characteristic is its intimate connection with the practical concerns of a society, the particular rules and purposes of its institutions, and the more personal relationships of its members. When, therefore, psychologists speak sometimes rather disparagingly about what they call common sense (see, e.g., Atkinson, 1964, Ch. 1), they usually ignore and oversimplify the the richness and complexity of the understanding that it contains. This is the first aspect of common sense for which it is difficult to see how psychology could provide an adequate substitute. For this sort of understanding is revealed in the *identification* of behaviour as well as in its explanation, there being no hard and fast line between them (see Melden, 1961, *passim*). To revert, for instance, to the case of the scientist: we could ask why Galileo was rolling balls down an inclined plane. If we were told that he was doing this in order to test a scientific hypothesis, we could then, in some other context, refer to what he was doing as 'testing a scientific hypothesis'. An action with a low-level purpose would be classified as one having a higher-level purpose. Similarly, in a means–end type of situation, an end like 'getting a promotion', which can be appealed to as an explanation of a person's hard work, could be used to characterise his behaviour at work. This is because the explanation and the identification of actions depend on the aspect under which the agent views what he is doing: as conforming to some standard or as bringing about some end. And this can be stated at different levels of generality or located at different points of prevision. To identify human behaviour, therefore, as well as to explain it in a commonsense way, we must know not only the general rules and purposes governing the type of activity under scrutiny; we must also know the agent's view of the matter, his information, what he sees as important in the situation. Whatever would we make of a person sitting down and moving bits of wood around unless we knew something about the rules of chess and the point of the game?

These are not particularly outlandish examples; for my contention is that much of human behaviour is like this. It is constituted by human beings manœuvering within a complicated network of purposes and rules that are appealed to for both the explanation and the identification of behaviour, depending on the context (cf. Winch, 1958, Ch. 11). The same sort of point can be made, too, about performances in which psychologists are interested, such as perception and memory, as has been made about activities, such as doing science, or actions, such as moving a piece of wood. For both perception and memory involve standards of reality, claims about what is really there or about what really happened; both involve classification of things or events as falling under concepts that are related in complicated ways to each other. All these presuppose elaborate conventions worked out over centuries, which are incorporated in our language. If we understood nothing of these elaborate conventions, human behaviour would be as unintelligible to us as it is to small children and to animals.

Of course, we do understand it, more or less. And this is not because we have learned any psychology; it is because we have been initiated from childhood onward into the various rules and purposes that are constitutive of human life (see Peters, 1966, Ch. 2). In learning to behave as human beings we at the same time take into ourselves the structure of concepts and categories without which we could make no sense of human life. In learning a language we gradually structure our consciousness with these rules for making sense of the world and relating ourselves to aspects of it in various ways. Our ability to reason scientifically, for instance, depends not only on gradually acquiring categories like those of enduring object, reality, and causality, but also on the incorporation of a critic into our consciousness so that we look for counterexamples to our expectations. All this has to be laboriously learned.

It is not surprising, therefore, if the psychologist can contribute very little to the understanding of particular actions and if his ability to predict what an individual will do in particular circumstances is little better than that of his nonprofessional colleagues. This is because success depends much more on detailed knowledge of the society and the individual in question, including his history and belief system, than on the devising of any new general laws. Lewin, it is true, emphasised the importance of the life space of a person at a given time; but he devised no satisfactory way of including all that would have to be known about this in his Galilean system. Indeed, how could he have done so? Furthermore, he neglected the importance of knowledge of the enduring attributes of a person, which only familiarity with his history could provide.

A similar point can be made about more recent work on achievement motivation. It is suggested that

'the motive to achieve success (M_S), which the individual carries about with him from one situation to another, combines multiplicatively with the two specific situational influences, the strength of expectancy or probability of success (P_S), and incentive value of success at a particular activity (I_S) to produce the tendency to approach success that is overtly expressed in the direction, magnitude, and persistence of achievement-oriented performance' (Atkinson, 1964, p. 242).

Atkinson points out that, whereas the first variable is a relatively general and stable characteristic of the person, values of the other two variables P_S and I_S depend on the individual's past experience in specific situations that are similar to the one that he now confronts. Assigning values to these variables must therefore depend on a fairly intimate knowledge of the individual concerned. This presents far greater difficulties than does formulating the commonsense assumptions enshrined in the generalisations. Indeed, I am inclined to say that if people in American society were not alive to these generalisations about achievement, one would ask questions about their general education rather than about their attendance at psychology courses!

Of course in coming to understand why individuals do what they do, or to predict what they will do, we make use not just of our detailed knowledge of their past and their individual systems of beliefs, purposes, and appraisals; we also rely, as I have emphasised before, on our familiarity with the general rules and purposes of the various activities and social institutions (such as science) that they have internalised in varying degrees. Much of this type of knowledge is specific to particular activities and institutions. It is because of this that we know what people are doing and roughly what to expect of them in restaurants, hotels, colleges, churches, and golf clubs. It is because of the importance of this sort of knowledge that, on getting to know people, we first orient ourselves to them by finding out their profession, marital status, and other affiliations. In this area of knowledge, social psychologists have much to contribute, which falls under the rather too general concept of role playing. It is difficult to see how any developments in psychology could reveal the unimportance of this sort of general knowledge; for as I have argued before, it is largely constitutive of the form of life in which we are engaged most of our waking lives. To dispense with it would be to put ourselves in the positions of dogs trying to take part in or to understand the proceedings of a law court.

It might be thought that much store is being placed on what might be called the conventional wisdom of the tribe. But the thesis here advanced is not about the indispensability of all the *content* of common sense; rather it relates to the indispensability of the types of concepts that it employs, namely, those belonging to the family of which 'wanting', 'following a rule', 'deciding', and so on are members. Particularly assumptions embedded in common sense (e.g. about what people invariably want) may well be mistaken and it is an important function of empirical psychology to provide evidence that may falsify such assumptions. Similarly, evidence should be provided as confirmations of common sense, though on occasions this might seem rather otiose.

Psychological theories, too, may extend and attempt to make more precise assumptions that are embedded in common sense (e.g. the work done by Atkinson and McClelland on 'achievement') and to suggest ways in which factors involved in such assumptions are combined and related to each other. Doubts of a conceptual sort might, of course, be raised about the type of relationship envisaged. It is not altogether clear, for instance, how far the use of algebra in a system like that of Lewin or Atkinson advances our understanding until the basis of the measurement is clear and one is sure that commensurables are being combined. The way in which 'beliefs', for instance, are related to 'wants' in giving an account of action is distorted if these are thought of as separable variables that can be quantified and causally related to each other; for to want something is always to want it under some aspect and the aspect falls under beliefs. (If I want to eat something, my seeing it under the aspect of 'food' is connected with various beliefs about its properties.) The connection, in other words, between beliefs and wants in so far as both are involved in 'motivated behaviour', is conceptual rather than causal. The strength and persistence of certain wants can, of course be measured. But if an attempt were made to isolate and quantify the belief component, all sorts of problems would break out. What could be done about the content of beliefs, for instance, and the grounds on which they are held? 'Strength' of beliefs is a notion that suggests quantification; but it is unintelligible apart from notions like 'evidence' and 'good reasons'; and how are logical notions of that sort to be expressed algebraically?

This general sort of point can be made with particular reference to the problem of quantifying a variable, such as P_S in Atkinson's system, which is a situational variable relating to the strength of expectancy or probability of success. Probability theorists have always found these sorts of sums very difficult; but when they occupy a twilight zone between rational grounds of belief and actual psychological potency, the algebra becomes even more problematic. And the more the notion of 'strength of expectancy' approximates to psychological potency, the nearer it gets to the notion of the 'incentive value of success' (I_S), which is represented as a distinct situational variable. Nevertheless, whatever one thinks of the algebra by means of which Lewin and Atkinson summarise their theories, the attempt to give more precision to common–sense assumptions is laudable enough. It would be more laudable still if it were accompanied by an attempt to break down further conceptually such common-sense notions as achievement, which incorporate at least three rather different notions, namely, the desire to master or succeed in anything that one attempts, the desire to master or succeed in anything that one thinks important, and the desire to do anything better than one's fellows.

2 MOTIVES, TRAITS AND ATTITUDES

Mention of the achievement motive brings to the fore the fact that there are, even at the common–sense level, a whole range of explanations of human behaviour that do not seem so clearly bound up with *specific* activities and institutions. We interpret a range of behaviour as directed toward making good a deficit of things such as food, water and affection. Other types of behaviour are classified in terms of character traits, such as honesty, punctuality, selfishness and considerateness, which are internalised rules widespread in society rather than confined to particular institutions, or in terms of higher-level traits, such as persistence, integrity, consistency and conscientiousness, which pick out the manner in which people stick to lower-order rules (Peters, 1962). At this general level, too, talk of motives is apposite; for this is a term that we use to ascribe purposes to people of a *personal* rather than specifically institutional sort. An ambitious man is one who is moved by the thought of getting ahead of others; a jealous man is one who is moved by the thought that someone else has something to which he thinks he has a right; an envious man is one who is irked by the thought that another has something that he wants.

The points that I have made about the dependence of our understanding of behaviour on the cognitive content that pervades particular forms of social life applies to this more general area of conduct as well. The difference is in the lack of specificity of the cognitive content, not in the essential features of the type of understanding that is involved. Without moral education and the development of a fairly sophisticated grasp of interpersonal relationships we would not know how to apply these concepts. How, for instance, would we know when to say that a person was jealous, as distinct from envious, unless we grasped notions to do with possession? How would we begin to understand the difference between remorse, guilt, and shame unless we could make fairly sophisticated moral distinctions?

What I have said, too, about the different functions of the discourse of common sense applies very much to concepts at this level; for our general terms, such as motive, intention, need and interests, reflect the complexity of our preoccupations. When, for instance, we say that somebody needs something – a bath, for instance, or oxygen or affection – we are combining a value judgement about the desirability of being clean, alive, or mentally healthy with the assertion that there is something absent, namely, a bath, oxygen, or affection, without which the desirable condition cannot be attained. Diagnostic remarks of this sort combine empirical hypotheses with value judgements. Similarly, as I have argued elsewhere (Peters, 1958, Ch. 2, and 1967), remarks about people's motives usually combine the suggestion that somebody's behaviour is up for assessment with a certain type of explanation of it. I was delighted to have confirmation of this point from an unexpected source when I read that one of Kelly's objections to the construct of motives is that he thinks that it is widely used as 'part of the language of complaint about the behaviour of other people' (Kelly, 1958, p. 46). The same sort of point can be made about the term 'intention', whose general function is to identify rather than to explain actions, usually in some kind of justificatory context, often where there is a suggestion of a mistake having been made. Stephen Toulmin, in a recent paper, has developed this point about the justificatory as distinct from the explanatory use of language (Toulmin, 1968).

Common sense also has concepts that operate at an even more abstract level than that of motives and traits. Sometimes we interpret people's behaviour in terms of attitudes, such as optimism, pessimism, cynicism and fearlessness, which exert a general influence on whole areas of their behaviour. We also talk about people's ideals and aspirations. There is little point in probing into the distinctions between these sorts of concepts. All that need be noted, for the purpose of the present argument, is their obvious connection with affectively tinged beliefs; they have a wide-ranging cognitive content.

I need hardly mention that in this area, much important work has been done by psychologists to supplement common sense. The work of McClelland and Atkinson on the motives of achievement and affiliation, as I have already noted, makes more precise use of commonsense concepts. Kelly's theory of personal constructs operates also at this level and, like most theories of this sort, is very important for the understanding of individual differences. It suggests that individuals tend to anticipate and to interpret the behaviour of others in terms of very general dichotomies, such as 'loving–hating'. The key to the general style of a person's behaviour is to be found by unearthing the system of constructs with which he operates. Other theories of personality types, such as those of Adler, Fromm and

Horney, make use of similar types of concepts. So do theories of attitudes such as those of Allport and Campbell. Such theories in no way supersede explanations in terms of the purposes and rules that structure the consciousness of members of a particular society. Rather they suggest that there are certain general orientations toward others and toward oneself that determine individual differences in behaviour within such systems. And this may well be true; for one of the important ways in which man differs from animals is that he acts not just in the light of a concept of his own nature and relationship to others, but in terms of a variable concept of these.

The view that we have of ourselves and of others as *persons*, as distinct from as occupants of a variety of institutional roles, is as important in influencing our behaviour as it is variable between people. That it should be so is not a notion unfamiliar to any keen common-sense observer. Psychologists, however, provide an additional dimension to this type of understanding by constructing causal-genetic theories about the origins of such general orientations in childhood. Freud's theory of character traits, for instance, was a theory about the genesis of certain exaggerated and distorted styles of rule following (Peters, 1962). It presupposes a pattern of rules operative in a society but suggests that individuals, because of early social influences, adopt a characteristic style of exhibiting them. This way of looking at such theories seems to me much more helpful than to suggest that the content of the individual's rule-governed behaviour can be deduced from such high-level orientations, that from one such 'genotype' many 'phenotypes' may be deduced (Brown, 1940, p. 79).

Such theories seem highly plausible on general grounds; for given the established importance of early learning, and given the fact that in early life interpersonal rather than institutional relationships predominate, it seems highly plausible to suggest that the early stances that we adopt in this interpersonal sphere, especially at crucial stages of conflict where we encounter general social norms, are likely to persist and to be of an all-pervading influence throughout our lives. One need not go along with many of the details of the Freudian scheme in order to accept the general plausibility of this imaginative idea. The problem in this area is not the dearth of interesting theories to supplement the conceptual scheme of common sense, but the intractable difficulties involved in devising tests to decide between them. There is the additional difficulty, too, that some of the theories in this area are expressed in too woolly a way to be testable.

3   THEORIES OF MOTIVATION AND THE ABSTRACT
POSTULATES OF COMMON SENSE

At this juncture psychologists may well be feeling rather fidgety; for
they will be thinking, nothing yet has been said about more ambitious
theories of motivation that operate at a much more abstract level
than common sense. Before passing to these, however, I want to
point out that this is an oversimple contrast. Common sense is
often thought of as a very mundane low-level system of beliefs. Yet a
little thought about its presuppositions scarcely supports this stock
assumption. This is particularly true in the sphere of human behaviour; for in so far as we are concerned in ordinary life with explaining what people do, as distinct from praising them, cursing them,
advising them, selecting them, giving them orders and so on, we take
for granted some very abstract assumptions in ascribing purposes to
people and in classifying their behaviour as being cases of following
certain rules. We assume that, other things being equal, a person who
wants something, and who has the information about means necessary
to attain it, will take what he judges to be the means. Deviations
require some special explanation. We assume, too, certain postulates
about rule following. There are appropriate as well as efficient ways
of performing most actions. In our society, for instance, we do not
expect people, without some special reason, to slam doors, but to
shut them in an appropriate manner. Similarly, in activities that are,
in the main, constituted by rules of appropriateness, we assume that a
person who knows what the rules are and who voluntarily participates
in an activity will act in the light of his knowledge of these rules,
other things being equal. We assume, as I have argued before
(Peters, 1958, Ch. 1), that man is a purposive rule-following animal,
who acts in the light of what Popper has called 'the logic of the
situation' (Popper, 1945, p. 90). A lot more work, of course, needs to
be done to tidy up these assumptions and express them more precisely, which would not be either appropriate or possible in an article
with as broad a coverage as this one. There have, however, been
several other philosophers who have attempted this (e.g. Hempel,
1962; Ayer, 1964; and Mischel, 1966). We do not, of course, learn
such basic postulates of human action by having them explained to
us like the postulates of mechanics. We learn them as what Freud
calls 'the ego' begins to be superimposed on 'the id'; they are gradually
built into us by others and by our transactions with the world as we
learn to want things in a full sense, which involves taking means to
ends, as we learn to interpret the world in causal terms, and as we

learn to follow rules. We learn these abstract postulates without first being able to formulate them by being initiated into a form of life that exhibits them.

Atkinson (1964, pp. 4–7) admits the intuitive validity of what he calls the 'common-sense of motivation'. He claims, however, that psychological theories transcend it in the same sort of way as Galilean explanations transcended the common sense of Aristotle. This, of course, is a familiar claim made by psychologists not just since Lewin wrote his notorious chapter on the subject (Lewin, 1935), but ever since Hobbes set himself up as the Galileo of psychology in the seventeenth century and suggested very much what Atkinson himself suggests at the end of his most erudite and illuminating book: that psychological phenomena could be deduced from the law of inertia (see Peters, 1956, Chs 4, 6). But nothing that Atkinson produces in the way of a plausible theory ever shows that these sorts of postulates about human behaviour have in fact been superseded; all that psychologists have done, who have been concerned with human behaviour rather than with pipe-dream extrapolations from animal movements, is to translate such assumptions into a more technical (and often pretentious) terminology. Lewin's dreadful jargon about life space, vectors and valences, for instance, enshrined first of all the astounding discovery, which he shared with Koffka and Köhler, that the behaviour of individuals is to be interpreted in terms of how they see a situation and their information about it, rather than in terms of the purely physical or geographical properties of their environment. Second, it translated familiar assumptions about wanting and avoiding things into a language that added nothing to what we already know and that suggested no deductions that would not readily be made from postulates expressed in the commonsense language. Was anything added, for instance, to the suggestion deriving from Freud that unfulfilled wishes tend to persist and to influence thought and action by translating all this into the language of tension systems and psychological forces? Did not Zeigarnik's work on interrupted tasks and subsequent work on substitute activities owe more to Freud's speculations, which could be expressed in commonsense language, than to the elaborate conceptual superstructure that Lewin erected in order to demonstrate that the Galilean era was dawning?

The same sort of point could be made about technically expressed decision theories that are now becoming fashionable. Admittedly they permit mathematics to be used, which may be useful in dealing with some areas of human behaviour. But do not assumptions about 'subjectively expected utility' make use of postulates belonging to the

the old commonsense family of wanting, having information about means to ends, deciding in terms of the relative attractiveness of alternatives, and so on? And does not all the valuable work done by McClelland and Atkinson (McClelland, Atkinson, Clark and Lovell, 1953; Atkinson, 1964) on achievement and affiliation motivation itself make use of most of the concepts connected with a purposive rule-following model?

My point is not, of course, to deny that a great deal of additional light has been thrown on phenomena of motivation by all the work that has been done under the aegis of these elaborate conceptual schemes. It is only to query the assumption, often made, that the conceptual scheme of common sense has been superseded. As far as I am aware, there is no important theory of human motivation that has seriously suggested that we can dispense with the family of concepts of which 'wanting', 'taking means to ends', 'following rules', and 'deciding between alternatives' are members. Some theorists (e.g. Tolman, Lewin) have verbalised these concepts in terms that sound more scientific; others (e.g. Hull) have suggested that postulates in this conceptual scheme could eventually be deducted from postulates about 'colourless' movements' which, as I have argued before, is a piece of metaphysics at least as old as Hobbes (Peters and Tajfel, 1955); others (e.g. Freud) have admitted its validity for a certain range of behaviour (the theory of the ego) but have supplemented it by another conceptual scheme (the theory of the id) to account for phenomena that it does not fit; others (e.g. McDougall) have been so impressed by this conceptual scheme that they have argued that behaviour is to be explained in terms of a finite number of innate purposes, thereby exalting a conceptual insight into a superfluous genetic doctrine; others (games and decision theorists) have elaborated this scheme and tried to quantify some of the variables; others (cyberneticians and information theorists), impressed by the similarities between purposive behaviour and self-regulating machines, have honoured such machines, and the human brain, with terms such as 'plans', 'standards', 'information', 'memory', and 'knowledge of results' in order to theorise about them.

Given, then, that the applicability of this conceptual scheme has usually been granted at some level of explanation, with what have theories of motivation usually been concerned? Surely with what have been thought to be further and more fundamental questions. Unfortunately, however, most of the work on motivation in the first half of this century has been dominated by the postulation and gradual refutation of an all-inclusive theory that provided answers, albeit mistaken ones, to most of these further and more fundamental questions. Koch gave a splendid caricature of this when he remarked in 1956 'there was a time not too many years ago when a direct pipe-line extended between Cannon's stomach balloon and the entire domain of motivational psychology' (Koch, 1956, p. 78). What he was referring to, of course, was the old homeostatic theory, the metaphysics of drive or need reduction, whose conceptual confusions and empirical mistakes I tried to catalogue in *The Concept of Motivation* (Peters, 1958). There is no need to go over any of that hallowed ground again. Nevertheless, most of the questions raised by the theory were legitimate enough, except perhaps that of a special explanation for the initiation of behaviour, which presupposed an antiquated view of the nervous system. Fundamental questions still remain about the energising and directedness of behaviour. In singling out hunger, thirst and sex, the classical theory was not on a wrong track; for there do seem to be very special conditions here that sensitize behaviour and make talk of drives not inappropriate. The mistake was to generalise the concept and to think of all behaviour as in some way 'driven'.

It was also a mistake to think that all other behaviour patterns are acquired by being conditioned on these basic drives. Unfortunately, those who established that some forms of behaviour are not so acquired tended to postulate other drives, like 'the drive to know' or 'extero-ceptive drives', or, as in the case of modern hedonists such as Young and McClelland, to generalise the model appropriate to positive preferences (e.g. for sugar). Worse still, even more metaphysical overall tendencies toward 'self-realisation' and 'growth' were postulated by people such as Rogers and Maslow to provide a more positive supplement to the old overall model of deficiency motivation (see Peters, 1958, Ch. 5). I suspect, too, that a similar hankering for an overall supplementary postulate to drive reduction prompts Hunt's recent suggestion that all these more positive aspects of motivation, covered by concepts, such as curiosity, novelty, competence and pleasure seeking, that are inconsistent with the old model of the organism stimulated into activity, and driven ultimately by biological needs, can be encompassed within some general postulate of intrinsic motivation 'inherent in information processing and action' (Hunt, 1965, pp. 196–7). It is also very strange to equate *this* assumption with what Hunt calls 'the ancient doctrine of rationality' (Hunt, 1965, p. 270), though it is encouraging to learn that he thinks that there might be something to be said for the ancient notion that man is a rational animal!

For anyone who accepts the indispensability of the purposive rule-following model in the explanation of actions, there are not only important further questions about how particular wants are acquired, but also questions about how children learn in general to want things and to follow rules, including especially those involved in the use of language, and to interpret the behaviour of others by means of these concepts. Psychologists have devoted little attention to this because of their concentration on animals, whose motor systems mature very quickly; philosophers tend to ignore it because of their preoccupation with language games and with concept formation. But the use of words in a language as distinct from babbling and reacting to words as mere noises presupposes that children already understand what 'wanting' is, at least in an intuitive sort of way; for they come to grasp that noises are made to mean something, that is, that they are at least instrumental to human purposes. It is interesting to note that Hunt spends a lot of time dealing with this in his reinterpretation of Piaget's account of the development of action in terms of his own all-inclusive theory of 'intrinsic motivation' (Hunt, 1965, pp. 246–60).

Once a child has learned to see things as instrumental to other things and to classify things in terms of important aspects, the role of motivation in learning becomes ubiquitous. For all sorts of things can be seen as related to something that is wanted, such as food, warmth and affection. How important this sort of extrinsic motivation is in the development of new wants, as distinct from forms of social learning such as imitation and identification, would be difficult to determine. Its importance in accounting for *persistence* in behaviour and for *change* in behaviour is also obvious enough; for to talk about motivation is to talk about the aspects under which things are wanted that explain some kind of persistence of activity or change of activity in respect of them. Obviously much of the detailed empirical work on motivation must consist in trying to answer such further questions about wants. Most of our actual daily behaviour, as I have argued before, is to be explained by reference to the myriads of rules and purposes that are constitutive of life in our particular society. But appeal to more general purposes is in place in asking further general questions about their acquisition and about individual differences in persistence and vigour within them and about changes from one pattern of behaviour to another. Perhaps one of the most important things that McClelland and his co-workers have done is to devise tests for studying the influence of a few important wants in noncontrived and complex situations such as that of the classroom

(McKeachie, 1961; Atkinson, 1964, p. 255) and even during remote periods of the past (McClelland, 1961).

In the realm of human as well as animal motivation much is made nowadays of various forms of intrinsic motivation, such as the tendency to explore, master things, and search for novelty. White's article, 'Competence and the Psycho-sexual Stages of Development' (White, 1960) and Hunt's 'Intrinsic Motivation' (Hunt, 1965) are perhaps two of the most interesting expositions of the emergence of these forms of motivation in childhood. These developments are certainly most encouraging in their rejection of the old model of extrinsic motivation; certainly, too, the new emphasis on cognition is salutary, whether or not theorists try to unify these tendencies by means of rather formal cognitive notions, such as familiarity, dissonance and incongruity. But what these types of theory tend to neglect is the valuable element in the old doctrine of hedonism that has been somewhat obscured by modern attempts to revive the doctrine by Young and McClelland (Young, 1955, 1961, Ch. 5; McClelland et al., 1953). There is no time here to enter into all the complications associated with the notion of 'pleasure' (see Kenny, 1965; Taylor, 1963). Suffice it to say that one of the main functions of the concept is to draw attention to things that are done or indulged in for what there is in them as distinct from things done out of habit or for some extrinsic reason. Given that there are things of this sort, it is very important to make a detailed study of the intrinsic features of various activities in virtue of which they fall into this category. Koch threw out this suggestion at the end of his contribution to the Nebraska symposium of 1956 (Koch, 1956). But as far as I am aware, no detailed work has been done to follow this up.

This may sound an academic sort of investigation to suggest, but for anyone actively engaged in education, it is far from academic in the pejorative sense of that word. In my view one of the main objectives of education is to get children going on various worthwhile activities so that they come to pursue them and continue with them for what there is in them as distinct from what they offer in the way of instrumental value. I need not elaborate on the difficulties of this enterprise in a consumer-oriented society in which most things are viewed in an instrumental sort of context, with wants of rather a material sort providing the most widespread reasons for doing things. It may well be that various forms of extrinsic motivation (e.g. grades, approval) have to be used to get children going, combined with appeals to the types of general intrinsic motivation in which there has been so much recent interest. But I doubt whether those sorts of motivation do much to get children really on the inside of activities so that they continue with them after they leave educational institutions. What we need to know is what is specific to, say, biology or cookery, toolmaking or astronomy, that will provide reasons for pursuing them that are not entirely idiosyncratic (see Peters, 1966, Ch. 5). If we knew more about this, we might come to know better how to present them to children. General talk about problem solving, discovery, mastery, curiosity, novelty and even more general talk about incongruity and dissonance, is about as much use in this context as is talk about self-realisation and growth in the context of educational aims.

4   COMMONSENSE CLUES TO PHENOMENA REQUIRING SPECIAL EXPLANATION

A further feature of common sense that is important for psychological theories is that it makes all sorts of distinctions in a variety of dimensions that intimate that there is something untoward, faulty, or lacking in a piece of behaviour that makes us unwilling to classify it as an action, activity, or performance in a full sense, or to apply one or other of the postulates of the rationality model to it. We have words, like 'involuntarily', 'unintentionally', and 'accidentally', that make distinctions in a rather different dimension from words like 'inadvertently', 'impulsively', 'carelessly', and 'automatically' (see Austin, 1955–6). We distinguish between jumping on purpose to avoid a puddle, jumping automatically when skipping, and jumping involuntarily when a face appears at the window or in response to a loud noise. Even the Greeks realised that dreams, visions, deliria and certain emotional states could not be accommodated within their commonsense explanations; indeed, they often accounted for them by suggesting that they were due to the agency of gods and goddesses. A strict behaviourist, of course, imposes a self-denying ordinance on himself that forbids him to take cognisance of such distinctions; but I think it would be extremely foolish for a less puritanically minded psychologist to refuse to avail himself of these clues provided by common sense. Indeed, one of the troubles about ordinary language is that some of the distinctions that we make in it are too subtle to be coped with by science, not that it is too crude as a form of communication. Psychology might be wiser to 'home in' on some of the important distinctions between phenomena suggested by common sense and develop special theories to explain groups of phenomena rather than to try to develop one type of theory to encompass all phenomena. A good example of such a special theory is that developed by Freud.

I have argued elsewhere (Peters, 1958, Ch. 3), following Ernest Jones, that Freud's originality as a thinker lay not in his discovery of 'the unconscious' but in his suggestion that it worked according to *different principles*, and in his use of it mainly to explain not everything but a special group of phenomena that had previously not been explained in psychological terms and among which a certain kind of 'family resemblance' is discernible. The phenomena are

'related to facial and other expressive movements and to speech, as well as many other processes of thought (both in normal and in sick people), which have hitherto escaped the notice of psychology because they have been regarded as no more than the results of organic disorder and of some abnormal failure in function of the mental apparatus. What I have in mind are 'parapraxes' (slips of the tongue or pen, forgetfulness, etc.), haphazard actions, and dreams in normal people, and convulsive attacks, deliria, visions and obsessive ideas or acts in neurotic subjects' (Freud, 1955, p. 166).

The family resemblance between these phenomena that Freud's theory explained is not that they are abnormal in the popular sense; for what, in this sense of 'abnormal', is abnormal about dreams and slips of the tongue? They are rather abnormal in the more recondite sense of not being explicable in terms of the norms of the rule-following purposive model. Slips of the tongue, motor slips and lapses in memory represent 'fallings-short' of standards of performance of which the agent is assumed to be capable and Freud himself gave careful criteria for the range of such phenomena (Freud, 1914, pp. 192–3). Conversely, compulsive and obsessional behaviour require special explanation because they are *excessively* rule ridden; either there seems no point to the exaggerated pattern of rule following, or the behaviour seems unduly influenced by the predominance of one sort of purpose. The rationality model cannot be applied in any straightforward way to such phenomena. Dreams, deliria, visions, hysteria and so forth, on the other hand do not rank as actions, activities, or performances at all. They are states that prima facie fall completely outside the range of application of the purposive rule-following model. Freud's genius consisted in seeing links between this wide range of phenomena requiring special explanation and relating them all to his hypothesis of unconscious wishes.

This introduces the second main point of Freud's originality, his use of the concept of 'wish'; for, as I have argued, Freud explained these phenomena in terms of wishes, not motives. In developing his theory of the primary processes of thought, Freud combined both a negative and a positive characterisation of them. Negatively he argued that they are unchecked by logical contradiction and causal association; they are unhampered by a proper sense of time, space and reality. Positively they are ruled only by a vague idea of emotional congruence based on the association of ideas with a discharge of tension. One cannot discuss his positive suggestions without going into his whole theory of sexuality and his antiquated tension-reduction model of psychic functioning; but his negative characterisation of wishes is instructive in that he reports, on the basis of introspection and clinical evidence, certain important points about wishes that could also be arrived at by conceptual analysis. For when we talk about wishes we are prepared to withdraw the applicability of a range of categories that go along with the rationality model. Typically we wish for things, like the moon, where realistic questions of taking means to ends do not have to be raised. We can even have wishes for states of affairs that are logically impossible, as in the case of an old colleague of mine who wished that he was monogamously married to eight women at once. Freud postulated that this form of cognition still persists in us, after we learn to think and act in accordance with the purposive rule-following model, the stages of which have been mapped by Piaget. Because of this, some of our more rational behaviour is 'overdetermined' when it follows the lines of such wishes which are consistent with more realistic wants; but forms of 'abnormal' behaviour, namely the classes listed above, which require special explanation, are to be explained in terms of the persistence of such wishes and the 'mechanisms of defense' that are adopted to deal with them.

When I first defended this interpretation of Freud's theory in *The Concept of Motivation* (Peters, 1958), my concern was mainly to attack the notion of an all-inclusive theory of motivation. I argued that Freud saw himself as putting forward a special theory to explain a limited class of phenomena. It was left to others, like Hartmann and David Rapaport (Rapaport, 1959, 1960), to say more about the development of the ego and to link this with developmental theories, such as that of Piaget, that elaborate in detail the stages at which the various categories characterising rational forms of behaviour are acquired. But when I came to do some work on emotions a few years later, I was struck by the similarities between this range of phenomena and those that Freud tried to explain. This suggested a possible extension of this type of explanation to cover a whole range of what I called 'passive' phenomena. I will now pass to the details of this suggested extension.

5   COMMON SENSE AND PSYCHOLOGICAL THEORIES OF EMOTION

I have argued throughout this article that in the sphere of our understanding of human behaviour, as distinct from that of our understanding of the natural world, we are in a special position that should make us beware of taking too cavalier an attitude toward common sense and the distinctions that we have found it important to make in ordinary language. This is also true in the sphere of emotional phenomena, and the history of psychological theories of emotion is an embarrassing reminder of what can happen if this rough and ready source of understanding is neglected.

If we ask ourselves, first of all, what we might naturally call 'emotions', we would give quite a long list that would include fear, anger, joy, sorrow, jealousy, envy, pride, wonder, shame, guilt, remorse and the like. We would not include hunger, thirst, pain, pleasure and an interest in symbolic logic. What sort of criteria are implicit in this selection? Surely the connection between 'emotion' and a class of cognitions that might conveniently be called 'appraisals'. These consist in seeing situations under aspects that are agreeable or disagreeable, beneficial or harmful in a variety of dimensions. Fear, for instance, is conceptually connected with seeing a situation as dangerous, anger with seeing it as thwarting, pride with seeing something as ours or as something that we have had a hand in bringing about, envy with seeing someone else as possessing what we want. We would not call hunger or thirst emotions because, although they too involve seeing the world in a certain light, this tendency is cyclic, depending on definite internal conditions; emotions, on the other hand, seem to be appraisals elicited by external conditions or by things that we have brought about or suffered. We do not think of pain and pleasure as emotions unless they are connected with some determinate aspect of a situation that is appraised as affecting us in the agreeable of disagreeable ways indicated by 'pleasure' and 'pain'. An interest in symbolic logic would be ruled out for many reasons, one of them being that emotions do not seem to be connected with specific activities but with general ways in which we view ourselves as related to others and to environmental conditions.

It is a depressing fact that most of the psychological work done on emotion during this century has taken little cognisance of this peculiarly intimate connection between emotions and specific forms of cognition, in spite of the fact that attempts to differentiate emotions in other ways have proved abortive. Ever since Darwin conducted experiments with photographs on facial expressions connected with emotions, attempts to distinguish them in this way have failed, although some general differences in terms of variables such as 'pleasant–unpleasant' and 'attending–rejecting' seem to be discernible (Woodworth and Schlosberg, 1954). Attempts to distinguish emotions by reference to physiological conditions have proved equally abortive, starting from the highly confused hypothesis about the relationship between emotion and changes in the viscera put forward in the James–Lange theory. Another connection also favoured by James and many other psychologists has been that with actions or tendencies to action that were alleged to be criteria of emotion. This connection, like that between emotion and specific facial expressions, was also asserted by Charles Darwin in his *The Expression of the Emotions in Man and Animals* (Darwin, 1872).

The explanation of this widespread neglect by psychologists of this most obvious lead-in to the study of emotion is not very recondite. Ever since the latter part of the nineteenth century, psychology has been trying desperately to make itself scientifically respectable. Physiological psychology had long been established as a scientifically respectable form of enquiry that was based on publicly observable 'data'. It was thought that concentration on facial expressions or on overt actions (e.g. flight in the case of fear) would provide equally reliable data, which were not dependent on the hazards of introspective reports. It is, I suppose, encouraging to read a long recent article by Leeper (Leeper, 1965), which elaborates the startling discovery that emotions are connected with cognitive cues, though they are not quite the same as perceptions! But his laboured explanation of how psychologists have been led to ignore this palpable point because of the general tendency of scientists to concentrate on what is palpable scarcely holds water (Leeper, 1965, pp. 37–40). What Leeper never brings out squarely into the open is the skeleton in psychology's cupboard, namely, Behaviourism, which as a methodological doctrine has exercised a stranglehold on academic psychology since the early part of this century. It was the concept of 'palpability' that went with this particular brand of dogmatic methodism, with all its conceptual confusions and antiquated notions of scientific method, that both restricted the questions that psychologists felt they could respectably raise about emotions and that occasioned them to ignore the obvious point that we cannot even identify the emotions we are talking about unless account is taken of how a person is appraising a situation. This is not to deny, of course, the importance of work done on the physiology of emotion. It is only to assert that the investigation of emotional phenomena has been hamstrung by a widely influential methodological dogma.

Another important facet of this very restricted approach to the study of emotion has been the tendency to take fear and anger as paradigms of emotion rather than, say, sorrow and pride, which probably cannot be experienced by animals that lack a developed conceptual scheme. This tendency had a highly respectable ancestry in Darwin's work, which gave prominence to these emotions, which have an obvious biological utility. These emotions, too, have palpable facial expressions connected with them and are accompanied by palpable signs of changes in the autonomic nervous system, such as goose pimples, sweating and flushing, some of which, such as the psychogalvinic response, are measurable by instruments. Also, if any emotions are closely connected with typical action patterns, these two are. If sorrow were taken as a paradigm, as it could not be by psychologists who concentrate on rats, the connection with action is, to put it mildly, difficult to discern. And what distinctive facial expressions are connected with envy or pride? Is it plausible to suggest that highly specific physiological changes, of the sort that often accompany fear and anger, accompany remorse?

These restricting influences on the study of emotion are still with us. Witness George Mandler's pronouncement, which provides the keynote to his chapter on emotion in *New Directions in Psychology*:

'Since antiquity, students of man have emphasised two facets which, in conjunction, appear to differentiate emotion from other human experiences: First, emotion involves action which is strongly influenced by certain environmental goals and events, and second, it usually presupposes bodily, visceral, or physiological reactions' (Mandler, 1962, p. 270).

In his treatment of emotion there is thus a significant contrast between the specificity of the references to the physiology of emotion and the amount of space devoted to the viscera, and the woolly and brief references to prior experience and to the 'content of our emotions', which 'is determined by the sort of things that go on around us, particularly the things people do and say to us' (Mandler, 1962, p. 338), which relate to 'social induction, and a vast category of presumptive stressors or emotional situations, mostly social in nature' (Mandler, 1962, p. 312). Consciousness is mainly considered in relation to the specific role played by the subject's awareness of his own physiological state. The complicated and highly ingenious experiments of Schachter were designed to exhibit the importance of consciousness in emotional behaviour only in this limited respect (Mandler, 1962, pp. 279–98). The distinctive appraisals connected with the different emotions receive no specific attention whatever.

Suppose that, resisting these historic influences in the scientific study of emotions, we stick to common sense and insist on both the connection between emotions and distinctive appraisals and a broad sample of emotions rather than only fear and anger. An interesting point then emerges if we study the list, namely, that most of the terms in the list can also be used to characterise motives, and obviously, as the terms 'motive' and 'emotion' suggest, there is a close family resemblance among these terms. Indeed this may be another reason that has led countless theorists to postulate an intimate connection between emotion and motivation, culminating in the dispute between Young and Leeper about the facilitating or disrupting effect of emotion on motivated behaviour. I have elsewhere summarised most of the important attempts to establish such a connection (Peters, 1961–2, Sect. 3) and do not wish to elaborate this theme here. What is of present interest is the proper way to conceptualise this undoubted overlap between the concepts.

In attempting to do this, I think, again, that the common sense that is embedded in ordinary language can help. For surely, in ordinary language we only talk about motives in certain contexts, when we are demanding an explanation of actions; we do not ask for motives for feeling cold, indigestion, or mystical visions. We talk about emotions, on the other hand, in contexts where things come over people, where individuals are passive rather than active. The phrases in which the term 'emotion' and its derivatives are not only natural but also indispensable are those used when we speak of judgements being disturbed, warped, heightened, sharpened, and clouded by emotion, or people being in command of or not being properly in control of their emotions, being subject to gusts of emotion, being emotionally perturbed, upset, involved, excited, biased and exhausted. In a similar vein we speak of emotional outbursts, reactions and upheavals. The suggestion in such cases is that something comes over people or happens to them when they consider a situation in a certain kind of light. This passivity frequently occurs when we appraise situations as dangerous and frustrating. Hence the obviousness of fear and anger as emotions and hence our slight reluctance to regard benevolence or remorse as emotions; for there are rarely marked symptoms of passivity when we think of people or situations under the aspects connected with these terms. What is common to both motives and emotions on this view is the distinctive appraisals that are necessary to characterise the states of mind as being cases of fear, jealousy, joy and so on. The difference lies in the fact that 'motive' is a term that we use to connect these appraisals with things that we do, 'emotion' with things that come over us. And we need not, of course, always connect these appraisals with either. We may, for instance, simply feel remorse or regret without being disposed to do anything in particular and without being particularly affected by our view of the situation. In such cases we simply view a situation under the aspect connected with the appraisal.

To put the difference between the concepts in this way is to suggest a conceptual connection between motive and action and between emotion and passivity. There is thus no conceptual connection, as many maintain, between emotion and action. Indeed, when such appraisals are related to emotion, they are typically connected with the functioning of our autonomic nervous systems, about which we usually speak in a metaphorical way, but in metaphors that are consonant with our passivity. We boil and fume with anger; we tremble and sweat with fear; we swell and glow with pride; we blush with shame and embarrassment; our eyes dilate with fear, sparkle with delight and moisten with sorrow. Often, of course, the motor system is involved, but when it is, the manifestations typically take on an involuntary character. Our knees knock with fear, our teeth chatter with fright and sometimes our limbs are paralysed.

There can, of course, be a *de facto* rather than a conceptual relationship between fear, anger and so forth, as emotions and action in the sense that they can disrupt, heighten and intensify motor performances. We can act in fear as well as out of fear. The preposition 'in' draws attention to the manner of acting rather than to the reason or motive for acting. 'He acted in anger' is different from 'he was angry', which merely interprets the action as being of a certain sort, as well as from 'he acted out of anger', which gives a reason or motive for acting beyond the initial characterisation of the action as being of a certain sort. A man can act in anger who is also acting out of pity. His manner of acting is affected by considering aspects of the situation, considerations that may distort or intensify his actions. And it is very nice when such gusts of emotions, as it were, speed us on our way rather than deflect us from our path. Thus there is no reason why fear or anger should not function both as motives and as emotions at the same time.

There are, too, the intermediary class of cases where people do not act altogether with reason, but where their reaction, which is typically of an unco-ordinated protopathic type, springs from an intuitive type of appraisal of a situation. An example would be when a person lashes out in anger or starts with fear. These are not reactions to stimuli, like jumping when one receives an electric shock, because of their cognitive core. Neither are they actions in a full-blown sense; for there is no appraisal of means to an end, no careful consideration of the end to be achieved. They are what we call 'emotional reactions'. They are dissimilar, too, from acting on impulse; for we act on impulse when there is no such appraisal of a situation as is involved in emotional reactions. To say that a man acts on impulse is at least to deny that he acts deliberately. But it is not necessarily to class what goes on as being subsequent to the sort of appraisal that is involved in emotion. A hungry man might put his hand out and grab a banana in a store. This might be an action on impulse but it would be very strange to describe it as an emotional reaction.

In a similar way, there can be and often is a *de facto* relationship between perception, memory and judgement on the one hand and emotion on the other. In such cases, the suggestion is that the appraisal that is conceptually connected with the emotion in question acts on the person so as to cloud or distort, or heighten or sharpen, the assessment that he is making. The appraisal of a situation as being in some way agreeable or disagreeable, which is involved in emotion, takes the attention away from or clouds over the relevant features of the situation, 'relevance' being defined in terms of whatever criteria are involved in the type of judgement that is being made. Or maybe it goes along with the criteria of relevance and thus enhances or sharpens the judgement, as in the case of a terrified sentry who spots an approaching enemy long before anyone else.

The widespread tendency to postulate a conceptual connection between emotion and action, which is shared by philosophers and psychologists alike, is due not only to the overlap between the concepts but also to the tendency to concentrate on some emotions rather than others. If sorrow, wonder and grief were taken as examples, this connection would surely be most implausible; for, as Koestler puts it: 'The purely self-transcending emotions do not tend towards action, but towards quiescence, tranquillity and catharsis' (Koestler, 1966, pp. 273–85). There are, of course, plenty of passive phenomena connected with the autonomic system that go with these emotions, for example, weeping, catching one's breath, a lump in the throat and so on. But one cannot *act* in any specific way out of wonder or grief; one is overwhelmed by it. Furthermore, even appraisals that can function both as motives and as emotions do not necessarily lead to action, or even tendencies to action. Jealousy, for instance, may affect one's judgement or memory; but it may not issue in action in the sense in which psychologists have thought of action.

The tendency to connect emotion with action is the main feature that I reject of the treatment of emotion by Asch and Arnold, whose writings on this subject I have otherwise found most illuminating. They above all psychologists have taken the cognitive aspect of emotion seriously and Asch's writings reinforced my conviction of the connection between emotion and passivity. Nevertheless, Asch seems to me to connect emotion too closely with motivation when he says

'Emotions are our ways of representing to ourselves the fate of our goals. They are a direct consequence of the understanding of our situation. One may say that emotions mirror the course of motivational events' (Asch, 1959, p. 112).

Similarly, Arnold, to whose erudition and insight on the subject of emotions I am greatly indebted, comes to the view in the end that an emotion is 'a felt tendency towards or away from an object' that is preceded by an appraisal of a situation as being of a sort that is harmful or beneficial to the agent. This attraction or aversion is, on her view, accompanied by a pattern of physiological changes organised toward approach or withdrawal (Arnold, 1961, Chs 9–12).

6 EMOTIONS, WISHES AND PASSIVE PHENOMENA

I have argued against the prevailing tendency to postulate a conceptual connection between emotion and actions or dispositions to action, although I have been ready enough to admit widely prevalent *de facto* connections in the case of some emotions. There is, however, an additional explanation of the closeness of this connection if we follow a previous suggestion that I have made (Peters, 1961–2, Sect. 4), that emotion is conceptually connected with the concept of 'wishing' rather than with the concept of action via the stronger and more determinate notion of 'wanting'. Wishing, I suggested, is a bare teleological notion whose object is some state of affairs that can be very indeterminately conceived. 'The moon' is the sort of object that can be wished for, because questions about what one would do with it if one had it do not have to be pressed. Also, mundane questions of 'taking means' to get it, which go along with wanting, need not be raised. Obviously, however, the concepts are very intimately connected, and if emotions are conceptually connected with wishes, the tendency to connect emotion with action via the notion of wanting would be readily explained.

My contention is that there is such a connection. If we consider emotions such as grief and wonder, which are the most intractable ones for those who try to connect emotion conceptually with action, the connection with wishes is quite obvious. A widow who is mourning her dead husband fervently wishes that he were alive. But what action could consummate a want of this sort? A lover overwhelmed by his love may wish himself to be fused into one with his beloved; but he cannot, strictly speaking, want what is logically impossible. Yet this is just the sort of way in which those deeply in love do express their feelings. And, surely, it is just because there is no appropriate action with which these sorts of appraisals can be connected that there is what we call a 'welling up' of emotion and some kind of discharge in internal visceral and glandular processes connected with the parasympathetic system. Similarly, a person strongly affected by fear or anger certainly has wishes such as 'Would that I were away from here' or 'Would that he were dead'. Such wishes may or may not follow the lines of wants exhibited in actions.

Magda Arnold has drawn attention to some other aspects of emotion that are very relevant in this context. She notes what I call its connection with passivity when she says

'Emotion seems to include not only the appraisal of how this thing or person will affect me but also a definite pull towards or away from it. In fact, does not the emotional quale consist precisely in that unreasoning involuntary attraction or repulsion?' (Arnold, 1961, p. 172).

She stresses its immediate or 'here and now' character and its connection with wild and intuitive judgements that often are inconsistent with our more rational understanding. These features of emotion are the ones to which Sartre paid most attention. He regards emotion as 'an abrupt drop into the magical' (Sartre, 1948, p. 90): 'Thus the origin of emotion is a spontaneous and lived degradation of consciousness in the face of the world' (Sartre, 1948, p. 77). This brings out well the connection between emotion and wishes; but it also emphasises a feature of appraisals connected with fear, jealousy, pity and so forth, when we employ the concept of emotion to connect them with our passivity. A jealous man's appraisals are not always wild or intuitive, any more than are those of a man who quite sensibly experiences fear when he hears the shriek of a bomb descending towards him. But the more we think of these appraisals as emotions, the more we tend to think of the appraisals as immediate and 'intuitive' and of our reactions as having an involuntary character. What we call emotional reactions provide a good example of both these features. For if we jump when we see what we take to be a face at the window, our appraisal is immediate and intuitive and our jump has an involuntary protopathic character. It is quite unlike the deliberate jump of a high jumper. When we 'jump for joy' we express a highly indeterminate wish; it would be difficult to describe us as wanting anything in particular. 'Lashing out' in anger is another good example of this type of phenomenon. The appraisal is not very discriminating and the movements do not attain the level of co-ordination and grasp of means to ends for them to qualify as actions that exhibit our wants.

The character of the appraisals in cases of emotion is very similar to that of those noted by Dember in his more stimulus- and response-ridden account of perceptual vigilance and perceptual defence (Dember, 1964, pp. 313–25). His problem is that of the 'mechanism' by reference to which the responsiveness to stimuli below the identification threshold could be explained. Dember's speculative solution is that identifying and affective responses are not learned in identical fashions. Affective responses are learned much earlier in childhood, before children have developed the conceptual apparatus necessary for identification, and can be aroused by stimulation that is not sufficiently informative to arouse the appropriate identification responses. When, however, the stimulation can arouse the identification responses, it will probably also arouse affective responses. If Dember's solution is generalised, it can be postulated that after the conceptual apparatus essential to life as a rule-following purposive agent has been developed, the individual still retains his capacity to respond much more 'intuitively' to affectively significant signs that may be fragmentary or well below the threshold of conscious discrimination. Such 'intuitive' awareness can have either a disrupting or a facilitating effect on more rational forms of appraisal, depending on whether the cues to which the individual is sensitive at the different levels are consonant or dissonant. This links some of the phenomena of perception with the type of distinction that Freud made between primary and secondary processes of thought (see Hilgard, 1966).

If these affective responses are connected at the start with strange wishes such as Freud postulated, then a link between emotional phenomena generally and those that Freud's theory was designed to explain can readily be suggested. The 'mechanisms' that Freud postulated as defences against such wishes have the same character. They are activated by an immediate type of appraisal and then strange things happen to us that cannot be categorised as actions or performances. In conversion hysteria, for instance, a man's arm becomes paralysed or he finds that he cannot see. In repression the memory of a traumatic experience just passes out of his mind; he does not intentionally suppress it. Similarly, a man who projects his fears onto something does not wittingly or purposely rig his environment; he just comes to see it under a different aspect. The phenomena are indubitably 'mental' because of their cognitive core; that is why the description of them as mechanisms is really inappropriate; but they fall into the category of passivity because of their unintentional involuntary character.

7   CONCLUSION

If the sort of conceptualisation presented in this article is not completely off-beam, it gives rise to a whole cluster of fascinating problems: for example, about the possibility, suggested by many past theorists, of there being a few primitive types of appraisals at the basis of our more sophisticated ones, about the transition from one level of appraisal to another and the connections established between them and actions that issue in motives, and about the whole subject of 'the education of the emotions'. But I must leave these and cognate problems for consideration on some other occasion.

For present purposes I hope I have succeeded in indicating the lines along which some of the phenomena that cannot be accommodated within the purposive rule-following model might be unified by being explained by this supplementary model of mental passivity. To suggest a further generalisation of the Freudian type of explanation to cover emotional phenomena is not, of course, to accept all the details of the Freudian conceptual scheme, much of which I find objectionable – especially the tendency to physiologise mental concepts. Perhaps one of Freud's greatest insights was to hit upon the importance of the concept of 'the wish' in the explanation of this realm of phenomena – another commonsense concept! To characterise the ways in which wishes work, however, our ordinary forms of description will not do, almost by definition; for the latter are couched in categories of what Freud called 'secondary processes'. From a commonsense point of view, too, the connections suggested between wishes and phenomena such as facial tics, parapraxes, paralysis, and a host of psychosomatic phenomena seem anything but obvious. Indeed, as I have argued before (Peters, 1965, p. 381), because there does not seem to be such a close conceptual connection between beliefs and passive phenomena as there is between beliefs and actions, there seems much more scope for the development by psychologists of novel empirical generalisations in the sphere of passivity than there does in the sphere of action.

It might be reasonably argued that I am not really suggesting two conceptual schemes. For in so far as these wilder types of appraisal are connected with bodily phenomena such as facial tics, paralysis and stomach ulcers, the connection is no more and no less intelligible than that between wanting to do something and the movement of our limbs. In this respect wants and wishes are equally mysterious in their mode of operation. On the other hand, in so far as such appraisals are connected via wishes with dreams, distorted judgements and perceptions, and the phenomena referred to as 'the mechanisms of defence', we dimly understand them by starting with secondary processes and thinking away the categorisations involved until we are left with the bare notion of a fulfilled wish. That is why we find notions like that of 'displacement' difficult to understand save by analogy with the lower-level operations of animals (Austin, 1956-7, pp. 29–30). The parasitic character of such descriptions explains the tendency to talk of the unconscious in terms of 'as if', or to say that it deals with the sort of things that one might want if a more determinate description of them were specified (MacIntyre, 1958). There are also phenomena, such as when we are 'driven' by hunger, or when actions are overdetermined, for example, when a surgeon takes obvious delight in using his instruments, that fall between the two models. Such considerations should encourage us to look at the various phenomena to be explained as lying on a continuum rather than as having always to be placed unambiguously as falling under the activity or passivity models.

Certainly, too, there are other phenomena that cannot be accounted for in terms of either of these two models. Reflexes, pains and nonemotional reactions are also passive phenomena; but they cannot be explained in terms of appraisals linked with wishes. Perhaps a more mechanical type of model is required to deal with these. Two conceptual schemes, however, are quite enough for one article. Indeed it might reasonably be said that they are at least one too many. It might have been better to dwell longer on the details of one of them and discuss more thoroughly many of the points that have been raised. But there is something to be said for a synoptic view at times – especially if it can be linked with common sense.

REFERENCES

Arnold, M., *Emotion and Personality*, Vol. 1 (London: Cassell, 1961).
Asch, S., *Social Psychology* (Englewood Cliffs, N.J.: Prentice-Hall, 1959).
Atkinson, J. W., *An Introduction to Motivation* (Princeton, N.J.: Van Nostrand, 1964).
Austin, J. L., 'A Plea for Excuses', *Proceedings of the Aristotelian Society*, Vol. LVII (1956–7).
Ayer, A. J., *Man as a Subject for Science* (Auguste Comte Memorial Lecture) (London: Athlone Press, 1964).
Bannister, D., 'A New Theory of Personality', in Foss, B. M. (Ed.), *New Horizons in Psychology* (Harmondsworth, Middlesex, England: Penguin, 1966).
Brown, J. F., *The Psychodynamics of Abnormal Behaviour* (New York: McGraw-Hill, 1940).
Darwin, C., *The Expression of the Emotions in Man and Animals* (London: Murray, 1872).
Dember, W. N., *The Psychology of Perception* (New York: Holt, Rinehart & Winston, 1964).
Freud, S., *The Psychopathology of Everyay Life* (London: Benn, 1914).
Freud, S., 'The Claim of Psycho-analysis to Scientific Interest', in *Collected Papers* (London: Hogarth Press, 1955).
Hempel, C. G., 'Rational Action', *Proceedings and Addresses of the American Philosophical Association*, Vol. 35 (October 1962).
Hilgard, E., 'Impulsive Versus Realistic Thinking', in Haber, R. N. (Ed.), *Current Research in Motivation* (New York: Holt, Rinehart & Winston, 1966).
Hunt, J. McV., 'Intrinsic Motivation', in Levine, D. (Ed.), *Nebraska Symposium on Motivation* (Lincoln, Neb.: University of Nebraska Press, 1965).
Kelly, G. A., *The Psychology of Personal Constructs*, Vol. I (New York: Norton, 1955).
Kelly, G. A., 'Man's Construction of his Alternatives', in Lindzey, G. (Ed.), *The Assessment of Motives* (New York: Holt, Rinehart & Winston, 1958).
Kenny, A., *Action, Emotion and Will* (London: Kegan Paul, 1965).
Koch, S., 'Behaviour as "Intrinsically" regulated' in Jones, M. R. (Ed.), *Nebraska Symposium on Motivation* (Lincoln, Neb: University of Nebraska Press, 1956).
Koestler, A., *The Act of Creation* (London: Pan Books, 1966).
Leeper, R. W., 'Needed Developments in Motivational Theory', in Levine, D. (Ed.), *Nebraska Symposium on Motivation* (Lincoln, Neb.: University of Nebraska Press, 1965).
Lewin, K., 'Aristotelian and Galilean Modes of Explanation', in Lewin, K. (Ed.), *A Dynamic Theory of Personality* (New York: McGraw-Hill, 1935).
McClelland, D. C., *The Achieving Society* (Princeton, N.J.: Van Nostrand, 1961).
McClelland, D.C., Atkinson, J. W., Clark, R.A. and Lowell, E. L., *The Achievement Motive* (New York: Appleton-Century-Croft, 1953).
MacIntyre, A., *The Unconscious* (London: Kegan Paul, 1958).

McKeachie, W. J., 'Motivation, Teaching Methods and College Learning', in Jones, M. R. (Ed.), *Nebraska Symposium on Motivation* (Lincoln, Neb.: University of Nebraska Press, 1961).

Mandler, G., 'Emotion', in Mandler, G. and Galanter, E. (Eds.), *New Directions in Psychology* (New York: Holt, Rinehart & Winston, 1962).

Melden, A. *Free Action* (London: Kegan Paul, 1961).

Mischel, T. 'Pragmatic Aspects of Explanation', *Philosophy of Science*, Vol. 33 (March–June 1966).

Peters, R. S., *Hobbes* (Harmondsworth, Middlesex, England: Penguin, 1956).

Peters, R. S., *The Concept of Motivaton* (London: Kegan Paul, 1958).

Peters, R. S., 'Emotions and the Category of Passivity', *Proceedings of the Aristotelian Society*, Vol. 62 (1961–2).

Peters, R. S., 'Moral Education and the Psychology of Character', *Philosophy* (April 1962).

Peters, R. S., 'Emotions, Passivity and the Place of Freud's Theory in Psychology', in Wolman, B. and Nagel, E. (Eds), *Scientific Psychology* (New York: Basic Books, 1965).

Peters, R. S., *Ethics and Education* (London: Allen & Unwin, 1966).

Peters, R. S., 'More about Motives', *Mind* (January 1967).

Peters, R. S. and Tajfel, H., 'Hobbes and Hull: Metaphysicians of Behaviour', *British Journal of the Philosophy of Science* (May 1955).

Popper, K. R., *The Open Society and its Enemies*, Vol. II (London: Kegan Paul, 1945).

Rapaport, D., 'The Structure of Psycho-analytic Theory: A Systematising Attempt', in Koch, S. (Ed.), *Psychology: A Study of a Science*, Vol. 3 (New York: McGraw-Hill, 1959).

Rapaport, D., 'On the Psycho-analyic Theory of Motivation', in Jones, M. R. (Ed.), *Nebraska Symposium on Motivation* (Lincoln, Neb.: University of Nebraska Press, 1960).

Sartre, J. P., *The Emotions* (Transl. by B. Frechtman) (New York: Philosophical Library, 1948).

Taylor, C. C. W., 'Pleasure', *Analysis*, Vol. 23 (1963), Supplement.

Toulmin, S. 'Reasons and Causes', in Borger R. and Cioffi, F. (Eds.), *Explanation in the Behavioral Sciences* (London and New York: Cambridge University Press, 1969).

White, R. W., 'Competence and the Psycho-sexual Stages of Development', in Jones, M. R. (Ed.), *Nebraska Symposium on Motivation* (Lincoln, Neb.: University of Nebraska Press, 1960).

Winch, P., *The Idea of a Social Science* (London: Kegan Paul, 1958).

Woodworth, R. S. and Schlosberg, H., *Experimental Psychology* (Rev. ed.) (New York: Holt, Rinehart & Winston, 1954).

Young, P. T., 'The Role of Hedonic Processes in Motivation', in Jones, M. R. (Ed.), *Nebraska Symposium on Motivation* (Lincoln, Neb.: University of Nebraska Press, 1955).

Young, P. T., *Motivation and Emotion* (New York: Wiley, 1961).

5

THE DEVELOPMENT OF REASON*

'The organisation of moral values that characterises middle
childhood is, by contrast, comparable to logic itself; it is the
logic of values or of action amongst individuals, just as logic
is a kind of moral for thought.'[1]

INTRODUCTION

I take it as axiomatic that, in talking about development, there must
be a prior conception of the end-product, and that the processes
which contribute to it must be sequential.[2] In the case, however, of
human development, if its physical aspects are disregarded, there is
an additional condition which derives from the fact that the processes are processes of learning. This involves coming up to a mark
in a variety of respects as an outcome of past experience, and between the attainment and the learning processes there must be some
intelligible connection. It is unintelligible, for instance, that an
understanding of Euclid could develop out of learning experiences
of standing on one's head, unless, say, the posture were conceived as
drawing one's attention to angles and their relationships. It is an
empirical question, of course, which particular experiences help
individuals or people in general to reach the particular level of
mastery, or understanding; but the outcome dictates certain types of
experience.

Now much of the more precise experimental work in child psychology has been done within the old stimulus-response (S-R) type
of conceptual framework on the assumption that the development of
thought can be explained in terms of variants of the old principles of
association such as recency, contiguity, frequency, etc. My view is
that such principles explain certain forms of human behaviour but,
in the main, those that are non-rational or irrational. At best they

* I am greatly indebted to Stanley Benn and to Geoffrey Mortimore for their
comments on this paper (to be published in their *Rationality and the Social
Sciences*) which led to its revision.

are to be regarded as primitive precursors of thought that may impede the later development of rationality.

I propose to ignore also physiological findings about the development of the brain, even though these deal, of course, with necessary conditions for the development of rationality. Theories such as those outlined by Woodward,[3] and the influential views of Miller, Galanter and Pribram[4] make use of a model of the nervous system, which is thought appropriate to deal with types of behaviour that the old S-R approach could not handle. As, however, this model credits the nervous system with plans, strategies, information, etc., it seems conceptually corrupt from the outset. For all such concepts are only properly attributable to conscious agents. Such models may suggest fruitful hypotheses, but their findings can all be translated into more straightforward terms. Indeed Woodward uses such models mainly to corroborate and supplement Piaget's findings.

The basic structure of my account of the development of rationality will be provided by the work of Piaget.[5] This is not simply because he has devoted most of his life to just this topic; it is also because he throws out at times certain suggestions about connections between the use of reason and its social context that I find both stimulating in themselves and appropriate as supporting some theses which I propose to advance in this essay.

1   THE END PRODUCT OF THE DEVELOPMENT OF REASON

In this section I shall give an account of the main features that mark a man out as rational. This will provide an account of the end-product of the developmental process, and so enable us to judge whether Piaget does justice to the complexity of the phenomenon of rationality, and whether he provides an adequate explanation of its development.

(a)   *Intelligence, Rationality and Reasonableness*

Intelligence and Reason   Piaget thinks that in his work he is tracing the development of intelligence. In a way, he is right; for though rationality involves much more than intelligence, it can be viewed appropriately as a development of it. We only describe thought and behaviour as intelligent or unintelligent in a situation in which there is some kind of novelty in relation to the belief structure or established behaviour routines of an agent. If a person, or animal for that matter, is just carrying out some established routine, questions of the behaviour being intelligent or unintelligent do not arise. Suppose, then, that something novel or unexpected turns up. The person who exhibits intelligence can do what Piaget calls 'assimilate' it. By that is meant that he deals with it by fitting it into his existing belief structure because of some similarity which he grasps. Alternatively, if the novelty is too discrepant to be dealt with in this way, he 'accommodates' it by making some adjustment to his expectations.

What additional features do being rational or reasonable possess? For we talk quite happily of animals and very small children as being intelligent or stupid, but we do not talk of them as being reasonable or unreasonable, rational or irrational. The difference is surely that we can understand rational behaviour and belief as informed by general rules. It is behaviour and belief for reasons – and for reasons of a certain kind. Rational behaviour and belief spring from the recognition, implicit or explicit, that certain *general* considerations are grounds for action or belief. Thus, the development of rationality allows an individual to transcend the present – to emerge from a level of life in which his actions and beliefs are determined by the particular immediate impulses and perceptions of his current experience. Current and future actions and beliefs come to be influenced not just by what occurs here and now, but by what an individual believes has been or will be the case in the past or in the future. The clearest cases are perhaps when an individual forms predictive beliefs on the basis of past observations, or makes plans for the future on the basis of various expectations.

This transcendence of the present is, of course, implicit in the more primitive use of intelligence, in that both perception and action are unintelligible without the use of concepts; we always see something as something and want it under some aspect. There is, therefore, an implicit relating to the past and future by means of general concepts. But in reasoning this relating is extended and made explicit. Inferences made in choosing or forming an opinion, and arguments to justify one's action or beliefs, all tacitly invoke rules which mark out certain general considerations as relevant grounds.

There is another way in which rationality involves the transcendence of the present. The considerations which influence the rational man need not, and usually will not, contain any temporal reference. The force of the consideration that p will not depend on p's being the case *now*. This second aspect of the transcendence of the present is linked with other ways in which rationality allows of the transcendence of the particular – the emergence from a level of life in which what determines actions or beliefs are considerations about the identity of persons or things, or of time and space. This feature stands out if note is taken of what the use of reason is usually contrasted with – authority, revelations, tradition. In these cases what is right or true is finally determined by appeal at an ultimate level to some particular man, body, or set of practices; it is not determined by appeal to general considerations. In the use of reason, by contrast, identity, as well as time and place, come to be seen as irrelevant sources of considerations.

Thus both 'rational' and 'reasonable' presuppose a background of reasoning which is not necessarily present when we talk about behaviour or beliefs as being intelligent or stupid. 'Stupid' is used simply when there is no grasp of a similarity which provides the basis for assimilation or of a difference too glaring to warrant it. There can, of course, be reasoning in cases where we use the term 'stupid' and the reasoning itself can be intelligently or stupidly done; but there does not have to be.

'Reasonable' and 'Rational'   There are certain distinctions to be made between 'rational' and 'reasonable' which are particularly important for one of the theses which I propose to develop in this essay. They are embedded, I think, in the ways in which we do ordinarily use these terms. But even should counter-examples be produced, I shall not mind. For the point of examining ordinary usage is not to spot some linguistic essence but to take one route to explore distinctions which may prove important in the context of a thesis.

How, then, do 'rational' and 'reasonable' differ, given that they both presuppose a background of reasoning? They obviously do, as can be gleaned by considering their opposites. 'Irrational' functions almost as a diagnosis, and requires special explanation. 'Unreasonable' is a much milder and more common complaint and does not seem to be associated in the same way with summoning the psychiatrist for advice. The difference, surely, is that 'rational' and 'irrational' have application to situations in which someone could have conclusive reasons for belief or action. 'Irrational' is usually applied to cases where there is a belief or action with no good reason or in the face of reasons. The irrational man is presumed to be aware of the considerations which would normally be deemed conclusive for believing or doing something; but, because of something that comes over him, he cannot bring himself to believe or do what is appropriate. Or alternatively, he believes something fervently, for which there is not the slightest evidence or does something for which there is no discernible reason. To call a man unreasonable who believed that his hands were covered in blood when the blood could not be seen and when he had washed his hands in hot water with detergent in it, would be to make too feeble a complaint. For 'unreasonable' is a weaker kind of condemnation: it presupposes that a person has reasons for what he believes or does; but it suggests that the reasons are very weak, and that he pays little attention to the reasons of others. A man who is unreasonable has a somewhat myopic or biased viewpoint; he either wilfully turns a blind eye to relevant considerations or weights them in an obtuse and idiosyncratic way. It would be unreasonable, for instance, to believe that it is not going to rain simply because there are patches of blue sky about, or that one will contract pneumonia simply by getting caught in the rain without an umbrella. Generalisations are used, but there is little attempt to test them or to consider them critically. The individual tends to be attached to beliefs that suit him, or that are based on authority, hearsay or a narrow range of considertions. It is a level of life to which epithets such as 'bigoted', 'short-sighted', 'prejudiced', 'wilful', 'pig-headed', 'obtuse', have obvious application.

Many of these epithets apply to actions in which there is the same suggestion of a limited form of reasoning with sketchy attention to evidence and to relevant considerations. It is unreasonable, for instance, to insist on driving from London to Birmingham by car if all one wants is to get there as quickly as possible; for there is the inter-city train service. Similarly it is unreasonable to do the football pools as the appropriate way of acquiring the money for one's summer holiday. In the sphere of emotion the same point holds. It is unreasonable, but not irrational, to be afraid of being shot at by a gamekeeper near a 'Trespassers Will Be Prosecuted' notice. It is unreasonable, but not irrational, to be jealous of one's son if he begins to occupy some of one's wife's time and attention.

The second important difference between 'unreasonable' and 'irrational' is that the former has a more explicitly social connotation. 'Reasonable' suggests a willingness to listen to arguments and relevant considerations advanced by others in public argument. There is, however, a second and stronger sense of 'reasonable' which implies that an individual is disposed to take account of the claims to consideration that other individuals have – that is, he is to some degree impartial in dealing with situations in which the rights and interests of others are at stake. 'Irrational' has no suggestion of a failure to give this kind of impartial consideration to the claims of others.

The possibility of a slide from the first to the second sense of 'reasonable' will prove to be very important in our understanding and appraisal of Piaget's treatment of the development of rationality in a man's practical life.

(b) *The Publicity and Objectivity of Reason*
The reference to the social aspect of 'reasonableness' introduces another cardinal feature of 'reason' which is its publicity. It is very easy to think of reasoning as the operation of a private gadget, or as the flowering of some inner potentiality. But this is an untenable view; for though there is a sense in which, as a mode of consciousness, it is private to the individual, its content and procedures of operation are public possessions. By that I mean that the concepts fundamental to its operation are shared concepts; children are introduced to them from the very beginning of their lives as social beings. They structure the experience of the world for them from the very start. With the learning of language, which is one of the main vehicles of reasoning, children are initiated into rules of syntax as well, which are also public possessions. Furthermore, developed types of reasoning, which involve criticism and the production of counter-examples, can best be understood as the internalisation of public procedures, and the different points of view of others. The individual, who reasons in this developed sense, is one who has taken a critic into his own consciousness, whose mind is structured by the procedures of a public tradition. He can adopt the point of view of what G. H. Mead called 'the generalised other'. This is a reflection in his consciousness of social situations in which the point of view of others has in fact been represented.

There is another public feature of reasoning which is crucial to its objectivity when it is applied to the world as in science, history, or morality. In these forms of reasoning, different points of view confront one another, each supported by reasons. But what counts as a reason depends not only on public rules embodied in concepts, syntax and forms of inference which structure common forms of discourse, but also upon there being some forms of experience which are generally taken to terminate disputes. In science, for instance, consensus can be reached on matters in dispute only because there is a prior understanding that what the research workers can all hear or see shall count as evidence for anyone. Similarly, in practical reasoning, it is because we respond alike to situations of danger, frustration, suffering, and the like, that we are able to agree in deliberation on what is to count as a reason for acting. Without such shared experiences and responses, neither explanation nor deliberation could get under way, since there would be nothing on which one could rely as an unproblematic anchoring point of discourse.

(c) *The Norms of Reason*

It has been usual, since the time of Hume, to contrast reason with passion. But, as I have argued elsewhere,[6] this contrast is a mistake. Integral to the life of reason are a related set of norms or standards with a range of correlative attitudes and concerns. What marks off rationality, as a level of life distinct from the non-rational, the irrational and the unreasonable, is the continual influence and interaction of these norms and concerns. I shall distinguish three aspects of the operation of the norms of reason.

(i) There is, first, the influence of the rational individual's concern for consistency and the avoidance of contradiction. This concern can be manifested in two ways in which a rational man forms and modifies his beliefs. He has to resolve and remove any putative inconsistencies between his existing beliefs and assumptions and any discrepant 'incoming' experience or piece of information. If something turns up which is novel he has either to latch on to some feature or similarity which will enable it to be subsumed under his existing assumptions, or, if it is too discrepant to be fitted in, he has to make an appropriate alteration to his assumptions. The second demand of the requirement of consistency is, of course, that in forming beliefs by an inference from antecedent convictions and assumptions, the individual avoids drawing conclusions which are inconsistent with his premises.

In the sphere of action the rational man, in choosing means to his ends, can be understood as concerned to secure consistency between his choices and his ends; and if he is acting on rules, between his choices and his rules. The demand for consistency is implicit in the requirement of reason that willing the end commits one to willing the means. One paradigm of rationality is the man who has a number of ends which cannot be simultaneously achieved: in devising a plan or schedule whereby the ends of highest priority are achieved, or all his ends are secured over a period of time, he can be seen as avoiding unnecessary conflict between his ends and as avoiding choices which unnecessarily conflict with and frustrate some of his wants. Presupposed by such rationality in choice is the agent's consistently ranking his ends and his rules in some order of priority. There is also a process – analogous to the adaptation of assumptions to some novel item of experience – of modifying ones' ends and rules in the light of circumstances. Rationality is, for example, evinced in qualifying an absolute disapproval of lying when confronted by a case where exceptional circumstances incline one to think that there are overriding grounds for lying – e.g. the immense amount of suffering likely to be brought about if the literal truth is told on a particular occasion.

(ii) The rational man also has a well-defined sense of what counts as a relevant consideration in the various contexts of belief-formation and choice. What counts as relevant can be given in a generalisation, as for instance a meteorological generalisation which indicates relevant grounds for the prediction that it is going to rain; or it may be given in a rule of conduct that indicates, say, the circumstances in which one ought to be polite. To accept such standards of relevance is to be disposed to take account of the considerations in question when they crop up, and to reject as partial or arbitrary choices or beliefs based on other considerations, such as may be suggested by extrinsic attractions or aversions. Rationality is also usually held to commit a man to rejecting as arbitrary *particular* considerations of time, place and identity. If one is considering whether it is going to rain, the mere fact that it is 10 a.m. and the place Christchurch does not count. Some additional features characterising the time and place of the prediction have to be added. Similarly, if one acts on the rule that one ought to be polite, the mere facts that it is 10 a.m., that one is in Christchurch and that one is talking to Mr Brown, have to be disregarded. Similarly, rational prudence involves taking no account of purely temporal considerations. As Sidgwick put it: 'Hereafter as such is to be regarded neither more than less than now.' There must be other than temporal considerations, even if they are as crude as 'if you wait you won't be able to have it at all' or 'if you wait there will be more of it'.

(iii) Finally, fully developed rationality involves not a comparatively passive taking account of considerations which are forced on one's attention, but an active enquiring and critical spirit. Many of the central norms of rationality relate to such activities. Thus the tendency to adapt assumptions to novel situations develops into the conscious attempt to check assumptions – nurtured, perhaps, by a caution born of past experience of being in error. This becomes of outstanding importance in systematic developments of reasoning about the world as in science or history. For instead of just being brought up short by the givenness of the world and having to accommodate to it if the novelty is to be dealt with, the individual becomes much more concerned about the warrants for his stock of assumptions and rules.

He pays explicit attention to what Bacon called 'the negative instance'. He makes sure that his assumptions and rules are well-grounded. And, in activities such as science, he makes explicit attempts to overthrow them by imagining counter-examples and seeing whether his assumptions and rules can stand up to such tests. He looks for evidence.

The same development can be discerned, too, in forms of practical reasoning, such as morality. Consider an individual who, through first-hand experience, becomes sensitive to the suffering brought about by social practices. No longer able to accept them uncritically, he sets about ruthlessly examining them against principles that common human experience establishes as relevant grounds for evaluation and decision.

Reasoning thus entails the recognition of the normative demands of consistency, relevance, impartiality and the search for grounds for belief and decision. It can readily be seen, too, that if it is going to operate in ways which are compatible with its over-arching τέλε of discovering what is true and what is best, other norms enter in. Clarity in stating assumptions is necessary if issues relating to consistency, relevance and respect for evidence are to be raised. Honesty is also required; for cheating would be completely counter-productive in the context of the determination to check the assumptions and rules concerned.

What status is to be accorded to these norms which are definitive of the use of reason? One can, in the fashion of a true English gentleman, say with Ryle that the individual is now subject to certain characteristic scruples.[7] One can talk less modestly about the intellectual virtues of consistency, clarity, impartiality, sense of relevance and demand for evidence or about the ethics of belief governed by the conviction that truth matters. Or one can talk about the rational passions that characterise the concern for truth.[8] These are just different ways of drawing attention to a group of values that are inseparable from the developed use of reason.

(d) *Action and Will*
In the sphere of action there is a continuum of virtues generated by the demands for consistency, relevance and the active search for grounds for belief and decision. They are closely connected with the concept of a self that endures through time. As we have seen, rationality in action is manifested in choosing means to ends, in the scheduling or planning of a series of choices over time in order to satisfy a number of conflicting wants, and in the delay of gratifica-

tion which is demanded by plans which give no special priority to the present. All such deliberation and planning involves the use of reason; and is subject to the demands of consistency and relevance, and the requirements of active rationality.

In putting such plans and policies into action, it is often the case that there is scope for the exercise of an additional family of virtues, which are intimately connected with what is often called 'the will', 'having character', or 'strength of character'. The virtues are those such as integrity, courage, perseverance and resoluteness. They are connected with reason in that all imply some kind of consistency in sticking to a principle or pursuing a policy or plan. The administrator refuses to abandon justice by accepting a bribe; his secretary heaves herself out of bed when the alarm goes with thoughts of the importance of being at the office on time flitting through her numbed consciousness. There is also the implication that these principles or policies are adhered to in the face of counter-inclinations or temptations. To give an account of such actions, which William James described as actions in the line of greatest resistance, reference must be made to the affective aspects of the demands of reason inherent in consistency and relevance as well as to the affective aspects of the principles and policies concerned.

2 PIAGET'S THEORY OF DEVELOPMENT

In the previous section, I have examined the principal components and the structure of the concept 'reason'.[9] Reason is the end-product of the process of development which is the subject of the rest of this essay. In particular, I shall examine critically the theory of development offered by Piaget. In this section I shall sketch the main outlines of the theory, focusing on those features that bear upon the distinction I have made between 'rationality' and 'reasonableness', on the publicity and objectivity of reason, on the acceptance of the norms of reason, and on the relation between the development of reason and action and will. These elements have figured prominently in my own account of the end-product; in my view it is the development of these features that most needs to be explained.

Pagiet distinguishes four stages, which I shall consider in turn.

(a) 0–2. The Copernican Revolution of Early Childhood
The first stage is what Piaget calls the intellectual revolution of the first two years. The child now apprehends the world as one in which enduring objects existing in time and space stand in causal relations, though causality is at first interpreted purely in terms of agency. At

the earliest stage, the child's consciousness is egocentric, since 'there is no definite differentiation between the self and the external world. . . . The self is at the centre of reality to begin with for the very reason that it is not aware of itself. . . . The progress of sensori-motor intelligence leads to the construction of an objective universe in which the subject's own body is an element amongst others and with which the internal life, localised in the subject's own body, is contrasted.'[10] It is only with the emergence of the concept of enduring objects that the child is able to objectify emotions and to differentiate them by reference to objects. The concept of a 'means to an end', which presupposes causality, also emerges at this stage. This is a prerequisite of any kind of rational action.

The thought of the very young child is non-rational in so far as it is not subject to such categories. One of Freud's most important contributions to psychological theory was just this distinction between primary and secondary processes; for he argued that the mind of the very young child is ruled by wishes in which there is no proper grasp of means to an end, and of enduring objects in a space–time framework having causal properties in relation to other objects.

At the primary Freudian level thought is determined purely by the affectivity of the wish. This makes possible a primitive form of associative thinking determined by affectively loaded similarities between objects in which no account is taken of their identity as substantive entities as distinct from their pleasing or displeasing features; there is no grasp of temporal or spatial considerations or of causality, which presupposes a sense of time and of objects, having stable characteristics. Without these concepts one could not have the capacity for rational belief or for the postponement of gratification which is indispensable to rational action. As Freud postulated the continuance of primary thought processes even in the adult, a more precise plotting of this intellectual revolution is very important. Some lapses from rational belief and action could be explained, Freud suggested, in terms of disruptions brought about by the persistence of this more primitive form of thought.[11] People succumb to impulses prompted by these unstructured wishes. And some more enduring forms of irrationality, such as schizophrenia, might be linked with the failure to acquire elements of the secondary conceptual apparatus, e.g. the concept of oneself and others as enduring objects, the distinction between appearance and reality.

(b) *2–7. Pre-operational Thought and Moral Realism*
The next stage in Piaget's developmental account is of great signifi-

cance for the social aspects of the development of reason; for it is at this stage (roughly 2–7) that language is acquired and: 'Thought becomes conscious to the degree to which the child is able to communicate it'.[12] In this stage, according to Piaget, the child internalises rules that are imposed on him by adults. What exactly is meant by 'internalisation' is no clearer than the way in which it actually happens. But this stage is of crucial importance in the development of man as a purposive, rule-following animal. Children somehow grasp, from the inside as it were, what it is to follow a rule. Language is obviously of great importance. It is a means of formulating rules, and a device for teaching children to follow them. But for the child himself the use of language still has partly an egocentric function. As Luria[13] has also demonstrated, the use of monologue helps the child to perform tasks as an adjunct to action; also, when children of this age talk together, their 'conversation' has the character of a collective monologue. But, on the other hand, language, together with imagery, enables the child to represent and rehearse actions, to reconstruct the past and to anticipate the future. It helps, too, to unite the child with others as it is a vehicle for concepts and ideas that are public. It aids his socialisation as well as providing a tool for individual projects.

The affective life of the child parallels this development in thought. He has interests of a predominantly practical character. He learns to evaluate himself and to develop levels of aspiration. Feelings are interchanged as well as words and fellow-feeling develops for those who share his interests. There is also respect for older people – especially parents – which, at this stage, is a mixture of affection and fear. Obedience is his first moral precept and values take the form of rules which are heteronomously accepted. What matters about them is their formulation rather than the intent which may inform them.

However, accommodation to others and to reality is still very rudimentary; for the child's thought is characterised by what Piaget calls 'intuition', in which judgements are made on the basis of perception rather than reason. 'One quality stands out in the thinking of the young child: he constantly makes assertions without trying to support them with facts.'[14] This stems from the character of his social behaviour, from his egocentricity in the sense of a lack of differentiation between his own point of view and that of others. 'It is only *vis-à-vis* others that we are led to seek evidence for our statements. We always believe ourselves without further ado until we learn to consider the objections of others and to internalise such discussions in the form of reflection.'

(c) *7–12. Concrete Operations, Autonomy and Will*

The next stage of concrete operations (roughly 7–12) is the crucial one for the development of reasoning proper. The child becomes able both 'to dissociate his point of view from that of others and to co-ordinate these different points of view'.15 True discussions between children are possible and 'ego-centric' language diappears almost entirely. 'One is hard put to say whether the child has become capable of a certain degree of reflection because he has learned to co-operate with others or vice versa.' The child is no longer so impulsive; he thinks before he acts. But this reflection is a kind of internal dialogue, that parallels actual discussions which the child holds with parents and peers. He has taken the objector, as it were, into his own consciousness.16 This fertile suggestion is, of course, as old as Plato who described thinking as the soul's dialogue with itself. It was also one of G. H. Mead's main contributions to developmental psychology.

The crucial difference in the child's thinking at this stage, which differentiates it from intuitive thought, is the capacity for reversibility or a rigorous return to the point of departure. When judging whether a flat cake of pastry weighs as much as a ball constructed out of the same amount of pastry, the child does not just go on what he can see. He can, as it were, return to the starting point and grasp that a ball can be remade from the material of the flat cake. He can objectify his own performances, both physical and intellectual, and conceive of himself going back to the beginning again, and perhaps doing them differently. This permits a range of rational operations.17 It also permits what Piaget calls the 'decentring' of egocentricity.

Piaget thinks that it parallels the capacity to see a situation from another's point of view, to go over the situation again, as it were, employing perhaps a different type of operation. It is thus possible to transcend the sense-bound character of pre-operational thought.

The construction of logic now beings. 'Logic constitutes the system of relationships which permit the co-ordination of points of view corresponding to different individuals, as well as those which correspond to the successive percepts or intuitions of the same individual.' 18 Piaget associates with this stage the development of a morality of co-operation and personal autonomy, in contrast to the intuitive heteronomous morality of the small child. 'This new system of values represents, in the affective sphere, the equivalent of logic in the realm of intelligence.'19

The morality of co-operation, replacing that of constraint, is one consequence of the child's new capacity to decentre. He sees that rules are alterable and, by his new-found ability to look at them from other people's point of view, is able to adjust his behaviour to others on a basis of reciprocity. He can also operate on his own rules and rethink them, thereby developing towards autonomy for himself and respect for others as rule-makers. The terms used to formulate a rule matter less than the intent which informs it; for the individual is now aware of himself and others as having intentions which are expressed in behaviour. The sense of justice based on strict equality takes the place of the previous emphasis on obedience. Thus honesty, a sense of justice, and reciprocity form a rational grouping of values that can be compared to the 'groupings' of relations or concepts that characterise logic.

At this stage of development, there emerges, as an equivalent to the regulative operations of reason, the will as a regulator of the affective life.[20] A young child will persevere in an activity when his interest is engaged; but interest is an intuitive regulator, not an intellectual one. Will, by contrast, is a kind of organisation of the emotions into a higher order motive, that transcends the momentary interest. So when a duty is momentarily weaker than a specific desire, the act of will consists not in 'following the inferior and stronger tendency; on the contrary, one would then speak of a failure of will or "lack of will power". Will power involves reinforcing the superior but weaker tendency so as to make it triumph.' Will acts, therefore, like a logical operation, when the conclusion of a piece of deductive reasoning is at odds with what appears to be the case; operational reasoning then corrects the misleading appearances by referring to previous states that are the grounds for the conclusion. Correspondingly, an act of will involves a decentring or detachment from the pressure of immediate interest, and so a decision taken in harmony with the personality as a whole.

(d) *Formal Operations*
The final stage is that of formal operations, which develop in adolescence. Logical operations, formerly restricted to concrete reality, to 'tangible objects' that could 'be manipulated and subjected to real action', can now be performed on general ideas, hypotheses and abstract constructions. Going beyond the logic of relations, classes and numbers, the logic of propositions is now possible, in which the system of inference is an abstract translation of that governing concrete operations. The adolescent starts by using this new range of abilities in the service of egocentric assimilation, but gradually learns to accommodate these systems to reality. He learns to predict

and to interpret experience by theorising instead of indulging in metaphysical egocentricity.

What Piaget calls the 'personality' of the individual now emerges which results from autosubmission of the self to some kind of discipline. Rules and values are organised in the light of a life-plan. There is a decentring of the self which becomes part of a co-operative plan dictated by ideals which provide standards for the operation of will.

3   CRITIQUE OF PIAGET'S ACCOUNT

In what follows I shall begin by focusing on Piaget's account of the development of rationality in an individual's practical life. In later sections, I shall redress the balance by concentrating on his account of epistemic rationality.

(a)   *Rationality and Reasonableness*
I shall begin my critique by considering how far Piaget's account pays due attention to the distinctions noted earlier between the notions of rationality and reasonableness and between the two senses of 'reasonable'.

The Explanation of Unreasonableness and Irrationality   Piaget's system permits a convincing account to be given of people who are unreasonable but not downright irrational. If there is some kind of fixation at the early egocentric stage beliefs tend to be infected with the arbitrariness and particularity characteristic of pre-operational thought. Little attempt is made to fit them into a coherent system or to test them out reflectively. Behaviour is governed by wants and aversions of an immediate, short-term character. The view-point of others impinges but little. Indeed the behaviour of others is seen largely in a self-referential way as it impinges on, threatens, or thwarts the demands of the greedy restless ego. The emotional life is not organised by stable sentiments. It tends to be gusty, and dominated by powerful self-referential emotions. There is, too, a bastardisation of will which is exhibited in wilfulness and obstinacy.

If, on the other hand, the fixation is at the transcendental stage of 'moral realism', the love of rule-following, of doing the right thing, is very much to the fore. The capacity for reasoning is enlarged because of the beginnings of classification and the desire to assimilate things into an established pattern. But another dimension of unreasonableness becomes possible because of the sanctity attached to what is established, which is reinforced by the fear of disapproval. The individual can be dogmatic, prejudiced and censorious because what is right is, for him, what is laid down by the group or by someone in authority. He is capable of a range of emotions beyond the ken of the purely egocentric man – loyalty, trust, shame. He can show courage, determination and other qualities of will in sticking to the code which he reveres. But he does so in a heteronomous way because of his fear of disapproval.

To explain the genesis of unreasonable behaviour I have used the Freudian conception of 'fixation', used by Freud himself in his later theory of the super-ego to explain distinctive forms of irrationality.[21] He was trying to explain the fact that some children seem to develop much more rigorous standards than their parents. This leads to obsessions and compulsions, which are irrational in the sense that rules are followed in a way which has no warrant in the situation. He tried to explain besides the fact that many people have a picture of themselves – what Adler called a 'guiding fiction'– which is quite out of keeping with the traits which they in fact exhibit. In his theory of character development, too, Freud was trying to explain not the genesis of character in the sense of what Kohlberg calls 'the bag of virtues' which people possess, nor 'having character', which is connected with virtues such as integrity, determination and courage, but rather the occurrence of various forms of irrationality. His contribution was in the tradition of characterology which goes back to Theophrastus. Either there is a subordination of traits to a dominant one, as in the sketch of the penurious man (Freud's anal character); or a whole range of traits is portrayed as being exercised in an exaggerated or distorted manner, as in the case of the pedant. Freud spotted similarities between these styles of rule-following and various forms of neurosis and assigned a common cause to both in his theory of infantile sexuality. Reason completely fails to exercise the 'decentring' function in relation to rule-following postulated by Piaget: the agent shows no capacity for impersonal appraisal of his behaviour, for making the kind of assessment that might be made by someone not centrally involved.

Reasonableness However, while Piaget allows for the kinds of belief and action which fall between the downright irrational and the totally rational, he gives no attention to the distinction between the two notions of reasonableness, outlined in section 1(a) (' "Reasonable" and "rational"') – between reasonableness as the disposition to take account of any relevant considerations advanced by others, and reasonableness as the disposition to give impartial consideration to the interests of others and their claims concerning those interests. The critical stage for Piaget in the development of reason is the stage of concrete operations which is characterised both by reversibility in thought and the ability to see other people's point of view, to internalise their criticism and so on. This is a thoroughly acceptable idea which stresses the public character of reasoning. It was not, of course, Piaget's discovery; but he demonstrated the details of this development in a brilliant way. He does not, however, make anything of the important distinction between seeing things from the point of view of others (what he calls decentring) which is essential to objectivity, and having *regard* for the point of view of others which presupposes some degree of active sympathy for them. He takes no account, in other words, of the possibility that a person might become a rational egoist. He assumes that a rational person will also be reasonable. In this respect, like Kant, he was a child of the Enlightenment.

The absence of any proper account of the development of sympathy is also a failure of Piaget's more specific work on moral development.[22] He makes mention, of course, of sympathy in the sense of the fellow-feeling that a child has at the heteronomous stage for those who share his interests. But this is really a feeling of fraternity rather than active sympathy for another individual. Sympathy also, in the sense of being able to reverberate in response to another's display of feeling, is presupposed in his account of decentring. For without this capacity it would be difficult to give any account of taking another's point of view in the affective realm. But both these forms of sympathy are possible without any concern for another person. And this, surely, is what a reasonable person must have in the second social application of the concept of 'reasonable'. For without this would his sensitivity to the claims of others be explicable? He would, of course, have a concern about consistency; he might appreciate, too, 'intellectually' that another person might have good reasons for his claims. But would this be sufficient to explain the fact that people are moved to act by consideration of the claims of others, especially if they are in conflict with their own? At this point, as is well known, Kant introduced the rational emotion of respect as explaining how people are moved to act out of consideration for law (i.e. consistency) and for other people as sources of law. But this raises the question in another form. For can a convincing account be given of the genesis of the 'moral' emotion of respect without postulating a 'natural' basis for it in compassion?

The same two criticisms can be made of Piaget's account of emotional development. Some people, of Augustinian leanings, are prepared to argue that there is a group of self-referential emotions, such as envy, jealousy and pride, which are extremely unamenable to education. They have, perhaps, a more Hobbesian view of human nature than Piaget. They may credit human beings with a general tendency to think of themselves first and foremost. Thus the objects or situations which are picked out by the specific appraisals of situations, which form the cognitive core of all emotions, always include some thought of oneself. This is perhaps an extreme view; but there is sufficient basis for the doctrine of original sin to suggest that, though human beings are capable of being moved by other types of emotion, egocentricity in this sphere is not just a skin that can be sloughed off in middle childhood. We may ask, then, for a justification for regarding the transcendence of egocentricity as an aspect of the development of rationality, and for an account of the way the grip of egocentric emotions can be loosened.

Presumably the grip of such emotions can be loosened by the development of what Koestler[23] calls the self-transcending emotions, such as love, awe, the sense of justice, and respect. But are the egocentric ones just precipitates of the egocentric period of early childhood? Or are they a more stubborn strand in the fabric of human nature? Or are they mainly the product of acquisitive, individualistic societies? Do we have just partially to 'decentre' them, e.g. by transferring pride to human achievements in general such as science or poetry, instead of directing it towards more trivial objects such as personal appearance and possessions? Or is it possible for them to slip from us like some of our childhood fears? Obviously they can be unreasonable or irrational in the sense that they can be felt for objects to which we have little claim or for situations which we have had absolutely no hand in bringing about (e.g. a man who feels proud of the sea). But can the development of reason alone rid us altogether of such self-referential emotions?[24] Indeed is our being subject to such emotions, as distinct from our directing them towards inappropriate objects, a matter just of being unreasonable or irrational? Is not lack of subservience to them connected with the development of moral, religious and aesthetic emotions of which Piaget takes no account?

(b) *Will and Autonomy*
Piaget had two connected insights both of which were rather vitiated by his elaboration of them. First, he saw that reasoning is basically a

social matter and is only explicable in terms of the public acceptance of norms. 'Logic', he says, 'is a kind of moral for thought.' But he then inappropriately, as I shall later argue, proceeded to attempt an explanation of its development in terms of an equilibrium model.

Secondly, he saw the logical or rational aspects both of morality and of the organisation of personality in terms of will. But he had too thin a concept of rationality to do justice to this insight. Thus his account of moral development, as has been seen, was marred by his failure to distinguish two applications of the concept of reasonableness, the formal and the substantive. The same sort of defect is to be found in Piaget's account of will which he sketches as a solution to the problem posed by William James, that the virtues of will such as courage, integrity, perseverance and resolution involve acting on principles in the face of strong counter-inclinations. Piaget assumed that there is a disengagement of affectivity from the self and a submission to discipline defined by the laws of co-operation.[25] These, like Rousseau's General Will, provide the assistance required to conquer insistent counter-inclinations. But why should there be this disengagement from the self? Surely rational egoists can exhibit great strength of will. They 'decentre' from instant gratification, however strong the immediate urge, and act in terms of prudence. McDougall, when confronted with James's problem, gives an answer in terms of support for duty from the self-regarding sentiment.[26] Why should not this provide an organisation of personality which is as capable of reinforcing duty as the Kantian type of ideal assumed by Piaget? As Hoffman points out,[27] Piaget's data relate only to the individual's judgement of others. Why should he evaluate his own behaviour in the same way? Impartiality may require it. But why should he not make a case for being specially placed with regard to the development of his own interests as others too are placed with regard to the development of theirs? Unless concern for others is written into the 'moral point of view' what is objectionable about a society of rational egoists?

There is, too, an even more fundamental valuative point underlying Piaget's whole account of personality development in which autonomy functions as the end-point. Kagan and Kogan[28] ask whether field-independence, which goes with autonomy, is a socially desirable form of development. Field dependents, they claim, are much more alert to the social nuances that surround them. They are better at remembering social words and faces. They are quicker at attaining consensus in a group, and more adept at interpersonal accommodation. They are, in brief, more likely to adapt harmoniously to society, whereas field-independents tend to be more aloof, awkward in personal dealings, and more prone to take a line of their own. If these different styles of cognitive functioning do depend on early family circumstances, they are in principle amenable to training. But which style should parents encourage?

Piaget, as a child of the Enlightenment, assumes that autonomy is the obvious ideal. And, though he acknowledges the importance of the social environment, he assumes that it merely hastens or impedes the development towards autonomy which he regards as almost a logically necessary sequence. There is a sense, of course, in which he must be right. For how could a child become autonomous if he had not first passed through a previous stage of rule-conformity when he learnt what it is to follow a rule? But there are some societies which definitely discourage development towards this final stage. By processes of shaming and indoctrination their members are prevented from developing very far towards autonomy. There are thus important valuative assumptions underlying not only Piaget's assumptions about the principles which give content to the organisation of personality, but also his assumptions about the autonomy which structures its form.

This raises major questions in ethics about the status of Piaget's developmental findings. Kohlberg, as a matter of fact, regards them as providing the basis for bridging the gap between 'is' and 'ought'.[29] To discuss this suggestion would open up vast issues which would require another paper to clarify.

(c) *Publicity and Objectivity*

It is often said that Piaget's biological preoccupations led him to neglect the social aspects of the development of reason. This is perhaps true of his account of the early experience of the child which is dominated by the model of assimilation and accommodation. But it certainly is not true of his account of the development of concrete operations in which, in his conception of 'decentring', he made a brilliant, if unoriginal, attempt to link the development of reason with reversibility and the capacity to adopt the standpoint of others. This is crucial to any account of the publicity and objectivity of reasoning.

There is, however, an omission in his account of objectivity, which parallels his failure to account for the development of reasonableness as distinct from rationality. This is connected with his predominating interest in logic and mathematics as the paradigms of reasoning, together with a Kantian type of moral system in which justice and consistency are the basis of all the virtues. Logic and mathematics are unusual forms of reasoning, in that the possibility of agreement on the outcome of a process of reasoning depends wholly on the acceptance of the canons of valid deductive inference. Rational agreement in most other developed forms of reasoning depends, besides, on a common acknowledgement of what is to count as a ground from which inferences can relevantly be made, and by which judgements can be properly supported. Scientific reasoning, for instance, depends upon the employment of sense organs, yielding evidence on which there can be agreement, since it is accessible to any observer and because anyone can appreciate its bearing on the truth or falsity of the propositions to which it relates. A similar point can be made about moral reasoning. The development of virtues such as justice and truth-telling could be fitted into the Piagetian scheme, as involved in 'decentring', because these might plausibly be grounded on formal conditions of rationality, like the exclusion of the irrelevant, impartiality and so on. But the development of a fuller conception of morality, which depends not merely on conceding to others the claims one makes on one's own behalf, but also a concern and respect for them, is possible only as one becomes sensitive and sympathetic to their sufferings and to their attempts to make something of their lives. And for this Piaget's account, which stops short at the capacity for looking at things from another person's standpoint, is inadequate.

The problem of objectivity is raised still more acutely by certain other forms of reasoning, notably those involved in religious and aesthetic judgement. Piaget deals with it only in the most general terms: one becomes capable of objectivity as one develops the capacity to look at situations from the standpoint of other subjects, likely to be differently affected by them. And from the appreciation of a diversity of viewpoints there can develop a capacity for the impersonal assessment of situations – for viewing them as *anyone* might, whose personal interests were not affected by them. Now this is necessary, but not sufficient for an account of reasoning. For there are still different modes of reasoning that need to be distinguished, each with its characteristic canons, determining what is to count in support of an inference of that specific type. Piaget considered science as well as logic and mathematics, but it raised no difficulty for him since he was able to rely on the fact that all men palpably possess sense-organs; and it is at least plausible to envisage men peering out on a public world of objects, which would consequently supply the content of a shared experience. But though the existence of objects to gaze at may be one condition for objectivity, it cannot be a necessary one. For the notion of objectivity can be applied just as readily to judgements made from a moral, a religious, or an aesthetic point of view. It may well be argued, therefore, that the shared responses of scientific observers are only a special case of what a repertoire of shared responses is like, and of the way it makes objective judgements in any field possible. Responses like the experience of awe in the face of contingency may supply a similar grounding for religious reasoning, and others like the sensitivity to suffering may similarly underpin moral reasoning, each in its own area providing a ground for agreement on objective judgement, corresponding to the evidence of the senses in science.

If this point about reasoning were accepted the way would be open for posing two further types of developmental problem which are of considerable educational significance. First, there would be a genetic story to be told about the origins of these shared responses and about their transformations at the different stages of development. This would be like asking, in Piaget's system, how the sporadic curiosity of the child becomes transformed into the disciplined search for the truth of the scientist, or how spontaneous sympathy becomes transformed into a steady concern and respect for others. Secondly, there would be the problem of setting out the norms which are constitutive of 'directed thinking' in these other modes of experience – e.g. neatness and elegance in the realm of the aesthetic. A developmental account would then have to be given of the emergence of sensitivity to them.

(d) Equilibration and the Norms of Reason

One of the most important questions to which Piaget's theory gives rise is why children progress through the various stages until they reach the end-point of autonomous beings making use of formal operations.

The Stimulation of Social Conditions   He links such development, of course, with social conditions which favour assimilation and accommodation by providing stimulation and novelty. His account of the role of language and his postulated link between the development of reasoning and critical dialogue should lead him to welcome the findings of sociologists such as Bernstein[30] and Klein,[31] who link the use of generalisations involved in reasoning, the tendency to plan for the future, and the general capacity for abstract thought with the different types of language and methods of social control employed in different strata of society.

A particularly interesting substantiation of this influence of the social environment on 'cognitive stimulation' is to be found in the study of Bruner and Greenfield.[32] The Wolof, a tribe in Senegal, were investigated for their ideas about the conservation of continuous quantities. Those who had not been exposed to the influence of Western schooling were unable to make distinctions such as that between how things are and how the individual views them. They had not the concept of 'different points of view' so important to operational thought. Also the concept of conservation is achieved much earlier by the Tiv, a tribe in Nigeria, whose children are encouraged to experiment with and manipulate the external world, unlike those of the Wolof. If the Wolof child wants to know anything he is told to ask someone, not to try to find out for himself. The child's personal desires and intentions, which might differentiate him from others, are not encouraged. What matters is conformity to the group. Thus the social pressures of the Wolof discourage the interaction with the environment which Piagetians regard as crucial for cognitive growth.

On Piaget's view, of course, the sequence of stages in the development of rationality is culturally invariant, and follows a *logical* sequence. Hypothetico-deductive thinking, for instance, presupposes a stage of classification; for without observed regularities there would be nothing to explain by reference to hypotheses. In a similar way the achievement of autonomy presupposes a stage at which an individual learns what it is to follow a rule. But this account of the invariant stages of development is consistent with the view that different social environments provide features which are more or less stimulating for such development. There will thus be individual and cultural differences in the rate and extent of development along a logically hierarchical sequence of stages.

However, Piaget holds that social conditions are not the crucial determinants of development; they merely facilitate or impede a progression that is to be explained in another way. Kohlberg, indeed, has elaborated this thesis about the connection between the social environment and 'cognitive stimulation' in his account of class differences and in his cross-cultural studies which reveal different rates and levels of development.[33] Why then do some children, with similar social backgrounds, remain 'embedded', as Schachtel[34] calls it, with a conventional heteronomous outlook? This issue is raised in a concrete way by the vast amount of research that has emerged from the experiments by Witkin[35] and his associates on individual differences in cognitive development. Witkin claims that individuals have very different capacities for analytic thinking and for abstracting from concrete perceptual situations. This influences the control of impulse, and the capacity for personal relationships, as well as intellectual skills. It is claimed that these abilities depend not on the development of linguistic sophistication, but most probably on early familial factors.

Equilibration   But why, in general, should *anyone* progress towards autonomy? For it is a progression in defiance of the deep-seated need for the security that a stable conformity provides. What general motivation is there for this type of development? Piaget's answer can be summed up in one word – equilibration. In his early work, in which he was particularly concerned with the way in which reasoning proper emerges from the kind of intelligence which men share with animals, Piaget used the biological model of assimilation and accommodation to cover both biological and rational processes. 'Assimilation' covers both nutrition, in which food is literally taken into the stomach, and understanding some new item of experience by subsuming it under existing assumptions. 'Accommodation' is used, too, both in its biological sense of fitting into an environment, and in an extended sense to describe the way in which a child adapts his concepts and assumptions to cope with some new experience that is too discrepant to be dealt with by his existing ones. In addition Piaget supposes that there is a general tendency towards stability, possessed by all organisms, which enables the organism to maintain a balance between assimilation and accommodation. This he calls 'equilibration'. The tendency of the body, demonstrated by Cannon, to maintain homeostasis, is parallelled by that of the mind to maintain in the individual's framework of belief, his behaviour routines and the rules informing them (what Piaget refers to as his 'schemata'), a more dynamic type of equilibrium. There is not a return to an existing equilibrium state but a constant movement towards new ones. A succession of strategies is developed for dealing in an affectively organised way with cognitive perturbations of increasing complexity as the child grows older. The entire process of cognitive development thus 'consists of reactions of compensation to perturbation (relative to previous schemas) which make necessary a variation of the initial schemas'.[36]

I have argued elsewhere[37] that this type of extension of the postulate of homeostasis is either a piece of metaphysics rather than science, or a redescription which does no explanatory work. Mischel,[38] too, has criticised this biological version of it using similar arguments. Homeostasis functions as an acceptable explanation at the physiological level only because it is possible to specify the deficit states that initiate the behaviour and the mechanisms by means of which equilibrium is restored, in ways independent of the behaviour explained. But in Piaget's theory, which transfers this type of explanation to the mental level, this is not done. It is claimed that the individual is prompted to assimilate or to accommodate by becoming aware of momentary disequilibrium between his schemata and the novel situation encountered. But such states of mental disequilibrium can only be identified by reference to the content of the schemata whose activity they explain. In other words, it is only by grasping the incoherence between what the individual already knows and the new material that one can understand that there is a problem for him. It seems, then, that 'the tendency towards equilibrium' is simply a somewhat misleading way of talking about the disposition to remove inconsistencies and get rid of contradictions. But nothing is added to our understanding of this disposition by introducing the model of restoring equilibrium at the mental level. To call this an attempt to re-establish equilibrium is not to explain why dissonance or inconsistency is motivating. It is simply to draw attention to its motivational properties by an inappropriate redescription.[39]

Assimilation and Accommodation   In my view, we can go no further in explaining the development of rationality than the ascription to man of two basic and closely related dispositions to respond to his experience. There is, first, assimilation, the constructive, classifying aspect of thought, the tendency to impose a conceptual scheme on experience and to generalise on the basis of similarities. Allied with this is the disposition to accommodate or to modify the scheme and the generalisations in the light of recalcitrant experience and information. The development of each process brings the various norms of reason into play. Assimilation can be seen as a tendency to strive for consistency in imposing a conceptual scheme on experience, picking out significant similarities. Assimilation requires, therefore, a sensitivity to the relevance or irrelevance of similarities from which a reflective concern to avoid arbitrariness and partiality can develop. We have already seen that the demand for consistency at work in the process of accommodation – the tendency to dwell on the novel or the discrepant and to adapt one's beliefs and assumptions accordingly. The development of accommodation involves the insistence on relevance, as distinct from purely associative similarities, the demand for clarity so that differences cannot be slurred over, and the demand for evidence or independent confirmation of the generalisation that has been advanced.

The primitive processes of accommodation and assimilation, then, generate thought as distinct from mere daydreaming or free association, i.e. a directed mental process guided by a concern, however primitive, for some basic requirements of consistency and relevance. I would want to argue that it is a conceptual truth that individuals with a tendency to assimilate and accommodate will be brought to think by features of their environment which are novel or discrepant (in terms of their conceptual scheme and/or generalisations).

There are a variety of interesting questions about these early stages in the development of reason which Piaget did not ask. For instance, in the development of reason the tendency to accommodate is of particular importance because of its connection with checking, criticism and looking for the negative instance. Psychologists have constructed a scale of reflection-impulsivity on which individuals show considerable and important differences.[40] For some children go for the first hypothesis that comes to mind; others reflect and check before committing themselves. They are more mindful of the possibility of the negative instance. This tendency seems to be a general one that is consistent over a variety of tasks. It affects the accuracy of recall and reading as well as the validity of reasoning. But it can be modified by training and by being exposed to models. What is the explanation of this basic difference between people that is so essential to the development of reasoning? The probable explanation is the extent to which children are afraid of making a mistake, rather than the strength of the desire to succeed; for this desire often occasions carelessness. This hypothesis is supported by some experiments, by a cross-cultural study, and by evidence from pathology.

The Norms of Reason   The above account of the development of rationality puts the emphasis squarely on the acquired grasp of various norms of reason. Now Piaget acknowledges the norms involved in the life of reason: he insists as much on the normative features of logic as on the logical features of morality. Yet, when confronted with the problem of explaining the development of rationality and giving an account of the motivation of the rational man he attempts to underwrite his account by a model taken from physiology.

None the less, there are the materials in Piaget's account for a more adequate approach. Piaget properly puts the twin processes of assimilation and accommodation at the centre of his account and, as we have seen, many of the central attitudes and norms of reason can be plausibly traced to the individual's initial dispositions to assimilate and accommodate. And while the equilibrium model is open to the criticisms I have discussed above, it can be seen as a misleading way of giving a central place to the general norm of consistency which is immanent in the processes of assimilation and accommodation. Piaget's recognition of the normative nature of reason opens the way for a satisfactory account of the motivation of the rational man; for the norms of consistency, relevance and the active search for grounds are, of course, motivating. But any complete account of rational motivation would need to distinguish at least two kinds of motivation. On the one hand there is the sheer enjoyment of construction, of getting things clear and right. This is, as it were, the hedonistic side of the ethics of belief. But, on the other hand, there is the more obligatory aspect, the demand that confusions and inconsistencies be removed, that conclusions be checked, that evidence be sought, and that irrelevance be expunged from argument.

The above is, however, no more than the bare outlines of a suggested approach to the development of rationality: substantial problems remain. For let us suppose that rationality does emerge from the primitive dispositions to assimilate and accommodate – tendencies for which an evolutionary account might be given in terms of their survival value. How does this combination of classifying and caution evolve into the conviction that one ought to be consistent, that one ought to look for the negative instance? How does a love of order become transformed into Kant's categorical imperative? How does caution about making mistakes emerge into what Russell calls 'cosmic piety', into the conviction of the givenness of the world and its regularities and the demand on man that he should check and recheck his assumptions? In brief what is to be made, in an explanatory system, of the τέλος, immanent in the development of reason, that truth matters?

The difficulties about such explanations parallel the difficulties in ethics generally about giving naturalistic explanations in terms of concepts such as 'want'. For we are really concerned with the emergence of the ethics of belief out of the egocentric, hedonistic world of the young child. 'Belief' is a concept that has a foot in both worlds; for though it is descriptive of a psychological state, in its developed form, where it is distinguished from expectations, which animals also have, it can only be explicated by reference to the acceptance of norms. For belief is a state of mind *appropriate* to what is true. But it is not the case that believers always *want* to find out what is true. Rather they feel that they *ought* to do so. The pursuit of truth as an absorbing activity characteristic of scientists and other academics must be distinguished from the state of mind of any reasonable being who feels that, though it may be bit of a bore, and though it may interfere with his wants, he ought to look into the evidence for some of his cherished assumptions.[41] This can only be represented as a case of wanting if the concept of 'wanting' is made purely formal so that it becomes analytic that, if anyone does anything, this must be something that he wants to do. And the fact that this move has often been made by naturalists to bridge the gap between interpersonal moral values such as justice and human wants adds little to its plausibility in the field of the intellectual virtues. Indeed it is even less plausible; for whereas there obviously is a conceptual connection between action and some concept of 'wanting', the connection between knowing, believing, doubting, etc., and such a concept is much more problematic.

Those who want to preserve some kind of naturalistic status for the intellectual virtues might admit the normative aspects of the final product but they might give an explanation of this in terms of socialisation. They might point to the fact that many cultures or subcultures discourage curiosity,[42] which may explain the limited development of reasoning in some people. Encouragement of curiosity involves not only approval of sporadic inquisitiveness, but also insistence on standards for its operation which become incorporated in a social tradition such as that of science. So social approval supporting traditions is the source of the normative aspect of the intellectual virtues. It transforms idle and sporadic curiosity about the explanation of things into self-critical reactions if explanations are not rigorously examined.

There are two difficulties about this type of explanation. The first was made very pertinently by Hume in the context of the attempt to explain morality in terms of a sense of duty, which was instilled in people by society. For this leaves over the problem of why society should attach such approval to some forms of behaviour rather than to others. There must, he argued, be some first-hand form of judgement to which attention is drawn by this social reinforcement, which generates a second-hand type of approval. And this is a judgement of the importance of consistency, etc., not just an expression of its attractiveness.

There is secondly the distinctiveness of such first-hand judgements from the second-hand conformity. In moral development a person may first of all behave justly because he is susceptible to rewards and punishments, and then to praise and blame. But he reaches a stage when he sees 'for himself' what makes a rule right or wrong. He sees the wrongness of causing suffering or of exploitation and judges social practices in the light of this first-hand type of appraisal. And, it is argued, the sort of guilt experienced when he does wrong or contemplates it, is qualitatively different from the guilt which is associated with the fear of punishment or of disapproval. The same sort of point can be made about the intellectual virtues. There is all the difference in the world between feeling that one ought to abandon a cherished belief when confronted with conclusive evidence against it, just because there is such evidence, and feeling that one ought to abandon it because one will not stand well with one's colleagues if one sticks to it. Skinner[43] suggests that scientists who allow themselves to be swayed by consequences that are not part of their subject matter, will find themselves 'in difficulties' because other scientists can easily check up on them. Their alleged 'finely developed ethical sense' is therefore a feature of the environment in which they work. But why do scientists make a fuss about cooking results in the service of self-interest? Why is their disapproval attached to this lack of authenticity in the first case? Surely because science, as an activity, is only intelligible on the assumption that truth matters. So we are back again at our starting point, namely the status of the norms definitive of the operation of reason which the person who cares about truth accepts as required by his quest. My tentative conclusion is that no attempt to reduce such virtues to naturalistic wants is plausible. Man is potentially a rational being and, as such, comes to subject his beliefs and actions to the normative demands of reason. The intellectual virtues are expressions of the normative demands of reason on his sensibility.

4 CONCLUSION

My main criticism of Piaget has been that, though he stresses the normative features of logic, he also tries to explain logical thinking in terms of a purely naturalistic conception of man. Thus his account of the development of reason does not just raise the usual doubts about giving a purely naturalistic account of conduct in the sphere of practical reason. It also raises even more fundamental questions about the status of man in the natural world as a creature that develops beliefs. Human beliefs and behaviour cannot be made intelligible without the basic postulate of the rationality of man. But this, in its turn, can only be made intelligible if we write into rationality the responsiveness to normative demands. What type of developmental account is appropriate for explaining the transition from the biological beginnings of reason to its norm-ridden end-product? Piaget's natural history of mind explicitly raises this question but does not solve it. It merely locates more precisely the points of perplexity.

REFERENCES

1. Piaget, J. (1968), p. 58.
2. See Nagel, E. (1957) and Peters, R. S. (1972c). For a sustained defence of this starting point in relation to conceptual development see Hamlyn, D. W. (1967) and (1972).
3. Woodward, W. Mary (1971).
4. Miller, G. A., Galanter, E. and Pribram, K. H. (1960).
5. The general background of Piaget's work will be assumed but, for the purpose of this essay, there will be a concentration on Piaget, J. (1968); for in this article, in which he reviews his work up to 1940, there is the most explicit attempt to link cognitive development with social and affective development, which is of particular relevance for the theses advanced in this essay.
6. See Peters, R. S. (1972a).
7. See Ryle, G. (1972).
8. See Peters, R. S. (1972a).
9. For a fuller explanation of more of its facets see Dearden, R. F., Hirst, P. H. and Peters, R. S. (1972).
10. Piaget, J. (1968). p. 14.
11. See Peters, R. S. (1972a), pp. 218–23. See also Peters, R. S. (1965).
12. Piaget, J. (1968), p. 19.
13. Luria, A. R. (1961).
14. Piaget, J. (1968), p. 29.
15. Ibid., p. 39.
16. Ibid., p. 40.
17. Ibid., pp. 48–54.
18. Ibid., p. 41.
19. Ibid.
20. Ibid., pp. 58–60.
21. See Peters, R. S. (1960).
22. See Hoffman, M. L. (1970) in his definitive article on 'Moral Development', who also makes this criticism. The same type of criticism is made of Kohlberg's extension of Piaget's theory in Peters, R. S. (1971), pp. 246–7, 259.
23. Koestler, A. (1966), pp. 273–85.
24. See Peters, R. S. (1972b), esp. pp. 474–80.
25. Piaget, J. (1968), p. 61.
26. See McDougall, W. (1942), Ch. IX.
27. Hoffman, M. L. (1970), pp. 280–1.
28. See Kagan, J. and Kogan, N. (1970).
29. Kohlberg, L. (1971).
30. See Bernstein, B. (1972).
31. See Klein, J. (1965).
32. See Greenfield, P. M. and Bruner, J. S. (1969).
33. See Kohlberg, L. (1968), (1969), (1971).

34. See Schachtel, E. (1959).
35. See Witkin, H. A., et al. (1962).
36. Quoted by Mischel as his translation of Piaget, J., 'Apprentissage et connaissance', in Greco, P. and Piaget, J. (Eds) (1959), p. 50; and in Mischel, T. (Ed.) (1971), p. 326.
37. Peters, R. S. (1958), Chs 1, 3, 4.
38. Mischel, T. (1972).
39. Berlyne (see Berlyne, D. E., 1960, 1965) indulges in a similar piece of metaphysics or redescription by extending the old drive theory to cover intrinsic as well as extrinsic motivation. Human beings have a 'drive to solve a problem' as well as hunger and sex drives. But there is the same problem of specifying the conditions of drive arousal independently of the problem-solving type of behaviour that they are supposed to explain. No specific internal conditions are specifiable and the appropriate environmental stimuli cannot be identified independently of the cognitive state of the problem-solver. There is, too, the objection that the mechanical model of 'drive' nullifies the important distinction between valid processes of thought and processes that simply proceed by chance associations – a distinction that Berlyne himself wants to preserve by his characterisation of directed thinking by notions such as 'legitimate' and 'appropriate' steps in the solution of a problem. But the model of man as a purposive rule-following animal cannot be reconciled with the model of an entity 'driven' by 'mechanisms'.
40. See Kagan, J. and Kogan, N. (1970), pp. 1309–19.
41. See Peters, R. S. (1973).
42. See Klein, J. (1965), Vol. 2.
43. Skinner, B. F. (1972), p. 174.

BIBLIOGRAPHY

Berlyne, D. E., *Conflict, Arousal and Curiosity* (1960).
Berlyne, D. E., *Structure and Direction in Thinking* (New York, 1965).
Berlyne, D. E., 'Children's Reasoning and Thinking', in Mussen, P. A. (Ed.), *Carmichael's Manual of Child Psychology* (New York, 1970), Vol. 1, pp. 939–81.
Bernstein, B. B., *Class Codes and Control.*, Vol. 1 (1971), Vol. 2 (1972).
Clifford, W. K., *The Ethics of Belief* (London, 1947).
Dearden, R. F., Hirst, P. H. and Peters, R. S. (Eds), *Education and the Development of Reason* (London, 1972).
Goslin, D. (Ed.), *Handbook of Socialisation Theory and Research* (New York, 1969).
Greenfield, P. N. and Bruner, J. S., 'Culture and Cognitive Growth', in Goslin, D. A. (Ed.), *Handbook of Socialisation Theory and Research* (New York, 1969), pp. 633–57.
Hamlyn, D. W., 'The Logical and Psychological Aspects of Learning', in Peters, R. S. (Ed.), *The Concept of Education* (London, 1967).
Hamlyn, D. W., 'Epistemology and Conceptual Development', in Mischel, T. (Ed.), *Cognitive Development and Epistemology* (New York, 1971), pp. 3–24.
Harris, D. B. (Ed.), *The Concept of Development* (Minnesota, 1957).
Hoffman, M. L., 'Moral Development', in Mussen, P. A. (Ed.), *Carmichael's Manual of Child Psychology* (New York, 1970), Vol. 2, pp. 261–355.
Kagan, J. and Kogan, N., 'Individual Variation in Cognitive Processes', in Mussen, P. A. (Ed.), *Carmichael's Manual of Child Psychology* (New York, 1970), Vol. 1, pp. 1323–42.

Klein, J. *Samples of English Culture* (London, 1965).

Koestler, A., *The Act of Creation* (New York, 1966).

Kohlberg, L., 'Early Education: a Cognitive Developmental View', *Child Development*, Vol. 39 (1968), pp. 1013–62.

Kohlberg, L., 'Stage and Sequence: the Cognitive–Developmental approach to Socialization', in Goslin, D. (Ed.), *Handbook of Socialisation Theory and Research* (New York, 1969), pp. 347–480.

Kohlberg, L., 'From Is to Ought', in Mischel, T., *Cognitive Development and Epistemology* (New York, 1971), pp. 151–235.

Luria, A., *The Role of Speech in the Regulation of Normal and Abnormal Behaviour* (New York, 1961).

McDougall, W., *An Introduction to Social Psychology*, 24th edn (London, 1942), pp. 150–79.

Miller, G. A., Galanter, E. and Pribram, K. H., *Plans and the Structure of Behaviour* (New York, 1960).

Mischel, T., 'Piaget: Cognitive Conflict and Motivation', in Mischel, T. (Ed.), *Cognitive Development and Epistemology* (New York, 1971), pp. 311–55.

Mischel, T. (Ed.), *Cognitive Development and Epistemology* (New York, 1971).

Mussen, P. A. (Ed.), *Carmichael's Manual of Child Psychology* (New York, 1970).

Nagel, E., 'Determinism and Development', in Harris D. B. (Ed.), *The Concept of Development* (Minnesota, 1957), pp. 15–24.

Peters, R. S., *The Concept of Motivation* (London, 1958).

Peters, R. S., 'Freud's Theory of Moral Development in Relation to That of Piaget', *British Journal of Educational Psychology*, Vol. 30 (1960), pp. 250–8.

Peters, R. S., 'Emotions, Passivity and the Place of Freud's Theory in Psychology', in Wolman, B. and Nagel, E. (Eds), *Scientific Psychology* (New York, 1965), pp. 365–83.

Peters, R. S. (Ed.), *The Concept of Education* (London, 1967).

Peters, R. S., 'Moral Development: a Plea for Pluralism', in Mischel, T. (Ed.), *Cognitive Development and Epistemology* (New York, 1971), pp. 237–67.

Peters, R. S., 'Reason and Passion', in Dearden, R. F., Hirst, P. H. and Peters, R. S., *Education and the Development of Reason* (London, 1972a), pp. 208–29.

Peters, R. S., 'The Education of the Emotions', in *Education and the Development of Reason* (1972b), pp. 466–83.

Peters, R. S., 'Education and Human Development', in *Education and the Development of Reason* (1972c), pp. 501–20.

Peters, R. S., 'The Justification of Education', in Peters, R. S. (Ed.), *The Philosophy of Education* (Oxford, 1973), pp. 239–267.

Peters, R. S. (Ed.), *The Philosophy of Education*, (Oxford, 1973).

Piaget, J. and Greco, P. (Eds), *Apprentissage et Connaissance* (Paris, 1957).

Piaget, J., *Six Psychological Studies* (London, 1968).

Piaget, J., 'Piaget's Theory' in Mussen, P. A. (Ed.), *Carmichael's Manual of Child Psychology* (New York, 1970), pp. 703–32.

Ryle, G., 'A Rational Animal', in Dearden, R. F., Hirst, P. H. and Peters, R. S. (Eds), *Education and the Development of Reason* (London, 1972), pp. 176–93.

Schachtel, E., *Metamorphosis* (New York, 1959).

Skinner, B. F., *Beyond Freedom and Dignity* (London, 1972).

Witkin, H. A., et al., *Psychological Differentiation* (New York, 1962).

Wolman, B. and Nagel, E. (Eds), *Scientific Psychology* (New York, 1965).

Woodward, W. M., *The Development of Behaviour* (Harmondsworth, 1971).

6

REASON AND PASSION*

INTRODUCTION

I once gave a series of talks to a group of psychoanalysts who had trained together and was rather struck by the statement made by one of them that, psychologically speaking, 'reason' means saying 'No' to oneself. Plato, of course, introduced the concept of 'reason' in a similar way in *The Republic* with the case of the thirsty man who is checked in the satisfaction of his thirst by reflection on the outcome of drinking. But Plato was also so impressed by man's ability to construct mathematical systems by reasoning that he called it the divine element of the soul. And what has this ability to do with that of saying 'No' to oneself? And what have either of these abilities to do with the disposition to be impartial which is intimately connected with our notion of a reasonable man, or with what David Hume called a 'wonderful and unintelligible instinct' in our souls by means of which men are able to make inferences from past to future?

It must readily be admitted that there are few surface similarities between the uses of 'reason' in these contexts. No obvious features protrude which might be fastened on as logically necessary conditions for the use of the term 'reason'. But beneath the surface there may be lurking common notions that are, or can be, of importance in our lives. To make them explicit is to give structure and substance to what is often called 'the life of reason' and to show that this is not

* My thanks are due to the Australian National University for the facilities provided for me as a Visiting Fellow which enabled me to write this paper, and to those colleagues whose comments enabled me to improve it.

inconsistent with a life of passion as is often thought. This seems eminently worth attempting at a time when many people seem hostile to reason. For those who demand instant gratification, who adopt some existentialist stance, who cultivate violence or mystical experience, or who merely do what others do, are all, in various ways, resisting the claims of reason on them. And what they are resisting is not just the demand that they should reflect and calculate; it is also the influence of passions and sentiments that underlie a form of life.

The plan of this paper will therefore be:

1. To set out briefly some central notions connected with the concept of 'reason'.
2. To enquire into the usual contrast between reason and passion.
3. To attempt a more adequate conceptualisation of this contrast in terms of different levels of life.

1   SOME GENERAL FEATURES OF 'REASON'

(a)   *Reason and Intelligence*

The view that what is distinctive of man is his rationality was more or less unchallenged from the time of the Greeks until the Copernican revolution in thought about man brought about by Darwin's theory of evolution. The continuity hypothesis suggested both that men were much more like brutes than had been previously thought because of the instincts which they shared with them, and that brutes were much more like men because they too possessed reason, albeit of an embryonic sort. What was really meant was that there are good grounds for thinking that some animals are intelligent.

What then is meant by saying that an animal or a man is intelligent? To qualify for being so called, behaviour has to take place in a situation to deal with which either there exists no established routine or which is different in some respect from a situation for which there exists a routine. We then say that behaviour is intelligent if there is evidence to suggest that the man grasps the features of the situation which, in the former case, are relevant to whatever he wants or is required to do, or those which, in the latter case, make it inappropriate for him to do what he usually does. The higher mammals such as dogs, cats and apes both respond to unfamiliar situations in ways which are relevant to obtaining what they want, and modify their standard responses when they no longer help them to satisfy their wants. So there is little reason to doubt that their behaviour displays intelligence, if we are prepared to accept the continuity hypothesis.

Why, then, would we not be prepared to go further and say that the behaviour of animals and young children is reasonable or unreasonable, rational or irrational? Surely because these words suggest the ability to reason in the sense of explicitly employing generalisations and rules in the forming of beliefs and in the planning of action. Man is rational, maintained Aristotle, in the sense that he imposes plans and rules on his behaviour and has a capacity for theorising. Animals and small children do not do any of these things in any explicit sense. Still less do they exhibit any tendency to link the past, present and future by means of generalisations and rules stated in a universal form. Young children lack a concept of the past and future and there is no reason to suppose that animals recall and remember as distinct from merely recognising things. Animals and young children live very much in the here and now; they lack the most general characteristic of reason which is the transcendence of the particular. (For detailed defence of some of these points, see Bennett, 1964.)

(b) The Transcendence of the Here and Now

The most obvious and all-pervading feature of reason is surely this transcendence of the this, the here, and the now. This is embryonic in any form of perception or action; for we always see something *as* something and want something under some aspect, and this classification implicitly relates the here and now to the past and future. But in reasoning this relating is extended and made explicit, mainly by the use of language. Explanation, planning, justification, all share in common this obvious characteristic. They connect what is, what is done, and what is to be done with the past and the future by means of generalisations and rules. This general feature of reason emerges clearly if we consider what reason is usually contrasted with – authority, revelation, tradition, etc. In these cases what is right or true is finally determined by appeal to some particular man, body or set of practices; it is not determined by appeal to general considerations.

A more formal way of making this point is to say that in the use of reason particularities of time, place and identity are irrelevant to the determination of what is true, correct or to be done. In science, for instance, which is a paradigm case of reason, appeal is made to a universal law which, in principle, anyone can test. Nothing depends on the identity of the individual who states or tests it. Similarly in prudential reasoning about conduct, when one says 'No' to oneself, there is a presupposition that, other things being equal, the mere position in time of the satisfaction of a desire is of itself irrelevant. This is a point well made by Sidgwick in his axiom of prudence 'that Hereafter *as such* is to be regarded neither more nor less than Now' (Sidgwick, 1962 edn, p. 381). Mabbott also stresses the function of reason in devising time-schedules for the satisfaction of desires, which is a device for avoiding conflicts (Mabbott, 1953, pp. 114–15). This presupposes that, other things being equal, mere position in time is an irrelevant consideration in the satisfaction of desires.[1]

The same sort of point can be made about identity in cases where we reason about the distribution of something good or bad. If I am going to benefit or suffer as a consequence of an action, some special characterisation of myself has to be given which relevantly differentiates me from others if the fact that *I* am going to suffer or benefit is to be regarded as having any special significance. This abstract principle of no distinctions without relevant differences is central to all forms of reasoning. Reason, in other words, is opposed to any form of arbitrariness.

(c) *The Public Character of Reason*
The irreconcilability of the use of reason with egocentricity and arbitrariness is a reflection of its essentially public character. It is public, not just in the sense that its vehicle is language whose concepts and rules of syntax are a public possession, but in the further sense that, even when it takes place in the individual's head, it is an internalisation of public procedures – those of criticism, the production of counter-examples, and the suggestion of different points of view.

Reason, in this developed sense, of course has its origin in the primitive tendency manifest in intelligence to 'accommodate' or to change assumptions because the differences encountered in a novel situation do not permit assimilation, or the fitting of it within existing assumptions. But in reasoning proper, this caution born of the frequent experience of being in error because of the differences between situations, becomes the principle enunciated by Francis Bacon that a search must always be made for the negative instance. Conscious, explicit attempts must be made to falsify assumptions, to find exceptions to rules; for only in this way can more reliable assumptions and rules gradually be built up. There must also be some form of public test to decide between competing assumptions. This means agreement not just about how answers are to be sought but also about the types of considerations that are to count as deciding between possible answers. Science is the supreme example of reason in action not just because of the opportunities for criticism which it provides, but also because of the agreement in judgements which it permits by means of its testing procedures. These guarantee objectivity and the escape from arbitrariness.

It is most implausible to suggest that these critical procedures develop naturally in children's minds as they grow up. History and psychology give no support to this flattering belief. In the history of man the overwhelming tendency has been for men to believe what they are told and to do what is expected of them. It is only at rare periods in history that sporadic curiosity and uneasiness about what is generally accepted have become embedded in a critical tradition. Psychologically speaking, too, the general proclivity of men is to believe what they want to believe, and to accept the approved view of the group. Francis Bacon was one of the first to note what has since become a psychological platitude, that the determination to look for the negative instance, to subject assumptions to criticism, goes against a deep-seated tendency of the human mind, which William James called 'the primacy of belief'. The determination to find out the truth, to get to the bottom of things, only tends to develop if people are brought up in contact with a critical tradition.

This means that what we call reasoning is not just the exercise of some inner potentiality. Maybe it presupposes curiosity, which is probably unlearned, and the use and understanding of language, which probably has an innate basis. But in some cultures curiosity is definitely discouraged and there is, too, all the difference in the world between curiosity, which may be sporadic, and the passion for truth that lies at the heart of developed forms of reasoning. Some cultures, in their child-rearing practices, perpetuate arbitrariness, and so discourage the development of an inquiring mind (see Klein, 1965, Vol. II, pp. 517–26). Even within one society, too, the type of language employed can seriously affect the capacity for reasoning. The elaborated code of the middle class, for instance, is a much more suitable vehicle for reasoning than the restricted code of the working class, which does not facilitate the communication of ideas or of relationships which require precise formulation (see Bernstein, 1961). The frequent use of generalisations, the appeal to principles and the development of criticism are reflections of a social situation in which ideas are discussed, proposals debated and orthodoxies challenged.

Thus the individual, who is accustomed to reason in this developed sense, is one who has taken a critic into his own consciousness, whose mind is structured by the procedures of a public tradition. A reasonable man is one who is prepared to discuss things, to look at a situation impartially from the point of view of others than himself, to discount his own particular biases and predilections. As G. H. Mead put it, he can adopt the point of view of the 'generalised other'. The disposition to adopt this point of view is a reflection in his consciousness of social situations in which the point of view of others has in fact been represented.

2   THE CONTRAST BETWEEN REASON AND PASSION

There are many other points that could be made about the use of reason, but enough has been said to deal with the contrast often made between reason and passion.

(a)   *Hume's Dichotomy*

Hume put generations of philosophers on the wrong track by his claim that reason is merely the ability to make inductive and deductive inferences whose basis is a 'wonderful and unintelligible instinct' in the soul of the individual. He contrasted reason, which is inert, with passions, which he regarded as psychological entities which move people to act. He did, however, draw attention to a special class of 'disinterested passions' which, because of their calmness and steadiness, are often mistaken for reason. He had in mind the attitudes which go with taking the point of view of the impartial spectator.

What Hume did not appreciate, however, was that these so-called passions are intimately connected with the use of reason rather than distinct entities that are liable to be mistaken for it; for the use of reason is inexplicable without them. Without the attitude of impartiality, for instance, the individual could not concentrate on relevant considerations and counteract his inclination to favour his own point of view or that of someone to whom he might be attracted or attached. He could not disregard the promptings connected with time, place and identity which, it has been argued, he must do if he is to use his reason. For to use one's reason is to be influenced by this type of passion.

It might be thought, therefore adapting Hume's view slightly, that the proper distinction to be drawn is between the calm passions associated with the use of reason and the more turbulent ones of a less disinterested type. And certainly the ordinary use of 'passions' does suggest some kind of turbulence. But this suggestion is not really tenable; for in some people the passions connected with the use of reason can be violent. When Bertrand Russell, for instance, was referred to as 'the Passionate Sceptic', the suggestion was that his passion for truth was anything but calm.

(b) *The Philosophical and the Ordinary Sense of 'Passion'*

What, then, is there in common between the philosophical conception of 'passion', as something that provides an inducement to act, and the ordinary usage of 'passion' which suggests some kind of turbulence or state of heightened feeling? And is there necessarily any contrast between reason and these states of mind? A clue to this may be provided by asking when a passion, in the philosophical sense, would normally be referred to as a passion in ordinary language. When, for instance, would a concern for fairness or an abhorrence of irrelevance be referred to as a passion? Usually, surely, when looking at a situation in a way which warrants the term 'fair' or 'irrelevant' is connected with things that come over us, which we may not be able to control. To have a passion for truth suggests more than just caring about it. It suggests that we are strongly affected by disregard of evidence, inaccuracy and deceit. We are subject to strong feelings if truth is disregarded in any way. This links the use of 'passion' with the Latin *patior* from which it is derived. It suggests being subject to something, being mastered or overpowered. Hence the connection in ordinary language between passion and turbulence; for it is often, though not always, the case that when we are affected in this way our state of mind is a turbulent one.

Given, then, that in ordinary language there is this link between 'passion' and passivity, why have philosophers referred to motives for action as passions? For a man who acts out of jealousy or ambition is not necessarily subject to strong feelings or in a turbulent state. The explanation, surely, is that there is something in common between being moved to act and being subject to feelings in this way. This is the non-neutral appraisal of a situation from which both derive. When we are jealous or fair we see a situation in a certain light which is not a matter of indifference to us. As a consequence we may act in an appropriate way or we may be assailed by pangs of jealousy or by feelings of indignation, or we may both act and be 'in a state' at the same time (see Peters, 1965, 1970). There is thus a close enough connection between 'passion', in the sense of being affected, and being disposed to act, to explain the use of the term 'passion' by philosophers to refer to that which moves us to act.

Suppose, then, that we leave on one side the philosopher's special use of the term 'passion' and concentrate on cases where there is some suggestion of passivity, of being subject to strong feelings, and so on. Is there necessarily a contrast between being in such states and reason? I might be overcome with passion; but would it *ipso facto* be unreasonable? Would it be irrational? To show that there is a contrast between reason and passion in its ordinary sense it would surely have to be shown to be either one or the other. We must therefore enquire what is meant by 'unreasonable' and 'irrational' and then see whether there is a contrast between 'reason' and 'passion' in this non-philosophical sense.

(c) *'Irrational' and 'Unreasonable'*[2]

'Irrational' and 'unreasonable' are similar in that they both presuppose a background of reasoning that is not necessarily presupposed when we talk about behaviour being stupid. 'Stupid' is used of behaviour that just shows little or no grasp of what is relevant to bringing about what is wanted or required. For instance, if a man wants to go to the theatre and omits to find out the time when the curtain goes up, it would be normal to say 'How stupid of him'. There can, of course, be reasoning in cases where we use the term 'stupid' and the reasoning itself can be intelligently or stupidly done; but there does not have to be. That is why we can use the word of dogs and small children.

In cases, however, where we use the words 'unreasonable' and 'irrational' we assume a background of reasoning that the person either actually performed or could have performed. Both presuppose some estimate of the alternatives which are open and some assessment of the comparative strength of considerations deriving from them as they apply to what the problem is. In the theatre case, for instance, the man's behaviour could be regarded as unreasonable if he failed to book seats because, though it was a very popular play, he had thought that there was no need to book seats as it was Monday and theatres are not usually booked up on Mondays. And what would make it unreasonable would be *both* the fact that he had reason for not booking *and* that there were other reasons which were more cogent – in this case that this was a very popular play, a fact which others had impressed upon him. A background of reasoning must also be assumed for the word 'irrational' to be used. Suppose, for instance, that the theatre which he wanted to visit was known to be booked up, and suppose he also knew that there was little likelihood of his getting a ticket at the door, and he then refused to accept tickets that were offered to him by one of his colleagues. This would be called irrational and some special explanation would have to be given for his refusal, e.g. some aversion to the colour of the tickets, or to his colleague.

'Unreasonable' and 'irrational' have, then, in common the requirement of some kind of background of reasoning before they can be applied and, in this respect, are different from 'stupid' which does not have to have such a background. What then is the difference between saying that behaviour is 'irrational' as distinct from 'unreasonable'? Can any general points be extracted from the example given? If we describe a person's behaviour as irrational we are suggesting that he is deviating from what I have elsewhere called the purposive rule-following model of behaviour with knowledge of what the standards of correct behaviour are (see, e.g., Peters, 1958; 1969, p. 145). He must be assumed to think that a certain course of action is the only one that is likely to get him what he wants or to be in accordance with a rule which he accepts. He then refrains from taking this course of action, knowing what he does. Practically always, in cases when we describe behaviour as irrational, we add the special explanation which accounts for this deviation, e.g. that he had some inner obsession or absurd scruple, or that he was overcome by emotion. 'Irrational' functions as a diagnosis as well as a complaint.

The charge of 'unreasonable', on the other hand, is different. Unlike 'unreasoning' it presupposes that a person has reasons for what he does; but it suggests that the reasons are very weak, and that he does not pay attention to the reasons of others. A man who does something which is unreasonable is not like the man who does something irrational in that he knows what the appropriate thing to do is but, because of something that comes over him, does not do it. On the contrary he has a very limited view of what considerations are of most weight in a situation. There is a suggestion that he has a somewhat myopic viewpoint on the situation and takes little account of considerations advanced by others. He falls down on the cardinal requirements of objectivity. 'Unreasonableness' has social dimensions which are not implicit in 'irrationality'.[3]

So much, then, for the lines along which meaning must be given to the terms 'unreasonable' and 'irrational' when applied to conduct. The same lines of analysis seem to fit the application of these terms to beliefs as well as to conduct. An irrational belief is one that is held wittingly in the face of conclusive evidence against it or one that is held with conviction when it is extremely problematical whether anything could count as evidence against it. An instance of the first type would be that of a man who believes that his hands are dirty in spite of having repeatedly washed them and in spite of no dirt being visible; an example of the second would be that of a man who believes that a wood is inhabited by fairies. A belief is unreasonable, on the other hand, if there are some considerations which might be produced to support it, but which are clung on to in spite of very strong reasons marshalled against it. If, for instance, a man persists in believing that the Labour Party will win the next election simply because Mr Wilson has said so, I think we might well describe his belief as unreasonable.

(d) *Being 'Unreasonable' or 'Irrational' and being Subject to Passion*
Given that this is how the terms 'unreasonable' and 'irrational' function, is there necessarily a suggestion that when we lapse from the proper use of reason we are in some way subject to passion? This does not seem to be the case at least when we are dealing with examples of being unreasonable. The man who bungled the business of getting the theatre tickets was not overcome by any passion; the man with the trusting faith in Mr Wilson's words might be in a very calm state. Conversely there is the obvious point that what we call emotions are good examples of passive states; but we can speak of them as being both unreasonable and irrational. This suggests that, on certain occasions, we can at least speak of them as reasonable, if not as rational. Suppose, for instance, that I discover, by a perfectly valid process of inference, that my friend has deceived me. I am struck dumb with indignation and my indignation is perfectly justified in the senses both that he really has deceived me and that there is some sort of appropriateness, which would need to be elaborated, between my understanding of the situation and my response. My reaction would be perfectly reasonable.

What, then, would make an emotion irrational or unreasonable? Emotions, such as jealousy, go with specific estimates of a situation. If there is absolutely nothing in a situation which gives a man grounds for thinking that someone else is after that to which he thinks he had a right, then it is irrational for him to be jealous. But if there are some grounds, but not good grounds, then jealousy is unreasonable. Othello's jealousy was unreasonable, not completely irrational, unless he is regarded as a pathological type of case; for there are people who are so threat-orientated that they interpret almost any situation in this self-referential sort of way. They rig their environment to match a permanent mood. We call such attitudes irrational because, from an objective point of view, as distinct from their point of view, there is absolutely nothing in their situation which deserves this type of interpretation. Othello's jealousy was not of this type. He had very flimsy grounds and steadfastly refused to look at the situation in a more objective way, to see it as others saw it.

These cases bring out the importance of having standards of appropriateness if the words 'unreasonable' or 'irrational' are to be used in the sphere of the emotions. These standards can be connected with judgements of appropriateness of two main types. We can say, for instance, that a reaction is inappropriate in the case of, say, jealousy, because there is nothing, or not much, in the situation which would justify anyone in thinking that this conformed to the general criteria that are conceptually connected with 'jealousy' e.g. that to which one thinks one has a right is, in some way, threatened by someone else. This is the type of case that we have so far considered. But it might be suggested that to be jealous *at all* is either 'irrational' or 'unreasonable'. This would either condemn completely or raise serious doubts about the judgement built into jealousy that there is something wrong or inappropriate in others venturing in various ways into one's own special domain. Some philosophers have held that all such transitory emotions are unreasonable, if not downright irrational. What enables them to say this is the complicated story which they tell about the situation in which we are placed in the world which makes the judgements involved in jealousy either completely inappropriate or lacking in cogency when compared with other considerations, depending on whether it was thought of as irrational or unreasonable. Such a philosopher might therefore say that falling in love with anyone is quite irrational; for it involves becoming attached to a particular person in the world, which is an absurdity for anyone who sees life under a certain aspect of eternity. We, on the other hand, might not see the state of mind in this cosmic context. We might regard falling in love as a-rational, just one of those things to which human beings are subject. Being in such a state would not qualify for being either reasonable or rational; for it would be denied that there are any standards of appropriateness by reference to which it could be judged. But, on the other hand, it *might* have little to do with passion either. For we might be little moved by it. Some impulses and inclinations might also fall into this category. Someone might just like looking at trees or at animals. Such a want might be neither reasonable nor unreasonable, and it might be so feeble that to call it a passion would also be a misnomer.

It does not seem, therefore, that the passive states, which we call emotions, are *necessarily* either irrational or unreasonable. Nevertheless there is a tendency for them to be. For as the appraisals, which are intimately connected with them, are of situations which are very important to us, they are often made rather intuitively and urgently, with little careful analysis of the grounds for making them. They are also the most potent *source* of irrationality in that attention to features which are relevant to making *other* sorts of judgements is often deflected by irrelevant appraisals which are conceptually connected with our emotions. The analysis of 'irrationality' brought out the point that it involves failing to do or believe what there are conclusive reasons for doing or believing, for which a special explanation is necessary. And the special explanation is very often in terms of some emotion to which we are subject, that makes us unable to follow the logic of the situation or argument. There is thus a much closer connection between being irrational and emotion than there is between emotion and being unreasonable.

In approaching, therefore, the type of distinction that people have wanted to make in terms of 'reason' and 'passion', we must abandon altogether the contrast between reason as an inert capacity and passions which move us to act. We must instead attempt to give a new description of the contrast in terms of different levels of life in which being reasonable, unreasonable, rational and irrational are placed in proper perspective.

3   LEVELS OF LIFE

There is a level of life at which young infants live all the time and primitive people part of the time, which might be called a-rational in that it has not reached the level at which experience is structured by categories of thought associated with reason. More often, however, we describe it as irrational because we assume a lapse from a rational level on the part of the person who is capable of functioning at such a level.

(a)   *Irrationality*
The most all-pervasive characteristic of this low-grade type of experience is that it is dominated by wishes and aversions. This, as I have argued before, was the most important insight which Freud contributed to psychological theory (see Peters, 1958, Ch. 3; 1965). He noted three main characteristics of wishful thinking.

1. It does not observe the principles of rational thought, e.g. it lacks

a sense of reality, it does not follow the causal principle, it is not bounded by any determinate spatio-temporal framework.
2. It proceeds by some principle of affective congruence in which, e.g., a snake stands for the male sex organ.
3. It is controlled only by strange 'mechanisms' of condensation and displacement.

Freud himself did not elaborate the cognitive aspect of wishing; he was more interested in the motivational aspect, the all-pervasive influence of the sex-instinct. But later theorists such as Arieti and Werner have studied the details of the primitive sort of cognition involved. Arieti draws attention not simply to the obvious characteristics of wishing which link it with magic and with the child's and maniac's conviction of omnipotence, namely the absence of a sense of reality and of causal connection in relation to the means necessary to obtain what is wished for; he also suggests that it proceeds by a more primitive, palaeologic form of thinking, in which classification is purely on the basis of the similarity of predicates without any importance being attached to the subject (see Arieti, 1967, pp. 109–12). It is thus a pre-Aristotelian type of thinking which can be found amongst some primitive people who identify men, crocodiles and wild cats because they have the common property of having an evil spirit. Young children between the ages of one and a half and three and a half are also prone to this type of thinking. The similarity picked out is one that is related to some primitive wish or aversion.

There are, of course, other features of low-grade thinking. But this particular feature of it will serve to make the main point which is that it manifests the combination of wish or aversion together with a low-grade form of classification and inference. This is frequent in pathological states. The man, for instance, who flares up or behaves in some other inappropriate way when confronted with an authority figure, is picking on one feature of similarity between his father, towards whom he had an aversion, and a whole succession of other men. Classification is based on an affectively loaded similarity without regard to identity. In delusions, too, such as that of the girl who thinks that she is the Virgin Mary, the wish to be perfect can be connected with one point of similarity, virginity. The same phenomenon is frequent in schizophrenia, in which a belief in regularities is based on coincidences in which there is one tenuous but affectively laden element of similarity.

In considering cases like these, one cannot say that the motivational element, as it were, determines the form of thinking; for even at this primitive level of motivation the wish or aversion is connected with the grasp of some feature of a situation that is distinguished. The point, however, is that the distinguishing is very faultily done. There is not a wish for or aversion to an *object* in the full sense of one that is identified by the normal subject–predicate form of thought. The inferences involved fasten on affectively charged similarities but take no account of differences. The cognitive and motivational aspects are bound together. The contrast is not between reason, which is meant to characterise normal rational behaviour, and passion which is a non-cognitive force that disrupts it. It is rather between high-grade type of experience, in which determinately conceived objects are wanted and realistic means taken to obtain them, and low-grade forms of experience, in which behaviour is influenced by wishes and aversions linked with primitive classification and thinking structured by some shadowy principle of affective congruence.

Another type of case which belongs to this family is when we are subject to some kind of emotional reaction. Suppose, for instance, that someone is sitting in a chair and looks up and sees what he takes to be a face at the window and gives an involuntary jump or cry. There are two interesting features of such reactions in extreme cases. On the one hand the perception of the situation tends to be wild and fragmentary as in the cases of palaeologic thinking already mentioned; on the other hand the movements made tend to be of a protopathic character, lacking the co-ordination involved in deliberate action. That is why we call such cases emotional reactions; we do not say that the individual is acting out of fear. Cases such as these link very well with the phenomena of vigilance and perceptual defence studied by psychologists. In such cases the individual reacts to stimuli even though they are below the identification threshold. Dember's speculative theory about such reactivity fits in very well with my suggestion of different levels of thinking each with its own type of affect. He claims that primitive affective responses are learned very early in childhood before children have developed the conceptual apparatus necessary for identification, and can be aroused by stimuli that are not sufficiently informative to arouse the appropriate identification responses (see Dember, 1964, pp. 313–25). There is a level of thinking and affect which precedes the development of the conceptual apparatus necessary for life as a purposive, rule-following agent, and which persists after the development of this apparatus which we associate with 'reason'. The individual thus retains his capacity to react much more 'intuitively' to affectively significant stimuli that are fragmentary and may be well below the threshold of conscious discrimination.

Another type of case, which has a similar explanation, is when a low-grade way of viewing and reacting to a situation interferes with a high-grade way. For instance, a man may be teaching a class effectively in accordance with the rules of appropriateness that govern an activity of this sort. An objection is put by one member of the class in what he takes to be a hostile, perhaps derisive, tone of voice. He is put off his stroke and reacts quickly with some sarcastic, person-centred reply which does nothing to further the understanding of the point under discussion. His quick, exaggerated reading of the situation follows the line of his underlying feeling of insecurity, and leads to his irrational response. He is unable to ignore whatever hostility might lurk behind the question and to carry on with the attempt to determine the truth of the matter under discussion. For this would have presupposed not simply an interest in the question under discussion but also a determination connected with a higher-order concern for truth, which was sufficiently strong to outweigh the feelings of insecurity aroused by some slight sign of hostility. Sometimes people are subject to semi-permanent moods which make them prone for days at a time to interpret the behaviour of others in this self-referential way, to fasten on the smallest clues which confirm their attitude of suspicion. And, in the case of the paranoiac, this attitude of mind is a permanent one. Here again it is not a case of a reasoning process simply being interrupted by an emotional reaction deriving from insecurity. It is a case of a lapse from one level of conduct at which the perception of the situation is structured in terms of one group of passions being replaced by another level of reaction which also has its own cognitive and affective components.

More commonplace phenomena which have a similar type of explanation are those when the judgement is warped or clouded through the influence of some unrecognised way of viewing the situation which leads to weight being given to factors which are irrelevant or only marginally relevant. The judge gives a faulty weighting to aspects of a case because his aggression or sympathy are aroused; the politician makes a feeble decision because of his need to be loved; flattery leads a businessman to overestimate the performance of his secretary.[4]

In such cases it is simple-minded to analyse the situation in terms of dispassionate judgement being clouded by emotion. What we have is not only the presence of passions which sidetrack the individual and lead to distortion of judgement by the intrusion of irrelevant features of the situation. We have also the absence or weakness of passions which help the individual to keep his eye on the ball. These fall into two classes. First there are those connected with the point of the activity in which the individual is engaged, e.g. the maintenance of justice, the promotion of the public interest, the maximisation of profit. Secondly, there are what might be called the rational passions, in the philosophical sense of 'passion', which demand that the individual should stick to the logic of the situation, get his facts right, ignore what is irrelevant, conceive the situation clearly, and so on. These latter sorts of passions are of cardinal importance in high-grade experience. They act as monitors maintaining rational thought and action.

The cases so far considered, in which we might talk about behaviour being irrational, have been those in which the lapse from reason is to be explained in terms of a low-grade cognition which is affectively charged. There are other types of case, however, where the defect is not straightforwardly one of the understanding but of will. If we speak of 'will' in this sense, as distinct from the sense in which we talk of people doing things 'at will' or 'willingly', we are drawing attention to the influence on behaviour of beliefs and principles of a settled, usually long-term type. 'Will' is exhibited when people are able to stick to principles, policies and programmes in the face of temptations, ridicule, tiredness and so on. Words such as 'determination', 'resoluteness', 'consistency' and 'integrity' come naturally to mind in such contexts – even 'ruthlessness', if ends are pursued resolutely, but with disregard for the claims of others.

In the literature on 'the will' (see, e.g., Flugel, 1946, Ch. 1) much is made of the sentiment of self-regard in accounting for this factor of control or 'ego-strength', as it is often called. But, whatever is to be said about the importance of this, there are surely other rather abstract but affectively charged considerations involved as well. Let me take an example to explain what I mean.

The most common case, perhaps, is that in which our condition is a mild form of that to which the psychopath is permanently prone. We want it now. The psychopath is basically a person who cannot postpone gratification. Intellectually he is aware of the future and of the probability of punishment if he satisfies a wish immediately and in some anti-social way. But this knowledge has for him only a theoretical reality. He thus goes ahead with immediate rape instead of waiting until he can find someone who will willingly co-operate. He lies and finds some immediately gratifying way out of a difficulty, or some temporary enhancement of his reputation. There are two important features of this condition. One is the obvious one of lack of strength of moral or social considerations that usually act as a countervailing influence; the other is the defect which prevents the future being real to him. It has been remarked earlier (section 1 (b)) that one of the cardinal features of reasoning is the transcendence of the here and now. This involves not simply the negative axiom of Sidgwick that, other things being equal, mere position in time of a satisfaction is irrelevant, which presupposes some abhorrence of the irrelevant if it is to be operative. It also presupposes something more positive which is central to the use of reason – a determination to take account of the facts. The situation of the psychopath, when the factor of time is left out, is that he discounts the known probability that something most undesirable will happen to him which he does not want at all. He is so overwhelmed by the present that he sees the situation without a proper sense of reality. One of the main passions that lies at the heart of reason is inoperative in his case, which is not simply that one should acquaint oneself with relevant facts but that one should also have a *concern* for them in formulating beliefs or deciding on courses of action. This failure to countenance future facts is the explanation of one class of cases that are called 'weakness of will', of which the psychopath is an extreme example.

Perhaps the most dramatic cases belonging to this category of lack of control are those of crimes of passion, irresistible impulses, etc. The husband comes home and finds another man in bed with his wife. There is nothing faulty about his understanding of the situation and most people would regard his emotional reaction as quite justified. Its strength and its translation into a motive for action is what leads him to the law-courts, when he kills the man, instead of the other man in the role of co-respondent. Here again what is at fault is his ability to control his immediate response and to let it flow in a delayed and approved institutional channel. The future is not sufficiently present to him as something that matters as well as the present.

(b) *Unreasonableness*
There are situations in life when it is possible to be rational as distinct from being merely reasonable. If someone wants a holiday, for instance, it is rational to save a certain amount of money out of every month's salary in order to pay for it. For this is a situation in which reasoning is involved and there are conclusive reasons for acting in one way rather than another. But such situations are less common than those in which we act in a condition of uncertainty

about what we want and think worth while, and about the best ways of achieving such ends. If, in such situations, we take account of reasons which are the best available in the circumstances, if due attention is paid to considerations produced by others, then we can be said to be reasonable. (See Oakeshott, 1962.)

Being unreasonable, therefore, is not connected, like being irrational, with a level of life on which reason gets no grip. Rather it is connected with a level of life when there are reasons, but the reasons are of a pretty low-grade sort. It is a level of life in which notions such as 'bias', 'prejudice', 'short-sighted', 'obtuse', 'wilful', 'bigoted' and 'pig-headed' have a natural home. Beliefs, at this level, tend to be infected with particularity. Little attempt is made to fit them into a coherent system and to make sure that they are consistent with each other. In so far as generalisations are employed, there is little attempt to test them, to consider counter-examples. The individual is attached to beliefs that suit him or that are based on authority, hearsay or a narrow range of considerations. The viewpoint of others is not seriously considered. This is especially manifest in social situations where people's claims are at stake. The unreasonable man shows lack of respect for others and is extremely partial and arbitrary in his approach.

In the sphere of the will the same kind of particularity infects the approach of the unreasonable man. He finds difficulty in sticking to a plan or policy because he lacks the capacity to detach himself from the present and to balance a present against a future satisfaction. It is not that the future is more or less unreal to him as it is to the psychopath. Rather the urgency or concreteness of the present particular asserts itself and disrupts his well-meaning plan. This tendency is particularly apparent in the case of conflicts of desires in deliberative situations before a course of action is decided upon. Mabbott points out that many conflicts can be satisfactorily settled by devising a time-schedule. But the unreasonable man finds difficulty in imposing such schedules on himself because he is so dominated by the present and by the concrete. There is probably lacking, too, another affective consideration which often accompanies the use of reason, the love of order, of consistency, of imposing some kind of system. This was very prominent in the Platonic conception of the harmony of the soul. For Plato the passion for order was one of the main features of reason. It is interesting that Freud also regarded it as one of the main affective sources of civilisation (see Freud, 1930, Ch. III).

It has been suggested that being 'unreasonable' is much more a social concept than being 'irrational'. This is so in two senses. First, there is a strong suggestion that the individual in question is ego-centric, that he does not pay much attention to the reasons of others. Secondly, while 'irrationality' has been explained largely in terms of the operation in us of a more or less unsocialised level of thinking, when we are subject to infantile wishes and aversions, 'unreasonable-ness', on the other hand, is connected with a form of behaviour that is exemplified at a primitive level of socialisation. The work of Josephine Klein in this field is of interest. She singles out certain abilities which, in the account of reason here given, are intimately connected with it: the ability to abstract and use generalisations, the ability to perceive the world as an ordered universe in which rational action is rewarded, the ability to plan ahead, and the ability to exercise self-control. She cites evidence from Luria and Bernstein to show that the extent to which these abilities develop depends on the prevalence of an elaborated form of language, which is found in some strata of society but not in others. She also shows how the beliefs and conduct of some working-class sub-cultures are affected by the arbitrariness of their child-rearing techniques (see Klein, 1965, Vol. II, pp. 487–526).

To be unreasonable is thus to exemplify or to revert to a level of life which is different from that connected with being irrational. It is similar, however, in that the type of cognition which it exemplifies goes with a distinctive form of motivation. It tends to be 'sense-bound', to be swayed by pleasures and pains of the moment. Emotions, usually of a gusty sort, are aroused only by particular people and situations. Spinoza's account of the state of human bondage is a good description of this level of life.

(c) *The Rational Passions*

Josephine Klein is mainly interested in the ways in which the develop-ment of language and child-rearing techniques affect the development of cognitive abilities definitive of reason. She sees such abilities as necessary for the operation of forms of motivation associated with prudence and with the desire for achievement. But attention must also be drawn to the importance of specific motivations which accompany the abilities operating at this level of life.

Much has been said in passing about the passions, in the philo-sophical sense of 'passions', peculiar to the life of reason. It is now time to draw together the threads and say something of a more positive sort. There is a level of conduct connected with the use of reason which is only intelligible on the supposition that we postulate certain distinctive passions as well as the ability to infer, demonstrate, etc. The obvious overriding one is the concern about truth, without which reasoning in general would be unintelligible. This is articulated in a number of appraisals which are affectively non-neutral. By this I mean that anyone who is concerned about truth must be concerned about correctness – about getting his facts right; he must care about consistency and clarity; he must abhor irrelevance and other forms of arbitrariness; he must value sincerity. And so on. A rational man cannot, without some special explanation, slap his sides and roar with laughter or shrug his shoulders with indifference if he is told that what he says is irrelevant, that his thinking is confused and inconsistent, or that it flies in the face of evidence. These passions, of course, are internalisations of principles which give structure and point to theoretical enquiries; but they are also involved in practical activities and judgements in so far as these are conducted in a rational manner.

Ryle gives a very good account of the development of such passions which he associates with the development of 'disciplines':

'A person's thinking is subject to disciplines if, for example, he systematically takes precautions against personal bias, tries to improve the orderliness or clarity of his theory, checks his references, his dates or his calculations, listens attentively to his critics, hunts industriously for exceptions to his generalisations, deletes ambiguous, vague or metaphorical expressions from the sinews of his arguments, and so on indefinitely. His thinking is controlled, in high or low degree, by a wide range of quite specific scruples. . . .

'Now, at last, we can begin to see more clearly than before how the ideas of rationality, reasonableness and reasons are internal to the notion of the thinking that needs to be graded as intellectual work. For this thinking essentially embodies the element of self-correction. Hunch, native sense of direction, following good examples, though indispensable, are no longer enough. The thinker cares, at least a little bit, whether he gets things right or wrong; he is at least slightly concerned to think properly' (Ryle, 1962, pp. 21–2).

Ryle associates these 'scruples', which help people to think properly, with the disciplines of subjects such as history and science which are practised and passed on by special institutions. But surely these 'scruples' are more precise articulations of the more generalised passions which begin to exert an influence when reasoning of a less precise sort gets under way, when children's curiosity leads them to ask for explanations, when their early delight in mastery gradually takes the form of the determination to get things right, and when primitive constructiveness passes into the love of order and system. When children become concerned about what is really there, when they learn to delay gratification with realistic thought about the future, passions are beginning to take hold of them which later become more precisely differentiated in the distinct disciplines.

In the interpersonal and moral spheres, too, which are central to the development of any human being, a corresponding care, scrupulousness and striving for objectivity and consistency can take place and transform more slapdash, sporadic and subjective types of reaction. The attempt to divine people's motives and intentions, to grasp what they are really about, can gradually take the place of a more impressionistic and self-referential reaction to them. Sympathy can pass into a steadier compassion and animal caution into a more reflective prudence.

To describe the transformation of 'natural' passions such as fear, anger and sexual desire would be, more or less, to attempt an Aristotelian analysis of the virtues; but more emphasis would have to be placed on the passionate side of reason than in Aristotle's account. Aristotle, unlike Plato who distinguished a level of desire appropriate to the life of reason, held that reason alone moves nothing. He was not sufficiently aware that the use of reason is a passionate business.

REFERENCES

1. It might be objected that the delay of gratification is unpleasant, and the longer the delay the more unpleasant it becomes. Apart, therefore, from extrinsic considerations connected with certainty of satisfaction, there are intrinsic considerations to do with the nature of desires that make delay undesirable. But this surely only applies to some desires, to those which Plato termed the 'necessary appetites', e.g. hunger. Failure to satisfy these is unpleasant. But this does not apply to the normal range of desires, e.g. my desire to go to Greece. If I thought that I could never satisfy this desire, that would be unpleasant. But whether I satisfy it next year or in five years' time does not seem to be of any great moment. Indeed many postpone the satisfaction of desires because they enjoy the pleasurable anticipation of satisfying them and because the satisfaction is greater at the end of such a build-up. Such considerations show that the case for propinquity in the satisfaction of desires cannot be based purely on the nature of desire. Thus this is not an objection to Sidgwick's main point.
2. This analysis of 'unreasonableness' owes much to Max Black, whose paper on 'Reasonableness' will shortly be published in Dearden, R. F., Hirst, P. H. and Peters R. S. (Eds), *Education and the Development of Reason* (London, Routledge & Kegan Paul, 1972).

3. I have assumed that, in the case of actions, 'unreasonable' and 'irrational' are judgements passed on conduct in relation to some end in view. But can the ends themselves be criticised in these ways? Certainly they can be criticised. They can be condemned as worthless, pernicious, trivial and so on. But can they be criticised as being unreasonable or irrational? 'Unreasonable' suggests always some sort of comparison. If an end is criticised as 'unreasonable', the suggestion is that some kind of monadic myopia is involved. There is inadequate account taken of other people's ends, or of other ends that an individual might have that are more important. There seems, therefore, no problem about criticising ends as unreasonable. But what about an end being termed irrational? It might, of course, be so termed if it was viewed in a context where its pursuit would frustrate some other end that the agent wanted much more. But could an end be deemed irrational in itself? Only, I suppose, if a man veered towards bringing something about without being able to give any account of the aspect under which it was wanted. Suppose, for instance, that every Thursday a man put every milk-bottle in sight on his garden wall. If we asked him whether he was doing this for target practice, or because he was collecting milk-bottles, or because he enjoyed looking at them there, and to every suggestion he replied 'No, I just want them there on Thursdays', I think that we might use the word 'irrational' of such an end. For what we call 'ends' of human action must conform to certain general standards. They have to be conceivable objects of interest, concern, enjoyment, approval and so on. If an individual persists in doing something and can produce no aspect under which he views it which makes intelligible that he should want it, we would, I think, regard such an end as irrational in itself and one that required some special explanation, e.g. in terms of an unconscious wish or aversion.

4. It might be said that such cases are very different from those previously considered because there is nothing particularly low-grade about being angry or sympathetic, needing love and liking admiration. This is perfectly true if a situation is clearly conceived under the aspects appropriate to these emotions, though it is a further question whether they are justifiable or not. But the hypothetical cases of the judge, the politician and the businessman are not of this sort. They are cases in which the individual does not clearly or explicitly view the situation under these aspects. He may be only fleetingly aware of them or may refuse to recognise his susceptibility.

BIBLIOGRAPHY

Arieti, S., *The Intrapsychic Self* (New York, 1967).

Bennett, J., *Rationality* (London, 1964).

Bernstein, B., 'Social Class and Linguistic Development, A Theory of Social Learning, in Halsey A. H., Floud, J. and Anderson, C. A., *Education, Economy and Society* (New York, 1961).

Dember, W. N., *The Psychology of Perception* (New York, 1964).

Flugel, J. C., *Man, Morals and Society* (London, 1946).

Freud, S., *Civilization and Its Discontents* (London, 1930).

Klein, J., *Samples from English Cultures* (London, 1965).

Mabbott, J., 'Reason and Desire', *Philosophy*, xxxviii (April 1953).

Oakeshott, M., 'Rationalism in Politics' and 'Rational Conduct', in *Rationalism in Politics* (London, 1962).

Peters, R. S., *The Concept of Motivation* (London, 1958).

Peters, R. S., 'Emotions, Passivity and the Place of Freud's Theory in Psychology', in Wolman, B. and Nagel, E., *Scientific Psychology* (New York, 1965).
Peters, R. S., 'Motivation, Emotion and the Conceptual Schemes of Common Sense', in Mischel, T. (Ed.), *Human Action* (New York, 1969).
Ryle, G., *A Rational Animal* (London, 1962).
Sidgwick, H., *The Methods of Ethics*, Paperback edn (London, 1962).

7

THE EDUCATION OF THE EMOTIONS

1 EMOTIONS AS FORMS OF COGNITION

I propose in this paper to confine myself to getting clearer about what is involved in the task of educating the emotions. I do not propose to address myself to further questions about the relevance of empirical work done by psychologists to implementing this task. This would, as a matter of fact, be a very difficult undertaking for two reasons. In the first place, most of the changes in emotion studied experimentally by psychologists could not conceivably be described as 'education'. Whatever else we understand by 'education' (Peters, 1966, Ch. I), at least we think of it as involving a family of experiences through which knowledge and understanding develop. Injecting adrenalin into the body, administering drugs, stimulation by electrodes and various methods of conditioning, do not of themselves bring about know-ledge and understanding. They may, of course, provide conditions which facilitate cognitive development. In this respect, like altering the temperature of a room or smiling at children, they may function as aids to education; but they are not themselves processes of education. A psychologist might concede this point about 'education' but conclude from it that the task of educating the emotions must therefore be an impossible one; for 'emotion' might convey to him only some general state of activation or arousal which had no necessary connection with knowledge, understanding, or belief. In this sphere of behaviour, therefore, it would follow for him that people could be stimulated or conditioned but not educated.

This brings me to my second reason for omitting to delve into empirical work done by psychologists on emotion, which is that the concept of 'emotion' employed by many psychologists fails to do justice to what I would regard as its central feature, namely its connection with a certain type of cognition. If we ask ourselves what we might naturally call 'emotions' we would give quite a long list which would include fear, anger, sorrow, grief, envy, jealousy, pity, remorse, guilt, shame, pride, wonder and the like. What sort of criterion underlies this selection? Surely, the connection between emotions and the class of cognitions that are conveniently called 'appraisals'. These are constituted by seeing situations under aspects which are agreeable or disagreeable, beneficial or harmful in a variety of dimensions. To feel fear *is*, for instance, to see a situation as dangerous; to feel pride *is* to see with pleasure something as mine or as something that I have had a hand in bringing about. Envy is connected with seeing someone else as possessing what we want, jealousy with seeing someone as possessing something or someone to which or whom we think we have a right. And so on. Emotions have in common the fact that they involve appraisals elicited by external conditions which are of concern to us or by things which we have brought about or suffered. (We would not, for reasons such as this, call hunger and thirst emotions.) They differ from each other because of differences in what is appraised. Fear, for instance, differs from anger, largely because seeing something as threatening differs from seeing it as thwarting, and these different appraisals have different consequences both physiologically and in the behaviour which may be their outcome. Clues to distinguishing emotions may be provided by overt signs such as facial expressions; but the history of experiments in this field has shown them to be unreliable signs. Also, the fact that we can say that facial expressions are reliable or unreliable as distinguishing marks of the different emotions itself reveals that we have other ways of identifying them. My thesis, however, about the appraisals involved in emotion is not that they provide very valuable evidence as to what the distinct emotions are; it is rather that these different appraisals are largely constitutive of the different emotions. By that I mean that at least a logically necessary condition for the use of the word 'emotion' is that some kind of appraisal should be involved, and that the different emotions must involve different appraisals. In other words, emotions are basically forms of cognition. It is because of this central feature which they possess that I think there is any amount of scope for educating the emotions.

Why then have psychologists concentrated on the physiological conditions underlying emotions, on expressions of emotions, and on some assumed link between emotion and action? Partly, I suppose, because Charles Darwin started a tradition of studying facial expressions with his famous, or notorious, experiments with photographs. But more importantly, because of psychology's endeavour to become a proper science based on publicly observable data. Physiological psychology had long been established as a scientifically respectable form of enquiry. It was also thought that concentration on facial expressions or on overt actions – for instance flight in the case of fear – would provide equally reliable data, free from the hazards of introspective reports. It is, I suppose, encouraging to read a long recent article by Leeper, which returns to common sense in connecting emotions with cognitive cues, but his laboured explanation of how psychologists have failed to see this because of the general tendency of scientists to concentrate on what is palpable scarcely holds water (Leeper, 1965, pp. 37–40). What Leeper keeps locked in the cupboard is psychology's skeleton, Behaviourism, which, as a methodological doctrine, has exercised a baneful and stupefying influence on academic psychology since the early part of this century. It was the concept of 'palpability' which went with this particular brand of methodological puritanism, with all its conceptual confusions and antiquated notions of scientific method, that both restricted the questions which psychologists felt they could respectably raise about emotions and which occasioned them to ignore the palpable point that we cannot even identify the emotions we are talking about unless account is taken of how a person is appraising a situation. I am not, of course, denying that there are important questions to ask in these fields – for instance, about the physiology of emotion and about expressions of emotion. I am only commenting on the restrictions placed on investigations into emotional phenomena. (See, for instance, Mandler, 1962.)

There is, too, another important historical point about the restricted study of emotion by psychologists, namely, the tendency to treat fear and anger as paradigms, rather than, say, sorrow and pride. The tendency of psychologists in the Behaviourist tradition to confine their work to animals as a matter of fact left them little alternative; for most emotions – for instance, pride, shame, regret, grief – are not experienced by animals because the appraisals involved in them presuppose a conceptual scheme beyond the range of animals other than man. Also, there was a highly respectable ancestry for the study of these two emotions in Darwin's work which gave prominence to them because of their obvious biological utility. But these two emotions are atypical in that they do have definite types of facial expressions connected with them and are accompanied by palpable signs of changes in the autonomic nervous system. Also, if any emotions are closely connected with typical action patterns, these two are. If sorrow were taken as a paradigm, the connection with action patterns would be difficult to discern. And what distinctive facial expressions are connected with envy or pride? Is it plausible to suggest that highly specific physiological changes accompany remorse or regret of the sort that often accompany fear and anger?

2 EMOTIONS AND PASSIVITY

Suppose, then, that we resist these historic influences, and, sticking to common sense,* insist both on the connection between emotions and distinctive appraisals and on a broad sample of emotions rather than confining ourselves to fear and anger. An interesting point, then, emerges if we study the list, namely, that most of the terms on the list can also be used as names of motives. This is not surprising; for obviously, as the terms 'emotion' and 'motive' suggest, there is a close family connection between the two terms. This has obviously been another reason which has led countless theorists to postulate an intimate connection between emotion and 'motivated behaviour', culminating in the historic dispute between Young and Leeper about the facilitating or disrupting effect of emotion on motivated behaviour. I have elsewhere summarised most of the important attempts to establish such a connection (Peters, 1961, Sect. 3), and do not propose to elaborate this theme now. What I propose to do instead is to state briefly what I take to be the proper way of representing the undoubted overlap between these concepts.

My suggestion is that what is common to the two concepts is the connection with distinctive appraisals. In cases where either the term 'motive' or 'emotion' is appropriate, the situation is appraised in the way which is established by the particular term – for instance, as dangerous in the case of fear, as having done something wrong in the case of guilt. In cases where we apply the term 'motive' this appraisal of the situation is regarded as providing the reason why we go on to *do* something. We talk about 'motives' only in contexts where an explanation for an *action* is given or demanded; we do not ask for motives for feeling cold, for indigestion or for mystical visions. The explanation takes the form of appealing to a postulated connection between the appraisal and the action pattern in question. If a person's motive for making damaging remarks about a colleague is jealousy, then he must see him as achieving, or likely to achieve

* For a sustained defence of paying careful attention to the distinctions embodied in the conceptual scheme of common sense see Peters (1958, 1969).

something to which he thinks he has a right, and he must act in the light of this view of his behaviour.

We talk about jealousy as an emotion, for instance, when a person is subject to unpleasant feelings that come over him when he views his colleague's behaviour in a certain light. Perhaps his perception of him is distorted by this view he has of him – perhaps his judgement of his character is warped by it – perhaps he gets into an emotional state at the mere mention of his name. The term 'emotion', in other words, is typically used in ordinary language to pick out our passivity. We speak of judgements being disturbed, warped, heightened, sharpened and clouded by emotion, of people being in command or not being properly in control of their emotions, being emotionally perturbed, upset, involved, excited and exhausted. In a similar vein, we speak of emotional states, upheavals, outbursts and reactions. The suggestion in such cases is that something comes over people or happens to them, when they consider a situation in a certain light, when they appraise it in the dimension suggested by terms such as jealousy, envy and fear. This passivity frequently occurs when we appraise situations as dangerous and frustrating; hence the obviousness of fear and anger as emotions and hence our reluctance to regard benevolence and ambition as emotions, for there are rarely marked symptoms of passivity when we think of people or situations under the aspects connected with these terms.

It is important, to avoid misunderstanding of my analysis of 'emotion' which some regard as a trifle eccentric, to be clear about the sort of analysis it is. What I am denying is that the terms 'emotion' or 'motive' pick out, as it were, distinctive items in the furniture of the mind. I am claiming, on the contrary, that they are terms we employ when we wish to link the *same* mental acts of appraisal with *different* forms of behaviour – with actions on the one hand and with a variety of passive phenomena on the other. The appraisals involved, however, need not issue in either motives or emotions. We can say, 'I envy him his equanimity' or 'I am sorry that you can't come to stay', without acting in the light of the relevant appraisal and without being emotionally affected in any way.

What is common to both 'motives' and 'emotions', therefore, is the distinctive appraisals which are necessary to characterise these states of mind as being cases of fear, envy, jealousy, etc. The difference lies in the fact that 'motive' is a term we employ to connect these appraisals with things we *do*, emotion with things that *come over us*. In strong cases of emotion our passivity is manifest in changes in the autonomic nervous system of which we speak in metaphors which are consonant with our passivity. We boil and fume with anger, we tremble and sweat with fear; we swell and glow with pride; we blush with shame and embarrassment. If the motor system is involved, the manifestations typically exhibit an involuntary character. Our knees knock with fear; we do not knock them. There is, too, the intermediary class of some reactions, which are typically of an unco-ordinated protopathic type, that spring from an intuitive, sometimes subliminal type of appraisal of a situation. An example would be when a person lashes out in anger or starts with fear. These are not reactions to stimuli, like jumping when one receives an electric shock, because of their cognitive core. Neither are they actions in a full-blown sense; for there is no grasp of means to ends, no consideration of possible ends of action. They are what we call 'emotional reactions'.

This analysis of the similarities and differences between motives and emotions suggests a conceptual connection between 'emotion' and 'passivity' and between 'motive' and 'action'. It thus denies a conceptual connection between 'emotion' and 'action' which is so often maintained by both philosophers and psychologists alike. The wide-spread tendency to postulate such a connection is due partly to the overlap between the two concepts already suggested, and partly to the tendency to take some emotions, for instance, fear and anger, as paradigms rather than others. If sorrow, grief and wonder were taken as paradigms, this connection would surely be most implausible, for as Koestler (1966, pp. 273–85) puts it: 'The purely self-transcending emotions do not tend towards action, but towards quiescence, tranquility and catharsis.' There are, of course, plenty of passive phenomena which go with these emotions – for instance, weeping, catching one's breath, a lump in the throat. But one cannot act in an appropriate way out of wonder or grief; one is overwhelmed by them. Perhaps one may *express* one's feelings in a symbolic way, as in mourning, or in some reverential ritual; but the appraisals do not function as motives for appropriate action as in the case of making reparation out of guilt. In the case of motives, the actions are appropriate because they remedy or retain what is unpleasant or pleasant about the situation which is appraised. To run away in the case of fear is to avoid what is unpleasant; to make reparation out of guilt is to attempt to remedy a wrong done. But if a man is overcome by grief because his wife is dead, what can be done of a specific sort, to remedy *that* situation? Expressions of emotion discharge the feeling through some sort of symbolic behaviour because there are no appropriate channels through which any relevant action can flow. Furthermore, even appraisals which can function both as motives and emotions do not necessarily lead to action, or even to tendencies to action. Jealousy and envy, for instance, may affect one's perception, judgement and memory; but they may not issue in actions in the sense in which psychologists have thought of actions. They may even be expressed in poetry.

To deny a conceptual connection between emotion and action is not, however, to deny *de facto* connections. In other words, though it is not part of our understanding of the concept of 'emotion' that there must be an action or tendency to action resultant on the appraisal of a situation, actions done out of a variety of motives can be contingently related to emotion; for one of the main manifestations of emotion is their tendency to disrupt, facilitate, heighten and intensify actions and performances. We can act *in* fear as well as *out of* fear; for there is no reason why an appraisal of the situation should not function as both an emotion and as a motive at the same time. The preposition 'in' draws attention to the manner of acting rather than to the reason or motive for action which is picked out by 'out of'. When the same appraisal functions both as an emotion and as a motive then the question is whether the emotional aspect of it is facilitating or disrupting, which depends largely on its strength. (This was one of the points of the controversy between Young and Leeper.) In cases where emotion influences an action or performance done out of another motive, the question is whether the appraisal from which the emotion derives is consonant with, or antagonistic to, that connected with the motive for the action. Fear may help a sentry acting out of a sense of duty to spot an approaching enemy long before anyone else; or it may lead him to imagine an enemy. But it is not likely to help him much if he is acting out of sexual desire in an off-duty period. Similarly, fear and envy felt for X are likely to warp and distort the moral judgements which Y may make of his actions. But they might also lead Y to notice aspects of X's behaviour which excape the notice of less biased observers. It depends on whether the appraisal involved in the emotion draws the attention away from or towards the relevant features of the situation, 'relevance' being defined in terms of whatever criteria make the actions and judgements concerned right or wrong, wise or foolish, valid or invalid, and so on.

3   EMOTIONS AND WISHES

My account of emotion obviously owes a great deal to Magda Arnold. It differs from her account in not postulating a conceptual connection between emotion and action; for she holds that an emotion is 'a felt tendency towards or away from an object' which is preceded by an appraisal of the situation as being of a certain sort that is harmful or beneficial to the agent (Arnold, 1960, Ch. 9–12). There is, however, another feature of her account that would give an additional explanation of the tendency to make a tight connection between emotion and action, namely, the connection which she suggests between emotion and wishing.

'Wish' is a teleological concept which is very closely related to 'want'. It differs, however, from 'want' in that the state of affairs wished for can be very indeterminately conceived. The moon is just the sort of thing that can be wished for, because questions about what one would do with it if one had it do not have to be pressed. Also, mundane questions of taking means to get it, which go along with 'wanting' need not be raised. Now 'wanting' is conceptually connected with action in the sense that action involves taking the means to a desired end. 'Wishing', however, only conjures up the vision of some indeterminately conceived end. But, obviously, the concepts are very intimately connected, and if emotions are conceptually connected with wishes, the tendency to connect emotion with action, or tendencies to action, via the notion of 'wanting' would be readily explained.

My contention is that there *is* such a conceptual connection between emotion and wishing. If we consider emotions such as grief and wonder, which are the most intractable ones for those who try to connect emotion conceptually with action, the connection with the weaker teleological concept of 'wish' is clear enough. A widow who is mourning for her dead husband *wishes* fervently that he were alive. But what *want* of this sort could issue in appropriate action? A lover, overwhelmed by his love, may wish that he were one with his beloved; but he cannot strictly speaking *want* such a logical impossibility. Yet these are just the sorts of thoughts that come into the heads of those deeply in love. Similarly, in cases where there is a possibility of appropriate action, the appraisal may only issue in a wish; it may not become a motive for action. A person strongly affected by fear or anger certainly has wishes such as 'would that I were away from here' or 'would that he were dead'. But nothing in the way of action or a tendency to action necessarily follows from this appraisal.

Magda Arnold also stresses the immediate, 'here and now' intuitive, undiscriminating types of appraisal that are characteristic of of emotion. These features of emotion are also emphasised by Sartre, who regards emotion as 'an abrupt drop into the magical' (Sartre, 1948, p. 90). This brings out well the connection between emotion and wishes, but it also emphasises a feature of appraisals which we associate with them when we regard them as emotions, namely, their undiscriminating character. A jealous man's appraisals are not always wild and intuitive, any more than are those of a man who quite sensibly experiences fear when he hears the shriek of a bomb descending towards him. But the more we think of these appraisals as *emotions* and hence stress our passivity with regard to them, the more we tend to think of the appraisals as immediate and 'intuitive, and of our reactions as veering towards the involuntary. 'Emotional reactions' illustrate both these features. If we jump when we see a face at the window, our appraisal is immediate and intuitive and our jump has an involuntary, protopathic character – quite unlike that of the high-jumper.

I have elsewhere (Peters, 1965, 1969) attempted to generalise this theory of passivity and to connect emotional phenomena via the concept of 'wish' with the sorts of phenomena explained by Freud in his theory of the wish, and with theories of the mechanisms underlying perceptual vigilance and defence suggested by more stimulus-response ridden theorists such as Dember. But this is not the place to develop this conceptualising any further. Enough has been done to enable me to address myself to the question of what must be involved in the task of educating the emotions. If the foregoing analysis is not altogether misconceived, there must be two interconnected aspects of this task. There will first be the development of appropriate appraisals, and secondly, the control and canalisation of passivity. I propose to deal briefly with each of these aspects in turn.

4   THE DEVELOPMENT OF APPROPRIATE APPRAISALS

(a)   *The Justification of Appraisals*

Although it may sound almost indecent to mention it in the company of psychologists, the education of the emotions is inescapably a moral matter. Most emotions and motives are, as a matter of fact, regarded also as virtues and vices – for instance, envy, benevolence, lust, pity. This is presumably because they are consonant with, or conflict with fundamental moral principles such as respect for persons and the consideration of people's interests. And there are many emotions which are conceptually connected with general moral notions – for instance, shame, guilt, remorse. There is also the point that 'education' suggests the initiation of people into what is worthwhile in a way which involves some depth and breadth of understanding and knowledge. It implies, therefore, not only a view about what is valuable in life, but also the all-pervasive principle of respect for truth. For the endeavour to develop knowledge and understanding would be unintelligible if there were no concern for truth and if educators generally were unmoved by the standards connected with its pursuit, such as those involved in relevance, clarity and cogency in argument, truthfulness in the production of evidence and impartiality towards people as possible sources of what might be true. Anyone who is concerned with the education of the emotions must necessarily approach his task from the standpoint of a moral position.

It might be thought that psychologists could have little to say about the appropriateness or inappropriateness of the emotions and motives that are taken to be desirable. But this is not altogether true. There are, so it seems to me, at least two respects in which psychologists might have something important to say about this. First, they might produce evidence about what is empirically possible in this sphere, human nature being what it is. There have been philosophers, such as Bertrand Russell (1929) who have held that jealousy is always inappropriate as an emotion, basically because it presupposes unjustifiable claims to a special relationship with another person. If psychologists could show that human beings were unable to avoid appraising situations in this way, that would be an important assertion to make. For there is a sense in which 'ought' implies 'can'. It is pointless to tell people that they ought not to feel in a certain way if, in general, human beings cannot avoid being subject to such feelings. This may be untrue about jealousy, but it may well be true about fear and anger, which obviously have a much more solid biological basis. The question then, for the educator, would not be whether, but with and of what, people should be angry or afraid.

Secondly, there is a strong case for saying that psychologists who have concerned themselves with mental health are in a position to offer well-substantiated counsels of prudence about certain emotions. They might say that the influence of some emotions is so all-pervasive that their presence or absence may seriously affect a person's capacity for doing what he thinks desirable, whatever his conception of what is desirable might be. They may say, for instance, that the absence of a capacity for love or the constant presence of a feeling of threat or insecurity might have such an all-pervasive influence on the person's life. Whatever else, therefore, we do about educating children, we should have particular regard for the development of the one and the avoidance of the other; for their presence or absence might be regarded as empirically necessary conditions for the satisfactory development of a whole range of other emotions and motives.

(b) *The Conceptual Prerequisites of Appraisals*

The point is often made nowadays by educators influenced by Piaget that children cannot form certain concepts unless they have first formed others, though it scarcely needs elaborate experiments to establish this. Nevertheless, even if one regards this as a matter for conceptual analysis as distinct from empirical investigation, it is certainly an important point to make in the sphere of the emotions. For what was made to look, in the writings of classical theorists such as Shand, as a kind of mental chemistry was in fact a crude attempt at making explicit conceptual priorities in the sphere of the emotions. For instance, just as one could not experience pride unless one had a concept of oneself, so one probably has to be able to experience pride before one can be subject to ambition and shame. Guilt presupposes a capacity to feel either fear of another or sympathy for another depending on whether it is the authoritarian or humanistic type of guilt.* Looking at the more complex emotions in this way in terms of the relationship between the concepts involved in the distinctive appraisals, raises in a more modern way the old issue about the possibility of all motives and emotions being generated out of a few simple ones; it also raises difficult empirical questions about the social processes by means of which the rationalisation and moralisation of appraisals takes place. The development of language is obviously of cardinal importance in this. To enter into the descriptions of a writer such as Henry James or George Eliot is to have one's capacity for making appraisals extended. We tend to think too much of human beings as having the capacity for making discriminations which are put into words by others. It is nearer the truth to say that we learn to make the discriminations by entering into the descriptions. It may, too, take a whole novel such as *Howard's End* to explore the range of an emotion like indignation.

(c) *False and Irrelevant Beliefs*

Most of our more complex appraisals do not presuppose just other appraisals; they also presuppose empirical beliefs of a more straightforward sort. I may just dislike someone for no apparent reason; but if I am jealous of somebody it is usually because I believe, perhaps falsely, that he has done something, or intends to do something, which threatens my claim to something or somebody. An obvious element, therefore, in the education of the emotions is the attempt to ensure that people's appraisals are not based on false beliefs.

* For the distinction see Money-Kyrle (1951).

To ensure this is not at all easy. To start with, as I have argued before, in so far as we are subject to something like jealousy as an *emotion*, the appraisal of the situation tends to be immediate and undiscriminating. We are predisposed often to interpret situations in a certain way, especially when we are in a frame of mind which we call a mood, and our beliefs may unreflectingly follow the lines of the appraisal. In a jealous frame of mind all sorts of beliefs are rigged to match our mood. Furthermore, the determination to examine the facts of the matter, to base our appraisals on well-grounded beliefs, is not a disposition that comes naturally to most men. As Bacon argued in the section on the Idols in his *Novum Organum*, the determination to look at the facts, to look for the negative instance which tells against our comfortable beliefs, goes against our inveterate tendency to believe what we wish to be the case. One of the main tasks of the education of the emotions, beginning with the development of what Freud called the ego, which he connected with the sense of reality, must therefore consist in fostering the capacity for objectivity. This is not just a matter of ensuring that children are well-informed; it is more importantly a matter of converting what natural curiosity children have into a concern for truth, and getting them to discipline themselves to submit what they think to public tests.

Psychologists, in my view, have told us too little about the conditions under which reasonableness, in the limited sense of the disposition to base conduct and appraisals on well-grounded beliefs, tends to develop. They have said much more about the antecedent conditions of various forms of irrationality; yet anyone who is seriously concerned with teaching children to be reasonable would like to know how positively to proceed as well as what to avoid. Nevertheless, in the area of irrational conduct, Freud and his followers have invented a technique which is best described as being once of re-education. The point is that the best way of characterising some forms of neurosis is to say that the patient is a victim of false beliefs.* Of course, according to Freud's definition of 'unconscious', the sufferer is not aware of what he believes. Rather, he once believed, for instance, that his father was going to damage him in some drastic way and repressed this belief which occasioned his fear of his father. In later life he has difficulty in dealing with various authority figures. The technique of re-education consists in getting him to recall vividly what he believed about his father and to see that, whether or

* The writing of both this section and succeeding two sections was helped by a preview which John Wilson of the Farmington Trust, Oxford, was kind enough to let me have of a book he has written on *The Education of the Emotions*.

not this was true of his father, it is not invariably true of authority
figures who remind him of his father.

Of course, not all types of irrational conduct have a similar explanation or can be influenced to any great extent by such a process of
re-education. An irrational aversion to a type of thing, for instance, a
rabbit – to use the classic case – might be set up by an association
between that type of thing and an unpleasant experience, for instance
a loud noise. This might establish a nameless dread that was reactiva-
ted whenever the individual encountered rabbits or animals with
similar characteristics. In such cases, it would be stretching things
to say that the person had beliefs about the rabbit which he repressed.
And if he was treated by some kind of reconditioning process it
would be inappropriate to describe this as a process of *education*.
For nothing is done about his beliefs; all that happens is that some
different sort of association is established to counteract or inhibit the
original one.

I am not, of course, making any claims for the success of psycho-
analysis as a technique, or chancing my arm on the extent to which
irrational conduct is susceptible of one type of explanation rather
than another. All I am claiming is that some irrational conduct and
appraisals can be represented as being derived from unconscious
beliefs that seem to undergo a kind of irrelevant generalisation, and
that, in so far as the 'cure' consists in getting the patient to understand and to acknowledge this, it can be properly represented as a
technique of re-education in the sphere of the emotions.

(d)   *The Recognition of Emotions*
In this process of re-education in psychoanalysis, the patient does
not just come to know theoretically that he at one time had some
belief about a person or a past event; he is also brought to relive his
previous experience which gives him some kind of additional insight into his condition. This kind of distinction is a very important
one in the general field of awareness of one's own and other peoples'
emotional states. There is a long-standing problem in the theory of
knowledge about the status of knowledge of persons which is partly
connected with the general problem of criteria of knowledge in this
field, and partly with the issue about whether there is any kind of
priority to be attached to knowledge of one's own case (see Austin,
1946; Malcolm, 1958; Ayer, 1954 and 1956). But whatever is said
about these very difficult matters, there is certainly an important
distinction to be made between knowing certain facts about oneself
and other people and the more imaginative type of entering into

one's own and other peoples' more recondite emotions, for which we use the term 'insight'.

Many claim that this imaginative ability is encouraged by taking part in games and drama, as well as by literature; but this is an *a priori* type of hunch rather than one substantiated by reliable empirical studies. As, however, one's ability to recognise emotions in oneself is a feature of being educated in this sphere, and as a criterion of being educated emotionally is the tendency for one's appraisals of others to be based on a realistic assessment of their condition, further knowledge about how this imaginative ability is developed is of crucial importance in the education of emotions. In this sphere, we are particularly prone to see what we fear or wish to be the case; our beliefs are likely to follow the lines of our moods and intuitive appraisals. If we lack the capacity for ascertaining what really is the case, we are very likely to remain in what Spinoza called 'The state of human bondage', at the mercy of our own prejudices and passivity.

(e) *Emotional Sincerity*

Often in such cases, we are not so much victims of ignorance as of insincerity, or *mauvaise-foi*, about which Sartre has written so much. 'Sincere' is applied to people and their speech and other forms of symbolic gestures (for instance, smiles). It can relate either to cases where one does not deliberately mislead people by one's utterances or symbolic gestures, or, more generally, to one's determination to reveal, as well as one can, what one's feelings, beliefs, etc., are. Often one has some strong motive for being insincere – for instance, fear, shame and the feeling associated with the feigned appraisal helps to develop a tendency towards deceiving oneself as well as others. For any educator, honesty and sincerity must be cardinal virtues, for he is concerned with the development of knowledge and understanding, and if people are concerned with finding out what is true, it must in general be the case that they are disposed to reveal their thoughts and feelings to each other. Without this, no kind of co-operative enquiry can flourish. How children are best encouraged to develop this disposition is an empirical matter about which it would be rash for a philosopher to make any pronouncement.

5 THE CONTROL AND CANALISATION OF PASSIVITY

So much for the appraisal aspect of the education of the emotions. I now propose to make a few observations about the other aspect of it, which is concerned with the management of our passivity. This is, to a large extent, a complementary aspect of the task of developing appropriate appraisals; for the task of freeing people from false and irrelevant beliefs, of enabling them to have insight into themselves and into others, and of encouraging sincerity are made doubly difficult because of the countervailing influence of more primitive, wild types of appraisal that warp and cloud perception and judgement and aid and abet self-deception and insincerity.

(a) *The Warping and Clouding of Perception and Judgement*
If, as Freud argued, the infant tends to life on in us with the wild and intuitive forms of appraisal characteristic of a more primordial condition of mind, even after the laborious development of the ego and the sense of reality, how can this ever-present influence on our perception and judgement be minimised?

There are, roughly speaking, three ways of tackling this task. The first would be to use some non-educational technique such as conditioning or the administering of drugs. At best these techniques would decrease a countervailing condition, or neutralise an existing condition, which might enable more positive educational techniques, that dealt directly with the development of beliefs and appraisals, to get a firmer grip.

The second approach would be that used by Freud and advocated by Spinoza, namely that of bringing a person to have some kind of insight into the sources of his irrationalities. Even Freud himself, though, never regarded this as a sufficient technique. Indeed he claimed that in some cases it even exacerbates the symptoms, like the distribution of menu cards at a time of famine.

A much more important positive approach is that envisaged by Spinoza in his saying that it takes an emotion to control an emotion. The predicament of most of us, an extreme case of which is presented by the paranoiac, is that we are too much subject to a kind of monadic myopia. Our interpretation of the world is inveterately self-referential. We find difficulty in peering out and seeing the world and others as they are, undistorted by our own fears, hopes and wishes. Better understanding of ourselves could not, of itself, remedy this condition. There are, however, certain appraisals which lack this self-referential character, notably love, respect, the sense of justice, and concern for truth. The development of what Koestler calls the 'self-transcending emotions' is probably the most effective way of loosening the hold on us of the more primitive, self-referential ones. To become effective, they must become stabilised in sentiments, rather than simply issue in sporadic emotions, the term 'sentiment' indicating a settled disposition to make appraisals of a certain sort. More precise knowledge about the conditions under which these sentiments are formed would, in my view, be one of the most important contributions which social psychology could make to educational theory.

(b)   *Motives and the Connection of Appraisals with Action Patterns*
In my preceding analysis of the similarities and differences between the concepts of 'emotion' and 'motive' I made the point that appraisals can be connected either with our passivity, which may have a distorting and disrupting effect on judgement and action, or with action patterns, in which case they function as motives. So one of the basic ways in which passivity is controlled is to develop appropriate action patterns with which the various appraisals can become connected. Thus a man who is subject to fear will have a settled disposition to act in an appropriate way. His chance of being overcome by passive phenomena is thereby lessened. This transformation of vague wishes into determinate wants and hence into relevant action is of manifest educational importance. To writhe with sympathy, to fume with moral indignation, to squirm with guilt or shame, may be more desirable than to be incapable of such feelings. But, it is surely more desirable still that these appraisals should also function as motives for doing whatever is appropriate. This is particularly important in the context of dealing with tendencies to action which issue from undesirable motives such as envy, hatred and lust. A vague tendency to say 'no' to oneself issuing from a feeling of guilt or shame, and unconnected with any disposition to act in an appropriate way, is singularly ineffective. Of more value are tendencies to action issuing from positive sentiments such as respect, benevolence and the sense of justice; for my guess is that the rather negative type of moral education, which issues from the puritan tradition is not particularly effective. In developing these more positive moral patterns of action the transition from second-hand, external sorts of appraisals to first-hand ones, which become linked with settled action patterns, is crucial. Much of what is moral is marked out by generalised appraisals such as 'wrong' 'good', and 'naughty'. Terms like these indicate that there are reasons for doing or not doing things but do not intimate at all clearly what the reasons are. Children have to be taught in such a way that they are led to see the reasons for and against courses of action built into them – for instance 'that's unfair'

and 'that is hurting him'. The development of such concrete first-hand appraisals, and linking them by on-the-spot training with patterns of action is one of the most important tasks of moral education.

Connected with the puritan tradition is the emphasis on 'character', or strength of will, which exhibits itself in higher order traits such as consistency, integrity, determination and so on. What is called 'weakness of will' is explicable in terms of emotions such as fear, anxiety and lust, which disrupt peoples' well-meaning intentions. Here again, one wonders about the puritan tradition. Strength of character is so often represented in negative terms, as saying 'no' to temptation, as standing firm, impervious to social pressure. My guess is that the influence of positive, self-transcending sentiments is just as important in the development of this as either prudence or the more negative superego types of appraisals.

(c) *The Expression of Emotions*
There is finally the problem of the discharge of passivity through the expression of the emotions. This may take the form of facial expressions and of changes in the autonomic system; or it may be handled in a more controlled way by appropriate speech and gesture of a voluntary sort. It was pointed out that some emotions, such as grief, can only be handled in this way, for there are no appropriate actions in relation to which the appraisals can function as motives.

The control and canalisation of emotions through speech and symbolic gesture is an extremely important intermediary in the sphere of emotion, which lies between extreme forms of passivity and appropriate action. In the case of many appraisals, such as those connected with hate, fear and lust, we would be in a very sorry plight if there were no intermediary between quivering in the passive state specific to the appraisals in question and launching into the relevant actions of murder, flight and rape. The mechanism of 'sublimation' is of obvious relevance here. Much of civilised life, including poetry, manners, wit and humour, consists in devising and learning forms of expression which enable us to deal with emotions in a way which is not personally disturbing or socially disruptive. Control can, of course, go too far. It is interesting to speculate, for instance, about what happens to those who are brought up with a prohibition on the public display of any emotion, either in gesture or in extravagant utterances, such as those of the poet. Do they become stunted in their capacity for experiencing emotion; or does it distort their judgement, facilitate or inhibit their actions in various subterranean ways; or do they tend to form deep and lasting sentiments for people, causes and places? And what of those who are encouraged always to display their emotions publicly? Is the transience of their emotional states matched by an inability to form stable sentiments? There are a host of empirical speculations in this area, but no well-established knowledge.

6 UPSHOT

This brings me to my final point which is really the point of writing this paper. Educational problems are not of the sort which can be solved by any one of the established disciplines such as philosophy, psychology, or sociology. They always raise questions to answer which there must be co-operation between people working in different disciplines. I have found that when I have done some work on the philosophical aspects of an educational problem, a host of empirical questions are opened up. If I ask my colleagues in psychology about such issues, they usually reply that no well-designed experiments have been done in this field. In many cases, this lack of research is due not to the fact that it would be impossible to test limited hypotheses, but to the fact that various puritanical traditions in psychology have discouraged work. And so we continue in our abysmal ignorance, dealing with the minds of our children in a haphazard way that would not be tolerated by those who deal with their bodies.

The area of the education of the emotions is a case in point. My contention is that most of the work in this field, with the notable exception of that of Solomon Asch and Magda Arnold, has been hamstrung by the behaviouristic and physiological traditions, and by the concentration on fear and anger as paradigms of emotions. My more positive intention has been to construct a conceptual map of the area which reveals, I hope, both what is distinctive of emotional phenomena and what needs to be known if we are to tackle more systematically the cluster of problems connected with this very important area of education.

REFERENCES

Arnold, M. B. *Emotion and Personality* (London: Cassell, 1960).
Asch, S. *Social Psychology* (Englewood Cliffs, New Jersey: Prentice-Hall, 1952).
Austin, J. 'Other Minds', *Proc. Aristotelian Soc.*, Suppl. Vol. 20 (1946), pp. 148–67.

Ayer, A. J., 'Our Knowledge of Other Minds', in *Philosophical Essays* (London: Macmillan, 1954).

Ayer, A. J., *The Problem of Knowledge* (London: Macmillan, 1956).

Koestler, A., *The Act of Creation* (London: Pan Books, 1966).

Leeper, R. W., 'Needed Developments in Motivational Theory', in Levine, D. (Ed.), *Nebraska Symposium on Motivation* (Lincoln: University of Nebraska Press, 1965).

Malcolm, N., 'Knowledge of Other Minds', *J. Philos.*, Vol. 55 (1958), pp. 969–78.

Mandler, G., 'Emotion', in Mandler, G. and Galanter, E. (Eds), *New Directions in Psychology* (New York: Holt, 1962).

Money-Kyrle, R., *Psycho-analysis and Politics* (London: Duckworth, 1951).

Peters, R. S., *The Concept of Motivation* (London: Routledge & Kegan Paul, 1958).

Peters, R. S., 'Emotions and the Category of Passivity', *Proc. Aristotelian Soc.*, Vol. 62 (1961), pp. 117–34.

Peters, R. S. 'Emotions, Passivity and the Place of Freud's Theory in Psychology', in Wolman, B. and Nagel, E. (Eds), *Scientific Psychology.* (New York: Basic Books, 1965).

Peters, R. S., *Ethics and Education* (London: Allen & Unwin, 1966).

Peters, R. S., 'Motivation, Emotion, and the Conceptual Schemes of Common Sense', in Mischel, T., *Human Action* (New York: Academic Press, 1969).

Russell, B., *Marriage and Morals* (London: Allen & Unwin, 1929).

Sartre, J. P., *The Emotions*, trans., B. Frechtman (New York: Philosophical Library, 1948).

8

C. A. MACE'S CONTRIBUTION TO THE PHILOSOPHY OF MIND

This is indeed a ridiculous position for a philosopher to find himself in – to have to talk about his teacher's philosophy in his presence when he is unable to reply. It must be particularly frustrating for Alec Mace. For he was always at his best when hemmed in by a pack of eager and often aggressive disputants, who were trying to pin him down to saying that people were constructions out of sense-data or some such preposterous view. 'But do sense-data or images exist?' he would ask. 'And what could be the sense of "exist" in such a question?' And so he got to work. As he put the matter himself: 'Hence the appropriate reaction to a philosophical remark is not to say "How true" or to say "What nonsense" but to say "Tell me more more".' And that is what he said, year after year, with great patience and acuteness, to a group of us who met with him every week to discuss problems in the philosophy of mind. Several quite well-known people came to his group at various times – John Passmore, Bill O'Neill, John Thompson, John Cohen, John Maze, Fred Smith, J. O. Wisdom, to mention only a few of those who are not on the Birkbeck permanent staff.

As a teacher Alec Mace was not only clear-headed, patient and constructive; he also had that unostentatious enthusiasm for his subject which is so much more genuine and enduring than some of the mannerisms and brands of lifemanship that emanate from other figures in twentieth-century philosophy. If only he could get clear about how to answer the question 'What is x trying to do?' he would say. Or alternatively: 'What is it to think about thinking? I really think that images are about the most puzzling phenomena in the whole universe!' His brow would pucker and a far-away look would come into his eyes as he gazed at the ceiling in the grip of such fascinating problems – rather like Thomas Hobbes goggling at the wonder of apparition. Not that he was unaffected by Cambridge. Indeed, his whole way of thought obviously owed much to G. E. Moore and he used to take a great delight in concocting fantastic examples to make his points. 'Supposing one looked up one morning and there was a typewriter hammering out propositions in the sky . . .' or 'Supposing one was playing billiards and the balls started making for the pockets like rabbits towards their burrows . . .'. He also shared the Cambridge set of values in which 'good' loomed larger than tiresome words like 'ought' and 'wrong'. I often think that he recoiled with the horror of a natural gentleman with thoroughly nice feelings from the modern talk of norms and man being a rule-following animal. Principles were things that might have to be formulated in order to clarify an awkward situation at staff meeting. It was almost indecent to regard them as written into the ordinary fabric of human judgement and behaviour.

The point about Alec Mace is that he cares about truth above all things. He was thus not a bit concerned to score points or to sprawl his personality over a seminar room. Neither was he much influenced by fashions. Like Raymond Chandler's hero, he has always been a quiet man working at his job. He never tired of trying to see what lay behind the jargon of pretentious theories and of noting that many classical theories were not refuted; they simply became outmoded. 'Nursery language, please', he used to say when confronted with a particularly pompous piece of pseudoscientific jargon. (He later modified this to the claim that anything worth saying in psychology could be said in language intelligible to a child of eleven; I never discovered what led to this mild concession.) And his writing, like his teaching, was a model of clarity, courtesy and elegance.

The positive aspect of Mace's concern for truth is his constructiveness, his attempt to reconcile conflicting view-points and to see what they have in common. This search for a harmony that lies beneath the appearances is, I suppose, Mace's most characteristic contribution to the philosophy of mind; it also explains what look like the most glaring anomalies in his thought. And if Mace has often seemed like a patient marriage-guidance counsellor trying to convince a warring couple that in spite of all appearances to the contrary, in spite of plates flying across the kitchen, continual infidelity and publicly delivered insults, they still love each other, there is a great need for his constructive spirit. In English philosophy the prevailing fashion is to be extremely critical of, even rude about, the efforts of others. Yet it is easy enough to see where others go wrong; it is often more difficult and more worth while to see where they may be right. As Mace himself so charmingly puts it:

'The philosopher needs time to remove the misunderstandings that arise from this opening clause. Elucidation follows the zig-zag course of an Hegelian progression: Thesis, Antithesis, and, perhaps, a Synthesis. But by saying this no doubt someone has been misled.'

This constructiveness in approach is extremely obvious in the three main spheres of Mace's contribution to the philosophy of mind – those of his analytic Behaviourism, his homeostasis, and his ethical naturalism. I propose to deal with each of these contributions in turn and to show how widespread his attempts at reconciliation have been.

Consider first the most glaring anomaly in Mace's thought. He has often described himself as an analytic Behaviourist; yet he has taken introspection more seriously and has had more to say about it than any other living philosopher. How has this come about? Let us start with his so-called Behaviourism. Like most modern philosophers Mace has been much influenced by the verificationist movement and by the Wittgenstein thesis that the meaning of mental concepts is not to be brought out by searching for inner states, entities, or processes to which such terms might refer, but by making explicit the public criteria of behaviour with which they are linked. Behaviourism therefore appealed to him as a doctrine because of its stress on public testability, though Mace took a certain sardonic delight in pointing out whenever possible that McDougall was just about the first person to lay out systematically the publicly observable hallmarks of purposive behaviour. But Behaviourism never appealed to him much as a methodological doctrine, as will be seen in a moment. It was the possibilities which it represented for philosophical analysis that excited him. He liked to suggest, I think in earnest, that thinking was a special form of doing; and generations of missionaries and cannibals were enlisted to substantiate what many would regard as a somewhat fanciful analogy. He also carried on a heavy flirtation with the offshoot of the Unity of Science movement known as Physicalism. He persisted for a long time with the view that the analysis of mental concepts is to be found either in behaviour or in dispositions to behave. Statements about perceiving, he suggested, could be analysed into statements about 'differential responses', statements about liking and disliking into statements about 'adient' and 'abient' responses. I have a suspicion that he now thinks that such attempts at analysis were almost hopeless; but I am not sure. I never could glean quite what he made of language; for he would be the first to see through the silly trick of extending the term 'behaviour' to cover it. For he used to say that one can use words to a certain extent as one likes; but certain usages are singularly unilluminating, as for instance the definition of 'work' as 'moving lumps of matter about'. The definition of language as 'verbal behaviour' would surely fall in the typically Macean category of 'the unilluminating'. But on such matters I am not clear what Mace thought and what he now thinks. And if he has changed his mind he is not the sort of man who would regard it as important to make a public recantation or to draw people's attention to what he thought or said at any particular time.

If Mace ever wished to withdraw he would, of course, always have his stress on introspection to fall back on, which was his version of the doctrine of inner sense and can be traced back through Stout to John Locke. How can this characteristic emphasis be squared with his Behaviourism? Roughly speaking Mace's view has always been that the Behaviourists were somewhat limited in their view of what constituted 'data'. Though he agreed with the general thesis that there is no separate entity called 'the mind' and no special type of process that might be called 'mental', he always insisted that psychology differed from other biological sciences in that we have a special way of observing our own bodily states, dispositions and acts, which rooks and rabbits do not share. This entailed both that mental concepts like 'perceiving' and 'striving' had to be unpacked in terms of introspective as well as overtly observable 'data' and that psychologists should not deprive themselves of this source of evidence in testing hypotheses. For there is no reason why different observers should not more or less agree on what they observe in this special way about themselves. To quote him:

'Introspection is a special case of the method of making use of the data of more than one sense. I observe that someone other than myself sees a thing, likes the look of it, and wishes to possess it, in the main by visually observing an extremely complex pattern of behaviour. I observe that I myself see it, that I like the look of it, and I desire to possess it by observing my own dispositions and inclinations. I observe these latter things by directing my attention to the felt tensions set up by these dispositions.'

This stress on introspective data goes right back to an early paper which Mace wrote on Hume's view of self-identity in which he pointed out what a sorry show Hume made of looking into himself to find the impressions from which the idea of self was derived. Here of course Mace stands in the James–Stout tradition of the bodily self. Indeed, he often quoted with relish James's location of the sensations connected with the spiritual self in cephalic movements and in the quivering of the epiglottis and respiratory tract. But Mace gave this strange doctrine a characteristic twist. He noted that

'The awareness of a material thing which is obtained through a visual sensation, v – whatever else it may require – at least depends in part upon some other datum, say a tactile datum, t, which is or at some time has been so presented that we can judge that the thing to which v "belongs" is identical with that to which t "belongs". Now one of the peculiarities of the awareness of the self obtained through awareness of our own acts is that the relevant somatic data are not presented in suitable relations to other data for such judgements to be made. We do not for example apprehend our "cerebral adjustments" both by somatic experiences and by touch or vision.'

As knowledge of self given through our awareness of mental acts is derived from a single modality of sense it has a rather peculiar diaphanous quality to it.

This is an intriguing point. Equally intriguing is Mace's frequent noting of the fact that although historically the distinction between primary and secondary qualities rested on criteria connected with peculiarities of the mathematical sciences, it was equally important to recognise that the primary qualities are in fact those which can be perceived by means of more than one sense. At times I have heard Mace suggest that the distinction between the mental and the physical is a particular case of the more general distinction between primary and secondary qualities. Smells, on this view, would be candidates for sitting at the right hand of the spiritual self. This is a typical Macean idea – an imaginative flash, a streak of impishness – but is there a serious far-reaching thesis underlying it? He was throwing off these fascinating suggestions when the Chair of Psychology was thrust upon him. After that the rest was not exactly silence; but certainly the training of minds and the patient attempt to convince rather brash behaviouristically-minded students that there was a perfectly respectable sense of 'mind' in which they could be said to have minds, left him too little time to pursue such fundamental questions in the philosophy of mind. Philosophers, whose estimate of Mace's contribution to the philosophy of mind was made clear by his election to the Presidency of the Aristotelian Society in 1948, have always regarded his absorption in the more mundane matters of running a Psychology Department as rather a pity. But in such matters of personal vocation who is to judge, save the man himself, what it is right for a man to do?

Mace, then, claimed that in a certain rather sophisticated sense he was a Behaviourist, though his stress on introspective evidence made his claim seem a trifle quaint. But he did not, as it were, play the benign house-agent and give the introspectionists an unlimited order to view the inner aspects of acts, dispositions and bodily states without supervision. On the contrary, he insisted on examining their credentials and often made rather whimsical remarks about their claims to be trained observers. He referred to the:

'pardonable hocus pocus concerning experimental procedures, the controlled conditions of quiet rooms, etc. Titchener was writing at a time when introspective psychologists felt it important to establish their scientific status. But whilst since that time experimental psychology has justified itself in quite a variety of ways, it has not established a single introspective observation in a laboratory which was not equally apparent to those who have carried out introspection in a psycho-analyst's consulting-room or for that matter in the homely arm-chair.'

And Mace thinks that this is so because of his conviction that 'the difficulties encountered in introspection reside not so much in observing the facts as in knowing how to describe them'. The classical problems of abstract ideas, the nature and status of mental images, and the problem of 'mental acts' derive from this fundamental difficulty.

'And from this we begin to get some inkling of what happened on the occasion of Titchener's blinding revelation when he read James Mill. "I can test this for myself", he said. Of course he could. He, too, could guess what words in the English language mean. He, too, could play the analytic game. . . . There is, accordingly, a prima facie case for the hypothesis: The problems of introspection are in part at least problems of analysis.'

Mace, of course, was not original in this view. For was he not one of

the few who stayed the course with Wittgenstein without incurring
his charismatic displeasure? And did not Wittgenstein proclaim:

'The confusion and barrenness of psychology is not to be explained
by calling it a "young science"; its state is not comparable with that
of physics, for instance, in its beginnings . . . for in psychology there
are experimental methods and *conceptual confusion*.'*

Mace's importance was in the fact that, unlike Wittgenstein and
some of his followers, he knew a lot of psychology and could substantiate this general thesis about it with a wealth of examples drawn
from its history. About ten years ago I tried to persuade Mace to
write a modern equivalent of Stout's *Analytical Psychology* – a
psychologist's charting of the 'logical geography' mapped from rather
a remote vantage point by Ryle in his *Concept of Mind*. He evinced
interest but muttered about the priority of his commitment to publish
his Tarner Lectures on Teleological Causation. So I started nagging
him about those and have been doing so on and off ever since. As a
matter of fact there was a period, about 1948 I should say, when he
actually did 'set himself' in the direction of publication. He revised
and read one or two of them as lectures. But they somehow got
wafted out of sight in the elevation of the department to the fourth
floor in the West.

Mention of the Tarner Lectures brings me to the second main
sphere of Mace's contribution to the philosophy of mind – that of
purpose, goal-directedness, motivation, homeostasis, and all the
other rather gruesome members of that family that are huddled together higgledy-piggledy in the psychologist's cupboard. I am not
altogether clear what Mace's views on these matters now are. But
he definitely has strong views. For when, a few years ago, I submitted
my manuscript of *The Concept of Motivation* to him for comment
he went off like a bomb. Page after page of excited and often out-
raged comment flowed from his feverish pen. This led me to remark
in my preface that his detailed and constructive comments convinced
me that he should have written the book himself. Perhaps he had.
The point is that we don't know; for his lectures to us on the subject
of teleological causation never got much beyond a preliminary
limbering-up operation on 'introspective evidence' and 'felt tendencies'. I suspect, however, that he reacted so strongly because I could
not accept what I have called his marriage guidance in this field – his

* Wittgenstein, L. *Philosophical Investigations*. Oxford: Blackwell, 1953, p. 232

attempt to make concepts like those of 'purpose', 'want' and 'need' snuggle down peacefully and respectably in the arms of homeostasis. For in this field, too, Mace has always been a reconciler. Just as he wanted to hang on to the objective emphasis of Behaviourism, while at the same time insisting that psychology was different from biology, in that human beings can introspect and by so doing enrich the meaning of mental concepts and obtain a special kind of evidence in relation to their own acts and dispositions, so also in the sphere of teleology Mace has, as far back as his paper 'Mechanical and Teleological Causation' in 1935, insisted on defining notions like 'purpose' in terms of objective criteria and underwriting them with some kind of biological or physiological theory. A process is teleological or purposive, he claimed, if there is an end-state, E, whose absence is a condition of persistent directed activity until it is attained or restored. Purposive behaviour, at the human level, which is described or explained in terms of a person's wants or needs, is a particular case of a more general type of behaviour in which the organism in question is conscious of and can plan means to the ends towards which its behaviour tends. Mace therefore extended the concept of homeostasis, which has a reasonably precise and testable application at the level of bodily functioning, to cover all forms of behaviour. Spiritual aspirations as well as sweating are to be explained in fundamentally the same kind of way. Mace was brought up on Stout's conative tendencies and McDougall's instincts; he tried to underpin this concept of purpose with a homeostatic principle which he delighted to trace back from Cannon to Spinoza.

This approach to human behaviour goes against modern trends in the philosophy of mind which, by concentrating on the analysis of concepts like 'intention', 'motive', 'knowledge', 'insight', etc., and above all on man's peculiarities as a rule-following and language-using animal, resist any attempt to describe or explain the full range of his behaviour in terms drawn from physiology or biology. In my *Concept of Motivation* I launched a sustained polemic against that yearning for over-all explanations which involve such conceptual extensions from the ground-floor upwards. (I have always thought that there was something rather distinctive about the fourth floor!) In so doing I may well have been trying to kill the father at whose knee I learnt just about all the psychology which I did not pick up by reading the stuff for myself. Mace would smile and remark characteristically: 'Lay off, Hypatia. Why must philosophy always play the part of psychology's nagging wife?' Fair enough. But why must it instead be cast in the role of the down-to-earth father who thinks that his son, when in search of a respectable union, should set so much store by breathing, sweating and bowel movements? Is the Wisdom of the Body really much like the Wisdom of the Mind?

Typically enough Mace himself was not unsympathetic to the wisdom of the mind as revealed in morals, religion and man's concern for values that pass beyond the level of the satisfaction of the 'necessary appetites'. Indeed, we have it from his own lips that a protracted argument over the objectivity of 'good' was one of the main bonds that held him and his wife together in the early years of their acquaintanceship. But, of course, he always tried to reconcile such rule-ridden activities and spiritual aspirations with man's physiological workings and biological tendencies. A man's good is that which would give satisfaction to the needs of any individual on the whole and in the long run. The crucial, norm-ridden concept of 'need' is interpreted in terms of his ubiquitous homeostasis and the whole range of ethical concepts (even those drawn from social ethics such as 'the common good') is encompassed in a somewhat emaciated equilibrium. 'Homeostasis, Needs and Values' represents, as it were, the climax of Mace's lifelong work at reconciliation, his homeostatic vision. It reveals in a majestic way his urbane audacity. For though there may be many psychologists still who would feel happy about passing from homeostasis to human behaviour, there must be very few philosophers who would wittingly ignore the age-old criticisms of naturalism in ethics and the modern stress on the logical gulf between nature and convention.

How is it that Mace can sustain such an unclouded vision of man as part of nature, striving at many different levels to persist in his own being? How can he be unmoved by the vision of man striving ceaselessly by artifice, convention and institution to perpetuate the thin brittle crust of civilisation? Because, I would suggest, he is at heart a metaphysician. But he is not, like Hobbes, a metaphysician of movement to whom life was but a motion of limbs, social life a race, and for whom happiness consisted always in proceeding. Mace is more like Spinoza – a metaphysician of equilibrium. Beneath the appearances of organisms and people, beneath the aspirations and institutions of man he always sees at work a tendency towards stabilisation and harmony. For him this principle, like the pleasure principle for Bentham, seems both an explanation of what men in fact do and a justification of what they ought to do. In his own thought and in his work with people he has always fastened on and sought to ally himself with this tendency which has not only an overt observable aspect but also a felt inner side. Indeed I should say that he really understands from the inside what Spinoza meant, which showed such great psychological insight, when he said:

'Blessedness is not the reward of right living; it is the right living itself. Nor do we delight in blessedness because we restrain our desires. On the contrary it is because we delight in it that we restrain them.'

And that is how I always picture Alec Mace, sitting at peace in his arm-chair trying to reconcile ideas, and to reconcile conflicts between people who were often petty-minded, neurotic and concerned with their own advantage. His attempts at reconciliation were never just manœuvres to paper the cracks. He always tried to arrive at the underlying issues and to get people to see what was just. And I am sure that, like Plato, he sees justice as some kind of proportionate arrangement. He believes almost passionately in the rationality of man and is convinced, again like Spinoza, that: 'In so far as men live under the guidance of reason, thus far only they always necessarily agree in nature.' I should say that he is about the most fair-minded man that it has ever been my privilege to meet as well as one of the most shrewd and humane. But these qualities, I feel sure, are his because of his profound convictions about the nature of man and society.

A good thing about his retirement is that it will at last give him time to work out in more detail the conclusions he has reached in all these different realms of thought, so that others may at last be able to share them. And if we don't always agree with what he says we will at least be able to fall back on his own words:

'It is characteristic of the greater amiability of contemporary philosophical discussion that philosophers are less disposed than hitherto to accuse each other of being *utterly*, if not culpably mistaken. It is in fact almost as difficult to be *utterly* mistaken as it is to be *absolutely* right. A philosopher nowadays can say almost anything he likes, but – and this is the snag – almost anything he says will be challenged as "misleading".'

9

THE PSYCHOLOGIST AND THE
TEACHER

In my last talk I made the point that educators badly need more reliable information about methods of passing on information and rules and that psychologists should be able to provide them with such information. Of all branches of psychology one would have thought that learning theory would be most relevant. Yet the fact is that very little of learning theory is of much interest or relevance to the educator. This is such a strange anomaly that it is worth while exploring why it is so. For it is intimately connected with the whole conception of psychology as a science.

One of the most awe-inspiring features of academic institutions is the tyranny of fashions. Ten years ago if one mentioned God in certain philosophical circles it was almost like swearing in an Edwardian drawing room, and if one suggested in certain places that psychology might after all be about the mind of man rather than about his bodily movements, there used to be muttering that one needed one's brain tested. I want to discuss the tyranny of such a fashion. For my thesis is, roughly speaking, that the relationship between education and theories of learning has been largely misconceived – colossally misconceived. Far from it being the case that educationists have a lot to learn from the theory of learning, I want to suggest that the psychology of learning could benefit enormously from a study of the practice of education.

The fashion which I have in mind has a respectable and ancient lineage. It dates back at least to the seventeenth century when Thomas Hobbes suggested that the behaviour of men could be explained in the same sort of way as the behaviour of bodies in motion. Men, after all, have bodies, and in their loves and hates they move towards and away from each other. Could not life be then nothing but motion of the limbs, thinking nothing but a movement of some substance in the head, and feeling the motion of some substance round the heart? Or could not men's ideas, as Hume suggested, be regarded as mental atoms bound together by mechanical laws of association which functioned as a parallel to the laws of gravity in the physical world?

Biology developed in the nineteenth century and the suggestion that men behaved like bodies in motion was, to a certain extent, modified by the suggestion that men behaved like animals as well. Theories of instincts and irrational urges supplemented the pushes and pulls of the old mechanical systems. And in modern learning theories, like those of Hull and Skinner, a strange explanatory brew was concocted in which vaguely conceived biological notions like 'need' jostled with mechanical concepts like 'stimulus', and a marriage of convenience was arranged between biology and mechanics which gave birth to the monstrous mongrel concept of 'drive'. Learning theorists were not at all modest about their claims. Hull, for instance, boldly proclaimed that a psychologist should start from 'colourless movements and mere receptor impulses as such' and eventually explain everything in terms of such concepts as 'familial behaviour, individual adaptive efficiency (intelligence), the formal educative processes, psychogenic disorders, social control and delinquency, character and personality, culture and acculturation, magic and religious practices, custom law and jurisprudence, politics and government and many other specialised fields of behaviour'.

In fact Hull developed some simple postulates which gave dubious answers to limited questions about particular species of rats.

This metaphysical movement was understandable. For man had been treated previously as lord of creation, a rational creature who had free-will and whose behaviour was not subject to laws at all. So those who reacted against the traditional concept of man, like most rebels, pushed their views to extremes. And maybe it was necessary. Maybe one does not really see how dotty an assumption is until someone attempts to work out its implications in detail. Maybe Hull and his fellow learning theorists have done a considerable service to psychology by exhibiting a sort of detailed dottiness.

What then is so dotty about the Hobbes–Hull–Skinner approach? This is another way of asking what was valuable in the old conception of man as a rational animal. For when Aristotle distinguished man from animals and plants by stressing his rationality he did not mean that men are not subject to impulse, incontinence and fits of brutishness. He meant that men lead a distinctive sort of life because they are capable of imposing plans and rules on their conduct. Man is a purposive, rule-following animal. He does not merely, like animals or machines, act *in accordance with* rules; he acts because of his *knowledge* of them. He forms intentions. We cannot bring out what we *mean* by a human action without reference to the ends which men seek and the plans and rules which they impose upon their seeking. Indeed most human ends are impossible even to describe without reference to social standards. Passing examinations, getting married and getting promotion are goals in terms of which one might explain quite a lot that goes on in the precincts of an academic institution; but how could one begin to bring out what is meant by such goals without reference to social standards? And what would *count* as a means to such goals if we had no rules of efficiency and of social appropriateness which help us to describe and explain what people are up to? If it were suggested – perhaps rather fancifully – that attending a lecture is a means to passing an examination, this implies that it may lead on to it in a way which going to the pictures will not and that it will lead on to it in a socially appropriate manner – unlike bribing an examiner.

Standards of correctness are, as a matter of fact, built into most typically psychological terms. To *remember* is not just to have something passing through one's mind; it is to be right about what happened in the past. To *know* is to have good grounds for what one feels sure about; to *perceive* is to see something that is really there. And even terms which are regarded as explanatory terms in psychology make no *sense* without reference to standards or rules. To say that a person *needs* something, for instance, is to say that he is suffering from sort of injury if he is without it. And what constitutes injury depends upon some standard or norm. To postulate a *motive* for an action is to point to a goal which explains a deviation from a conventional expectation. If we ask what a man's motive is for getting married or giving a Christmas present we are suggesting that he is going to the altar or giving the present for reasons which are not the conventional ones.

Now we can never give an adequate explanation or description of such actions or performances in mechanical terms such as 'stimulus' and 'drive' beloved by learning theorists. For a reference to *movements* alone will never do the trick. What movements are either necessary or sufficient for describing what we mean by things like signing a contract, catching a bus, or winning a girl's affection? Movements, of course, are involved; but they only count as part of an action because they are grouped together as leading up to a goal or falling under a rule. From the point of view of *mere movements* how does one distinguish arriving at a lecture punctually out of habit, on principle and for a purpose? The movements might be the same in all cases; but we recognise them as very different types of action. The concept of an action is inseparable too, from the concept of 'knowing what we are doing'. And this makes no sense at the level of mere movements. Furthermore the concept of an action is inseparable from that of intelligence which gives another reason for objecting to the mechanistic programme. Men will vary their movements towards a goal according to relevant differences in a situation. And provided that they get to the goal almost any movement within a certain range will count to class it as an example of an action of a certain sort. Human actions can therefore be described as intelligent or stupid, efficient or inefficient, correct or incorrect; but movements are things that just happen. Such descriptions do not apply to them unless they are seen in the context of an action. There cannot therefore be an adequate description or sufficient explanation of human actions which employs only concepts such as 'stimulus' and 'drive' which belong to a logically different category.

Of course there are some movements which are *necessary* conditions of human actions and performances. The truism that we cannot think without a brain can be enlarged into a story about the excitation of phase sequences in the cell assemblies of the association areas of the brain. But we cannot begin to describe what we mean by performances such as remembering, perceiving and knowing in such terms. For how can we get notions like being right about the past or having good evidence for what we say by studying the movements of the body or brain? We have to understand human conventions and human language and the criteria in terms of which actions and statements are assessed. And these cannot be gleaned by doing physiology or by studying animals. For animals have no institutions; they have no history; they do not even speak and hand down conventions by means of speech and records. They probably have not even got a concept of the past and future.

On grounds such as these it seems to be obviously absurd to think that conditioning theories in the Hull–Skinner tradition could be of much interest or relevance to *educationists*. For educationists are mainly concerned with handing on the rules and traditions of civilisation and with getting children to learn or get things right. Nevertheless it would be a mistake to think that classical learning theory is of no relevance at all. For there are, perhaps, some things that *happen* to us rather than things which we do, knowing what we are doing, which can be explained in mechanical terms. After all, if we fall off a cliff our movements towards the ground are explained in terms of the laws of motion. But that does not mean that everything which we do can be explained in similar terms. Human beings salivate, like dogs – though this would scarcely be classed as a human action. It may therefore be that things which happen to us like salivation and eye-blinks can be sufficiently explained in mechanical terms – though I am not even sure about that. But one has to be very careful. For a blink, *qua* movement, is not all that different from a wink if you are looking at a person's profile. Yet the different words signify a difference between an action and something that happens to you – and to confuse the two might be fraught with dire social consequences. And it is absurd – logically absurd – to suppose that a deliberate wink in the middle of a staff-meeting has the same *sort* of explanation as the blink, which might be evinced if a psychologist puffed air at someone's eyeball. Similarly there are yawns and yawns. And if a lecturer sees someone yawning it is a real issue as to whether it is something that is happening to the man because of the heat of the room or something which he is doing deliberately to show that the lecturer is rather labouring a point. A deliberate yawn, like a wink, is something that is done for the sake of some end; it has conventional significance in certain social contexts. But a blink or a yawn may be things that happen to a man which have a more or less mechanical explanation. The beginning of wisdom in psychology is to realise that human goings-on are not all of a piece. There cannot therefore be any *one* type of explanation for them, any one type of learning. People who try to explain a clever finesse at Bridge in the same sort of way as they explain leaping up when you sit on a thistle do not fail because they have not tried hard enough. They fail because they are trying to do something that is logically impossible – rather like doing a lot of physics and chemistry to find out what the good life is.

Aristotle, as a matter of fact, provided also a most suggestive model for psychology which takes account both of man's rule-following and of things which need some other sort of explanation. He suggested that there are levels of soul – the rational, the animal and the vegetative. The lower is a necessary condition of the higher; but the higher modifies the way in which the lower operates and cannot be sufficiently explained in terms of it. And by 'soul' he did not mean a ghost in a machine. He meant a striving towards ends at different levels, which presupposes different levels of bodily organisation, and different categories of explanation. We should not therefore suppose that much that human being do could be explained in terms of a very simple category like movement. On the other hand we should not assume that everything can be explained in terms of the categories of rationality. The question always to ask about human behaviour is what *level* or *type* of explanation is relevant to what has to be explained. Is it a case of an action falling within the purposive rule-following category? Or is it the animal type of desire? Or is it even the vegetable in us at work?

How then, if we abandon the notion of an all-inclusive mechanical theory in psychology, is the task of psychology to be conceived? Well, the basic sciences of man must be rather like social anthropology – a study of the rules and goals by reference to which human actions are described and explained. After all, most of our understanding of others derives from our understanding of the sorts of goals that men pursue in a given society and the sorts of means that are regarded as efficient and appropriate for attaining them. We know roughly what to expect when the chairman gets to his feet because we are familiar with the conventions for the conduct of meetings. But a visitor from a country without scientific and cultural institutions might be rather at a loss. He might think that the lecturer was going to dance or to smell out a witch or something. Now supposing we did start dancing. Or supposing that his performance broke down – that he got stuck and stood staring in a stricken way at the ceiling. Surely a psychologist should be called in at this point. For psychology is necessary to supplement the social sciences – to explain *deviations from*, *breakdowns in*, and *individual differences* in *adaptation* to the particular rules and goals in terms of which we give content to our rule-following purposive model of explanation.

And this is where education comes in. For surely one of the most obvious explanations of human differences in adaptation, and of breakdowns and deviations in performance, is that the conditions under which the rules are passed on are very different. Education is surely best described as the passing on of the information, skills and traditions which are necessary to intelligent behaviour within a society, together with those higher-order skills and traditions which are necessary for assessing, criticising and modifying such rules and skills when necessary. The educative processes should therefore be one of the main subjects for psychologists to study. For parents and teachers are at the key points where individual differences are generated as the rules and goals of a society are passed on. For just as the very learning of a language or of science, history and mathematics opens up a common world for us, a form of life which we share with others; so also does the *manner* in which we are initiated into the paths cut by human language and conventions determine to a large extent the ways in which we walk differently along them. The social scientist and historian exhibits the structure of the form of life; the psychologist is concerned with the ways in which individuals adapt themselves to it and deviate from it. That is why I started by saying that I thought that we cannot begin to understand *human* learning unless we make a very careful study of the various educational techniques which, to a large extent, determine individual differences.

Now the psychologist who is concerned about the importance of learning theory for education often casts himself in the role of a Galileo, working on simple experiments in a laboratory in order to discover the basic laws of a theoretical science which could be handed on for teachers to apply. Pavlov is for him the paradigm – although it is worth noting that when Professor Luria was over here from Moscow recently he stated categorically that Pavlov, in his later years, proclaimed explicitly that his laws were relevant only to animal learning. Human learning, he maintained, needs a quite different set of laws. Luria then went through the Pavlovian laws and demonstrated how all of them were false at the human level. Human beings, astounding to relate, use language, and because of this there must be quite a different set of laws for human learning. In a very revealing passage Tolman, one of the earlier and more impressive learning theorists, once let the cat out of the bag when he said:

'Let me close now with a final confession of faith. I believe that everything important in psychology (except perhaps such matters as the building up of a super-ego, that is everything save such matters as involve society and words) can be investigated in essence through the continued experimental and theoretical analysis of the determiners of rat behaviour at a choice point in a maze.'

But what a hollow confession of faith is this! For what is there of importance in human behaviour that does *not* involve society and words?

There is a case to be made for Galileo in psychology if all that is meant is that psychologists should reduce their problems to as simple terms as possible; formulate bold hypotheses about their solution; and subject them, if possible to crucial tests. But there is nothing, in my view, to be said for following Galileo in psychology if this implies *also* attempting to use mechanical concepts and laws to explain all human behaviour – laws which have to be formulated by studying how rats or dogs behave in very circumscribed conditions. Psychology has been too long haunted not by the ghost *in* the machine but by the ghost *of* the machine.

There is, however, a very different picture of the psychologist's job in relation to education, which has a more practical and common-sense orientation. It maintains that most educational psychology is systematic common sense and that there is little in psychology that good teachers do not know already. The psychologist's job is to order what is already known and to give explanations of rather queer things like the phi-phenomenon or perceptual constancies which teachers have noted but have not taken to be of much theoretical interest.

Now I sympathise very much with this point of view; but it needs touching up and enlarging a bit. Teachers, as we all know, have a lot of hunches; but if asked to produce good evidence for them, they would be rather at a loss. I remember a teacher at a conference remarking that she had just read Professor Vernon's *Backwardness in Reading* and that she knew it all already. She was delighted to find so many of her hunches confirmed. But she did not mention what other hunches she had for which there was little evidence.

So one of the main tasks of psychology is to systematise and test the hunches of practical people like teachers, probation officers, welfare workers and industrialists. In the educational sphere the pioneering work of Piaget should prove of great importance. For Piaget has tried to map the various steps in the ascent of the child to the rational level. Piaget is of vital importance to educationists because he takes language and concept formation very seriously. He claims, quite rightly, that speech and argument make possible a new level of thought. Furthermore he attempts to arrive at maturation levels at which certain types of concepts like that of quantity, weight and volume can be grasped. In his earlier work on causality he showed how thinking starts by proceeding according to pre-rational principles where no account is taken of cause and effect as we understand it, or of logical connectedness, in this way providing confirmation of Freud's theory of the wish which works according to pre-rational principles. Also in his work on moral judgement he suggested generalisations about the differences in the child's attitude to rules at different ages, whether the rules relate to morals or to playing marbles.

Now it is most important for teachers to know what concepts and skills are within the grasp of a child at a certain age. Professor Vernon, in her recent book, claims that in about 70 per cent of cases the main cause of backwardness in reading is that a child is made to read before reaching the required level of development. But the teacher also wants to know what techniques facilitate the grasp of the skill or concept in question and what sorts of conditions impair performances and lead to breakdowns *in addition* to the general one of instruction before the appropriate level has been reached. What Piaget says, for instance, of the new process needed to link concrete problems with the verbal statement of the problem may be very relevant here – especially to the age at which we teach mathematics and to the techniques by means of which we teach it. If mathematics is a special sort of abstract language, what techniques are best for bridging the gulf between this and fiddling around with oranges?

To take another example from a field with which I am more familiar – that of moral training. Piaget distinguished what he called the transcendental stage when children never question the validity of rules, from the autonomous stage where they no longer regard rules as externally imposed, but as alterable conventions that have some point to them. He seems to assume an automatic maturation from one level to another. But the fact is that a great number of human beings, even in our culture, do not emerge from the transcendental stage. Now given that we want children to develop to the autonomous stage, what techniques of passing on rules are likely to encourage or impair such development? Here, I would suggest, the work of the Freudians on the super-ego and the origin of character-traits is very relevant. For the period of the formation of the super-ego roughly corresponds to Piaget's transcendental stage. And the theory of the super-ego and of character-traits is, roughly speaking, a theory which explains why people don't reach the autonomous stage, why they become compulsive, guilt-ridden and obsessed. And it uses the concept of being 'fixated' at various stages of growth. And this 'fixation' may well be due to the sort of training received at the various stages. Indeed it might be because they had received some form of 'conditioning'. The trouble about the theory of 'conditioning', when generalised indiscriminately beyond the level of salivation and eyelid blinks, is that it obscures the important question of what sort of phenomena *are* explicable in terms of a process like that of conditioning as distinct from one of training.

Now Piaget suggested that marbles and morals are more or less on a par as far as the child's attitude goes. Is his attitude to the rules of mathematics or music likely to be so different? Could it be that there are certain general principles about *techniques* which operate in all these seemingly different spheres? I know well enough that there are certain very general *necessary* conditions which apply to most spheres – such as the linkage with need and interest, the emotional relationship with adults and with other children, and the picture which the child has of himself, and so on. This is the perpetual swan song of people like Jersild. But granted all this, whether it is chess, mathematics, music, or morals that have to be passed on, there is surely a lot to be said about the *techniques* of passing on the relevant rules in such a manner that the child will follow them and learn to apply them *intelligently* instead of in a purely mechanical manner. When I used to teach Latin I experimented constantly with this sort of thing. But, like most teachers, I relied on hunches and intuition. My suggestion is that Piaget provides a fruitful framework to keep learning theorists busy for another fifty or hundred years.

But the systematisation and testing of such hunches is only part of the job of psychologists. For, as I remarked earlier, there are also odd phenomena which we come across that do not seem to fit into the ordinary model of common-sense explanation. And occasionally a psychologist of genius, such as Freud, lights upon an area of such phenomena and develops a special theory to explain departures from our rule-following, purposive model. Freud's great contribution to psychology was to provide a subsidiary theory for a number of phenomena which have a certain family resemblance. There were first of all things like hysteria, dreams, visions and fantasy. These are sorts of things which are not done 'on purpose', of which it would be odd to say that they were done for the sake of some end. Then there are slips of the tongue, lapses of memory, motor slips and stumbles, and perceptual mistakes. These represent *breakdowns* of or *lapses* from performances. When we describe them as 'unintentional' we bring out that they are not to be explained in terms of our purposive rule-following model. And then there are things like obsessions and compulsions which are either acts which are palpably inefficient in relation to their stated purpose, or which have a very queer kind of purpose. Freud's genius consisted in linking these everyday phenomena with various types of insanity and giving the same sort of explanation for all of them – in terms of unconscious wishes and the mechanisms of defence against them.

Freud, in my view, provides a paradigm for the progress of psychology. For here we find problems arising in a practical context and a special explanation being provided for them to supplement the purposive rule-following model (which roughly corresponds to Freud's theory of the ego and the reality-principle). I am also prepared to admit that Pavlov provides another such paradigm provided that we see his type of explanation as one that must be given only for certain sorts of things that happen to us like salivation. What I object to is when the unconscious wish or conditioned response is taken not as a brilliant hypothesis to explain certain limited phenomena but as an all-inclusive postulate to explain things as various as salivation, pressing a lever, cutting potatoes with a knife, talking, being honest and decent, being taken in by a business man, and making a clever finesse at Bridge.

In the light of this development of a common view about the job of psychology I can explain a bit more what I meant when I said at the beginning that far from it being the case that educationists have a lot to learn from learning theory, learning theory has a great deal to learn from the study of the practice of education. I meant, of course, negatively, that generalisations of the stimulus-response model of classical learning theory were of little relevance to problems in the classroom; but I meant positively something like this. Teachers, roughly speaking, are specialists in the various educational techniques by means of which information, skills and traditions are handed on. Very little is known, in my opinion, about the most effective techniques for handing on these things at different ages. For what subjects and at what ages is drill and the use of authority effective – and effective for what? Do such techniques, if used at early ages, whether for mathematics or for morals, incapacitate the child for rational rule-following later on? Or are they a necessary preliminary without which later instruction will not be effective? What about reward and punishment? Do artificial incentives early on militate against the acquisition of skills in relation to genuine objectives later? How much can be learnt through imitation and by the 'discipline of the task' without much talk and chalk? What sorts of techniques, applied at various ages, lead to impairment of skills, breakdowns, blocks and compulsive habits? What about the influence of social factors like the arrangement of the class, the attitude of the teacher and the developing picture which the child has of itself in relationship to others?

Such matters are part of the air which educationists breathe. But how much has been definitely established about such matters? It was very interesting to note that Professor Luria at Moscow has been working on problems in this field – on the age at which orders help the child to master a manipulative task, on the difference made by instructions with an explanation, on working on your own as distinct from working with others and so on. Along lines such as these

I would suggest that a large part of the psychology of learning should develop. The *different* educational techniques – rational instruction, the use of authority, imitation, learning by experience, and reward and punishment, should be distinguished. And they should be studied in relation to the acquisition of all sorts of different skills and the passing on of different types of information and rules.

But it would be as mistaken to assume that we can explain *all* learning in terms of such a model of training by conscious techniques as it would be to assume that we can explain it all in terms of conditioning. We must remind ourselves again of Aristotle's levels of soul – the rational, the animal and the vegetative. Modern psychology could help to tidy up these levels and to state the laws according to which we operate at them. As Freud and Piaget have shown, children are at a transitional stage between the animal and the rational level. Physiology, conditioning theory, the Freudian wish and so on, suggest laws for functioning at such different levels. And when we get breakdowns in performance or defects and lapses, these can be seen as the animal, the child and, perhaps, the vegetable in us taking over. Different types of learning characterise different levels. And there might well be generalisations about general conditions – e.g. suggestibility, fatigue, motivation – which apply at all levels.

The employment of this type of explanatory model together with the abandonment by psychologists of their Galilean dreams might well have two types of beneficial effects. On the one hand learning theory might benefit enormously by the careful experimental study of situations under which human beings learn all sorts of different things rather than by a concentration on highly artificial situations where rats and dogs learn very limited things. On the other hand the careful generalisations developed by psychologists might really be of some use to teachers and other practical people who have the function of passing on the skills and knowledge essential to civilisation. Indeed, the psychology of learning might even cease to be an embarrassment to distraught lecturers who have the thankless task of trying to teach aspiring teachers how to teach.

10

SURVIVAL, THE SOUL OR PERSONAL RELATIONSHIPS*

REVIEW OF *Beyond Freedom and Dignity by* B. F. SKINNER

This book was proclaimed in *Science News* as 'one of the most important happenings in twentieth-century psychology', which is perhaps a revealing verdict on the history of psychology in this century. For Skinner's attitudes and ideas belong to the nineteenth century. Basically he is a Utilitarian who values happiness and who thinks that it is attainable if the environment can be more systematically controlled. Things can be fixed up all right for human benefit by the employment of a technology of human behaviour. This technology embodies the old inductivist view of science that generalisations are gradually built up out of systematic experimentation. The principles employed are the old principles of the association of ideas dressed up in their modern guise of the conditioning of responses which subserve the survival of the individual and the species.

Survival, of course, now seems a more urgent question than it did to nineteenth-century perfectibilists. In this respect Skinner's attitudes are less confident, less infected by a belief in the inevitability of progress. For he is very much a contemporary American as well, a member of a nation that has lost its nerve and shed some of its old arrogance. There is the Vietnam war, pollution, the blacks, the student drop-out, drugs and the threat of over-population. These are beginning to look like predicaments, not like problems that can be solved or fixed up – at least not until men are more persuaded of the possibilities opened up by Skinner's technology of behaviour.

Skinner passionately wants to persuade his contemporaries that salvation lies in submitting to control of the environment for their

* Reproduced from the *Times Educational Supplement* by permission.

own good; but he is thwarted by their obstinate attachment to their freedom and dignity as human beings. Hence his book. And here again his adversary comes straight out of the nineteenth century. For he claims that their attachment is due to their belief in 'autonomous man', which he interprets as implying a belief in a little man within a man. The old Behaviourists, like J. B. Watson, were of course scared stiff of the soul. Hence their onslaught on the immaterial stuff of consciousness of which it was alleged to be composed. Skinner, somewhat quaintly, ascribes similar beliefs to those who nowadays believe in the autonomy of the individual. He sets up straw men to attack who are musty with the smell of Victorian haylofts. I do not think that he wilfully or wickedly misrepresents his adversaries; he is not that sort of man. Basically he is a simple fellow who is too unsophisticated in these matters to understand what they say nowadays.

Skinner admits that the 'literature of freedom' has done much to eliminate aversive practices. But it has placed too much emphasis on changing states of mind instead of the circumstances on which they depend. And, more importantly, escape is sought from all controllers – even from those who control the environment for people's good. Such squeamishness spells race suicide and is based on the superstition of the little man within who is subject to no constraints. These pre-scientific hang-ups are now a luxury that men must do without if they are to survive, though historically they have done some good. Belief in freedom, for instance, has led to opposition to punishment, which is an ineffective form of control; for it induces people not to behave in certain ways but does not shape their behaviour in a positive direction. The individual has to find his own path – and gets credit for it to boot because of the mysterious workings of conscience, another stronghold of autonomous man.

But the alternatives to punishment proposed by freedom-lovers are also ineffective because they are tied to the superstition of autonomy. Permissiveness, for instance, exonerates the teacher or parent from responsibility for control and simply leaves the child to be controlled by other features of the environment. Socratic midwifery gives the teacher more power and the individual credit. So both are satisfied, but at the cost of more precise knowledge about factors in the environment which are the real determinants of learning. Guidance relies on horticultural metaphors. There is control all right; but it is cloaked by the pretence that the shaping is brought about by inner growth. Dependence on things, as advocated by Rousseau and Dewey, is more effective and saves a lot of time and energy. People, too, can be used as things for shaping others. But the teacher must be careful to arrange such things. Finally there is the more high-minded policy of changing people's minds by urging or persuading them. This is ineffective; for it is really only the changing of behaviour that counts. Mind manipulators overlook past contingencies that are in fact operative and attribute efficacy to the man within.

Skinner sees that hard-headed shaping of behaviour presupposes some view of value; for when is a man in good shape? His answer is Bentham's translated into behaviouristic jargon. Pleasure is positive reinforcement and this becomes both the standard of right and wrong and the throne to which the chain of causes and effects is fastened. Good things are positive reinforcers; so behavioural science is the science of values. Men are guided by their concern for happiness – i.e. by personal reinforcers, that have survival value. They reinforce their fellows who act 'for the good of others' – i.e. who do things that reinforce others. Practices develop that have long-term reinforcing effects. Morals are therefore basically a matter of good husbandry, of fixing things up for human benefit. People tell the truth because they are reinforced for so doing. The scientist does not cook his results because others will check them. This is how men in fact behave and, presumably, how they should – though Skinner, like Bentham, is not altogether clear about the difference.

In the evolution of culture the most important criterion of 'progress' is thus the emergence of enhanced sensitivity to the consequences of behaviour, and increasing ability to predict them. Culture must now be more consciously designed so that long-term goods are promoted. The ingenuity that has produced cars and space-crafts must be turned to fixing up the ghettos, pollution and the use of leisure. Man must accept the view of himself that behavioural science has revealed. It is indeed more appropriate, when contemplating him, to exclaim 'How like a dog' rather than 'How like a god'. God is not dead; for he was never alive. But man will exterminate himself if he does not pay attention to providing the reinforcement contingencies which will shape his survival and turn his back on all the superstitions associated with his own autonomy.

Obviously those who believe in freedom will not take kindly to this paternalistic paean. Neither will their hackles subside when Skinner assures them that controllers are themselves controlled – the master by the slave, the parent by the child, and that a system can be worked out in which controllers have to submit to their own controls. But between their snarls of fitting indignation they can reflect that Skinner's hard-headed *naïveté* performs a useful service. I do not mean just that his uninhibited approach leads him to draw attention to matters that the tender-minded are apt to gloss over – e.g. the amount of manipulation involved in progressive methods, the inescapability of some form of social control, the ham-handed character of much reform inspired by a hatred of control and injustice. I mean rather that he pushes an instrumental approach to life to its limits and thus reveals a vision of life that is the logical outcome of presuppositions that many seem to share with him.

The Utilitarians, in the main, were not prepared to be completely consistent. They worried about the implication that justice and truthtelling had to be defended instrumentally by reference to their alleged consequences in terms of human happiness. J. S. Mill stood fast on liberty and was half-hearted in his attempt to provide a Utilitarian underpinning for it. He saw its connection with the pursuit of truth, whose connection with the pursuit of happiness he did not explore. Skinner, however, is quite uninhibited. He was nurtured in a cultural *milieu* which enabled William James to proclaim that truth is that which enables the individual to glide happily from one experience to another, and John Dewey to assert that truth is that which works. Happiness becomes the criterion both of what is right and of what is true. Man, the fixer, is the measure of all things. The good life is a smooth flow of positive reinforcement.

But Skinner has pushed this ancient arrogance even further. For, because of his quaint sensitivities about the soul, descriptions as well as justifications are couched in instrumental terms. He thinks states of mind causally inoperative; so he tends to describe them in terms of their overtly observable antecedents and consequences. The result is that, on occasions, one does not literally know what he is talking about. This comes out very clearly in his treatment of human dignity. Understandably he can give no account of this value; for it is connected with the view that we have of a man as having a point of view, as a person who is not to be used or manipulated for his own or anyone else's good. Skinner is reduced to just jibbering about it and to scattering reinforcements around like bird-seed. For it not only starkly confronts his whole instrumental outlook; it also activates his horror of consciousness.

Skinner's set of descriptions are really an attempt to discourse with kings of science whilst retaining the common touch of ordinary speech which is founded on quite different presuppositions. He even fudges things with the use of that blessed term 'the environment'. For what effects people generally are not just the physical properties of things or people but how they view them. 'Responses', too, save at the level of very simple movements, cannot be distinguished without reference to the individual's view of his situation. When he waves his arm, for instance, is he signalling, expressing irritation, or performing a ritual? The basic trouble with Behaviourists is that they have never had an adequate concept of 'behaviour'. Presumably, too, in writing his book Skinner is trying to change people's beliefs about themselves. But he thinks attempts to change people's minds an ineffective way of trying to influence them. How, then, can he justify what he is doing in writing his book, or even give an account of it in terms of his own theory?

Those who believe in 'the autonomous man' do not necessarily subscribe to a belief in the soul. They agree with Skinner that behaviour has 'causes' but they wish to distinguish those that involve the individual's understanding and decisions from those that do not. They also, like Piaget, probably want to distinguish between levels of behaviour – between the level when people (especially children) are induced to act for the sake of reward or approval from the level when they can also act because of genuine reasons connected with the situation itself. Some people, for instance, go to concerts because they genuinely enjoy listening to music, though others may go because of wanting to keep up with their neighbours. Because, in their past, they too may have gone for such extrinsic reasons, it does not follow that they are still just under the influence of that type of 'reinforcement'. Skinner, of course, would probably call all this 'reinforcement'; but that is because, in the face of the refutation of his theory, he has extended the meaning of 'reinforcement' so that it includes every possible form of motivation. So like many other psychological concepts (e.g. 'drive') it ends up by explaining nothing.

In morals, too, it may be the case that, at a certain stage of development, people learn to tell the truth or to keep their promises by being positively reinforced. But they also have to understand what it is to tell the truth and what a promise is. Eventually they may come to see that they should tell the truth because, unless this were the general rule, what is true could not be discovered and communicated. And truth matters – whatever its consequences for survival. For it is one of the values that define a tolerable form of survival. The autonomous man is the person who attempts to be 'authentic' or genuine in his attitudes and beliefs, who tries to free himself from sole dependence on the extrinsic reinforcers so beloved by Skinner. So he values truth and subjects what he is told to constant criticism. He abhors a society, like Skinner's Utopia, in which people believe what it pays them to believe and gladly submit to Pavlovian paternalism.

The value, therefore, of Skinner's naïve fanaticism is to have pushed instrumentalism to its logical limits. He has really no interest in how things are or in people's perspectives on the world. He is concerned only about how things and people will be and in their past as a guide to future manipulations. For him, as for the Puritans whom he despises, salvation lies always ahead, even though it is now downgraded to survival. At the end of his book he says that 'no theory changes what it is about; man remains what he has always been'. But this ignores one of the most important truths about man which is that he alone of creatures lives in the light of theories about himself and behaves differently because of them. The danger is that men may come to believe what Skinner says. They may use their freedom to deny others their dignity.

REVIEW OF *Freedom to Learn: A View of What Education Might Become* BY CARL R. ROGERS

It is, to a certain extent, inevitable that a person's thinking about education will be an extrapolation from a situation with which he is most familiar. Perry (1965) has developed this point with regard to what he calls the 'traditional' and the 'child-centred' models of education. It is not surprising, therefore, that Carl Rogers's views about education should reflect, in the main, his experiences as a therapist. What is surprising, however, is that an author who strongly advocates openness to the experiences of others should put together a collection of papers that are meant to be of general relevance to educational problems in such a seeming state of ignorance and innocence about educational theory and practice. Freedom is fine; and so is self-directed exploration. But there are other values, both in life and in education – truth, for instance, humility and breadth of understanding.

Carl Rogers's book about education exemplifies both the strengths and weaknesses of his own emphasis. He builds on what he learns and values and much of what he says is perceptive, if rather repetitive; but his passionate assurance is not clouded by any hint of what he does not know and he even seems unaware of the light that others have already shed on some of the positions that he has made his own. Surely, one reflects, as one reads about self-directed learning, work contracts, and the problem-solving approach, Carl Rogers must have heard of the Dalton plan. Surely he has battled his way through Dewey and Kilpatrick as have most American educators; surely he is not so uneducated as to have missed out on Cremin's *The Trans-*

formation of the School. But then, as one reads on, one begins to understand the free-floating character of the book, its lack of any proper historical, social, or philosophical dimensions. It is not really an attempt to think systematically about the actual problems of teaching and learning in a concrete historical context. It is Carl Rogers 'doing his thing' in the context of education. Much of the book was actually given as distinct papers and addresses on specific occasions. These various addresses are strung together with other chapters in which Rogers restates his now familiar themes about the organism, interpersonal relationships, self-enhancement, etc., and tries to demonstrate their general relevance for education. This exposition is prefaced by three case studies in which a sixth-grade teacher, a college professor of psychology, and himself try experiments in facilitating learning.

So much by way of general comment on *Freedom to Learn* as a serious sortie into educational theory. But what is to be made of Rogers's specific themes, when due allowance has been made for the limitations of their launching pad? Most of them are to be found in Chapters 4–7, after Rogers has presented his case studies in Part I. He gets off to a very shaky start in contrasting teaching, which he thinks unimportant, with the facilitation of learning, which is the proper concern of the educator. He is led to make this rather stark contrast because the dictionary tells him that teaching means 'to instruct' and 'to impart knowledge and skill' – some, e.g. Oakeshott (1967), actually wish to *contrast* 'instruct' with 'impart' – and because he thinks that it is concerned only with the passing on of a static body of knowledge and skill. The Australian aborigines managed all right with teaching because of their unchanging environment; it is, however, useless for modern man because his environment is constantly changing. The goal of education for us must therefore be the facilitation of change and learning.

Every aspect of this thesis is dubious. If Rogers had thought more about the concept of 'teaching', or if he had taken the trouble to examine what modern philosophers of education had written about it, instead of just looking it up in the dictionary, he would have grasped that 'teaching' is a much more polymorphous concept than this. Was not Socrates teaching the slave in *The Meno*, even though he was not telling him anything? He would have grasped, too, that it is not only knowledge that can be imparted but also modes of thought and experience by means of which knowledge has been acquired and by means of which it can be criticised and revised. Also what is the point, on his own showing, of equipping people to *seek* knowledge, if no value is to be accorded to its acquisition? It may be salutary, at a time of change, to stress the importance of learning how to learn. But this goal is not inconsistent with acquiring information. My guess, too, is that, in spite of change, modern man needs to acquire much more of it to survive than ever was required by the Australian aborigine.

Having got teaching out of the way, Rogers is then able to give voice to his excitement about a real community of learners, which is worth quoting because, apart from its style, it could have come straight out of Dewey. 'To free curiosity; to permit individuals to go charging off in new directions dictated by their own interests; to unleash the sense of enquiry; to open everything to questioning and exploration; to recognise that everything is in process of change – here is an experience I can never forget' (p. 105). How, then, is this process of real 'self-initiated, significant, experiential, "gut-level" learning' to be facilitated? And, at this point, Rogers makes his distinctive contribution. It is through 'certain attitudinal qualities which exist in the personal relationship between the facilitator and the learner' (p. 106). Findings in the field of psychotherapy apply in the class-room as well. Rogers then outlines the qualities that a facilitator of learning should exhibit to learners, qualities that parallel those of a client-centred therapist to his patients – genuineness, being a real person with his pupils, prizing the learner and caring for him, empathic understanding and trust. Rogers claims that 'individuals who hold such attitudes, and are bold enough to act on them, do not simply modify class-room methods – they revolutionise them. They perform almost none of the functions of teachers. It is no longer accurate to call them teachers. They are catalysers, facilitators, giving freedom and life and the opportunity to learn, to students' (p. 126).

This is surely an extremely important point to make about teaching. If we avert our eyes from the naïve contrast between 'teaching' and 'the facilitation of learning' there remains a strong case for saying that personal relationships between teacher and pupil, of the type advocated by Rogers, do seem to facilitate learning. This needs to be said loudly at a time when educational institutions are becoming larger and more impersonal and when students are increasingly being treated as subject-fodder and as operatives to be slotted into the occupational structure. Teachers can function as human beings as well as teachers; and if they do so, learning is probably facilitated.

Rogers, however, does not seem altogether clear about what makes a relationship a personal one as distinct from a role relationship. What seems to me distinctive of a personal relationship is that a response is made to another individual just as a human being – not as an occupant of a role, not as a sharer in a common quest, including that of learning, not even as another moral being who is regarded with respect as the subject of rights (Peters, 1970). Yet Rogers constantly speaks of such relationships as if he views them, in an educational situation, mainly as facilitators of learning. But if they are entered into by the teacher *because he sees them* as facilitating learning they surely cease to be proper personal relationships; for the aspect under which the other is viewed, as a learner, now makes them a species of role relationship. Their spontaneity can thus be spoilt and endless possibilities for *mauvaise foi* are opened up. There is thus inherent in the teacher–pupil relationship a paradox akin to the paradox of hedonism. Learning is facilitated by the teacher entering into personal relationships with his pupils; but such relationships must not be viewed by the teacher as facilitating learning. Indeed a pupil would surely resent being at the receiver end of a 'personal relationship' with a 'facilitator' that is viewed as aiding his learning, much more than being subject to a straightforward attempt to instruct him. Rogers seems unaware of these difficulties because he does not appreciate that being a facilitator of learning is just as much a role relationship as instructing and that what makes an action a performance of a role is the aspect under which it is viewed by the agent. In other words, Rogers's ideal teacher must, to a certain extent, be capable of forgetting, in his dealing with pupils, that he is a facilitator of learning. He must, from time to time, just respond to his pupils as fellow human beings. This response is something that is valuable in its own right.

Rogers's preoccupations with personal relationships between teacher and pupil are very salutary because progressives, who stress freedom and self-initiated learning, sometimes stress too much 'do it yourself' methods. Rogers, of course, advocates these, but he is more than mindful of the bond between teacher and taught that is one of the most potent influences in the development of knowledge, sensitivity and skill. He does not, however, bring the teacher's role fully out into the open because he is squeamish about direction, and superficial about knowledge. He believes in the growth and self-actualisation of the individual. He finds that his clients and pupils move towards genuineness, acceptance of self, openness to others and self-direction. In other words the self that is realised is not any old self, but one that exemplifies moral values as old as Socrates. Rogers seems to see this as some sort of spontaneous unfolding of dormant potentialities. But he surely must appreciate that there are dormant potentialities for all sorts of other selves and that the emergence of this type of self is very intimately connected with the steady influence of persons such as Rogers. Rogers is, of course, an inveterate moralist who passes on his values more by exemplifying them than by trying to instruct others in them – except, of course, when he writes books. This kind of influence is a form of 'direction' – perhaps a much more effective form than explicit instruction. I myself share Rogers's moral convictions. But I do think that their ethical status should be made explicit and that some sort of justification of them should be attempted. I also think that persons who believe in them should stop being so squeamish about the manifest 'directiveness' involved in passing them on to others – especially if they are teachers.

Rogers's squeamishness about the role of the teacher is connected with his tendency to regard teaching as just instruction in a body of knowledge or code of behaviour. He does not appreciate that a more important aspect of teaching is the initiation of others into modes of thinking and experience that lie behind such bodies of knowledge and codes of behaviour. In teaching science, for instance, one does not just pass on facts and laws; nor does one seek simply to encourage the nebulous sort of adaptability, or learning how to learn, that Rogers advocates. One attempt to get others on the inside of a public form of thinking in which assumptions are challenged and techniques mastered for deciding who is right. Specific types of concepts and truth criteria have to be understood. Above all the passion for truth must be conveyed that gives point to the search for evidence, the abhorrence of irrelevance, incoherence and arbitrariness, and the love of clarity and precision. Similarly moral education is not just a matter of imposing rules such as those prohibiting stealing and the breaking of promises; it is also a matter of sensitising persons to principles such as respect for others, truthfulness, fairness, freedom and the consideration of interests, which are presuppositions of moral experience. Rogers's valuations are intimately connected with this form of experience. It is one that has taken the human race thousands of years to develop and that is constantly threatened by powerful and more primitive tendencies within human nature. It is institutionalised in democratic institutions at their best, and will be perpetuated only if it also is fostered in the consciousness of countless individuals.

Rogers does no service to the tradition that he had inherited by suggesting that his values are private possessions that develop miraculously within the individual soul. And he does a positive dis-service by minimising the role of the teacher as one of the main trans-mitters of these public forms of life. Rogers contrasts the teacher, who imposes his values, with the facilitator of learning, who sets people free to discover their own. Both pictures are inadequate; for both ignore the public forms of experience underlying, e.g. scientific, moral and aesthetic achievements and discoveries. The teacher, ideally speaking, is a person whose experience and special training has given him some mastery of one or other of these modes of ex-perience. Rogers himself manifestly has achieved this in the particular mode of interpersonal understanding. His function, in the same way as that of any other teacher, is to initiate others into this form of experience so they can manage on their own. But, as with 'creative' artists or scientists, they cannot do so without being introduced in a whole variety of ways, with which good teachers are familiar, into the mode of experience in question. It is against this general background of the role of the teacher that Rogers's important insights about personal relationships are to be seen in proper perspective.

In Part III Rogers outlines some assumptions about learning and its facilitation and discusses graduate education in the light of them. Generalisations are put forward about the importance of relevance to the learner's purposes, about learning through doing and participa-tion, and about the relationship of threats to the self to learning. Much of this discussion is very apposite; but there is nothing very novel in it. What is missing, however, is any sense of the great differences between the sorts of things that have to be learnt – skills, attitudes, principles, facts, etc., within different modes of experience. Some generalisations such as those of Rogers can be made about general conditions of learning. But equally crucial for education are the specific features of different types of learning that derive from differences in what is being learnt – these differences affect very much the role of the 'facilitator'.

Part IV includes a personal confession of what is most significant to Rogers in 'being in relationship', some thoughts about the 'valuing process', a chapter on Freedom and Commitment in which he out-lines his views on free will in contrast to those of Skinner, and an account of the goal of the 'fully functioning person'. There is no mention of any of the recent work done on moral development and Rogers's handling of the issues in ethics that he raises is so superficial, limited and confined to his own frame of reference that it would be difficult to know quite where to begin in discussing them. The book ends with a model for revolution in which Rogers recommends T groups, etc., for educational administrators, teachers and faculty members. This is mildly reminiscent of Plato's suggestion that society can be saved only if philosophers become kings or kings become philosophers. But Plato did know something about politics and institutional change.

REFERENCES

Oakeshott, M., 'Learning and Teaching', in Peters, R. S. (Ed.), *The Concept of Education* (London: Routledge & Kegan Paul, 1967).
Perry, L. R., 'What is an Educational Situation?', in Archambault, R. D. (Ed.), *Philosophical Analysis and Education* (London: Routledge & Kegan Paul, 1965).
Peters, R. S., 'Teaching and Personal Relationships', in French, E. L. (Ed.), *Melbourne Studies in Education* (Melbourne: Melbourne University Press, 1970).
Hirst, P. H. and Peters, R. S., *The Logic of Education* (London: Routledge & Kegan Paul, 1970), Ch. VI.

A LETTER FROM DR ROGERS

Dear Dr Effrat:

It was very gracious of you to send me, in advance of publication, the review of my book *Freedom to Learn*, by R. S. Peters.

The main theme of the review comes through loud and clear. Professor Peters regards me as being basically an educational ignoramus: uninformed in philosophy of education; in the rationale of teaching and instruction; in the place of historical content in education; in ethics and morality. He seems particularly distressed by the fact that I speak from my own experiences as a facilitator of learning and a therapist, rather than drawing on the writings of others.

Professor Peters has a perfect right to his own perception of and opinions about the book. Your readers, however, might wish to know that there are also other evaluations that have been made of it. I have permission of the author and editor to quote three brief paragraphs from a review written by Professor Samuel Tenenbaum, an educator and a long-time friend and biographer of William H. Kilpatrick. He is thus obviously knowledgeable in some of the fields in which Professor Peters regards me as ignorant. His review was published in *Educational Leadership* in October 1969.

'*Freedom to Learn*, by Carl R. Rogers, is not really a textbook in the conventional sense. It is a human document. It is a statement, in many instances impassioned, in which Carl Rogers communicates his deepest feelings, convictions and insights that have come to him after a lifetime of living, thinking and working in his discipline. Seldom does a book on education appear that so excites the imagination as to what is possible in education, so liberates the reader from viewing education in conventional ways. . . .

'. . . Dr Rogers sees the teacher as one who can release students as well as himself for growth. He, the teacher, also becomes a learner, eagerly seeking, as do his students, new meanings and insights. For Carl Rogers, education is not a mass of facts presented on examination papers, but a becoming process whose goal is ever richer and more meaningful living. In achieving these ends, the teacher is anything but an authoritarian figure, the processor of truth and wisdom, there to transmit it to students ignorant of this truth and wisdom. Each student in a good educational arrangement is given freedom to find his own truth and wisdom; and the adventure and the excitement lie in *not knowing*, in teacher and student finding out together. . . .

'. . . In *Freedom to Learn*, one gains not only a philosophy and methodology of what is good education but also what is the life good to live.'

What can one make of such sharply divergent opinions as those of Professor Peters and Professor Tenenbaum? Personally, I am reminded of the similarly polarised opinions that greeted my first books on psychotherapy. I gradually realised that when vital issues are raised in a professional field, violently opposing views are stirred up. I can only hope that this is the reason *Freedom to Learn* is controversial, and it is my wish that educators will read the book and form their own opinions.

Sincerely,
Carl R. Rogers

Part Two

ETHICAL DEVELOPMENT

11

FREUD'S THEORY OF MORAL
DEVELOPMENT IN RELATION TO
THAT OF PIAGET

INTRODUCTION

In dealing with the vast field of the psychology of morals, Kant's aphorism is particularly apposite: that percepts without concepts are blind and that concepts without percepts are empty. On the one hand there has been a great deal of investigation by psychologists, such as the Hartshorne and May *Character Investigation Inquiry*[1] without adequate conceptual distinctions being made; on the other hand moral philosophers have developed many conceptual schemes which seldom get much concrete filling from empirical facts. The aim of this paper is to explore how psychological theories of moral development might be unified and seen in relation to each other by making certain conceptual distinctions. Such distinctions are necessary for getting clearer about what the theories in fact explain, and for rendering the percepts less blind. I propose to attempt this by setting out Piaget's theory very briefly and by dealing with Freud's theory in relation to it.

1 PIAGET'S CONTRIBUTION

(a) *Exposition*
Perhaps Piaget's most important contribution was to make explicitly a distinction which people who speak of the psychology of morals are too prone to forget. This is the distinction between what might be called conventional morality and the following of a rational moral code. By 'conventional morality' I mean just doing the done thing, or doing what one is told. If a justification for following a particular rule is asked for, the individual appeals to an authority or to what

others do or say is right. Usually, however, the question of the validity of such a code does not arise, as in a closed, tight-knit, society, where norms tend to be undifferentiated. By a 'rational moral code' I mean one for which the individual sees that there are reasons, which he sees could be otherwise than it is, which he follows more reflectively.

Now Kant, of course, made this sort of distinction when he contrasted the autonomy with the heteronomy of the will; and Piaget, both in his moral theory and in his theory of knowledge, has a Kantian point of view. What he did was to pour into the mould of this conceptual distinction a rich filling taken from observation of children at different ages. He showed that the distinction actually has application.

Piaget studied the attitude of children to the rules of both marbles and morality and found a correlation between them.[2] At the 'transcendental stage' the rule appears as something external and unalterable, often sacred. At the autonomous stage it is seen to be alterable, a convention maintained out of mutual respect which can be altered if the co-operation of others is obtained. Constraint is replaced by reciprocity and co-operation. A lie is no longer just something 'naughty' which adults disapprove of, a prohibition which goes very much against the egocentric wishes of the child, a command stuck on to a mental structure of a very different order from that of the adult, whose letter has to be adhered to, but whose intention is incomprehensible. It now becomes an action which destroys mutual trust and affection; truth-telling becomes a rule which the child accepts as his own because of the reasons which can be given for it. To summarise the main features of Piaget's contributions:

(i)   Piaget insists that there *is* something of the sort which Kant described as morality proper, distinct from custom and authoritative regulation.
(ii) Piaget assumes, so it seems, some process of maturation. There is a gradual transition from one mental structure to another.
(iii) He assumes that this development in the child's attitude to rules is parallelled by his cognitive development in other spheres – e.g. the grasp of logical relations, and of causal connections.

(b) *Comments*
Piaget can be criticised both for what he did do and for what he did not do. Amongst the former type of criticism should be included those of J. F. Morris[3] and D. MacRae[4] who have maintained that many different sorts of things are included under the concept of

'autonomy' which are not only distinct but which also have not all a high mutual correlation. And, of course, much in general could and has been said about Piaget's methods of investigation.

More interesting, however, are criticisms of what Piaget did not do. For instance, he could have investigated whether the transition through the different stages of morality *is* just a matter of maturation, or whether it depends on specific social or family or educational traditions. In a lecture which he delivered to UNESCO in 1947[5] he assumes both that value judgements become more equitable with age and that the development depends on general features of the culture. But he makes no attempt to establish this in any detail. E. Lerner[6] has investigated this question and finds a correlation between the sort of development which Piaget outlined and the social status of the parents and the extent to which coercive techniques of child-rearing were employed.

Havighurst and Taba[7] also studied the moral attitudes of adolescents in a mid-West town and of children in six American Indian tribes and tried to relate them to methods of training, cultural factors, etc.

Such studies are suggestive but very inconclusive. From them three very general observations could be made about Piaget's work.

(a) Piaget's distinctions provide a useful framework for research. The details, however, of this descriptive apparatus need clarifying and tightening up – e.g. his concept of the autonomous stage.

(b) Given that some such transition sometimes occurs, much more needs to be established about the conditions which favour or retard it. These would include a variety of social factors, but of particular importance would be the techniques for passing on the rules of a society. As far as I know, Piaget says nothing about the ways in which parents and teachers help or hinder children in the transition to the autonomous stage.

(c) Piaget says nothing of the extent to which the relics of the 'transcendental stage' persist in the adult mind, and the conditions which occasion a complete or partial failure of the transition to autonomy in a society where such a development is common, and encouraged.

As Freud, so it seems to me, said a great deal in an indirect way about such matters, it is appropriate to pass to his contribution.

2 FREUD'S CONTRIBUTION

Piaget, I have stressed, explicitly made the distinction between conventional morality and following a rational code. In Freud this distinction is only implicit and the features of a rational code are not explicitly sketched.

Philip Rieff, in his recent book,[8] makes much of what he calls Freud's ethic of honesty and of his uncompromising egoism. He suggests that Freud believed in the generalisation of the frankness that is a necessary procedural requirement for psycho-analysis. A man must admit his nature, be quick to detect dishonesty and sham in himself and in others. He must accept his natural needs and have a deep suspicion of 'moral aspirations' such as Freud so often encountered in dealing with middle-class women at the turn of the century. Freud's 'education to reality' and 'the primacy of the intelligence', which he explicitly advocated, go no further than what should be called prudence, rather than morality proper as Piaget understood it. For Freud, on Rieff's view, heralded the advent of psychological man, the trained egoist.

Rieff's account of Freud the moralist, is interesting not only in stressing the cool rationality of Freud's own moral outlook but also in giving a certain interpretation of it. This interpretation is highly disputable. For, although Freud described the principle of impartiality or justice as a cloak for envy,[9] he actually said of himself: 'I believe that in a sense of justice and consideration for others, in disliking making others suffer or taking advantage of them I can measure myself with the best people I know.'[10] This looks very much like the confession of a rational Utilitarian code such as one could find in Sidgwick – or, indeed, in Piaget. It does not sound like the confession of a man who believed only in prudence or rational egoism.

It is therefore difficult to say whether Freud himself subscribed to a rational moral code such as that sketched by Piaget, or only to the cautious prudence attributed to him by Rieff. But, from the point of view of this article, it does not matter. For what I want to begin by stressing is that Freud assumed *some* form of *rational* code, both in his dealings with others generally and in his therapeutic practice. For the aim of psycho-analysis is to strengthen the ego by making unconscious conflicts conscious and by helping people to make decisions of principle with full cognisance of the irrational sources of their promptings and precepts. It is only his basic assumptions both about the distinction between rational behaviour and being at the mercy of the super-ego, and about the *desirability* of rational behaviour, that make his talk of 'education to reality' intelligible and his therapeutic practice square with his theory about morals.

As a matter of fact, the distinctions which he made between the ego, super-ego and id, were ways of making the distinction between behaving rationally and behaving in other ways. He equated the ego with reason and sanity; he says it 'tests correspondence with reality', 'secures postponement of motor discharge', and 'defends itself against the super-ego.' When we ignore the pictorial model which Freud's concepts suggest, we see that their main function is to distinguish between acting rationally when we take account of facts, plan means to ends, and impose rules of prudence on our conduct, in contrast to being at the mercy of the id, when we act impulsively or are driven to act, or being at the mercy of the super-ego when we are obsessed or goaded by the irrational promptings of past authorities.[11]

If we bear in mind this basic conceptual framework we can see, roughly speaking, that Freud's contribution to moral psychology falls under three main headings.

(i) In the theory of the id and the unconscious we find a description of typical occasions when we are deflected from conscious aims, when we cook up rationalisations as a cloak for following our inclinations, when we act unaccountably 'out of character', and when we seem to suffer from a general inability to decide between different possible courses of action, to control our impulses, or to carry out intentions however well-meaning. Such investigations throw great light on what might be called the *executive* side of moral action. I do not intend to say anything more about this side of Freud's work, in spite of its intrinsic interest. I propose to concentrate on the extent to which Freud deals with defects on what might be called the legislative or judicial aspects of morals. This implies something amiss with the sorts of rules which we apply to given cases or with the inability to see when rules fit particular cases. Such defects are to be found.

(ii) In Freud's theory of the super-ego.

(iii) In Freud's theory of character-traits.

These I now propose to discuss.

The Super-ego   The first and obvious point to make about Freud's theory of the super-ego is the extent to which his account of the formation of conscience corroborates Piaget's findings about the child's attitude to rules at the transcendental stage. Freud, it might be argued, went further and showed the mechanisms such as introjection, identification and reaction-formation, by means of which these externally imposed sacrosanct commands come to be interiorised by the child and the standards adopted of that parent with whom identification takes place. This would explain the perfectly familiar procedure of standards being passed on from generation to generation by contact with the earliest admired figures who exert some kind of discipline and provide a model for the child to emulate. Freud, it might be commented, stressed the 'inner voice' aspect of conscience because he took for granted a way of passing on rules which, as has often been pointed out, was prevalent in a patriarchal society where the father exerted discipline in an authoritarian manner, with a lot of *voice*, and where he was taken as the exemplar of conduct. Freud's theory looked after both the negative notion of taking the voice of prohibition into ourselves and the more positive modelling of our conduct on that of some loved and admired figure.

But a closer look at Freud's theory of the super-ego does not altogether confirm this rather obvious interpretation. Even in the matter of the authoritative voice, Freud showed very little interest in the empirical question of how rules were, in fact, passed on, in whether they were in fact taught with a lot of voice. Indeed, he seemed to take the social environment and educational techniques as more or less constant. He was mainly interested in the mind of the child, in the mechanisms of defence – introjection and reaction-formation – by means of which the child either took the parent into himself, in the form of the ego-ideal, as a safeguard against losing a loved object, or took over the parent's reactions to his sexual wishes as a way of dealing with the danger which they represented. He did not simply use his theory to explain how the traditions of a society are handed on by being taken into the child. For most of his theory was used to explain phenomena which were both different from this and different from each other.[12]

On the one hand, he was interested in the fact that some children develop *more rigorous* standards than those demanded by their parents; on the other hand, he tried to explain the familiar feature of types like the arrogant or humble man who have a picture of themselves, an ego-ideal – what Adler called a 'guiding fiction' – which is quite out of keeping with the traits which they, in fact, exhibit. These phenomena, too, he explained in terms of mechanisms which the child employs to deal with wishes in a social environment which is viewed as being more or less constant. The over-conscientious child is one who has turned his aggression inwards; the ego-ideal is the product of narcissism or outgoing love turned inwards. The obsessional and the melancholic exhibit extreme forms of this type of character. In other words, Freud was here concerned with people who had an exaggerated or distorted style of rule-following. This style of rule-following prevents the development towards a more rational way of following rules such as was sketched by Piaget in his account of the autonomous stage.

In his account of the super-ego, therefore, Freud's theory is an important supplement to that of Piaget. For Freud tries to explain why it is that people, as it were, get stuck at the transcendental stage. Some get stuck as a person might who conforms in a colourless way to the standards that are passed on; others exaggerate or distort the standards in question and are incapacitated for rational rule-following later. Of course, in all of us there is left what Freud called a 'precipitate' of parental prohibitions. Following rules in a rational manner can only be viewed as the end-point of a continuum. My point is that Freud assumed some such end-point and gave special explanations for people who got stuck in strange ways a long way down this continuum.

Freud as a Characterologist   Freud's theory of character-traits, too, supports this sort of interpretation. For here again he developed a genetic theory to explain why it is that another defective style of rule-following which impedes the development of ego strength gets laid down in infancy. The picture of the ego wedged between insistent wishes on the one hand and parental prohibitions on the other is again the conceptual framework for the theory. There are, he held, three main periods at which conflicts are likely to occur, the oral, the anal and the genital stages. The techniques or mechanisms employed by the child to regulate his dangerous wishes develop into traits of character. Freud suggested[13] that cleanliness and orderliness were reaction-formations against wishes for organ pleasure; interest in money was a sublimation, money being a substitute object; and obstinacy was a continuation of reaction to parental pressures. Similarly sarcasm, scepticism and food faddism were regarded as oral traits.

I have often been puzzled about what Freud thought he was explaining in this theory. Was he explaining the development of what we call character? Have the carefulness of the calculating determined business man, which is in accordance with the logic of the situation, and the hoarding of the miser, which is not, a similar explanation, the difference being only one of degree? His theory was that anal character-traits are produced by fixation at this stage of sexuality. Did he assume that those who are not fixated but who pass through this stage in accordance with some assumed norm of development, go forward with a minor imprint of orderliness or obstinacy stamped upon them?

In order to get clear about what Freud's theory explained it is first necessary to make some distinctions. By 'character' we can mean, first of all, the sum total of a person's traits like honesty, considerateness, punctuality and so on. We speak of giving a servant a 'character' in this sense. Presumably, too, the famous *Character Education Enquiry* of Harsthorne and May was concerned with the investigation of character in this non-committal sense. For little more was investigated than the incidence of traits like honesty, deceit and so on.

When characterologists, on the other hand, talk of types of character, they usually mean more than just the sum total of traits. They see a certain arrangement of traits which are usually subordinated to one, as in the case of the penurious man. Alternatively, a whole range of traits might be displayed in a distorted or exaggerated manner, as in a pedantic person.

But we can speak of people 'having character' in a third sense, when we speak of a type of consistency which is imposed on other traits by adherence to higher-order principles such as those of prudence or justice. Roback, in his classic on the psychology of character[14] spoke of character in this third sense. So also did McDougall, in what he said about the function of the self-regarding sentiment. Freud's concept of the strong ego is very similar.

Now Freud's theory of character-traits is obviously to be seen in the context of characterology. Indeed, Ernest Jones speaks of his *Character and Anal Erotism* as a contribution to this sort of speculation and notes its literary style.[15] He was surely explaining men who had types of character, men in whom certain traits were so dominant that they provided a unifying pattern. And this, of course, explains the connection between certain types of character and neurosis. Obsessionals, he claimed, manifest exaggerations of anal traits, just as schizophrenics do of oral traits. Freud, I suggest, was perfectly familiar with the penurious character who crops up over and over again in characterology. His genius consisted in spotting the similarity between this pattern of traits and a type of neurosis and assigning a common cause to both. He was put on to this by the findings of his *Three Essays in the Theory of Sexuality* which just preceded his paper on character-traits.

This type of explanation would account not only for obvious types of character, but also, to a certain extent, for the business man who always tends to be a bit more cautious or more optimistic than the facts warrant. There are standards governing decisions like those of the judge, the business man and the examiner. The usual assumption is that people learn these standards on some kind of apprenticeship basis; they gradually manage to master the know-how necessary for making rational judgements about such matters. We do not have to tell the Freudian story, surely, about all cases of caution in business, of rigour in marking or severity and leniency of sentence. But when we note a characteristic bias one way or the other, when there is a consistent deviation in one sort of dimension, it then begins to look as if the Freudian type of explanation is relevant.

Of course, it might well be asked what the evidence is for Freud's speculations anyway. That is another matter, with which I am not here concerned. For it surely presupposes the prior question as to what the theory was meant to explain. I have tried to show that it is to be seen as explaining only types of character, not people who *have* character. Freud's concept of the strong ego would cover what is usually meant by 'having character' together with hints thrown out by people like Abraham about the 'genital character' which describes roughly what I have previously referred to as the end-product of Freud's assumed continuum.[16] Such a person would be one who has not become fixated at any of the previous stages and who has passed through in a relatively smooth way to a more rational way of following rules in accordance with higher-order principles like those of prudence, impartiality and consideration for others which I mentioned previously as characterising Freud's implicit assumptions about a rational moral code.

3 FREUD'S OMISSIONS

Part of Freud's moral psychology, then, can be considered a supplement to that of Piaget in that, both in his theory of the super-ego and of character traits, he gives special explanations of why people do *not* attain the rational level of rule-following. I have argued that in his implicit assumptions about morality and in his concept of the ego he assumes a norm of development towards what might be called 'having character' in an autonomous way – regulating behaviour intelligently, consistently, with integrity and without self-deception in accordance with principles of prudence, impartiality, respect for others and so on. In his special theories he explains how it is that people fail to mature in this way because they get fixated at some earlier period and develop a type of character or because they come to adopt rules in an exaggerated or distorted way at the period of super-ego formation – Piaget's transcendental stage.

But as far as I know there is no positive theory in Freud of the conditions under which this desirable development towards rationality tends to take place. There are, of course, suggestions about very general necessary conditions – e.g. a proper love relationship in early life with a mother-figure, as stressed much later by Bowlby.[17] To be deprived of this is likely to lead to distractability, unreliability, and lack of self-inhibition which are almost definitions of having *no* character, both in the sense of colourless conformity with standards and of autonomous self-direction. But there is no positive theory about *techniques* of child-rearing and the passing on of rules which tend to favour rational development, which Freud treats almost as a maturation norm.

Are there, for instance, certain techniques of child-rearing which tend to create 'fixation'? On Freudian theory 'fixation' is usually regarded as being the product of too much or too little organ pleasure at the early stages. And there are, of course, many cross-cultural studies of weaning and toilet training.[18] But what is the evidence about techniques for the passing on of rules at the later stages covered by Freud's theory of the super-ego and Piaget's theory of the transcendental stage? Plenty is known about methods of child-rearing in the tribes studied by anthropologists; but there is very little established knowledge about what goes on in the various strata of European society. A start has been made along these lines in America[19] and A. N. Oppenheim is at the moment engaged on an ambitious project to remedy just this defect in our empirical knowledge about our own society.

It is pretty pointless to try to rectify our ignorance on such matters by appealing to conditioning theory and to far-fetched analogies between the behaviour of animals and men. For there are many quite different ways of passing on rules to children of which conditioning is only one. So conceptual confusion is only increased if these different ways of passing on rules are not distinguished as a preliminary to investigating what the result is of using different techniques at different ages. The type of instrumental conditioning used on animals, for instance, must be distinguished from that form of training in which rewards and punishments are promised and threatened and not just administered. This, in its turn, must be distinguished from the use of authority which presupposes the use of the voice, but, in giving commands rather than in promising and warning. Then there is imitation, suggestion and learning 'by experience' as well as rational instruction. Given such initial distinctions questions like this could be asked: to what extent do various techniques for passing on rules, when used at early ages where rational explanation and instruction are out of the question, incapacitate the child for rational instruction at later ages? If Piaget is right in saying that there is a correlation between a child's attitude to the rules of marbles and to moral rules as he develops, can any generalisations be made about ways of learning rules which, in general, help or hinder the development towards the more rational stage?[20] Luria, when he recently visited England, reported experiments which he was doing on the use of different techniques for passing on manipulative skills at different ages. He has been studying the use of the authoritative voice, the use of instruction with an explanation, and so on, in these very limited contexts. Could anything be done to supplement Freud's and Piaget's work along these lines? Do some techniques – e.g. conditioning – lead to break-downs, blocks and compulsive habits at later stages? Do they encourage types of character rather than help to develop character? And what sort of training leads to the colourless conformity of the man who never really emerges from Piaget's transcendental stage?

4   DEVELOPMENT OF FREUD'S THEORY

These omissions in Freud's theory are connected with a more general weakness – the lack of any detailed theory of the development of the ego, of rationality in general of which morality is a particular case. In the main those who have followed him, like Melanie Klein,[21] have revised some of the details of his theory about the development of the super-ego – for instance, the age at which it is formed. Others like Horney[22] and Fromm[23] have criticised his theory on the grounds that it is too biologistic and takes too little account of social differences, or that it treats infantile sexuality and the mechanisms adopted to deal with it as determinants of, rather than occasions for, the development of more general orientations.

There are, however, two other lines of development which are particularly relevant to the thesis of this article. There is, first, Money-Kyrle,[24] who claims that Freud's treatment of moral psychology is one-sided because he dealt only with the authoritarian conscience. There is also the humanistic conscience which is traceable back to the 'guilt' experienced in hurting and hating the mother, the first object of a child's love. If the child learns this first lesson, that the good and the bad are often different aspects of the same object, and if he fears lest what is good may be injured by his own efforts or omissions, he has the beginning of a conscience which is more rational and realistic. Whatever is to be made of Money-Kyrle's genetic speculations, which owe much to Melanie Klein, his theory is interesting in that he sees the connection between rationality and what he calls the 'humanistic' conscience and in that he tries to connect different types of 'conscience' – e.g. that of the obsessional, the hypomanic and the hypoparanoid, with different types of falling off from rationality.

There is, however, a second and even more relevant line of Freudian thought represented by Erikson,[25] Hartmann[26] and Rapaport,[27] who have developed the theory of the autonomous ego which was rather embryonic in Freud's writings. Erikson has tried, in very general terms, to map the development of the autonomous ego and to make generalisations about conditions which favour or hinder it. Rapaport has tried to sketch a conceptual model which does justice to the autonomous ego, to show the conditions necessary for the development of autonomy, and to connect his theory with other findings, such as those about stimulus deprivation, hypnosis, 'brainwashing' and Piaget's views on the origins of intelligence in children. This line of development is still exploratory. But a conceptual scheme based on it might help to unify the theories of Piaget and Freud in general as well as in the moral field.[28] It might, for instance, help to clarify Piaget's conception of the autonomous stage. It might also help to connect their investigations with others in the field, and cast some light on what particular investigations in it actually explain; for in this ill-explored field of moral development what is needed more than in almost any other field in psychology is a combination of concrete investigations with conceptual clarity. And this is the point from which my paper started.

REFERENCES

1. Hartshorne, H. and May, M. A., *Studies in the Nature of Character* (3 vols) (New York: Macmillan, 1930).
2. Piaget, J., *The Moral Judgment of the Child* (London: Kegan Paul, 1932).
3. Morris, J. F., 'The Development of Adolescent Value-judgments', *Brit. J. Educ. Phychol.*, Vol. 28 (1958).
4. MacRae, D., *The Development of Moral Judgment in Children*, Ph.D. Thesis (Harvard University, 1950).
5. Piaget, J., *The Moral Development of the Adolescent in Two Types of Society, 'Primitive and Modern'* (UNESCO, 1947) (quoted by J. F. Morris, op. cit.).
6. Lerner, E., *Constraint Areas and Moral Judgment of Children* (Menasha, Wisconsin, 1937).
7. Havighurst, R. and Taba, H., *Adolescent Character and Personality* (New York: Wiley, 1949).
8. Rieff, P., *Freud, the Mind of the Moralist* (New York: Viking Press, 1959), Chs IX, X.
9. Freud, S., *Group Psychology and the Analysis of the Ego* (London: Hogarth Press, 1949), pp. 86–8.

10. Jones, E., *Sigmund Freud, Life and Work* (London: Hogarth Press, 1955), Vol. II, p. 464.
11. For further development, see Peters, R. S., *The Concept of Motivation* (London: Kegan Paul, 1958), Ch. III.
12. For classic exposition of the theory of the super-ego and ego-ideal, see Flugel, J. C., *Man, Morals and Society* (London: Duckworth, 1945), Chs II-VI.
13. Freud, S., 'Character and Anal Erotism', in *Collected Papers* (London: Hogarth Press, 1942), Vol. II.
14. Roback, A. A., *The Psychology of Character* (London: Kegan Paul, 1928), Ch. XXV.
15. Jones, op. cit., p. 331.
16. Abraham, K., *Selected Papers on Psycho-Analysis* (London: Hogarth Press, 1949), Chs XXII–XXV.
17. Bowlby, J., *Child Care and the Growth of Love* (London: Penguin Books, 1953).
18. See, for instance, Whiting, J. W. M. and Child, I. L., *Child Training and Personality* (New Haven: Yale University Press, 1953); and A. Kardiner's various works.
19. Sears, R., Macoby, E. and Levin, H., *Patterns of Child-Rearing* (New York: Row, Peterson, 1957).
20. Similar issues are raised and discussed in Harding, D. W., *Social Psychology and Individual Values* (London: Hutchinson, 1953).
21. Klein, M., 'Early Development of Conscience in the Child', in *Contributions to Psychoanalysis* (London: Hogarth Press, 1948).
22. Horney, K., *New Ways in Psycho-analysis* (London: Kegan Paul, 1949).
23. Fromm, E., *Man for Himself* (London: Kegan Paul, 1948).
24. Money-Kyrle, R., *Psycho-analysis and Politics* (London: Duckworth, 1951).
25. Erikson, F., *Childhood and Society* (New York: Norton, 1950).
26. Hartmann, H., *Ego-Psychology and the Problem of Adaptation* (London: Imago, 1958).
27. Rapaport, D., 'The theory of Ego-autonomy: a Generalisation', *Bull. Menninger Clinic*, Vol. 22 (1958), pp. 13–35.
28. Rapaport, D., 'The Conceptual Model of Psycho-analysis', *J. Personality*, Vol. 20 (1951). See also Rapaport's, 'The Psychoanalytic Theory of Motivation', in the 1961 *Nebraska Symposium on Motivation*.

12

MORAL EDUCATION AND THE PSYCHOLOGY OF CHARACTER[1]

1 REVIVAL OF INTEREST IN 'CHARACTER'

It would be interesting to speculate why particular lines of enquiry flourish and fade. The study of 'character' is a case in point. In the 1920s and early 1930s the study of 'character' was quite a flourishing branch of psychology. It then came to an abrupt halt and, until recent times, there has been almost nothing in the literature on the subject. Perhaps it was the notorious Hartshorne and May 'Character Education Enquiry',[2] and the inferences that were mistakenly drawn from it, that killed it; perhaps it was the preoccupation with something more general and amorphous called 'personality'; perhaps it was the mixture of metaphysics and methodological neurosis centred around the rat. Who knows? Anyway, the study of character is very much with us again as is revealed not merely by Riesman's *Lonely Crowd*[3] but also by the recent study by Peck and Havighurst called *The Psychology of Character Development*.[4] The *British Journal of Educational Psychology* has also, for some time, been running a symposium on 'The Development of Moral Values in Children'.

Philosophers, too, are beginning to emerge cautiously from the central areas where their recent 'revolution' has been concentrated, and have begun to look with chastened souls and sharpened tools at more peripheral problems with which, traditionally, philosophers have been concerned – problems in aesthetics, political philosophy, and in the philosophy of education.[5] They have even begun to think again about moral education. In this field, ever since Aristotle, the training of character has always featured as a corrective to pre-occupation with the cultivation of the intellect and with vocational training. A re-examination of the concept of 'character' should therefore permit a fruitful cross-fertilisation between some modern developments in psychology and philosophy, which might be of interest to educators.

2 CHARACTER AND CHARACTER-TRAITS

It is no accident that the concept of 'character' is appropriately used in contexts of individual adaptation; for etymologically the word 'character', like the word 'trait', which is often associated with it, is connected with making a distinguishing mark. 'Character' comes from the field of engraving; hence we talk naturally of the delineation of character. 'Trait' comes from the cognate field of drawing. In their figurative sense, when applied to human beings, they are both used to bring out what is *distinctive* about people.

It seems to me, too, that there is another important similarity between the term 'character' and the term 'trait' which often leads to hyphenation. Their significance is primarily adverbial. They usually indicate a *manner* or *style* of behaving without any definite implication of directedness or aversion – unlike the terms 'motive', 'attitude', and 'sentiment'. 'Trait', however, covers countless manners of behaving. Allport claims that 18,000 words in the English language are trait names.[6] Traits of character are obviously a selection from these – for example traits like selfishness, honesty, punctuality, considerateness and meanness. Such terms, like all trait terms, are primarily adverbial in significance. They do not, like greed or sexual desire, indicate the sort of goals that a man tends to pursue, but the manner in which he pursues them. A man who is ruthless, selfish, honest, punctual, considerate, does not necessarily have any particular goals; rather he behaves in a certain manner, according to or not according to certain rules. And, I suppose, the connection with regulation is fundamental for bringing out what distinguishes character-traits from other sorts of traits – for instance those which we describe as a matter of temperament. Character-traits are shown in the sort of things a man can *decide* to be, where it may be a matter of forcing himself to do something in the face of social pressures or persistent temptations. In this way a man's character is contrasted with his nature. A man just is stupid or lacking in vitality; he cannot decide to be either of these. But he can decide to be more or less honest or selfish.[7] His inclinations and desires, which are part of his 'nature', may suggest goals; but such inclinations and desires only enter into what we call a man's 'character' in so far as he chooses to satisfy them in a certain manner, in accordance with rules of efficiency like persistently, carefully, doggedly, painstakingly, or in accordance with rules of social appropriateness like honestly, fairly, considerately and ruthlessly. Greed is not a character-trait if it means just an appetite for money or food; but it becomes a character-trait as soon as it carries the suggestion that this appetite is exercised ruthlessly or selfishly at someone else's expense, in other words in a certain manner. A craving for a beef-steak, a lust for a pretty girl reveal a man's nature, not his character. His character is revealed in what he does about them, in the manner in which he regulates, or fails to regulate them.

The point is often made that talk of character occurs in contexts of praise and blame. Indeed psychologists since McDougall have perhaps shied off character because of it. To quote Allport: 'Character enters the situation only when this personal effort is judged from the standpoint of some code'.[8] But my guess is that the fundamental connection is between character and some sort of personal effort. The judgement from the point of view of a code comes in because it is largely for his efforts and decisions that a man is praised or blamed rather than for his desires and inclinations. Nowell-Smith, too, stresses the connection between character and praise and blame when he says: 'Pleasure and pain, reward and punishment, are the rudders by means of which moral character is moulded; and "moral character" is just that set of dispositions that can be moulded by these means'.[9] Stupidity and vitality cannot be moulded by this sort of regulation; so we usually do not regard them as traits of character. But this is surely a mistake; for Nowell-Smith's statement that moral 'character *is just* that set of dispositions that can be moulded by these means' suggests that the connection is a necessary one. But we can surely be completely hazy about the spheres in which praise and blame, reward and punishment, are in fact effective; and yet we can talk quite confidently about a person's character. Also there are many 'dispositions' which can be altered by praise and blame that might not be regarded as part of a man's 'character' – e.g. his wants and wishes. There may well be, of course, a close connection between what a person can decide to do or force himself to do by personal effort and what he can be made to do by praise and blame or by reward and punishment. But the connection is a contingent one.[10] And there may indeed be, via the notion of decision, a necessary connection between a person's character and those dispositions which can *in principle* be moulded by praise and blame; for moulding by praise and blame presupposes the decision of the moulded, in a way which something like brain surgery does not.

There is surely the point, too, that if any term is to be linked with social assessment Allport's favoured term 'personality' is an obvious candidate. Allport, of course, uses the term as an omnibus technical term to cover more or less everything that a man is; but such a generalised usage leaves rather high and dry the perfectly good use of the term in ordinary language which, like the term 'character', picks out certain distinctive features of a man. For a man's personality is very much the mask or appearance which he presents to others; a man 'with personality' or 'with a strong personality' is a man whose behaviour is assessed as impinging in certain ways on others. It has not the same suggestion of inner effort and decision as has 'character'. A man's personality flowers or develops; it is not built up by his decisions as is his character. The criteria of assessment are, of course, very different. But certainly to say of man that he has 'personality' is to praise him as much as to say that he has 'character'. But it is to praise him according to different criteria. What Allport means, surely, is that character is connected inseparably with the following of rules. But as one of the most important things to say about man is that he is a rule-following animal, the concept of 'character' should be one of the most indispensable terms in psychology.

This brief excursion into the comparison between the terms 'character' and 'personality' has shown that it is difficult enough to decide what in general we mean when we speak of a person's character as distinct from his nature, his temperament and his personality; but the matter is further complicated by the fact that there seem to be at least three ways in which we can talk of 'character'. We can speak (a) in a non-committal way of a man's character, we can speak of him (b) as having a type of character, and we can speak of him (c) as having character. These distinctions, so it seems to me, are important for discussing matters concerned with the psychology of character, so it will be necessary to elucidate them in more detail.

3   THREE WAYS OF SPEAKING OF 'CHARACTER'

(a) *The Non-committal Use*
I suppose the most common use of 'character' is when we use the term as a way of referring to the sum-total of a man's character-traits. An individual is brought up in an elaborate system of codes and conventions. To speak of his character is to speak of the particular selection of rules which he has, as it were, absorbed in regulating

his conduct both in relation to others and in pursuit of his more personal ends. If a servant is given a character – or was – her future employer is informed of the particular traits which she tends to exhibit, the part of the code which is, as it were, stamped upon her. And it was presumably with 'character' in this sense that the abortive Hartshorne and May enquiry was concerned.

(b) Types of Character

In the second way of speaking of 'character', some distinctive pattern of traits is indicated or some distinctive style in which the traits are exhibited. We speak of the anal character, for instance. Presumably this second way of speaking of a type of character is connected with characters in a play. Characters, in this sense, are depicted or delineated either with some dominant trait emphasised or with a typical exaggeration or distortion of a range of traits. Parsimony, for instance, not only is an exaggeration of the 'normal' trait of being careful with money; but in characters like L'Avare it becomes generalised over a whole range of behaviour. This is the sense of 'character' beloved of characterologists.[11] Usually a style of life is sketched which is related to some central trait. Alternatively a whole range of traits is exhibited in a consistently distorted or exaggerated manner. Some of Hardy's characters illustrate this other way in which one can have a type of character; they have a peculiarly obsessive style of following rules like men who are excessively punctual, polite and precise. Freud's theory of character-traits is largely an attempt to trace the genesis of character in this second sense.[12] However, not all 'types of character' present such a depressing picture. There is the 'genital character' of the Freudian school, whose behaviour shows consistency but of a different order. For he regulates his following of rules in accordance with principles of a higher order like those of prudence or respect for persons, and varies them intelligently, making distinctions and exceptions to match relevant differences in the situations in which he is acting. In the case of the penurious man, by contrast, there is no such intelligent adaptation. Similarly the other anal type of character, who has a characteristic exaggeration or distortion of a range of traits, behaves in a way which is irrelevant to changes in situations. The norm-ridden man, like the pedant or over-scrupulous man, always goes further in regulation than the situation warrants. There is, too, the further point that argument and persuasion seem to make little difference to the style in question. And if the rule-following is backed by justifications, they can usually be regarded only as rationalisations. For no counter-arguments or fresh evidence will bring about any change.

The distinctiveness and consistency of the rule-following of the autonomous or 'genital' type of character, on the other hand, is of quite a difficult sort. Such a man will not necessarily be careful with money on all occasions. Indeed he may well present an *appearance* of inconsistency to the observer. He may be frugal in entertaining his friends but more lavish in entertaining his family; he may not insist on tidiness at home but may insist on it in his office. But these variations in rule-following cannot be correlated either with the strength of his inclinations or with the strength of social pressures. He follows rules for which he sees some point and he modifies them to take account of relevant differences in situations; and the point to a large extent, is determined by his adherence to higher-order principles, e.g. that of the consideration of interests. And we usually have to see his behaviour from the inside, from his point of view, before we understand it. Roback, in his classic on *The Psychology of Character*, defines 'character' as 'An enduring psychophysical disposition to inhibit instinctive impulses in accordance with a regulative principle . . . the man of character in the full sense of the word exercises a distributed inhibitory power in keeping with a general principle which subsumes under its authority more specialised maxims'.[13] Inhibition', here, perhaps conveys too negative a suggestion. For 'character' can be shown in encouraging and shaping natural tendencies; it need not always be revealed in their inhibition.[14]

(c) *Having Character*

We come now to the third way of speaking of 'character' which is clearly different from having a type of character. For Kant had something else in mind when he said: 'Simply to say of a man "he has character" is not only to say a great deal of him, but to extol him; for that is a rare attribute which calls forth respect towards him and admiration.' And clearly this sense of character is quite distinct from my first non-committal sense; for a man might well exhibit traits like honesty and truthfulness; yet we might still say of him that he had no character. When Pope said that most women have no characters at all, he was not, surely, saying that they were dishonest, selfish and mendacious. Presumably he was suggesting that they were fickle, inconstant and sporadic in conforming to standards because they were so much at the mercy of their moods and inclinations. Or he might have been suggesting that they took their standards entirely from their husbands or from the clique in which they happened to collect. We speak of integrity of character. A man who has it is not credited with any definite traits; but the claim is made that, whatever traits he exhibits, there will be some sort of control and consistency in the manner in which he exhibits them. He will not give way to his inclinations, be easily corrupted, or take his colour from his company. Similarly we speak of strength and weakness of character which is a way of measuring the degree to which a person can be side-tracked, tempted, coerced, corrupted, or altered by ridicule. Character-traits, in the first and non-committal sense of character, could be merely the imprint of the social code on a man. Such a man, like the Spartans, could behave consistently in a particular social group; but when he went abroad he would fall an easy victim to the corrupting influence of potentates, priests and profligates. Or, like Rousseau, without the constraining influence of the General Will, he would be at the mercy of his vacillating inclinations. But a man who has character, in this third sense, would have developed his own distinctive style of rule-following. This would involve consistency and integrity. It is significant that typical descriptions of men of character dwell not so much on the rules which they follow, the particular traits of a substantive sort which they exhibit, but on the manner in which they follow or exhibit them. When we talk of a person's character a trait like honesty springs to mind; but when we speak of a man as having character, it is something like integrity, incorruptibility, or consistency. These descriptions relate to traits that are necessary conditions of 'having character', but they can apply to different 'types of character' and to a great variety of lower-order traits. They describe the style, not the content of a man's rule-following. And though, as Kant points out, to say that a man has character is to praise him, we can say that he has character but that he is bad. Robespierre and the robber-barons had character. Conversely we can often find something to praise even in a consummate villain if we can apply such 'style' descriptions to his behaviour. A Quaker lady was once told that she would find something good to say even about the Devil. To which she replied: 'Well, he is persistent'.

It is therefore very important for educators to get clearer about what they have in mind when they speak of 'the training of character'; for it is quite possible for different educators to stress this and to have quite different conceptions of an ideal man. They might all be agreed on the desirability of developing traits like consistency, integrity and persistence; yet they might disagree vehemently about which substantive traits were desirable as well as about the type of character that was to be encouraged. Quaker educators and supporters of the 'Outward Bound' movement all emphasise the training of character. But they subscribe to very different conceptions of an ideal man. It is therefore necessary to look more carefully into the relationship between types of character and the notion of 'having character'.

4 TYPES OF CHARACTER AND 'HAVING CHARACTER'

The analysis of 'having character' already sketched has defined this notion against two main species of 'the heteronomy of the will', to use Kantian language. It rules out, first of all, the man who is at the mercy of his passing inclinations, whose behaviour shows very little sign of being rule-governed. It rules out, secondly, the man whose behaviour is rule-governed, but whose rules are those of the company which he is keeping. Modern typologies of character pick out men such as these. Riesman's anomic, tradition-directed and other-directed types of character spring to mind. Peck and Havighurst speak of amoral and conforming types of character. The former is the psychopathic type who follows his whims and impulses, regulating them only sporadically. The latter is a man who has no generalised or thought-out principles about, for example, being honest. He is often found in stable folk societies and what are called 'shame cultures'. There is, however, an ambiguity about this type of character. For such a man could be one who has no settled principles of his own and who acts *in accordance* with a principle such as 'When in Rome live like the Romans'. Chameleon-like he would adapt himself to any company that he was keeping out of fear or need for approval. But he might also, as a matter of *policy*, act on a principle such as 'One ought always to follow those rules that others follow' or 'One ought always to follow the rules laid down by the Church, the leader or the local community group'. We would say of the former type of conformist that he had no character. But we might say of the latter that he very definitely had character. Presumably many Jesuits, army officers and organisation men fall into this latter category. They would really be 'inner-directed men' though their supreme principle would always enjoin them to do what someone else laid down.

Usually, however, men who have character exemplify other types of character distinguished both by Riesman and by Peck and Havighurst. Riesman speaks of the 'inner-directed' type of character. Such a man acts consistently on internalised rules. Typically he is a Puritan. His moral philosophy is that of Price's or Sir David Ross's 'intuitionism'. He does what his inner voice tells him that he should even though the heavens fall. He is not, overtly at any rate, swayed by his desires and inclinations; he is impervious to what others think of him and cannot be shamed into conformity. He feels *guilt* only about departing from his inner convictions about what is right. His policies are rigid and, if he is an extreme case of this type of character, he will be a compulsive or an obsessive. But he has character all right. Indeed Sargant in his recent book,[15] claimed that such people, together with detached cynics, were the most impervious to systematic brain-washing.

The irrational type of inner-directed character must be distinguished from the more rational type, often called, as by Riesman, the autonomous character. There is, in this type of character, a less rigid type of rule-following; for the rules are applied intelligently and often revised in the light of higher-order principles. If the supreme principle is one such as 'One ought always to further only one's own interests' the man will be what Peck and Havighurst call an expedient type of character. He will be Philip Rieff's interpretation of the Freudian ideal of 'the psychological man' of cautious prudence.[16] If, on the other hand; the supreme principle is 'One ought to consider interests impartially' he will be a Utilitarian, and if it is 'One ought to consider only the interests of others' he will be an altruist. Peck and Havighurst ignore the distinction between these latter two types in their conception of the rational-altruistic type of character. All three types of character are 'inner-directed' and can have character if their behaviour is consistently rule-governed and if they adapt their rules intelligently in the light of their supreme principles.

5   THE COMPLEX TASK OF MORAL EDUCATION

This analysis, though sketchy, should be sufficient to indicate how complex the business of moral education must be. To simplify the approach to it I propose to use a model, though I am well aware that this, like all such models, fails to fit the phenomena at certain places. Instead of conceiving society, as Plato did, as the individual 'writ large', I propose to conceive of the mind of the individual as a focus of social rules and functions in relation to them. A child, if we are to trust Freud, starts life with a strange amalgam of wishes and mental processes which can scarcely be called thoughts because they do not proceed in accordance with canons of logical or causal connectedness. Wishes become wants when social standards defining ends and efficient and socially appropriate ways of attaining them become imposed on this autistic amalgam. With the development of the 'ego' and 'super-ego' these unruly wishes are regulated, shaped and transformed by considerations of prudence and social appropriateness. The child's 'character' emerges as the particular style of rule-following which he develops. And there develop, too, further functions in relation to such rules.[17] There will be, in other words, not only rules which govern the behaviour of the individual but there will also be 'writ small' legislative, judicial and executive functions in relation to them. The following clusters of problems will therefore have to be considered by the educator.

(a) Which rule is it vital for the growing child to absorb? What character is he to have in the first and non-committal sense of 'character'? Next the educator will have to consider what *type* of character should be promoted. This will cover the question of (b) the legislative function, i.e. some procedural principles for modifying and revising rules as well as (c) the question of the judicial function. For the child could learn to apply rules in a rigid rule of thumb manner or could develop discrimination and judgement. Finally the educator will presumably want the child to develop 'character' in the third sense. This will present itself (d) as the problem of developing a stable executive function in the mind of the child.

To discuss moral education within this sort of framework it is necessary to indicate, to start with, the point of view with which one approaches the problem. My concern is for the development of an autonomous type of character who follows rules in a rational discriminating manner, and who also has character. To do this a man must subscribe to some higher-order principles which will enable him both to apply rules intelligently in the light of relevant differences in circumstances and to revise rules from time to time in the light of changes in circumstances and in empirical knowledge about the consequences of their application. The most important higher-order principles which, in my view, are capable of some sort of rational justification, are those of impartiality and the consideration of interests. For these are presupposed in any attempt to justify the rules of practical discourse.[18] These higher-order principles, though pretty formal in character, provide a very general criterion of relevance for justifying particular rules and for making exceptions in particular cases. The ideal is that the individual will develop as Kant put it 'as a law-making member of a kingdom of ends'. He must not only come to know what is in general right or wrong; he must also go beyond the level of what Plato called 'ὄρθη δόξα, so that he sees why such rules are right and wrong and can revise rules and make new ones in the light of new knowledge and new circumstances. To do this he must both be introduced to the basic rules of his community and to the higher level principles which enable him to exercise a legislative function.

(a) *The Content of Basic Rules*

The criticism is often levelled against the advocacy of a rationally held moral code that it would lead to moral anarchy. But why should it? For if the higher-order criterion of the impartial consideration of interests affected by rules is applied it will be seen that there are some rules which are so important for anyone living in a society that they could be regarded almost as definitions of a society. For a society is a collection of individuals united by the acceptance of certain rules, and though many of them relate to 'my station and my duties' (e.g. what ought to be done *qua* husband or *qua* teacher) there are also (leaving aside the law) a number of more general rules binding on anyone who is deemed to be a member of the same society – e.g. rules about non-injury, veracity, the keeping of contracts, etc. I imagine that the Natural Law theorists were attempting to outline such a system of basic rules. It would be difficult to conceive of any social, economic, or geographical changes which would lead one to think that such basic rules should be abrogated, though, of course, exceptions could be made to them under special circumstances. Such basic rules are to be contrasted with others which clearly do depend upon particular circumstances. Obviously, for instance, the rule that one should be sparing in the use of water is defensible only in times of drought. The fact that it is diffcult to be sure to which category particular rules belong (e.g. about sexual relations) does not affect the general usefulness of the distinction. Presumably Hare had some such distinction in mind when he begged moral philosophers to address themselves to the question: 'How shall I bring up my children?'[19] The educator has therefore to make up his mind which *are* basic rules and he has to pass on these rules very firmly at any early age.

(b) *The Legislative Function*

Immediately, however, the believer in a rational code runs into another criticism. For it is argued that he is committed to introducing the child from the very start to the reasons for rules, to building in procedural rules which will enable the child to exercise a legislative function for himself. This might lead to endless and abortive arguments with children who treat this as an occasion for outwitting their parents. Now there is no doubt that 'progressive' parents do sometimes proceed in this way and are, not doubt, in danger of developing moral imbeciles as a result. But the believer in a rational code should surely proceed in a rational manner in passing it on to others, and there are at least three good reasons why he is not committed to such a disastrous policy.

In the first place there is an obvious practical reason. Children at an early age, before 'the dawn of reason', are capable of doing considerable harm to themselves and to others. It is as socially essential that they should observe certain rudimentary rules from a very early age as it is individually essential to their survival that they should learn to look both ways before they cross the road.

The second reason is a psychological one; for the evidence from psychologists such as Piaget[20] and Luria suggests that children up to about the age of seven are incapable of appreciating that rules could be otherwise and that there are reasons for rules. Questions about the *validity* of rules make little sense to them. It is therefore pretty pointless making their acceptance of rules at an early age depend upon their seeing that there are reasons for them. And it is also pretty pointless discussing moral education as Hare[21] does by the use of analogies such as that of teaching people to drive cars. For it is probable that most of the formative stages of moral education take place before this sort of rational instruction makes much sense to a child.

The third reason is a philosophical one. It is difficult to see quite what could be meant by developing a legislative function in relation to rules unless the child first of all has some practical examples of rules to work with. And it is no good having understanding of them in the way in which an anthropologist might have understanding of the rules of a strange tribe. He must have experience of rules whose function is to regulate his inclinations; he has to learn what such rules amount to in concrete situations. Legislation as a social process has always developed gradually out of an amorphous mass of custom. Certain rules are selected and more precisely formulated. An analogous development must take place in the mind of the child.[22]

The child, then, has to develop habits of regulation which permit the gradual development of second-order habits of assessment of rules. It could be that the constant barking out of commands, backed by frequent punishment, on the part of his parents, incapacitates him for this. His regulation becomes so associated with fear of punishment that he is rendered incapable of ever developing a more rational form of regulation. And surely 'That is wrong' followed by a slap can function in just the same way as 'Don't do that' followed by a slap. It is not clear that much depends on whether or not the parents use one form of words rather than another to pass on rules; what does matter, however, is what the parent does or says if the child asks why he should conform to what is proposed. For what makes an utterance a command rather than a moral injunction is the sort of backing that goes with it. Commands presuppose authority. Their backing is therefore either an appeal to authority of the form 'because I say so' or the use of punishment, or both. Moral rules are backed by an appeal to reasons such as 'because your sister will be hurt'. Much depends, too, on whether the tone of voice is reasonable or threatening. In other words it is what goes with the form of words, not the form of words taken by themselves that is crucial. It might well be that the 'inner voice' type of conscience, so prominent in the Freudian theory of the super-ego, is a product of authoritarian methods of child-rearing where commands and punishment are much in use. It is difficult to see how, for people brought up systematically in this manner, words like 'ought' and 'wrong' could ever come to be backed by reasons of a morally relevant sort, though they might become associated with appeals to authority or fear of punishment.

The question, then, is not whether to pass on basic rules to children at an early age, but which rules to pass on and how to do so. The child has to learn to regulate his impulses and to understand also that there are reasons for doing so. He has later to develop a second-order habit of assessing rules in the light of such reasons and developing a code of his own. Yet, in the early stages of his learning to regulate his impulses, he is incapable of appreciating what the real reasons for doing this are. This is indeed the paradox to which Aristotle referred when he said:

'But the moral virtues we do acquire by first exercising them. . . . We become just by performing just actions, temperate by performing temperate actions, brave by performing brave actions. . . . A difficulty, however, may be raised as to what we mean when we say that we must perform just actions if we are to become just, and temperate actions if we are to become temperate. It may be argued that, if I do what is just and temperate, I am just and temperate already. . . .[23]

It is only in recent times that the empirical investigation of the effect of various types of child-rearing has been undertaken. Already some interesting suggestions have been made about such matters.[24] It may well be that conformists and 'inner-directed' men of the irrational sort are victims of too many orders, too much punishment, or of too much permissiveness. Rational morality, in which reasons are given for rules, only has a chance to develop if appropriate methods of training permit the *differentiation* of types of rule which is presupposed. What *are* appropriate methods is largely an empirical question which psychologists, in time, ought to be able to answer.

(c) *The Judicial Function*

A man can know what, in general, is right and wrong and also be clear why it is so; but he may be nevertheless what might be called an ideologue – a man with no judgement about the application of rules to particular cases. He may be like this, as Aristotle stressed when talking of the young, because he has no experience of the concrete details of life. But he may have such experience and yet lack judgement like a professor in politics or a theoretical psychologist dealing with his fellow human beings. For rules do not dictate their own application. Situations can be seen in all sorts of different ways. Sending a child to a private school can be interpreted as being unfair, selfish or considerate. Often rules conflict and judgement is required to see in what circumstances a man is justified in making an exception to a rule.

Scheffler and Frankena make much of the contrast between moral education as concerned with the passing on of rules as distinct from 'patterns of action'. But they say nothing about the crucial question of judgement. How it is developed it is difficult to say. Probably Aristotle was right in stressing that it is learnt on some kind of apprenticeship system. And this is surely the burden of Oakeshott's thesis about political education.[25] It is reasonable to assume that it cannot be learnt by drill or sermons. Some suggest that the study of history, by providing a series of cases of men making decisions, might help towards the development of judgement. Machiavielli obviously thought this. Nowell-Smith has recently floated out this time-honoured suggestion.[26] But what is the evidence for this thesis?

Though there is little to be gleaned from a study of psychology about how people do develop judgement, there is a certain amount to be learnt about why they don't. For studies of 'types of character' suggest that some people are rendered incapable in infancy of ever developing in this way. It is as if they acquire unadaptive and unintelligent habits. The Puritan, for instance, whose traits are developed as a reaction-formation against his sexual wishes, will apply his code rigorously and in an undiscriminating manner. Guilt will attach even to his legitimate sex relations with his wife. Similarly the idealist will rig the world to suit his standards. He will be so considerate and charitable that, even when confronted with a really slick operator, he will consistently ascribe to him well-meaning intentions. These are mild cases of reaction-formations against sexual and aggressive wishes which have become magnified into unintelligent rule-following. In extreme cases, of course, the wishes haunt the man as obsessions. His world may become full of possible sources of danger – girls he may seduce, filthy words he may utter, children he may strangle, windows he may jump out of – and so he develops elaborate habits of self-correction. He may indulge in endless routines, self-imposed duties and punishments. He now does not simply apply rules unintelligently which have point in certain contexts; his view of the world is so distorted that he constantly manufactures occasions for the compulsive application of rules. The case of the miser is also a typical example of the development of such an obsession which completely warps a man's judgement.

There is much speculation but little established knowledge about what leads to the development of such reaction-formations. They may result from parental attitudes which contain a strong need for certainty and correctness, from a tendency to load the child too early with responsibilities and decisions, or from unwise handling at the anal stage of development.[27] Or they may result from too much permissiveness on the part of parents. But more empirical knowledge of this sort would only tell us why some people don't develop good practical judgement. It would not tell us why others do. To understand this we would probably have to study the training of judges and administrative civil servants rather than child-rearing techniques. For my guess is that the most the school and home can do in this matter is to guard against permanently crippling their clientele.

(d)   *The Executive Function*
We come now to cases where there is the gap between moral knowledge and patterns of action which both Scheffler and Frankena dwell on in their discussions of moral education. How are such cases to be described and how are they to be explained?

From the point of view of description it is important to distinguish between the different types of gap that may exist. When dealing with the legislative function in section 5(b) above the point was made that a child must come to understand rules not in an inverted commas sense or as an anthropologist might come to understand the rules of a strange tribe. 'Promises ought to be kept', for instance, must not simply appear to him as something that others say; it must present itself to him as a reason for doing something in a particular case, for regulating some wayward inclination. And, if the legislative function is properly developed, it is to hoped that he will come to see that there are reasons for having this general rule. Now a man may know what he ought to do in general and have the judgement to see that a rule applies to his particular case; yet he may ruthlessly and doggedly do what he knows to be wrong. He may feel twinges of guilt and remorse about doing it, but he still persists. He wants to do something else much more – e.g. get rich, enjoy sexual experience. This is the case of what we call a wicked man. He is to be distinguished from at least three other sorts of men. There is first of all another sort of man whom we might, perhaps, be more disposed to call evil than wicked. He is not sidetracked by wayward inclinations. He has his own code and pursues it in a determined fashion. But his code includes things like thrashing children and keeping his wife in subjection, which others would regard as palpably wrong. Secondly there is the man of weak will. He knows what is right and wants desperately to do it. He also has the judgement to see what is right in a particular case. But because of his emotional instability he cannot always do it. He is not like the wicked man who wants something else more than to do what he knows to be right. Rather he is side-tracked by emotions like fear, or he hesitates because of jealousy. There may, too, be more recondite explanations of his failure. But he does not, like the wicked man, pursue what he knows to be bad in a consistent determined way. The third case is that of the psychopath who can really only speak of what he ought to do in an inverted commas sense. For although he vaguely understands other people when they talk of what ought to be done, moral language does not really bite on his behaviour. For he cares little, if at all, about doing what he ought to do. Indeed he probably has no consistent policy in relation to his own interest either. The wicked man, on the other hand, is not impervious to obligations; he cares about them only to a limited extent.

How is the case of the wicked man to be explained? John Rawls, I think, gives the clue to this in his most interesting treatment of the moral emotions.[28] His thesis is, actually, primarily a conceptual one in that he wishes to establish a conceptual connection between moral feelings and natural attitudes. He thinks that a necessary condition of the moral feelings of shame, remorse and guilt is the existence of natural attitudes such as self-esteem, compassion and love. We could not, for instance, understand what shame was unless we also had the concept of self-esteem; for self-esteem includes the disposition to feel shame in certain circumstances. Similarly love is exhibited in a tendency to feel guilt or remorse in certain circumstances, as well as in other things. Now whatever the case may be for conceptual connections of this sort there is certainly a very strong case to be made for psychological connections between moral defects in this area and between the absence or weakness of moral feelings and between moral feelings and natural attitudes. The wicked man indeed could be almost described as the man who feels too little remorse or guilt about his actions which he knows to be wrong. Remorse is usually felt for actions which have dire consequences for others; the capacity for feeling remorse therefore presupposes that we have sympathy for others or love for them. Similarly guilt can be felt in relation to a breach of rules that issue either from an authoritative source or which are thought of as being fixed on a basis of reciprocity. The former kind of guilt is expressed to the desire to confess and ask for forgiveness which is a way of restoring the relation of love and trust which this sort of guilt presupposes. The latter is expressed in the desire to apologise, to make reparations, to admit one's faults, which are ways of restoring mutual trust. Such mutual trust and fellow-feeling is presupposed in the autonomous type of morality characterising an 'open' society. It is important to distinguish these types of 'conscience' as Money-Kyrle[29] has stressed in his distinction between the authoritarian and humanistic types of conscience, a distinction which my accounts of the different types of character allows for. But it is also important to stress that both types of conscience presuppose the development of attachment to others learnt in the first instance from parents and developing into fellow-feeling for the members of a peer-group if the child develops from what Piaget calls the 'transcendental' to the 'autonomous' stage of morality.[30] Much of this development must come about by simple imitation and by means of the rather indeterminate process called 'identification'[31] by psycho-analysis which leads to the formation of an 'ego-ideal'. But this is not the whole story; for it does not account completely for the development of sympathy and more spontaneous sentiments. Money-Kyrle, whose theory owes much to Melanie Klein, traces the development of the humanistic conscience back to 'guilt' experienced in hurting and hating the mother, the child's first object of love. But this is rather a dubious hypothesis; for a child of this age cannot feel guilty; for this presupposes that one already has the notion that something is wrong which children of this age obviously do not have. It looks rather like the time-honoured psychological practice of projecting some sort of conceptual connection (the sort that Rawls is trying to make) into the psychological matrix of infancy. Nevertheless there is a strong case to be made for a bond of some sort between mother and infant as being a necessary psychological condition for the development of sympathy. This occurs before the later period when the 'ego-ideal' begins to be shaped.

But this right relationship with the mother at an early age could only lay a foundation for love and, hence, for the later development of guilt and remorse when the child begins to grasp moral concepts. What can be done, subsequent to this, to kindle concern about the consequences of actions in so far as they affect others? How can the example of parents and teachers, which is essential to imitation and identification, be supplemented? My guess is that in our civilisation stories from the New Testament, in which the supreme importance of love is most graphically portrayed, have contributed much. Plato maintained that all moral education must begin with religion in the sense that vivid stories are the most effective and appropriate way of presenting moral truths to children before the dawn of reason. In a similar vein many modern American educators, who are vitally concerned about the development of a 'democratic' habit of mind, advocate the early presentation of the most arresting stories about moral heroes such as Washington, Lincoln and Jefferson. But what permanent effect do such stories exert? Is it similar to that of television serials or different because of the personal rapport which usually accompanies a story? A serious examination of the effectiveness of such age-old techniques is vital if anything concrete is to be established about the moral education of children in our civilisation. For at this stage habits must be formed and feelings awakened which are necessary conditions for rational morality at a later stage. Little is needed to kindle the desire for money, fame, or sexual indulgence which are obvious lures for the wicked man. It is much harder to develop sympathy and imagination so that doing what is right has a positive appeal and is not based purely on fear of consequences. Sympathy and imagination, too, are necessary not simply for caring about rules sufficiently to feel guilt or remorse if they are broken. They are necessary also for the sensitive exercise of the judicial function in making relevant exceptions to rules and for seeing situations as falling under different rules. It is regrettable, therefore, that so little has been definitely established about how sympathy and imagination are developed. For our knowledge about such matters to date comes largely from psycho-analytic speculation and from the hunches of practical men.

So far we have dealt only with the wicked man who knows what is wrong but who, because of the weakness of his sense of guilt or remorse, is too little repelled by the thought of doing wrong to recoil from it. But there are, unfortunately, some men who do not even make the grade necessary for wickedness to be a possibility for them. In extreme cases such people are called psychopaths who are the limiting case of people who have no character called 'amoral' types by Peck and Havighurst. For them moral rules are for ever framed in inverted commas. This, it is thought, is largely due to the fact that they seem incapable of real love and affection and hence of any serious twinges of guilt or remorse.[32] The usual explanation of such characters is in terms of maternal deprivation at certain ages which seems to correlated with traits like 'distractability', 'unrealiability', and 'lack of social conformity' which are almost definitions of having no character.[32]

Weakness of character, as distinct from an almost complete lack of it, is a quite different phenomenon. This type of person knows what is right and wants to do it but constantly fails. The explanation is not in wants which are stronger than his concern to do what is right. Rather he is the man who either seems constitutionally lacking in persistence or who seems to be a constant victim to various forms of passivity. Perhaps he is beset by insecurity which makes him veer from his course at the hint of social disapproval; perhaps unconscious wishes constantly deflect him from attaining his ends; perhaps he is the victim of strange moods. To speculate on the causes of such conditions would be a lengthy undertaking, though, as a matter of fact, psychological theories bear on this problem, if in rather a negative way. For although it is a presupposition of rational action that a man who wills the end must also will the means if he knows what they are, most work done in this field (e.g. by the Freudian school) has tended to explain only why people don't live up to this ideal postulate. As I have argued elsewhere too little thought has been given to the positive conditions of training which are likely to produce a strong ego, to switch from Kantian to Freudian terminology.[34]

But even if we knew the conditions which favour the development of strength of character as well as those which occasion weakness, we would still have to decide to what type of character such strength of character should be harnessed. If this rather lengthy analysis has done nothing else it has at least brought out this point which any

educator who talks of the training of character should bear constantly in mind. Indeed the main point of the paper has been to use
the analysis of the concept of 'character' to point to the many
ambiguities which beset discussions of moral education in general
and the training of character in particular. I have tried to show how
complicated this task is and how limited and unsubstantial our
knowledge is about the process of initiating children into the
traditions of rational thought, judgement and determined policies
without which the thin crust of rationality cannot be perpetuated.
For my model of the mind is, in an important sense, more than a
model. Plato once said that philosophy was the soul's dialogue with
itself. Similarly a person who has developed a legislative function,
as I have called it, is a person who has taken the assessment of rules
into his own mind. He has been initiated into a rational tradition
stretching right back to Socrates. That is why the model of the
educator as an artist producing an end product out of material or of
the gardener tending a process of growth are both out of place. For
moral education is a matter of initiating others into traditions and
into procedures for revising and applying them; these come to be
gradually taken in as habits of mind. It is also a matter of spreading
the contagion of sympathy and imagination so that such traditions
bite on behaviour. But I think that we have little established knowledge about the crucial conditions which favour the initiation into
this distinctive form of life.

REFERENCES

1. This paper was read at a conference on 'Education and the Concept of
   Character' organised by Harvard Graduate School of Education in May
   1961.
2. Hartshorne, H. and May, M. A., *Studies in the Nature of Character* (New
   York: Macmillan, 1930), 3 vols.
3. Riesman, D., *The Lonely Crowd* (Yale University Press, 1950).
4. Peck, R. F. and Havighurst, R. J., *The Psychology of Character Development*
   (New York: Wiley, 1960).
5. See Frankena, W., 'Towards a Philosophy of Moral Education', *Harvard Ed.
   Rev.*, Vol. 28, No. 4, Fall 1958); and Scheffler, I., *The Language of Education*
   (Illinois: Thomas,1960), Ch. V.
6. Allport, G. W., *Personality* (New York: Henry Holt, 1937), p. 303.
7. I am indebted to Mrs Foot for this point which she stressed when replying
   to an early version of this paper which I read to the Oxford Philosophical
   Society in March 1958.
8. Allport, op. cit., p. 51.
9. Nowell-Smith, P. H., *Ethics* (Harmondsworth: Penguin, 1954), p. 304.
10. Nowell-Smith was kind enough to read and comment on an early version of

this paper and said that what he says on p. 304 has to be supplemented by what he says about parental smiles and frowns on p. 213. But I am not sure that more detailed specification of this sort affects the main point that I am making.

12. See Peters, R. S., 'Freud's Theory of Moral Development in Relation to that of Piaget', *Brit. Journ. Ed. Psych.*, Vol. XXX, Pt III (November 1960).
13. Roback, A., *The Psychology of Character* (London, Kegan Paul, 1928), p. 452.
14. I am grateful to Sidney Morganbesser for pointing this out to me in his comments on my paper at the Harvard Conference.
15. Sargant, W., *The Battle for the Mind* (Melbourne: Heinemann, 1957).
16. Rieff, P., *Freud, the Mind of the Moralist* (New York: Viking Press, 1959). Chs IX, X.
17. See Peters, R. S., *The Concept of Motivation* (London: Kegan Paul, 1958), pp. 62–71.
18. For attempts towards such a justification see Benn, S. I. and Peters, R. S., *Social Principles and the Democratic State* (London: Allen & Unwin, 1959), Ch. 2; Griffiths, A. P., 'Justifying Moral Principles', *Proc. Aris. Soc.*, Vol. LVIII (1957–8); and Sidgwick's discussion of the principles of Justice, Egoism and Rational Benevolence in his *Methods of Ethics* (London: Macmillan, 1874).
19. Hare M., *The Language of Morals* (Oxford: Oxford University Press, 1952), pp. 74, 75.
20. Piaget, J., *The Moral Judgment of the Child* (London: Kegan Paul, 1932). See also Peters, 'Freud's Theory of Moral Development in Relation to that of Piaget'.
21. Hare, op. cit., pp. 65–8.
22. I am well aware that a rule becomes a legal rule if it is laid down by some one in authority, whatever his *reasons* for laying it down as such. This is one of the points where my analogy of course breaks down.
23. Aristotle, *Nichomachean Ethics*, Chs 3, 4.
24. See Sears, R., Macoby, E. and Levin, H., *Patterns of Child Rearing* (New York: Row, Peterson, 1957).
25. See Oakeshott, M., 'Political Education', in Laslett, P. (Ed.), *Philosophy, Politics and Society* (Oxford: Blackwell, 1956).
26. See Nowell-Smith, P. H., *Education in a University* (Leicester University Press, 1958).
27. See White, R., *The Abnormal Personality* (New York: Ronald Press, 1956), pp. 300–3.
28. In a paper entitled 'Moral Feelings and Natural Attitudes' read at the Harvard Conference referred to above, but not yet published.
29. Money-Kyrle, R., *Psycho-analysis and Politics* (London: Duckworth, 1951).
30. Piaget, J., *The Moral Judgment of the Child* (London: Kegan Paul, 1932).
31. See Sears, Macoby and Levin, op. cit., pp. 372–6.
32. White, op. cit., pp. 377–9.
33. Bowlby, J., *Child Care and the Growth of Love* (Harmondsworth: Penguin, 1953).
34. Op. cit., *Brit. Journ. Ed. Psych.*

13

REASON AND HABIT: THE PARADOX
OF MORAL EDUCATION

The debate about whether and how virtue can be taught is a long-standing one in the history of ethics; but right at the very start, when Socrates and Protagoras were discussing the matter, Socrates characteristically made the point that the answers to the questions depended on what is meant by 'virtue'. Is it the 'correct opinion' and conventional behaviour of well-brought-up people? Or is it conduct based on a grasp of fundamental principles? In more recent times Professor Oakeshott has made a similar contrast between two forms of the moral life.[1] A habit of affection and behaviour, characteristic of the gentleman, is contrasted with the reflective application of a moral criterion. There is a corresponding difference in what is emphasised in moral education. On the one hand there is an emphasis on habit, tradition and being properly brought up; on the other hand there is emphasis on intellectual training, and on the development of critical thought and choice.

It is not, however, necessarily the case either that these divergent accounts of morality are completely incompatible with each other or that there can be no *rapprochement* between their different emphases in matters of moral education. Indeed Aristotle attempted to combine both, but was led into a paradox about moral education which resulted from his attempt to stress the role both of reason and of habit. It is my intention in this paper both to combine these two emphases in moral education and to deal with the resulting paradox.

First of all it is necessary to follow Socrates' advice and attempt to get clearer about what morality is. This might be done by examining the uses of 'moral' and its cognates in ordinary language. But it would be a long and detailed task for which there is little time in this lecture; for 'morality', like 'education', means very different things to different people.

Why is it, for instance, that 'morals' suggest something to do with sex and selfishness whereas we speak of 'unethical' conduct on the part of doctors, business men and advertisers? Does 'unethical' suggest the subtle peccadilloes of the more cultured type of man who misses the mark slightly in the way in which a Greek aristocrat might have done, whereas 'immoral' suggests the more brutish plungings of the Roman? 'Morality', too, can cover the crude rigorous code of the Puritan as well as the more rational intelligent code of the scientific humanist. When Freud expressed agreement with Vischer's saying that, 'Morality is self-evident',[2] was he speaking of a crude code whose origin he did much to lay bare in his doctrine of the super-ego, or was he speaking of his own more rational humanistic code?

Behind, however, these vagaries of ordinary usage lies a distinctive form of discourse which has developed to answer distinctive forms of questions. These questions are concerned with what ought to be and with what ought to be done. This is a particular branch of what philosophers call practical discourse. Now practical discourse is not only concerned with answers to questions about what ought to be or what ought to be done. Commands, for instance, are also practical in that they are ways of getting people to do things by means of speech. But they differ from that form of practical discourse in which words like 'ought', 'good', 'right', and 'wrong' occur because there is no implied link with reasons. Saying, 'Shut the door', or, 'Shut up', has a different social function from saying, 'You ought to shut the door', or, 'Silence is a good thing'. Words like 'ought' and 'good' guide behaviour: they do not act as goads or stimuli for reactions. And they guide it with the suggestion that there are reasons for doing whatever is prescribed.

This is not, by the way, what is called a linguistic argument, if by that is meant an argument based on how we actually use words. Rather it is an argument of a Kantian form which attempts to arrive at what is presupposed by our use of different linguistic expressions. Nothing depends on using the *word* 'ought' or 'good', just as nothing depends on using the *word* 'moral' or 'ethical'. But once discourse or thought begins to get differentiated, as when, for instance, we begin to distinguish science from mythology and metaphysics, we can try to get behind these verbal distinctions to see what the differences are in the activities which are so picked out. In the particular case of 'ought', 'good', and other such words, if we ceased to use these words and still wanted to get people to do things by means other than twisting their arms, hypnotising them or giving them orders, we would have to devise a new family of words to do this job.

Morality, then, is concerned with what there are reasons for doing or not doing, for bringing into or removing from existence. But this is only the start of the story; for what makes the reasons relevant ones? Supposing it is said that one ought not to slash people with razors, which is to suggest that there are reasons for not doing this. We inquire what the reasons are and are told that people bleed as a result and blood is red and that is why we should not do it. This would be a reason; but it would not appeal much to us as a good reason because it presupposes the principle that the redness in the world ought to be minimised, which most of us would regard as a somewhat bizarre principle. We would be more inclined to accept a reason like 'it hurts' because we regard the principle that *pain* ought to be minimised as more acceptable than the principle that *redness* ought to be minimised.

It is not my job in this paper to pursue the fundamental problem in ethics of why one such principle is more justifiable than another. I am using this gory example only to bring out the double point that principles are needed to determine the relevance of reasons and that some principles seem more justifiable than others. Our moral principles might be picked out as those which are for us fundamental or overriding in such a structure of rules backed by reasons.

It is manifest enough, however, that in respect of such a structure of rules we can be more or less prepared to justify, revise, or adapt them to changing circumstances. We can guide our lives by a host of rules which seem to us self-evident, or which might be backed up by the very general principle that we ought to do what others do or that we ought to do what X, who is in authority or an authority, says. Or we might try to live by a more rational and thought-out code. For men are creatures of habit and tradition in varying degrees. In a similar way we may be more or less intelligent in the application of rules to particular cases. This is the field of judgement, and whereas some men proceed with fine discrimination, others plod along bone-headedly by rules of thumb. Finally we can do what we should mechanically and with heavy hearts without caring overmuch for what we are doing, like reluctant housewives peeling potatoes. Or we can do what we should with more spontaneity because we genuinely care about that for the sake of which we are acting. In brief, the legislative, judicial and executive aspects of our moral life can be more or less rationally, intelligently and spontaneously conducted.

Professor Niblett, in the first lecture in this series, stressed the importance of making clear where we stand in moral matters. But I do not merely appeal to the august authority of the Dean in order to justify myself in stating very briefly where I stand – the appeal to authority is seldom a good reason for doing anything! The fact is that I cannot explain what I consider the paradox of moral education to be unless I *do* make clear where I stand.

I am a staunch supporter of a rationally held and intelligently applied moral code. Such a code seems peculiarly pertinent at the present time; for, as we have learnt in previous lectures, this is a time of rapid social change, of shifting standards both in regard to general social rules and in regard to activities which are thought to be worthwhile, to which we are introduced in the curricula of schools and universities. My objection to intuitionist and traditionalist positions in morals is not based, of course, on these contigent facts about the social situation. My appeal to the social situation is to support the plea of pertinence. For it is just such facts about changing standards and shifting situations which often lead people who think of morality along intuitionist lines to embrace some subjectivist position and to talk about their feelings or commitments as if morality were a matter of private taste, or falling in love.

I was particularly struck by the peculiar phenomenon of American academics who took what sociologists said about moral relativism so seriously that they would never say that anything was right or wrong; instead they would self-consciously produce their blessed 'commitments' rather like the White Rabbit producing his watch from his waistcoat pocket. Of course this Existentialist type of reaction is to be seen in the context of the massive pressure to conform in America about which so much is said in the literature about the 'other-directed' man. The experiments of Solomon Asch and Stanley Milgram have shown the immense force of such social pressures which can make most men disavow even the plain evidence of their senses. Autonomous judgements requires considerable courage in such circumstances and, if asserted, can have a snowball effect which loosens the chains of conformity. These experiments are particularly relevant to the phenomenon of the teenage culture which we have in our midst. But my point is that the assertion of the individual against such pressures need not take the form of rather self-conscious talk about his commitments. After all some things may just be right or wrong, good or bad. The peculiar pertinence of a rationallly held moral code is that it can combine a degree of non-relativeness at one level with a degree of adaptability at another. Let me elucidate in a bit more detail both what I mean and where I stand.

To hold a rational code a man must subscribe to some higher-order principles which will enable him both to apply rules intelligently in the light of relevant differences in circumstances and to revise rules from time to time in the light of changes in circumstances and in empirical knowledge about the conditions and consequences of their application. The higher-order principles which, in my view, are capable of some sort of rational justification, are those of impartiality, truth-telling, liberty, and the consideration of interests. For these, I would argue, are presupposed by the very activity of giving reasons in practical discourse. These higher-order principles, though pretty formal in character, provide very general criteria of relevance for justifying particular rules and for making exceptions in particular cases.

Now just as it is possible for a scientist to stand firm on procedural principles like those of putting his theories up for public criticism, going by the evidence in deciding their truth and not cooking evidence, and yet be willing to change the substantial content of such theories, so also is it possible for a man who holds a rational code to stick firmly to his principles at the procedural level – i.e. the principles of impartiality, liberty, truth-telling and the consideration of interests, and yet to revise what he thinks about the substantial content of rules at a lower level – e.g. about smoking, gambling, or birth-control.

The criticism is often levelled against the advocates of a rationally held moral code that it would lead to moral anarchy. But why should it? For if the higher-order criterion of the impartial consideration of interests affected by rules is applied it will be seen that there are some rules which are so important for anyone living in a society that they could be regarded almost as definitions of a society. For a society is a collection of individuals united by the acceptance of certain rules, and though many of them relate to 'my station and its duties' (e.g. what ought to be done *qua* husband or *qua* teacher) there are also (leaving aside the law) a number of more general rules binding on anyone who is deemed to be a member of the same society – e.g. rules about the keeping of contracts, etc. I imagine that the Natural Law theorists were attempting to outline such a system of basic rules. It would be difficult to conceive of any social, economic, or geographical changes which would lead one to think that such basic rules should be abrogated, though, of course, exceptions could be made to them under special circumstances. Such basic rules are to be contrasted with others which clearly do depend upon particular circumstances. Obviously, for instance, the rule that one should be sparing in the use of water is defensible only in times of drought. The fact that it is difficult to be sure to which category particular rules belong (e.g. about sexual behaviour) does not affect the general usefulness of the distinction. So in a rational code there would be procedural rules which could be regarded as presupposed by the very activity of giving reasons for rules; there would then be basic rules which would be those which could be justified under any conceivable social conditions; then there would be more relative rules which would depend, for their justifiability, on more contingent facts about particular social, economic and geographic conditions. From the point of view of moral education it would be particularly important to pass on procedural rules and basic rules. Hence, presumably, the importance which Hare attaches to the question to which he thinks moral philosophers should address themselves very seriously: 'How should I bring up my children?'[3] For in a time of rapid change it is important to pass on both a minimum equipment of basic rules together with procedural rules without which exceptions cannot be rationally made to basic rules or decisions taken about rules of a more relative status.

And so we pass to moral education. But before we do so I want to draw out one of the implications for moral education which is implicit in the position which I have outlined. If one of the fundamental principles of morality is that of the consideration of interests, moral education will be as much concerned with the promotion of good activities as it will be with the maintenance of rules for social conduct, with what ought to be as well as with what men ought to do. Such good or worthwhile activities were emphasised by the Ideal Utilitarians, such as Moore and Rashdall, who tended also to emphasise things like the pursuit of truth, the creation of beauty, the enjoyment of sensitive personal relationships, which defined the way of life of Keynes and other members of the Bloomsbury set at the beginning of this century. They rightly regarded the extension of such activities and of the outlook which goes with them as one of the main constituents in a civilised life. It would be a very difficult task and quite beyond the scope of this paper either to make a list of such activities or to show conclusively why the pursuit of them is in any man's interest.[4] Nevertheless it is precisely these sorts of activities into which we strive to initiate children in schools. We do, presumably, aim at passing on poetry rather than push-pin. So the promotion of such activities will be as much a problem for those interested in moral education as the passing on of more general rules of conduct.

Now within these worthwhile activities it is generally possible to make the same sort of distinction between matters of procedure and matters of substance which I have made in the case of a rational code. Professor Oakeshott, in his fascinating essay entitled 'The Teaching of Politics in a University', makes a very similar distinction between what he calls the 'language' and 'literature' of a subject. To quote him:

'It is the distinction, for example, between the "language" of poetic imagination and a poem or novel; or between the "language" or manners of thinking of a scientist and a text-book of geology or what may be called the current state of our geological knowledge. . . . Science, for example, in a university, is not an encyclopaedia of information or the present state of our "physical" knowledge; it is a current activity, an explanatory manner of thinking and speaking being explored.'[6]

In such 'languages' are implicit various canons, or what I call rules of procedure, which permit the criticism, evaluation, and development of the 'literature'. The business of moral education consists largely in initiating people into the 'language' so that they can use it in an autonomous manner. This is done largely by introducing them to the 'literature'. And so we come to the paradox of moral education.

What then is the paradox of moral education as I conceive it? It is this: given that it is desirable to develop people who conduct themselves rationally, intelligently and with a fair degree of spontaneity, the brute facts of child development reveal that at the most formative years of a child's development he is incapable of this form of life and impervious to the proper manner of passing it on. Let me spell out these facts in a little more detail.

First, a fair amount of evidence has accumulated to demonstrate the decisive importance of early learning on later development. I refer here not simply to the evidence of Freudians, Kleinians, Bowlby and Harlow who have been concerned, roughly speaking, with the importance of early learning on the development of character and personality; I also refer to evidence produced by more physiologically minded psychologists such as Hebb.

Secondly, both the Freudian theory of the super-ego and Piaget's theory of the transcendental stage of the child's development converge to suggest that up to a certain age rules appear to a child as something external and unalterable, often sacred. Freud went further than Piaget in suggesting mechanisms, such as introjection and reaction-formation, by means of which these external sacrosanct rules come to be interiorised by the child and the standards adopted of that parent with whom identification takes place. It is not till later – well after the age of seven or eight – that what Piaget calls the autonomous stage develops when the notion dawns that rules can be otherwise, that they are conventions maintained out of mutual respect which can be altered if the co-operation of others can be obtained.

No doubt a similar point could be made also about a young child's attitude to the 'literature' of subjects such as geography, history and science. In so far as his minimal concepts of space, time and causality enable him to grasp information handed on which belongs to the 'literature' of these disciplines, he will tend first of all to regard them as pronouncements from an oracle. Until he is gradually initiated into the 'language' of the subjects, by means of which he can begin to evaluate the literature, he will remain in the position of primitive people in respect of their attitude to the traditions of their tribe.

Thirdly, there is evidence to suggest – e.g. from Luria's experiments with manipulative tasks – that the giving of reasons has very little educative effect before a certain age. The explanations given by adults bite very little into the child's behaviour, though commands do have an effect at an earlier age.

Nevertheless, in spite of the fact that a rational code of behaviour and the 'language' of a variety of activities is beyond the grasp of young children, they can and must enter the palace of Reason through the courtyard of Habit and Tradition. This is the paradox of moral education which was first put so well by Aristotle in Book 2 of his *Nicomachean Ethics.*

The problem of moral education is that of how the necessary habits of behaviour and the deep-rooted assumptions of the 'literature' of various forms of good activities can be acquired in a way which does not stultify the development of a rational code or the mastery of the 'language' of activities at a later stage.

I am assuming, by the way, like Aristotle, that children gradually acquire these desirable forms of life by some on-the-spot apprenticeship system. I am also assuming something about the factor which I previously picked out when I stressed the spontaneous enjoyment that goes with such a form of life. Spinoza put this in a very general way when he declared that, 'Blessedness is not the reward of right-living; it is the right living itself; nor should we rejoice in it because we restrain our desires, but, on the contrary, it is because we rejoice in it that we restrain them.'[6] In the jargon of modern psychology this

is to say that a rational code and worth-while activities are intrinsically not extrinsically motivated.

Now education, at any rate at later levels, consists largely in
initiating people into this form of life – in getting others on the
inside of activities so that they practise them simply for the intrinsic
satisfactions that they contain and for no end which is extrinsic to
them. That is why one gets so impatient with the endless talk about
the aims of education and the modern tendency to speak about
education in the economic jargon of 'investment' and 'commodity'.
No one, of course, would deny that many skills and much information have to be passed on to sustain and increase productivity in an
industrial society; it is also the case that if money has to be raised
from hard-headed business men or from an over-taxed and material-
istically minded public, the instrumental aspects of what goes on in
schools and universities may have to be stressed. But anyone who
reflects must ask questions about the point of keeping the wheels of
industry turning. And the answer is not simply that it is necessary for
survival or 'living' – whatever that means. It is necessary for the
maintenance and extension of a civilised life whose distinctive outlook and activities are those which are passed on in schools and
universities. In such institutions there is no absolute distinction
between teacher and learner. It is a matter of degree of skill, knowledge, insight and experience within a common form of life. So there
is an important sense in which 'life', by which is usually meant that
which goes on outside the class-room, is for the sake of education,
not education for life. This point was well made by the philosopher
who was castigated by the Marxist for trying to understand the world
rather than to change it. When asked what he proposed to *do* when
he had achieved the classless society the Marxist admitted that he
might then get round to the sort of thing that the philosopher was
doing. To which the philosopher replied: 'I guess I am ahead of my
time then!'

Now anyone who has managed to get on the inside of what is
passed on in schools and universities, such as science, music, art,
carpentry, literature, history and athletics, will regard it as somehow
ridiculous to be asked what the point of his activity is. The mastery
of the 'language' carries with it its own delights, or 'intrinsic motivation', to use the jargon. But for a person on the *outside* it may be
difficult to see what point there is in the activity in question. Hence
the incredulity of the uninitiated when confronted with the rhap-
sodies of the mountain-climber, musician or golfer. *Children* are to a
large extent in the position of such outsiders. The problem is to

introduce them to a civilised outlook and activities in such a way that they can get on the inside of those for which they have aptitude.

The same sort of problem can be posed in the case of their attitude to rules of conduct. Is it the case that children have to be lured by irrelevant incentives or goaded by commands so that they acquire the basic habits of conduct and the 'literature' of the various activities without which they cannot emerge to the later stage? Is it the case that we have to use such irrelevant 'extrinsic' techniques to get children going so that eventually they can take over for themselves, without needing any longer such extrinsic incentives or goads? Or does the use of such extrinsic techniques militate against intelligent, spontaneous, and intrinsically directed behaviour later on?

It might be argued, for instance, that the various maturation levels bring with them the possibility of a variety of intrinsic motivations falling under concepts such as competence,[7] mastery and curiosity. Then there is the ubiquitous role of love and trust; for psycho-analysts such as Bowlby suggest that the existence of a good relation-ship of love and trust between parent and child during the early years is a necessary condition for the formation of any enduring and consistent moral habits.[8] Whether love, the withdrawal of love, approval and disapproval, constitute extrinsic or intrinsic motiva-tions in respect to the development of habits is too complicated a question to consider here. Nevertheless it may well be that the use of such intrinsic as distinct from extrinsic motivations may be crucial in determining the type of habits that are formed. For the formation of *some* types of habit may not necessarily militate against adaptability and spontaneous enjoyment. However, it is often thought that, because of the very nature of habits, dwelling in the courtyard of Habit incapacitates a man for life in the palace of Reason. I now propose to show both why this need not be the case and why people can be led to think that it must be the case.

Aristotle was not alone in stressing the importance of habits in moral training. There is William James's celebrated chapter on the subject in which the purple passage occurs:

'Could the young but realise how soon they will become mere walking bundles of habits, they would give more heed to their con-duct while in the plastic state. . . . Every smallest stroke of virtue or of vice leaves its never so little scar. The drunkard Rip Van Winkle, in Jefferson's play, excuses himself for every fresh dereliction by saying, "I won't count this time!" Well! he may not count it, and a kind Heaven may not count it: but it is being counted none the less.

Down among his nerve cells and fibres the molecules are counting it, registering and storing it up to be used against him when the next temptation comes. Nothing we ever do is, in strict scientific literalness, wiped out.'[9]

The evidence from early learning reinforces James's graphic, if depressing, homily. The formation of sound moral habits in respect of, for instance, what I have called basic moral rules might well be a necessary condition of rational morality. It can, however, seem to be antagonistic to rational morality because of an interesting sort of conceptual confusion and because of the development, through a variety of causes, of specific types of habit. I will deal first with the conceptual issue and then proceed to the more empirical one.

What, then, do we mean by 'habits' and is there any necessary contradiction in stressing the importance of habit in moral matters while, at the same time, stressing the intelligent adaptability which is usually associated with reason, together with the spontaneous enjoyment associated with civilised activities?

The first thing to get clear about is that habits, like motives or emotions, are not as it were part of the furniture of the mind in the way in which the yellow, green and black are part of a snooker set. These terms are higher-order ones by means of which we say all sorts of extra things about people's actions, feelings and so on. 'Habit' is a term which we use to say extra things about people's *actions*. They must pick out the sorts of things that we could, in principle, have reasons for doing and the sorts of thing that, in principle, we could stop doing if we tried. It would be odd to talk about a heart-beat or a nervous tic as a habit. Forms of passivity such as stomach-aches or feelings of pity or fear are not properly described as habits either.

When we describe an action as a 'habit' we suggest, first of all, that the man has done this very thing before and that he will probably do it again. We are postulating a tendency to act in this way. 'Habit' also carries with it the suggestion not only of repetition but also of the ability to carry out the action in question 'automatically'. A man can automatically stir his tea or puff his pipe while discussing the latest developments in Cuba and if you ask him whether he puts his left sock on before his right, or vice versa, he may say that he requires notice of that question. And if you ask him to pay attention so that he can tell you in what order he makes a series of movements when hitting a good drive at golf he will probably put the ball into the neighbouring wood. This is not a tip for the life-man; it is support for the Duke of Wellington who proclaimed: 'Habit a second nature! Habit is ten times nature!' The art of living consists, to a large extent, in reducing most things that have to be done to habit; for then the mind is set free to pay attention to things that are interesting, novel and worthwhile.

Of course not all things done automatically are necessarily habits. If a man hears a scrabbling at the window and sees what he takes to be an escaped gorilla peering at him, he may 'automatically' dial 999 while wondering where he has put the bananas. But we would not describe dialling 999 as a habit. Automatic writing need not be one of a person's habits; for 'automatically' picks out only part of what is meant by 'habit' and only in the weak sense that it suggests that is the sort of thing that a man *can* do automatically. Getting up at eight does not cease to be one of a person's habits if, on occasions, he pays careful heed to what he is doing and leaps out of bed briskly the moment the alarm-clock tolls the knell of the dawning day.

What are the implications of this analysis for the development of adaptability which is the hallmark of skilled and civilised activities? What we call a skill presupposes a number of component habits. A fielder at cricket, for instance, may be very skilful and show great intelligence in running a man out by throwing the ball to the bowler rather than to the wicket-keeper. But to do this he would have to bend down, pick the ball up, and contort his body with his eye partly on the ball and partly on the position of the batsmen. But unless these component actions were more or less habits he would not be able to concentrate on using them in the service of the higher strategy of the game. But – and this is the important point – all these component actions would have to be capable of being performed with a degree of plasticity to permit co-ordination in a wide variety of very different overall actions. The concept of 'action' is 'open-ended' in many dimensions. We could describe the man as moving his arm, as throwing the ball at the wicket, or throwing it at the bowler's end, or as running the batsman out, depending on the aspect under which the fielder conceived what he was doing. In what we call 'mechanical' actions a man will always conceive the movements as leading up in a stereotyped way to a narrowly conceived end. In intelligent actions the component actions are conceived of as variable and adaptable in the light of some more generally conceived end. The teachers who have taught me most about golf and about philosophy are those who have insisted on conveying an overall picture of the performance as a whole in which the particular moves have to be practised under the aspect of some wider conception, instead of concentrating either on drilling me in moves which are conceived in a very limited way or going simply for the overall picture without bothering about prac- tising the component moves.

Now the type of habits which would count as moral habits *must* be exhibited in a wide range of actions in so far as actions are thought to be constituted by the sorts of movements of the body that are usually associated with skills. Consider, for instance, the range of such actions that can fall under the concept of theft or malice. What makes an action a case of theft is that it must be conceived of as involving appropriating, without permission, something that belongs to someone else. A child, strictly speaking, cannot be guilty of theft, who has not developed the concept of himself as distinct from others, of property, of the granting of permission, etc. It takes a long time to develop such concepts. In the early years, therefore, parents may think that they are teaching their children not to steal, whereas in fact they are doing no such thing. They may be teaching the child something else, e.g. to inhibit actions of which authority figures dis- approve, or to inhibit a narrowly conceived range of movements. At the toilet training stage, for instance, children may pick up very generalised and often unintelligent habits _ e.g. punctilious con- formity to rules, unwillingness to part with anything that is theirs. But this is not what the parents were trying to teach them. For the children probably lack the concepts which are necessary for under- standing what the parents *think* that they are teaching them, namely the rule of cleanliness. To learn to act on rules forbidding theft, lying, breaking promises, etc., is necessarily an open-ended business requiring intelligence and a high degree of social sophistication. For the child has to learn to see that a vast range of very different actions and performances can fall under a highly abstract rule which makes them all examples of a type of action. If the child has really learnt to act on a rule it is difficult to see how he could have accomplished this without insight and intelligence. He might be drilled or forced to act in *accordance with* a rule; but that is quite different from learning to act *on* a rule.

So it seems as if the paradox of moral education is resolved. For there is no *necessary* contradiction between the use of intelligence and the formation of habits. How then does the antithesis between the two, which is frequently made, come about? Partly, I think, through the existence of certain explanatory expressions such as 'out of habit', and partly because of certain empirical facts about a special class of habits.

To take the point about explanatory expressions first. In explaining particular actions or courses of action we often use the phrase 'out of habit', 'through force of habit', or 'that is a matter of sheer habit'. This type of phrase does not simply suggest that what the man is doing is a habit in the sense that he has a tendency to do this sort of thing and that he can do it automatically. It also implies that in this case:

(i) The man has no reason for doing it which would render the action other than one conceived in a limited way. He could of course be raising his arm to attract someone's notice. He might indeed produce such a reason for doing it if asked. But to say that he raised his arm on this occasion 'out of habit' or through 'force of habit' is to deny that, on this occasion, such a reason which he might have, was *his* reason. Raising his arm *simpliciter*, we are saying, is just the sort of thing that he tends to do.

(ii) The clash with the idea of spontaneity, which is also often associated with 'habit', comes in also because to say that a man cleans his teeth or washes up 'out of habit' or 'through force of habit' is to exclude the possibility that there is any enjoyment in it for him, that he is doing it for pleasure, for what he sees in it as distinct from what he sees it leading on to. It is, in other words, to rule out intrinsic motivation. It is to explain what he does, roughly speaking, in terms of the law of exercise, and to rule out any variant of the law of effect.

It would follow from this that the things which we are wont to do out of habit tend to be pretty stereotyped and narrowly conceived things, which are usually fired off by familiar stimuli. Often a superficially similar cue can release a whole train of such stereotyped movements when the circumstances are relevantly dissimilar. I remember the ghastly sensation of trying to ride a motor-bike and side-car after being trained on a motor-bike. As I automatically banked my body over and the bike went inexorably towards the gorse-bushes on the moor that stretched beside the road, my brother yelled at me: 'Imagine that you are steering a ship, not riding a motor-cycle.' He was thereby following the correct educative procedure which I have referred to above in order to release me from the force of habit.

Given, then, that the explanation 'out of habit' or 'from force of habit' rules out the possibility of a further extrinsic end by reference to which an action could be deemed to be intelligent and given that 'out of habit' also rules out explanations in terms of pleasure, enjoyment, or any kind of intrinsic motivation, it is obvious enough why the intelligent adaptability of a rational code as well as spontaneous delight in practising it and in pursuing worth-while activities are in stark opposition to things that are done 'out of habit'. But, as

I have tried to show, they are not so opposed to habits as mere descriptions of types of action. Habits need not be exercised out of force of habit.

The fact, however, that they very often *are* brings me to my empirical point, which is that there are a great number of things which we do in fact do out of habit, and this is essential if our minds are to be set free to attend to other things. Remember the Duke of Wellington. It is also the case that in some people whom, in extreme cases, we describe as compulsives, the force of habit is so strong that it militates against intelligent performance and disrupts the rest of a man's life. Tidiness and cleanliness are in general sound moral habits because they save time and health and permit efficient and intelligent performance of countless other things. But if a woman is so obsessed with them that she tries to impress the stamp of the operating theatre on the nursery and bedroom of young children, she may well have reached the point where her habits disrupt not only her domestic bliss but also her own capacity for intelligent adaptation and for enjoyment of things that are worth enjoying.

And so we stand at the door of the nursery which is the gateway to moral education. For it is here, in all probability, that the pattern of character-traits and the manner of exercising them is laid down. It is here that habits are first formed in a manner which may lead to the development of compulsives, obsessives, Puritans, and impractical ideologues. To explain how this probably happens would involve a careful examination of cognitive development and the role of extrinsic and intrinsic motivation in childhood. I could not begin to tackle this vast subject in this paper. I have only tried to explain and to resolve the *theoretical* paradox of moral education, not to develop a positive theory of rational child-rearing.

Aristotle put the matter very well when he said:

'But the virtues we get by first exercising them, as also happens in the case of the arts as well. For the things we have to learn before we can do them, we learn by doing them, e.g. men become builders by building and lyre players by playing the lyre; so do we become just by doing just acts, temperate by doing temperate acts, brave by doing brave acts. This is confirmed by what happens in the State; for legislators make the citizens good by forming habits in them . . . by doing the acts that we do in our transactions with other men we become just or unjust, and by doing the acts that we do in the presence of danger, and by habituating ourselves to feel fear or confidence, we become brave or cowardly. . . . It makes no small difference then, whether we form habits of one kind or another from our very youth; it makes a great difference or rather all the difference. . . .'[10]

But from the point of view of moral education it makes all the difference, too, at what age and in what manner such habits are formed, especially under what aspect particular acts are taught. For it is only if habits are developed in a certain kind of way that the paradox of moral education can be avoided in practice. This is a matter about which psychologists and practical teachers will have much more to say than philosophers. For I have only tried to resolve the theoretical paradox of moral education in a theoretical manner.

Bacon once said that the discourse of philosophers is like the stars; it sheds little light because it is so high. But when it is brought nearer the earth, as I hope it has been in this paper, it still can only shed light on where empirical research needs to be done and where practical judgements have to be made. It is no substitute for either. I hope that subsequent papers in this series will enrich our knowledge and increase our wisdom in relation to these more mundane matters.

REFERENCES

1. Oakeshott, I. M., 'The Tower of Babel', in *Rationalism in Politics* (London: Methuen, 1962), pp. 59–79.
2. See Jones, E., *Sigmund Freud, Life and Work* (London: Hogarth Press, 1955). Vol. II, p. 463.
3. Hare, R., *The Language of Morals* (Oxford: Oxford University Press, 1952). pp. 74–5.
4. See Griffiths, A. P. and Peters, R. S., 'The Autonomy of Prudence', *Mind* (April 1962).
5. Oakeshott, M., *Rationalism in Politics and Other Essays* (London: Methuen. 1962), pp. 308, 311.
6. Spinoza, *Ethics*, Pt V., Prop. XLII.
7. See, for instance, White R., 'Competence and the Psychosexual Stages of Development; in *Nebraska Symposium on Motivation* (1960).
8. See Peters, R. S., 'Moral Education and the Psychology of Character', *Philosophy* (January 1962).
9. James, W., *Principles of Psychology* (Macmillan, 1891), p. 127.
10. Aristotle, *Nicomachean Ethics*, Bk II, Chs 3, 4.

14

CONCRETE PRINCIPLES AND THE
RATIONAL PASSIONS

INTRODUCTION

In education content is crucial. There is some point in raising aloft the romantic banners of 'development', 'growth', and 'discovery' when children are being bored or bullied. Romanticism is always valuable as a protest. But another sort of trouble starts when romantics themselves get into positions of authority and demand that children shall scamper around being 'creative' and spontaneously 'discovering' what it has taken civilised man centuries to understand. Some synthesis has to be worked out between established content and individual inventiveness. The basis for such a synthesis is to be found mainly in those public historically developed modes of experience whose immanent principles enable individuals to build up and revise an established content and to make something of themselves within it. In science, for instance, merely learning a lot of facts is a weariness of the spirit; but a Robinson Crusoe, untutored in a scientific tradition, could not ask a scientific question, let alone exhibit 'creativity'. Originality is possible only for those who have assimilated some content and mastered the mode of experience, with its immanent principles, by means of which this content has been established and repeatedly revised.

The same sort of Hegelian progression is detectable in morality. 'Morality' to many still conjures up a 'code' prohibiting things relating to sex, stealing and selfishness. The very word 'code' suggests a body of rules, perhaps of an arbitrary sort, that all hang together but that have no rational basis. To others, however, morality suggests much more individualistic and romantic notions, such as criterionless choices, individual autonomy and subjective preferences. Whether one experiences anguish in the attempt to be 'authentic', produces one's commitment, like the white rabbit producing his watch from his waistcoat pocket, or proclaims, like Bertrand Russell, that one simply does not *like* the Nazis, the picture is roughly the same – that of the romantic protest. Synthesis must be sought by making explicit the mode of experience which has gradually enabled civilised people to distinguish what is a matter of morals from what is a matter of custom or law, and which has enabled them to revise and criticise the code in which they have been brought up, and gradually to stand on their own feet as autonomous moral beings. This they could never have done without a grasp of principles.

It is the details of this sort of synthesis that I propose to explore in this essay as a preliminary to discussing moral education; for it is no good talking about moral education until we have a more determinate conception of what is involved in being 'moral'. Because they are uncertain about this, many well-meaning parents and teachers are hamstrung in their attempts at moral education. If they incline toward the code conception, they tend to be authoritarian in their approach; if, on the other hand, they favour some variant of the romantic reaction, they may expect that children will go it alone and decide it all for themselves. A more adequate view of morality should reveal the proper place for both authority and self-directed learning in moral education. But I shall not have space to deal with details of such educational procedures in this essay – only to explore a middle road between these two extreme positions and to view the general contours of moral education from this vantagepoint.

1 THE FUNCTIONS OF PRINCIPLES

There are some, like Alasdair MacIntyre, who seem to hold that we have no middle way between allegiance to a surviving code and some kind of romantic protest. For, it is argued, moral terms such as 'good' and 'duty', once had determinate application within a close-knit society with clear-cut purposes and well-defined roles; but now, because of social change, they have broken adrift from these concrete moorings. A pale substitute is left in generalised notions such as 'happiness' instead of concrete goals, and duty for duty's sake instead of duties connected with role performances that were manifestly related to the goals of the community. So we have a kind of moral schizophrenia in the form of irresolvable conflicts between 'interest' and 'duty' and no determinate criteria for applying these general notions, because their natural home has passed away. It is no wonder, on this view, that those who have not been brought up in one of the surviving tribalisms make such a fuss about commitment and criterionless choice; for there is nothing else except those ancient realities to get a grip on.

(a) *The Emergence of a Rational Morality Based on Principles*

But even if this is how concepts such as 'good' and 'duty' originated, why this nostalgic fixation on those stuffy, self-contained little communities, such as Sparta, where they could be unambiguously applied? Could not one be equally impressed by the Stoic concept of a citizen of the world, by the law of nations forged by the Roman jurisprudents, and by the labours of lawyers such as Grotius to hammer out laws of the sea against piracy? The point is that both science and a more rational, universalistic type of morality gradually emerged precisely because social change, economic expansion and conquest led to a clash of codes and to conflict between competing views of the world. Men were led to reflect about which story about the world was true, which code was correct. In discussing and reflecting on these matters they came to accept higher-order principles of a procedural sort for determining such questions.

MacIntyre, it is true, applauds those like Spinoza who drew attention to values connected with freedom and reason. He admits the supreme importance of truth-telling; he notes the massive consensus about basic rules for social living first emphasised by the natural law theorists, which H. L. Hart has recently revived as the cornerstone of a moral system. Why then is he so unimpressed by this consensus that he gives such a one-sided presentation of the predicament of modern man? Mainly, so it seems, because an appeal to such principles and basic rules cannot give specific guidance to any individual who is perplexed about what he ought to do.

(b) *Difficulties About Concrete Guidance*

Two connected difficulties are incorporated in this type of objection to principles. The first, already mentioned, is that no concrete guidance can be provided by them for an individual who wants to know what he ought to do. This is usually illustrated by the case of the young man who came to Sartre wanting guidance about whether he should stay at home and look after his aged mother or go abroad and join the Free French. How could an appeal to principles help him? Well, surely he only had a problem because he already acknowledged duties connected with his status as a son and as a citizen. Would Sartre have said to him 'You have to decide this for yourself' if the alternative to joining the Free French had been presented as staying at home and accepting bribes from the Germans for information? And surely if what is claimed to be missing is a principle for deciding between these duties, there are principles which would rule out some reasons which he might give for pursuing one of the alternatives. Supposing, for instance, he said that he was inclined toward going abroad because he wanted to determine precisely the height of St Paul's Cathedral. Would Sartre have applauded his exercise of criterionless choice?

The existentialist emphasis on 'choice' is salutary, of course, in certain contexts. It is important, for instance, to stress man's general responsibility for the moral system which he accepts. This needs to be said against those who smugly assume that it is just there to be read off. It needs to be said, too, in the context of atrocities such as Belsen. It also emphasises the extent to which character is destiny and the role which choices play in shaping the individual's character. In this kind of development, conflict situations are particularly important, and if fundamental principles conflict there is not much more that one can say than that the individual must make up his own mind or use his 'judgement'. But we do not decide on our fundamental principles such as avoiding pain or being fair; still less do we 'choose' them. Indeed, I would feel very uneasy in dealing with a man who did. And why should a moral theory be judged by its capacity to enable the individual to answer the question 'What ought I to do now?' as distinct from the question 'What, in general, are there reasons for doing?' Do we expect casuistry from a moral philosopher or criteria for making up our own minds?

The more important difficulty is the one MacIntyre has in mind, that fundamental principles such as 'fairness' or 'considering people's interests' give us such abstract criteria that they are useless because they always have to be interpreted in terms of a concrete tradition. I am very sympathetic to this objection, but I think that it also applies in varying degrees to all rational activities. To take a parallel: all scientists accept some higher-order principle such as that one ought to test competing hypotheses by comparing the deduced consequences with observations. But this does not give them concrete guidance for proceeding. It has to be interpreted. To start with, what is to count as an observation? The amount of social tradition and previous theory built into most observation procedures, especially in the social sciences, is obvious enough. And how is the importance of one set of observations to be assessed in relation to others? This is not unlike saying in the moral case: Consider impartially the suffer-

ing of people affected by a social practice. But what is to count as
suffering and how is one person's suffering to be weighed against
another's? But do difficulties of this sort render the procedural
principles of science useless? If not, why should fundamental moral
principles be regarded as useless?

Fundamental principles of morality such as fairness and the consideration of interests only give us general criteria of relevance for
determining moral issues. They prescribe what sort of considerations
are to count as reasons. Within such a framework men have to work
out arrangements for organising their lives together. And just as in
science there is a fair degree of consensus at a low level of laws, so in
the moral case there are basic rules, e.g. concerning contracts, property and the care of the young, which any rational man can see to be
necessary to any continuing form of social life, man being what he is
and the conditions of life on earth being what they are. For, given
that the consideration of interests is a fundamental principle of
morality and given that there is room for a vast amount of disagreement about what, ultimately, a man's interest are, there are nevertheless certain general conditions which it is in any man's interest to
preserve however idiosyncratic his view of his interests. These include
not only the avoidance of pain and injury but also the minimal rules
for living together of the type already mentioned. Above this basic
level there is room for any amount of disagreement and development.
People are too apt to conclude that just because some moral matters
are controversial and variable, for instance sexual matters, the whole
moral fabric is unstable. It is as if they reason: In Africa men have
several wives, in Europe only one, in the U.S.A. only one at a time;
therefore all morals are a matter of taste! As evils, murder and theft
are just as culture-bound as spitting in the street!

The point surely is that stability and consensus at a basic level are
quite compatible with change and experiment at other levels. Indeed
to expect any final 'solution', any secure resting place in social or
personal life, is to be a victim of the basic illusion which is shared by
most opponents of democracy, that of belief in some kind of certainty or perfection. But in determining what are basic rules and in
seeking above this level ways of living which may be improvements
on those we may have inherited, we make use of principles. Such
principles have to be interpreted in terms of concrete traditions; they
cannot prescribe precisely what we ought to do, but at least they rule
out certain courses of action and sensitise us to features of a situation
which are morally relevant. They function more as signposts than as
guidebooks.

(c)   *The Nature of Principles*

A place for principles in the moral life must therefore be insisted on without making too far-flung claims for what they can pre-scribe without interpretation by means of a concrete tradition. Indeed I want to insist on the importance of such traditions for the learning of principles as well as for their interpretation. Before, however, this theme is developed in detail, more must be said about the nature of principles in order to remove widespread misunderstandings.

First of all, what are principles? A principle is that which makes a consideration relevant. Suppose that a man is wondering whether gambling is wrong and, in thinking about this, he takes account of the misery caused to the families of gamblers he has known. This shows that he accepts the principle of considering people's interests, for he is sensitised to the suffering caused by gambling rather than horror-struck at the amount of greenness in the world created by the demand for green tables. He does not, in other words, accept the principle of the minimisation of greenness. He may or may not be able to formulate a principle explicitly. But this does not matter; for acceptance of a principle does not depend on the ability to formulate it and to defend it against criticism, as some, like Oakeshott, who are allergic to principles, suggest. Rather it depends on whether a man is sensitised to some considerations and not to others.

Of course, formulation is necessary if one intends to embark on some moral philosophy in the attempt to justify principles. And it might well be said that the task of justifying them is a crucial one for anyone who is according them the importance I am according them. As, however, the central part of my *Ethics and Education* was con-cerned with this very problem it would be otiose for me to present more than a thumbnail sketch of the arguments here. What I argued was that there are a limited number of principles which are funda-mental but non-arbitrary in the sense that they are presuppositions of the form of discourse in which the question 'What are there reasons for doing?' is asked seriously. The principles which have this sort of status are those of impartiality, the consideration of interests, freedom, respect for persons, and probably truth-telling. Such prin-ciples are of a procedural sort in that they do not tell us precisely what rules there should be in a society but lay down general guidance about the ways in which we should go about deciding such matters and indicate general criteria of relevance. It was argued that these principles are presuppositions of what is called the democratic way of life, which is based on the conviction that there is a better and a worse way of arranging our social life and that this should be determined by discussion rather than by arbitrary fiat.

Even if it is granted that arguments along these lines might be sustained for a few fundamental principles, further difficulties might still be raised. It might be said, for instance, that stress on the importance of principles in morality implies rigidity in the moral life. A picture is conjured up of Hardy-like characters dourly doing their duty whilst the heavens fall about them. Certainly some kind of firmness is suggested by the phrase 'a man of principle'. But here again, there are misunderstandings. A man of principle is one who is *consistent* in acting in the light of his sensitivity to aspects of a situation that are made morally relevant by a principle. But this does not preclude adaptability due to differences in situations, especially if there is more than one principle which makes different factors in a situation morally important.

Another time-honoured objection is that principles are products of reason and hence inert. We may mouth them or assent to them, but this may be a substitute for acting in a morally appropriate way. Part of the answer to this objection is to be found in the answer to the criticism that links having principles with the ability to formulate them and to defend them. But there is a further point that needs to be made. Notions such as 'fairness' and 'the consideration of interests' are not affectively neutral. 'That is unfair' is an appraisal which has more affinities with an appraisal such as 'that is dangerous' than it has with a colourless judgement such as 'that is oblong'. Pointing out that someone is in pain is not at all like pointing out that he is 5 feet 6 inches tall.

The strength of the emotive theory of ethics derives from the fact that moral principles pick out features of situations which are not affectively neutral. This, however, does not make them inconsistent with living a life guided by reason; for this sort of life presupposes a whole constellation of such appraisals, e.g. that one should be consistent, impartial and truthful, that one should have regard to relevance, accuracy and clarity, and that one should respect evidence and other people as the source of arguments. It is only an irrationalist who welcomes contradictions in an argument, who laughs with delight when accused of inconsistency, or who is nonchalant when convicted of irrelevance. Science and any other rational activity presuppose such normative standards which are intimately connected with the passion for truth which gives point to rational activities. Unless people cared about relevance and had feelings about inconsistency science would not flourish as a form of human life. The usual contrast between reason and feeling is misconceived; for there are attitudes and appraisals which are the passionate side of the life of reason.

So much, then, for the usual objections to the conception of the moral life in which prominence is accorded to principles. I hope I have said enough to establish their place in it. I now want to show how they can be seen to function in relation to concrete traditions to which MacIntyre ascribes so much importance and how they can save us from the existentialist predicament which he views as the logical alternative to being encased in a surviving code.

2   THE COMPLEXITY AND CONCRETENESS OF THE MORAL LIFE

A man who accepts principles is too often represented as living in some kind of social vacuum and attempting to deduce from his principles a concrete way of living. This is an absurd suggestion. To start with, the disposition to appeal to principles is not something that men have by nature, any more than reason itself is some kind of inner gadget that men switch on when the occasion arises. If thinking is the soul's dialogue with itself, the dialogue within mirrors the dialogue without. To be critical is to have kept critical company, to have identified oneself with that segment of society which accepts certain principles in considering its practices. Rationality, of which science is a supreme example, is itself a tradition. Rational men are brought up in the tradition that traditions are not immune from criticism.

But criticism, thinking things out for oneself, and other such activities connected with a rational type of morality, cannot be exercised without some concrete content. For how can one be critical without being brought up in something to be critical of? How can one think things out for oneself unless one's routines break down or one's roles conflict? Adherence to principles must not be conceived of as self-contained; it must be conceived of as being bound up with and modifying some kind of content. Scientists cannot think scientifically without having any content to think about.

(a)   Complexity
In an open society this content is considerably more complex than in those small, self-contained communities where, according to MacIntyre, concepts such as 'good' and 'duty' had their natural home. The notion, for instance, that people are persons with rights and

duties distinct from those connected with their roles is an alien notion in such close-knit communities. But once this is admitted, as was widely the case with the coming of Stoicism and Christianity, the content of the moral life becomes immediately much more complicated. For the norms connected with treating people as persons begin to interpenetrate those connected with roles and with the accepted goals of life. In trying to get a clear idea, therefore, about the contours of our moral life it is necessary to consider its complexity before we can grasp the concrete ways in which principles enter into it. At least five facets of our moral life must be distinguished.

First of all, under concepts such as 'good', 'desirable', and 'worthwhile', fall those activities which are thought to be so important that time must be spent on initiating children into them. These include things such as science, poetry and engineering and possibly a variety of games and pastimes. Most of these are intimately connected not only with occupations and professions but also with possible vocations and ideals of life. In our type of society they provide a variety of options within which an individual can make something of himself if he is encouraged to pursue his own bent as the principle of freedom demands.

Second, under the concepts of 'obligation' and 'duty', fall ways of behaving connected with social roles. Much of a person's moral life is taken up with his station and its duties, with what is required of him as a husband, father, citizen and member of a profession or occupation.

Third, there are those duties, more prominent in an open society, which are not specifically connected with any social role but which relate to the following of general rules governing conduct between members of a society. Rules such as those of unselfishness, fairness and honesty are examples. These affect the manner in which an individual conducts himself within a role as well as in his non-institutionalised relationships with others. They are personalised as character traits.

Fourth, there are equally wide-ranging goals of life which are personalised in the form of 'motives'. These are purposes not confined to particular activities or roles, which derive from non-neutral appraisals of a man's situation. Examples are ambition, envy, benevolence and greed. An ambitious man, for instance, is one who is moved by the thought of getting ahead of others in a whole variety of contexts. Both traits of character and motives can be thought of as virtues and vices. The traits of fairness and honesty are virtues; those of meanness and selfishness are vices. The motives of benevolence and gratitude are virtues; those of greed and lust are vices. Both character traits and motives, when looked at in a justificatory context, incorporate considerations that can be regarded as fundamental principles. Examples would be fairness and benevolence, which can be appealed to in order to criticise or justify not only other traits and motives, but also conduct covered by activities and role performances.

There are, finally, very general traits of character which relate not so much to the rules a man follows or to the purposes he pursues as to the manner in which he follows or pursues them. Examples would be integrity, persistence, determination, conscientiousness and consistency. These are all connected with what used to be called 'the will'.

The point in spelling out this complexity of our moral life is to rid us straightaway of any simple-minded view that moral education is just a matter of getting children to have 'good personal relationships' or to observe interpersonal rules like those relating to sex, stealing and selfishness. It emphatically is not. To get a boy committed to some worthwhile activity, such as chemistry or engineering, is no less part of his moral education than damping down his selfishness; so also is getting him really committed to the duties defining his role as a husband or teacher. These duties, of course, must be interpreted in a way which is sensitised by the principle of respect for persons; but no adequate morality could be constituted purely out of free-floating personal obligations.

(b) *Concreteness*

So much for the complexity of the content of the moral life which is to form the basis for any rational morality that appeals to principles. Let me now turn to the matter of concreteness in the interpretation of fundamental principles and moral ideals. The burden of the attack on principles by people like MacIntyre and Winch is to be found in Edmund Burke; it is that they are too abstract. 'The lines of morality are not like the ideal lines of mathematics.' My contention is that principles can be conceived of and must be conceived of as entering into the moral life in a perfectly concrete way without making them completely culture-bound.

Impartiality   The most fundamental principle of all practical reasoning is that of impartiality. This is really the demand that excludes arbitrariness, which maintains that distinctions shall be made only where there are relevant differences. This is essential to reasoning, in that what is meant by a reason for doing A rather than B is some aspect under which it is viewed which makes it relevantly different. But though this principle gives negative guidance in that it rules out arbitrariness, making an exception of oneself, and so on, it is immediately obvious that it is quite impossible to apply without some other principle which determines criteria of relevance. The most obvious principle to supply such criteria is that of the consideration of interests, which is personalised in virtues such as benevolence and kindness.

The Consideration of Interests   In practice the rays of this principle are largely refracted through the prism of our social roles and general duties as members of a society. If we are teachers, for instance, considering people's interests amounts, to a large extent, to considering the interests of children entrusted to our care. I once taught with a man who had such a wide-ranging concern for people's interests that he used to tell his class to get on with some work and to sit there with them, writing letters to old scholars, in order to get them to subscribe to an 'Aid to India' fund. His present scholars were, of course, bored to death! He certainly had a somewhat abstract approach to considering people's interests!

Most Utilitarians, following Mill and Sidgwick, have stressed the importance of Mill's 'secondary principles' in morality. The Utilitarian, Mill argued, has not got to be constantly weighing the effects of his actions on people's interests any more than a Christian has to read through the Bible every time before he acts. The experience of a society with regard to the tendencies of actions in relation to people's interests lies behind its roles and general rules. The principle that one should consider people's interests acts also as an ever-present corrective to, and possible ground of criticism of, rules and social practices which can also be appealed to when rules conflict. This point is well made by Stephen Toulmin in his book on ethics. A man could stick too closely to his role and accept too uncritically what was expected of him generally as a member of society. He might be very much an organisation man or a man of puritanical disposition, riddled with rules that might have lost their point, or without sensitivity to the suffering caused by unthinking insistence on the letter of the law. What would be lacking would be that sensitivity to suffering caused by actions and social practices which finds expression in virtues such as benevolence, kindness and what Hume called 'the sentiment of humanity'.

Freedom   Giving interpersonal support to the consideration of interests is the principle of freedom which lays it down that, other things being equal, people should be allowed to do what they want, or that, in other words, reasons should be given for constraining people in their pursuit of what they take to be good. This combines two notions, that of 'wants' and that of 'constraints', and immediately the concrete questions crowd in 'What is it that people might want to do?' and 'What sorts of constraints should be absent?' What, too, is to count as a constraint? Is it the want to walk about nude or to speak one's mind in public that is at issue? And are the constraints those of the bully or those of public opinion? The situation becomes even more complicated once we realise that, men being what they are, we are only in fact free from obnoxious constraints like those of the bully if we are willing to accept the milder and more leveling constraints of law. And so concreteness asserts itself. The principle only provides a general presumption, albeit one of far-reaching importance. At what point we decide that there are good reasons for constraining people because, for instance, they are damaging the interests of others, is a matter of judgement.

Closely related to the principle of freedom are ideals like 'the self-development of the individual' and personal autonomy. But here again, concreteness is imperative, for what can 'development' mean unless we build into the concept those modes of experience that it has taken the human race so long to evolve? And what sort of 'self' is going to develop? Granted that this must come to a certain extent from the individual, who does this partly by his 'choices', must not this 'self' be fairly closely related to the normal stock of motives and character traits which are called virtues? And is it not desirable that higher-order character traits, such as persistence and integrity, be exhibited in the development of this 'self'? And how can the pressure for independence and the making of choices arise unless the individual genuinely feels conflicting obligations deriving from his occupancy of social roles and his acceptance of the general rules of a society? And what point is there in choice unless the individual thinks that what he decides can be better or worse, wise or foolish? And if he thinks that any particular act is not a pointless performance he must already accept that there are general principles which pick out relevant features of the alternatives open to him.

All of this adds up to the general conclusion that the ideals connected with the principle of freedom are unintelligible except against a background of desirable activities, roles and rules between which the individual has to choose and that any proper choice (as distinct from random plumping) presupposes principles other than freedom in the light of which alternatives can be assessed.

Respect for Persons　The same sort of point can be made about respect for persons, another fundamental principle which underlies and acts as a corrective to so many of our formalised dealings with other men. Indeed, much of the content of this principle has to be defined negatively in such concrete contexts. To show lack of respect for a person is, for instance, to treat him in a role situation as merely a functionary, to be impervious to the fact that he, like us, has aspirations that matter to him, is a centre of evaluation and choice, takes pride in his achievements, and has his own unique point of view on the world. Or it is to treat him merely as a participant in an activity who is to be assessed purely in terms of his skill and competence in that activity. Worse at something becomes generalised to worse as a human being. In a similar way an excess of group loyalty or fellow-feeling can make a man seem not just different in some respects but generally inferior as a human being. Respect for persons, too, is at the bottom of our conviction that some motives are vices – lust, for instance, and envy and a certain kind of humility.

So much, then, by way of a brief sketch to illustrate the way in which I conceive of fundamental principles as entering into the moral life in a manner perfectly consistent with its complexity and concreteness. I now want to end by outlining my conception of moral education, which goes with this conception of the moral life.

3 MORAL EDUCATION

One or two general remarks must first be made about the meaning of 'education'. There is a well-established generalised use of 'education' which refers, roughly, to any processes of 'rearing', 'instruction', 'training', etc., that go on at home and at school. But there is a more specific sense of education which emerged in the nineteenth century in which education is distinguished from training and which is used to pick out processes that lead to the development of an 'educated man'. In this more specific sense, education involves getting people to make something of themselves within activities that are thought to be worthwhile, in a way which involves an understanding that has some kind of depth and breadth to it. In this more specific sense of education, employed by most educators when they are thinking about their tasks, all education is, therefore, moral education, if we are to include the pursuit of good in morals and not just confine it to codes and more general dealings with other men. Again, we will have to leave on one side the vexatious question of justification in the sphere of 'the good', of why, in other words, chemistry is more worthwhile than baseball or sun-bathing. We can pursue the implications of this view of education without getting immersed in that issue, which is a veritable 'Serbonian bog where armies whole have sunk'.

The first implication is that educating people has very much to do with getting them 'on the inside' of what is worthwhile, so that they come to pursue and appreciate it for what there is in it as distinct from what they may conceive of it as leading on to. It is in relation to this criterion of education that I want to make sense of notions such as commitment and being authentic, which starkly confront the instrumental attitude of 'What is the use of it?' and 'Where is this going to get one?' I have sympathy for the philosopher who was pressed at an interview for a chair to commit himself to the view that philosophy must have some practical use – whatever that means. He exclaimed in exasperation: 'Look, we may have to say that sort of thing in order to get money from governments and businessmen for universities, but for heaven's sake do not let us become victims of our own propaganda.'

The second implication is that educating people must involve knowledge and understanding. To be educated is not just to have mastered a know-how or knack, even if it is in the sphere of some very worthwhile activity such as cookery or ballet dancing. The Spartans were highly trained and skilled, but they are almost paradigms of a people who were not educated. Though depth of understanding is necessary to being educated, it is not sufficient, for a scientist can have a deep understanding of the 'reasons why' of things and still be uneducated if all he understands is a specialised branch of science. 'Education is of the whole man' is a conceptual truth in that being educated is inconsistent with being only partially developed in one's understanding – with seeing a car, for instance, as only a piece of machinery without aesthetic grace, without a history and without potentialities for human good or ill. Let me now relate these two implications to the different facets of the moral life in order to show the indispensability of both content and principles and the proper place for the romantic ideal.

(a) *Commitment and Authenticity*
One of the great enemies of education, in this specific sense, is second-handedness and instrumentality; hence Whitehead's polemic against inert ideas. What seems deplorable is not just that children should

mug up some science because it is the done thing or in order to get good grades but that teachers should grind through their day with that dreadful fixed smile, or that people should be polite without sensing the point of it. Doing the done thing for conformity's sake seems a stifling corruption of the moral life, and it is inherently unstable outside a confined context; for a second-hand form of behaviour is very susceptible to temptations and disintegrates when external pressures and incentives are withdrawn. This is tantamount to saying that moral education is centrally concerned with the development of certain types of motives, especially with what I have called the rational passions. When looked at in a justificatory context, some of these, e.g. benevolence, respect for persons and the sense of justice, function as fundamental principles. But if such principles are to be operative in a person's conduct, they must become *his* principles. That means that they must come to function as motives, as considerations of a far-ranging sort that actually move him to act. Let us now consider the different facets of the moral life in the light of this commitment criterion of education.

Activities and Role-performances The trouble with the situation in which we are placed in education is not just that children do not always come to us glistening with a desire to learn what is worthwhile or with a predisposition toward mastering their duties; it is also that they are incapable of first-hand attitudes toward these activities and role performances until they are sufficiently on the inside of them to grasp them and be committed to what they involve. Although a child may have some degree of curiosity there is a great difference between this and the passion for truth which lies at the heart of an activity such as science, and until he feels strongly about this all-pervading principle that permeates science, it is difficult to see how his viewpoint can be anything but a bit external. He must, to a certain extent, be induced to go through the motions before he is in a position to grasp their point, and the point is given by the underlying principle, which personalises one of the rational passions. To be rational is to care about truth; similarly, in the interpersonal sphere he must come to care about persons as centres of evaluation.

Of course there are all sorts of devices for bringing this about. In the old days, teachers, modelling the school on the army, used to employ a variety of coercive techniques. The progressives, in revolt, model the school more on the supermarket and try to gear their wares to children's wants and preferences. Then there are the less dramatic devices of stimulating by example and employing general guiding words such as 'good' and 'ought', which suggest that there are reasons but do not intimate clearly what the reasons are. The teacher's hope is that the proper reasons for doing things will become the pupil's actual reasons. This may come about by some process of identification. Admiration for a teacher may be turned outward toward involvement in the activities and forms of behaviour to which he is committed, or an existing predisposition in the child, such as curiosity, may be gradually transformed by appropriate experience into the rational passion of respect for truth. This is likely to be greatly facilitated if the enthusiasm of the peer group is also enlisted, but this takes time and training. Let me illustrate this.

To be on the inside of an activity such as science or philosophy is not to have just a general curiosity or a merely abstract concern for truth. It is to be concretely concerned about whether particular points of view are true or false. These particularities are only intelligible within a continuing tradition of thought, which has been developed by people who adhere to a public stock of procedural principles. It is because of this concrete concern that they care desperately about things like the relevance of remarks, cogency in argument and clarity of exposition; for how can one get to the bottom of anything without a concern about standards such as these which are indispensable to serious discussion? Sporadic curiosity is not enough; it has to be fanned into a steady flame and disciplined by adherence to the standards which regulate a common pursuit. The problem of education, as Whitehead saw only too well, is not just that of contriving the initial romance, it is that of bringing about acceptance of the precision and discipline required to wed a person to a pursuit. In this the support of the peer group is probably as important as the example and insistence of the teacher.

The judgement and skill which come with first-hand experience render activities more absorbing and worthwhile. The cultivation of personal relationships, for instance, and even sitting on committees, can become more and more absorbing as occupations for those who have a shrewd grasp of human behaviour. Politics, as an activity, was quite different when practised by Caesar rather than by Pompey, because of the skill and understanding Caesar brought to it. Although it is satisfying sometimes to relapse into routine activities requiring little effort (a point, I think, which Dewey appreciated too little), and although there is something to be said for occasional incursions into simple, and sometimes more brutish forms of enjoyment, it would be intolerable for a rational man to spend most of his life in such a circumscribed way. A minimum task of moral education is surely to equip people so that they will not be perpetually bored. Therefore, the case for skill and understanding, on grounds purely of individual satisfaction, is a strong one. There is also the point that, as soon as knowledge enters in as an important ingredient in an activity, an additional dimension of value, deriving from the concern for truth, is opened up.

In a pluralistic society like ours there must be a high degree of consensus at the level of those fundamental principles which underlie democratic procedures and, as I have already argued, it is obvious enough that there must be agreement about a level of basic rules which provide conditions necessary for anyone to pursue his interests. But above this level there is bound to be controversy. In this sphere of 'the good' or of personal ideals, with which we are at the moment concerned, there are any number of options open to individuals. And the principle of freedom demands that there should be. It is in this sphere that talk of commitment and authenticity is particularly pertinent. One man may develop a lifelong passion for science. Another, more influenced by the Christian ideal, may find that his main sphere of commitment is in the sphere of personal relationships and the relief of suffering. Another may opt for an aesthetic type of activity.

On the other hand, another person may find almost complete fulfilment in devoting himself to the fulfilment of a role, that of a teacher for instance. There has been a lot of loose talk, deriving from Sartre's celebrated example of the waiter, about the incompatibility of authenticity with occupying a role. Playing a role, which involves either simulation or second-handedness, should not be confused with a genuine commitment to a role. And, of course, as has been emphasised repeatedly, there is no role which can *completely* contain one's concerns and duties as a human being.

Interpersonal Rules In the interpersonal sphere there may have to be firm insistence from the start on rules like those of keeping contracts, not stealing, punctuality and honesty. And why should children not *enjoy* mastering these rules as well as those of games? Unless, however, the reasons behind these rules eventually become the individual's reasons, the job is only half done. And this does not mean fostering a theoretical grasp of the conduciveness of such rules to the general good. That kind of notion never induced anyone to do anything except to preach theoretical revolution. Neither does it mean being swept by occasional gusts of sympathy when it dawns that somebody has suffered because he has been let down. It means, on the contrary, a steady but intense sensitivity to the consequences of actions, a constand and imaginative realisation that in interpersonal relations one is dealing with persons who also have their unique point of view on the world and that this is something about them which matters supremely. In other words, it means the development of motives which personalise fundamental principles. It means also the development of judgement about particular moral matters that can only come to a person who has really got on the inside of this mode of experience. Making decisions and choices is too often represented as agonising. For those who have attained some degree of wisdom it can be both a challenge and a delight.

It is not for a philosopher to pronounce on how children can be got on the inside of this more rational form of life, or on how the rational passions, which personalise fundamental principles, can best be awakened and developed. That is a matter for psychologists. The philosopher's role is only to indicate the sort of job that has to be done. But what he *can* say is that all talk of commitment and being authentic is vacuous unless this sort of job *is* done; for it is pointless to mouth these general injunctions unless concrete provision is made to implement them. What is to be lamented about young people today is not their lack of idealism but the difficulty of harnessing it to concrete tasks. Demonstrations, like mourning, are often symbolic expressions of feelings that have no obvious channel of discharge in appropriate action.

The Will   The importance of the rational passions can also be shown in the sphere of what used to be called 'the will', where notions like those of integrity, determination and resoluteness have their place. Of course this form of consistency is possible for people who adhere conscientiously to a simple code, perhaps because, like the colonel in *The Bridge on the River Kwai*, they accept unthinkingly some role-regulating principle such as 'one ought always to obey orders' or 'an officer must always care for his men'. But such consistency is also possible for people with a more complicated morality if they genuinely care about the considerations which are incorporated in fundamental principles. Strength of character is so often represented in negative terms as saying no to temptation, as standing firm, as being impervious to social pressure. My guess is that rational people are able to do this only if they are passionately devoted to fairness, freedom and the pursuit of truth, and if they have a genuine respect for others and are intensely concerned if they suffer. The rational passion for consistency itself is also an important positive type of motivation. Indeed it has an all-pervasive influence on a rational person's beliefs and conduct. So much, then, for the first aspect of education, which concerns commitment to what is worthwhile. I now pass briefly to the second: that concerned with depth and breadth of understanding.

(b) *Depth and Breadth of Understanding*
In any worthwhile activity or form of behaviour there is a mode of acting or thinking, with its underlying principles, and some kind of established content which incorporates the experience of those who are skilled in this sphere. Depth is provided partly by the principles immanent in the mode of experience and partly by the degree to which it has been possible to discern the one in the many in the content.

The sin, of course, of the old formalism was to hand on content in a second-hand way without encouraging children to get on the inside of activities and to master the appropriate mode of experience for themselves. The converse sin of the progressive was to imagine that children could go it alone without any proper grasp of content or of the underlying mode of experience with its immanent principles. A more modern sin is to assume that a mode of experience, or a methodology, can be formalised and handed out and children saved the trouble of mastering any content. Don't bother, it is said, to teach children any historical facts, just teach them to think historically. This reminds me of the yearning, which one so often encounters, that one should hand out rules for Clear Thinking in twelve easy lessons or that one should set out philosophical method in advance of dealing with particular philosophical arguments. Enough, I hope, has been said about the intimate relationship between principles and concrete content to avoid that particular rationalistic delusion.

In the interpersonal sphere of morality there is, of course, a basic content, which every child must master, of rules to do with non-injury, property, contracts and so on; but depth of understanding in this sphere is rather different. It is not like depth of understanding in the sciences, which consists in grasping more and more abstract theories; for in morality one comes very quickly to non-arbitrary stopping points in fundamental principles, such as the consideration of interests. Depth consists rather in the development of the imagination so that one can become more acutely aware of content to be given to these principles. What, for instance, is a man's interest? Above the level of physical and mental health what is to count? Surely not just what he thinks his interest to be? And so we start trying to understand various forms of worthwhile activity and personal ideals, not only in general but in relation to the capacity of particular individuals.

Respect for persons also opens up endless vistas for the imagination in making us vividly aware of the extent to which we drag our feet in failing to treat individuals and classes of people as persons in a full sense. It opens up, too, the whole realm of our understanding of persons. For understanding a person is more than being able to interpret his behaviour in terms of wide-ranging psychological generalisations – even if there were any such generalisations that had been established – and it is not a mystic confrontation of 'I' with 'thou', about which there is little coherent that can be said. It is something about which a great deal can be said which is of cardinal importance for the moral life – about the way in which an individual's outlook is shaped by his roles, about his traits and about his motives and aspirations. But most of this sort of knowledge we obtain by being with a person and sharing a common life with him, not by delving in psychological textbooks. This sort of knowledge is probably the most important sort for any moral agent to have; for our detailed appraisals of people are very closely intertwined with explanatory notions. Indeed, I made the point earlier that most motives and traits are also virtues or vices. And it may take a whole novel such as *Howards End* to explore concretely the range of an emotion like indignation.

Breadth of understanding, however, is of equal importance to depth in any concrete approach to the moral life. It has been argued that this life itself is a complex affair involving roles, activities, motives and interpersonal rules. It also involves the disposition to be critical of this wide-ranging content in which any generation must necessarily be nurtured. The individual, too, may be confronted with conflicts arising from this heritage. How is he to be critical in an intelligent way about a social practice or about a particular feature of government policy unless he has some understanding of history and of the sorts of facts and unintended consequences of actions with which the social sciences are concerned? How is he to choose realistically between alternatives open to him unless he knows some facts?

It is absurd to encourage children to be critical and autonomous and not to insist on them learning facts which may inform their criticism and choices. In England, at the moment, we have all sorts of variants on the topic-centred curriculum, which is meant to induce moral commitment and to sensitise children to social issues. Discussion, of course, is the thing; it is regarded as almost sinful nowadays to instruct children in anything! But too often all that such discussions achieve is to confirm people's existing prejudices. They are not used as launching pads to dispatch children to the realm of some hard facts in the light of which they might make up their minds in an informed manner.

The same sort of point can be made about the necessity of breadth if children are to choose for themselves the sphere of activity within the wide range of what is desirable, to which they are to become personally committed and which may form the nucleus of a personal ideal. Not only must they have some breadth of content in order to be provided with concrete samples of the sorts of things between which they must choose; they must also make a concrete study of some of the forms of experience which have a special position in informing their choice. By this I mean studies such as literature, history, religion and the social sciences, which, if imaginatively entered into, enlarge one's perspective of the predicament of man and so put one's own choice in a less abstract setting. The romantic ideal must at least have a classical background, if it is to function as more than a mere protest.

CONCLUSION

It might be said that my conception of moral education is indistinguishable from the ideal of a liberal education. I do not mind putting it this way provided that 'liberal' implies no wishy-washiness and is used with awareness of the distinct emphases that it intimates.

A liberal education, to start with, is one that stresses the pursuit of what is worthwhile for what is intrinsic to it. It is hostile to a purely instrumental view of activities, to the bonds that link whatever is done to some palpable extrinsic end. The moral life, I have argued, rests upon rational passions which permeate a whole range of activities and which make them worthwhile for their own sake.

A liberal education is secondly one that is not narrowly confined to particular perspectives. I have argued both for a broad interpretation of the moral life and for the necessity of breadth of understanding to give concrete backing to the ideal of freedom, which is the most obvious ideal of liberalism.

Thirdly, a liberal education is one that is incompatible with authoritarianism and dogmatism. This is because a liberal education is based ultimately on respect for truth which depends on reasons and not on the word or will of any man, body or book. This means, of course, not that there is not an important place for authority in social life, but that it has to be rationally justified – as indeed it can be in the bringing up of children. The use of authority must not be confused with authoritarianism. Respect for truth is intimately connected with fairness and respect for persons, which, together with freedom, are fundamental principles which underlie our moral life and which are personalised in the form of the rational passions. The central purpose, however, of my essay, has been to show that adherence to such principles is a passionate business and that they can and should enter in a very concrete way into a man's activities, roles and more personal dealings with other men.

15

MORAL DEVELOPMENT: A PLEA FOR PLURALISM*

INTRODUCTION

Much of moral philosophy in the past has been unconvincing because it has not dwelt sufficiently on the different views that can be taken about what is morally important. It has been bedevilled by monistic theories such as Utilitarianism, or some version of Kant's theory, in which the attempt is made to demonstrate that one type of justification can be given for everything which there are reasons for doing or being. Keeping promises, telling the truth, the pursuit of poetry rather than of push-pin, being courageous and being just have all been fitted into a monolithic mould provided by some fundamental principle. The result has been an artificial type of theory that has never quite rung true. Utilitarians, for instance, who have usually been decent people with developed moral sensitivities, have invented highly dubious, and quite untested empirical speculations to demonstrate that their conviction that they should be just and truthful, which would never really dream of giving up, rests on alleged consequences to human welfare.

There is a danger of a similar fate befalling theories of moral development. It may well be that some generalisations have been established about certain aspects of moral development; but these may be peculiar to the limited range of phenomena studied. It would be unfortunate if these generalisations were erected into a general

* My thanks are due to the Australian National University for the facilities provided for me as a Visiting Fellow which enabled me to write this article, and to Geoffrey Mortimore of the Philosophy Department of A.N.U., whose thesis on *Virtue and Vice* put me on the track of some important differences between virtues, and whose comments helped me to revise a first draft of this article.

theory of moral development without account being taken of the differences exhibited by the phenomena that have not been studied.

In developing this thesis I shall use Kohlberg's cognitive stage theory as my point of departure; for his work in this field seems to me to be by far the most important which has been done to date. Yet I have certain doubts about it. Some of these derive from his failure to spell out certain points in more detail; others derive from the thought that there is much more to morality than is covered by his theory, and that his generalisations may be true only of the area of morality on which he has concentrated his attention. My article will be divided, therefore, into five main parts: exposition of Kohlberg's theory; some doubts about details; virtues and habits; is Kohlberg prescribing a morality?; and Freud and moral failure.

1 EXPOSITION OF KOHLBERG'S THEORY

Kohlberg claims, like Piaget, that there are invariant sequences in development which hold in any culture. He produces evidence to show, for instance, that in any culture children begin by being unable to distinguish dreams from real events. They then grasp that dreams are not real; then that they cannot be seen by others, and take place inside the dreamer; then that they are immaterial events produced by the dreamer, like thoughts (Kohlberg, 1968b, pp. 1024–9). He makes two points about this sequence which, he claims, hold for all proper developmental sequences. First, he claims that this sequence could not have a different order. It depends upon the relationships of concepts such as 'unreal', 'internal', 'immaterial', which it would take too long to explicate. Secondly, he claims that this sequence cannot be fully explained in terms of the teaching of adults; for if adults taught anything about dreams, they would tend to use concepts about them appropriate to a much later stage, which would not explain how children go through the earlier stages. Also, the same sequence can be observed in cultures where adults have different beliefs about dreams.

Piaget has, of course, extensively illustrated this thesis about invariant order depending upon relationships between concepts in the case of mathematics and elementary physics, and, to a more limited extent, in the moral sphere, where Kohlberg has elaborated this thesis. He holds that, though there is a difference between cultures in the *content* of moral beliefs, the development of their *form* is a cultural invariant. In other words, though there is variation between cultures about whether or not people should, for example, be thrifty or have sexual relationships outside marriage, there are cross-cultural uniformities relating to how such rules are conceived – for example, as ways of avoiding punishment, as laid down by authority. Children, Kohlberg claims, start by seeing rules as dependent upon power and external compulsion; they then see them as instrumental to rewards and to the satisfaction of their needs; then as ways of obtaining social approval and esteem; then as upholding some ideal order; and finally as articulations of social principles necessary to living together with others – especially, justice. Varying contents given to rules are fitted into invariant forms of conceiving rules. Of course, in many cultures there is no progression through to the final stages, the rate of development will vary in different cultures, and in the same culture there are great individual differences. All this can be granted and explained. But Kohlberg's main point is that this sequence in levels of conceiving rules is constitutive of moral development and that it is a cultural invariant.

How, then, does Kohlberg think that this type of development occurs if it is not the result of teaching? He rejects maturation theories as non-starters except in the case of abilities such as walking. He also rejects three types of socialisation hypotheses. First, he claims that a whole mass of empirical studies have failed to confirm the findings of the psycho-analytic school. There are no correlations, for instance, between parental modes of handling infantile drives and later moral behaviour and attitudes. There are no correlations between the amount of reward given and moral variables. Findings on parental attitudes give no clear support for the theory that early identifications are central to a moral orientation. The only established correlation, he claims, is between what he calls 'induction', which often goes along with the withdrawal of love, and moral guilt. By 'induction' he means cognitive stimulation connected with the awareness of the consequences of actions. Similarly, there is a correlation between maternal warmth and the development of conscience. But this operates, he maintains, by providing only a climate for learning (Kohlberg, 1964).

Secondly, he maintains that the evidence from the classic Hartshorne–May study shows overwhelmingly that the theory of habit generalisation put forward by psychologists with a learning theory type of orientation has no validity. What came out of this mammoth enquiry was that the traits such as honesty are situation-specific. Moral learning of this sort can only bring about specific forms of behaviour conformity. It cannot bring about predictable behaviour over a wide range of situations, such as is found in a person who has emerged to the principled stage of morality. He also claims that learning theorists have produced no evidence whatever about the influence of early forms of habit training on later adult behaviour.

Thirdly, Kohlberg rejects Piaget's hypothesis, which he got from Durkheim, that the peer group plays a decisive role in moral development in the sense that its norms are internalised by the individual. There is a correlation between the development of a principled morality and peer-group participation. But Kohlberg argues that this is because of the stimulation which such a group provides for the individual to reflect upon situations (Kohlberg, 1968a).

How then does Kohlberg think that these Kantian categories, which provide forms of conceiving of rules at the different stages, evolve? He rejects Kant's own view that they are innate moulds into which specific experiences are fitted (Kohlberg, 1968b, p. 1023). He argues that they develop as a result of interaction between the child and his physical and social environment. To understand how this happens it is necessary, therefore, to analyse, first, the universal structural features of the environment; secondly, the logical relationships involved between the concepts; and thirdly, the relationship between the particular child's conceptual scheme and the type of experience with which he is confronted. In order for development to take place there must be an optimal amount of discrepancy between the two.

This interactionist theory of development is applied to the moral sphere. Kohlberg thinks that the stages of development represent culturally invariant sequences in the child's conception of himself and his social world.

'It implies, then, that there are some universal structural dimensions in the social world, as there are in the physical world. . . . These dimensions are universal because the basic structure of social and moral action is the universal structure provided by the existence of a self in a world composed of other selves who are both like the self and different from it' (Kohlberg, unpublished manuscript).

He follows Baldwin and Mead in ascribing great importance to role taking and the dawning of reciprocity in the development of this understanding of the social situation in which we are placed. Social and moral understanding develop *pari passu* with other forms of cognitive development. And just as contact with the physical world gradually stimulates the child, for example, to classify it in terms of objects having causal relationships with others, so also in the social and moral case, the child is led gradually to grasp principles which must obtain if individuals are to live together and to satisfy their claims as social beings who are both similar to and different from others.

In support of his thesis, Kohlberg claims that the main factors which have been shown to correlate with the development of a principled, predictable morality are intelligence, moral knowledge (that is, knowledge of the rules of a society), the tendency to anticipate future events, the ability to maintain focused attention, the capacity to control unsocialised fantasies, and self-esteem. The major consistencies in moral conduct represent decision-making capacities rather than fixed behaviour traits (Kohlberg, 1964).

It is difficult to know where to begin in criticising a theory which is so varied in its claims, but an obvious strategy which matches Kohlberg's manner of presentation suggests itself. Questions can first be asked about the acceptability of his positive theory. Then, as he puts this forward as an alternative to theories which stress habit formation and to Freudian theory, questions can be raised about his grounds for dismissing theories of this sort. It might well be, for instance, that if morality is not as unitary an affair as he suggests, there is some place for habit formation in some of the areas of morality which he rather disregards. Similarly, he assumes that Freud was trying to answer the same sorts of questions about moral development as those on which he and Piaget have concentrated. But if Freud was in fact concerned with a different range of questions, then Kohlberg's criticisms of Freud might not be altogether apposite. This is the strategy which I will, in fact, use in commenting upon Kohlberg's theories. Doubts will first be raised about some of the details of his positive theory; doubts will then be raised about his dismissal of other theories in the field; and these doubts derive from the thought that Kohlberg adopts too simple and too monolithic an approach to moral development.

2 SOME DOUBTS ABOUT DETAILS

If Kohlberg's cross-cultural claims are confirmed, they are the most important findings in the psychology of morals since those of Piaget, which have often been criticised for being culture-bound. Most people, on reflection, would be prepared to concede that there is some kind of culturally invariant order of development in the case of mathematical or scientific forms of experience; but they would regard morality as much more relative to culture both in its form and in its content. Nevertheless, leaving aside the validity of the empirical findings, there are some conceptual difficulties about Kohlberg's account which could, perhaps, be dispelled if he were to spell out in more detail what he has in mind.

Let us start by probing into what he claims to be the two main features of all proper developmental sequences as applied to this particular case, namely that the order of conceptual development could not be otherwise for logical reasons and that development does not depend upon teaching.

(a) *Order of Development and Logical Relations between Concepts*
In his account of stages of moral development, Kohlberg has, for a variety of reasons, elaborated Piaget's three stages of egocentric, transcendental and autonomous morality into six stages by making a sub-division within each stage. The egocentric stage, for instance, is subdivided into the stage when rules are seen as dependent upon power and external compulsion, and the stage when they are seen as instrumental to rewards and to the satisfaction of the child's needs. He claims that this order of stages could not be otherwise than it is because of the logical relationships between the concepts. What can this mean in this particular case? In a general way the claim might seem to hold of Piaget's three stages. For instance, it is difficult to see how an autonomous morality could come before a transcendental one, for an autonomous morality implies that one can raise questions about the validity of rules and accept or reject them after reflection. Unless, therefore, one already has been introduced in some way to rules and knows, from the inside, what it is to follow a rule, there would be no content in relation to which one could exercise one's autonomy. But surely a similar point cannot be made so easily about connecting rules with power and external compulsion as distinct from connecting them with rewards and with the satisfaction of needs. It may be empirically true that children do conceive of rules in these different ways in this order. But what is there in the concepts concerned which might convert this discovered order into some kind of logical order? That there must be some explanation of this sort seems a reasonable hypothesis; how else could the culturally invariant order be explained? For instance, one might plausibly suggest that the conceptual structure required for seeing rules as means to getting rewards must be more sophisticated than that required merely for seeing them as ways of avoiding things that are unpleasant. Children have, for instance, to have a more determinate

conception of the future; they have to be able to conceive of things as positively pleasant, rather than as things which either hurt or ease an unpleasant condition of need. As a matter of empirical fact, their behaviour can be influenced by external compulsion and interference much sooner than it can be influenced by offering them rewards, and it could be shown that this is no accident, because of the conceptual structure required to see things as rewards. A similar analysis could probably be given of why seeing rules as connected with rewards must come before seeing them as connected with approval, for, conceptually speaking, 'approval' is a much more sophisticated notion than 'reward'. I have no doubt that some detailed work on the concepts concerned could reveal the kind of connections that have to be revealed. Kohlberg links these stages of moral development with a theory of role-taking and with more general features of a child's developing understanding of other people in relationship to himself. It may well be that he can, by means of this type of analysis, make it intelligible why the child *must* conceive of rules in the order in which they in fact conceive of them. But it is incumbent on Kohlberg to spell out these connections explicitly at every point. Otherwise his theory fails to carry conviction; for it does not manifestly satisfy one of the two main conditions which, on his own view, a proper developmental theory must satisfy, namely, that the temporal order of the stages should reflect some kind of logical order in the forms of conception characterising each of the stages.

(b) Teaching and Moral Development

The second condition which a proper developmental theory must satisfy is that the progression from stage to stage is not brought about by the teaching of adults. Kohlberg claims that the transition from one level of understanding to another can be aided by cognitive stimulation which helps to establish an optimal amount of discrepancy between what the child has already mastered and what he has yet to master. But this cannot be brought about by explicit teaching.

This seems, at first, to be rather a startling point which has a counter-intuitive thrust to it, to put it mildly. Surely Kohlberg cannot mean, it might be said, that saying things to children such as 'That's not fair' plays no part in helping them to develop the concept of 'fairness'. How could children ever learn such a complicated concept unless the word was used by someone in situations in which the concept had application? It is difficult to be sure what Kohlberg is asserting because he gives no account of what he means either by 'teaching' or by 'cognitive stimulation', with which he contrasts teaching. He suggests that much of the *content* of morality is passed on by example and instruction, but the *form* is something which the individual has to come to understand for himself with appropriate stimulation from others and from typical concrete situations. This, he claims, provides the appropriate psychological rationale for Socrates' conception of education, in which the learner is gradually brought to see things for himself – not haphazardly, but in a tightly structured situation (Kohlberg, 1970).

In making this sort of contrast, Kohlberg surely displays an over-rigid conception of what teaching is. Socrates was teaching the slave all right even though he was not telling him things. He was asking him leading questions, getting him to concentrate on some things rather than on others, putting questions in sequences so that the slave came gradually to make certain crucial connections. 'Teaching' surely can be applied to a great variety of processes which have in common the feature that something is marked out, displayed, made plain so that someone can learn. Information, skills and attitudes are taught in different ways. But, if they are taught, there is always some process by means of which attention is drawn to the different types of things that have to be mastered. In the case of the learning of principles, which is what Kohlberg is talking about, this marking out can also be present. But it can only take the learner a certain way. If information which has to be memorised is being imparted, the teacher can instruct the learner explicitly in what has to be learned; in teaching a skill the particular movement can be demonstrated explicitly for the learner to copy and practice. But when what is being taught is a principle which provides some kind of unity to a whole number of previously disconnected items, the teacher can only put the matter this way and that until the learner comes to 'see' it or understand it. If, therefore, the teacher is trying to get the child to 'see' something that is characteristic of one of the developmental stages, all he can do is to draw attention to common features of cases and hope that the penny will drop. He cannot get him to memorise some explicit content, or practice some movement, as in the case of imparting information or training in a skill.

There is another feature, too, of this kind of learning which makes the notion of *specific* teaching inapplicable. A child may be brought to grasp a principle by being confronted, in a variety of ways, with particular examples. But once, as Wittgenstein put it, he knows how to go on, there is no limit to the number of cases that he will see as falling under this principle. There is a sense, therefore in this sort of learning, in which the learner gets out much more than anyone could possibly have put in. Kohlberg's objection to *specific* teaching is therefore readily explained; for, in this sense, principles just are not the sorts of things that can be regarded as applying to only a specific number of items which could be imparted by a teacher.

It looks, therefore, as if Kohlberg's thesis about the impossibility of adults bringing about conceptual development by teaching is either false or a conceptual truth. It is false if a normal, non-restrictive concept of 'teaching' is being employed; for it is manifestly the case that children's understanding can be accelerated by a variety of processes such as presenting them with examples and so on. Kohlberg may call this 'cognitive stimulation'; but most people would call it 'teaching'. It is a conceptual truth if a restricted concept of 'teaching' is being employed, which rules out the processes by means of which adults help to get the child into a position where he can grasp a principle. Understanding a principle is just not the sort of thing that can be imparted by instruction, example, training and other such processes.

There is a further point, perhaps, about the actual effectiveness of leaving the child alone to make his own connections, as distinct from trying to lead him to the brink as Socrates did with the slave. My guess is that what one says about this will depend very much on the types of principles that are being learnt. If one takes, for instance, the forms of conception that are features of the different developmental stages, it is not obvious what can be done about these – for example, coming to see a rule as connected with approval rather than with rewards. Kohlberg, however, like Piaget, regards other principles as of equal developmental importance – for example, that actions should be assessed in terms of their intentions rather than in terms of their objective consequences, as in the case of the child who thinks that what is crucial about breaking cups is whether the breaker intended it, as distinct from the number of cups that are in fact broken. In a sense, both these are 'formal' notions, but in very different ways, and it could be that the teaching of adults, in the non-restrictive sense of 'teaching', could play a larger part in helping children to grasp the latter principle than the former.

Kohlberg's thesis about the learning of principles, however, though it looks like some kind of conceptual truth about learning, is a very important one to emphasise at a time when there is much pointless controversy between those who emphasise 'activity' and 'discovery' methods and those who emphasise more traditional methods of instruction and training. The general point must first be made that the method used is limited severely by what it is that has to be learnt. Discovery methods have little application to the learning of skills or to the acquiring of information. However, in so far as there are principles which have to be understood in the type of learning that is taking place, the sorts of methods included by Kohlberg under 'cognitive stimulation' have manifest application. They also apply to the grasping of those principles – for example, of causality or of the relevance of intended consequences in morality – which constitute *one* type of what Kohlberg calls the 'form' of experience. Instruction, training and learning by example seem much more appropriate in learning what he calls the 'content'. This is a particular example of the general thesis that there need be no conflict between these different approaches to learning. The possible methods will depend largely on the details of what has to be learned (see Peters, 1969).

3 VIRTUES AND HABITS

Kohlberg maintains not only that character traits such as honesty are comparatively unimportant in morals, but also that processes of habit formation, by means of which they are assumed to be established, are of secondary significance. The considerations which led him to this somewhat surprising view are as follows.

1. The Hartshorne–May investigation cast doubt upon the existence of stable character traits. In the case of honesty, low predictability was shown of cheating in one situation from cheating in another. The tendency of children to cheat depended on the risk of detection and the effort required to cheat. Non-cheaters thus appeared to be more cautious rather than more honest. Peer-group approval and example also seemed to be an important determinant (Kohlberg, 1964, pp. 386–7).

2. Kohlberg claims that his own studies show that the decision not to cheat has something to do with the awareness of universal moral principles, not with principles concerned with the badness of cheating *per se*. Other good predictors of resistance to cheating are factors to do with ego strength. He concludes that the crucial determinants of moral development are cognitive. There are different conceptual levels in morality, and stability of character depends upon the level attained by the individual.

(a) Traits and Principles
Before discussing the role of habit in morality, something must

first be said about the dichotomy which Kohlberg makes between traits and principles. In his account of moral development a principled morality is contrasted with a morality of character traits. This is a strange contrast. Surely, being just or fair are paradigm cases of character traits. They are as much character traits as being honest, which is the virtue with which justice is often contrasted in Kohlberg's work. Yet fairness and justice are also paradigm cases of moral principles. To call something a 'trait' of character is simply to suggest that someone has made a rule – for example, of honesty or of justice – his own. Whether a rule, which can also be regarded as a trait of character if it is internalised, is a principle depends on the function which the rule or consideration, which is personalised in the trait, performs. To call justice or concern for others principles is to suggest that backing or justification is provided by them for some more specific rule or course of action. We might, for instance, appeal to considerations of justice to back up a decision to give women the vote; gambling might be condemned because of the suffering which it brought on the relatives of gamblers. In these cases, justice and concern for others would be functioning as principles. Honesty, too, often functions as a principle in that it can be appealed to in condemning fraud and many other forms of deceit. The contrast, therefore, between traits of character and principles rests on no clear view of how the term 'principle' functions.

There is, however, an important contrast which Kohlberg does not make between traits, such as honesty and justice, and motives such as concern for others. As we shall see, there are important differences between virtues which are motives and those which are character traits. But one obvious difference needs to be noted at this point: that concern for others develops much earlier in a child's life and does not require the same level of conceptual development to be operative as does justice or even honesty. Prima facie, too, there are grounds for thinking that it can be learnt or encouraged by the example of others. Of course, concern for others can be exhibited at different levels which vary according to a person's imagination and sophistication about what constitutes harm or welfare. But it certainly can get a foothold in a person's moral life earlier than justice, because it is not necessarily connected with rules and social arrangements, as is justice. This was one of the reasons which led Hume to distinguish the artificial from the natural virtues. It may, of course, take time for children to grasp that reasons for rules can fall under it *as a principle*. Kohlberg's stage theory may apply to it in so far as it comes to function as a principle – that is, as providing considerations that give backing to rules. But a different account must be given of how children become sensitised to such considerations than is given of how they come to be concerned about justice.

In talking about a principled morality we must not only distinguish motives from character traits such as justice and honesty. We must also note the peculiarities of a certain class of character traits that are both content-free and which do not, like motives, introduce teleological considerations. These are traits such as consistency, persistence, courage, determination, integrity and the like. They are of a higher order and relate to the ways in which rules are followed or purposes pursued; they prescribe no particular rules or purposes, as do honesty and ambition. In ordinary language this group of character traits is intimately connected with what we call 'the will'. Kohlberg suggests that 'ego-strength' variables correlate with the development of a principled morality. But this must necessarily be the case, for part of our understanding of a 'principled morality' is that people should stick to their principles in the face of temptation, ridicule and the like. But a different account must surely be given of their development than of that of a virtue like justice, for though it may be a necessary condition of a stable, principled morality that people should both be able to understand what justice is and assent to it, and that it should come to function as a principle for them in the sense of providing justifying reasons for a whole range of behaviour, it is nevertheless not sufficient. There are many who can do all this but who still lack the courage, determination, integrity and persistence to carry out what they see as just.

It looks, therefore, as if there is little validity in Kohlberg's distinction between principles and character traits. But a more positive finding of this brief examination is that there are distinct classes of virtues, the differences between which may prove to be important in considering the relationships between virtue and habit. To summarise, there are (a) highly specific virtues, such as punctuality, tidiness and perhaps honesty, which are connected with specific types of acts, and which lack any built-in reason for acting in the manner prescribed – that is, are not motives, unlike (b) virtues, such as compassion, which are also motives for action. There are, then, (c) more artificial virtues, such as justice and tolerance, which involve more general considerations to do with rights and institutions. Finally, there are (d) virtues of a higher order, such as courage, integrity, perseverance, and the like, which have to be exercised in the face of counter-inclinations.

When, therefore, Kohlberg criticises a character trait type of morality on account of the specificity of character traits, it looks as if his criticism is based on the peculiar features of the character trait of honesty, on which most research has been done. Dishonesty has to be understood in terms of fairly specific situations such as cheating, lying and fraud. This is a feature of all type (a) virtues. Other virtues and vices, however, such as benevolence, cruelty and integrity, are not tied down in this way to specific types of action, although about all such virtues the more sophisticated point could be made that what is to count as cases of them will vary from culture to culture. Kohlberg's criticism, therefore, depends on the peculiarities of a particular class of character traits.

In general, however, this criticism follows analytically from the meaning attached to a principled morality; for principles pick out very general considerations, such as unfairness or harm to people, which can be appealed to in support of a number of rules. As many type (a) character traits, such as thrift, punctuality, chastity and the like, represent internalised social rules whose justification depends upon appeal to more general considerations picked out by principles, their specificity, when compared with principles, is not surprising, for it is implicit in what we mean by a principle. But here again this depends very much on the examples taken. Punctuality and thrift manifestly require some further justification in terms of principles. Fairness and unselfishness, on the other hand, are also character traits, but there is nothing particularly specific about them. Indeed, they are internalisations of considerations which would normally be appealed to as principles. Consistency, integrity, determination and the like are, as we have seen, character traits as well, but of a higher order and in no way tied down to specific acts.

It is important to realise too, that although principles pick out abstract considerations that can be appealed to in contexts of justification and moral uncertainty, for the most part they enter into our lives in a much more concrete, specific way. For most of us, for instance, the principle that we should consider people's interests is to be understood by reference to specific roles such as that of a father, teacher, citizen, etc., with the specific duties that are constitutive of them, and in following the more general rules that are internalised in the form of punctuality, tidiness, thriftiness and the like. This was a point well made by Mill in his stress on the role of 'secondary principles' in morality.

(b) *The Role of Habit*
Kohlberg's contention that specific character traits, such as honesty,

which function as habits, are of little significance in the moral life, is paralleled by his claim that learning theorists have produced no evidence of the influence of early forms of habit training on adult behaviour (Kohlberg, 1966). Most of the evidence is negative – the effect of exposure to Boy Scouts, Sunday School, etc., and of the effect of earliness and amount of parental training on habits such as obedience, neatness, etc. (Kohlberg, 1964, p. 388). This type of learning seems to be short-term, situation-specific and reversible.

This lack of importance assigned to habit goes against a whole tradition of thought about moral development stemming from Aristotle. He too assigned a central place to cognitive factors in moral development in so far as he characterised this in terms of the gradual emergence of practical reason. But he conceded a major role to habits in morals and in moral education. He maintained (Aristotle, Bk 11, Ch. 1) that the capacity given to us by nature to receive virtue is brought to maturity by habit. We acquire virtue by practice. Just as we become builders by building houses, so 'we become just by doing just acts, temperate by doing temperate' acts, brave by doing brave acts' (Aristotle, Bk 11, Ch. 1). It is therefore of great importance to see that children are trained in one set of habits rather than another. In their early years they cannot, of course, act bravely or justly in a full sense for they lack the appropriate knowledge and dispositions. But through instruction, praise and blame, reward and punishment by men who are already courageous and just, they can acquire action patterns which gradually become informed by a growing understanding of what they are doing and why.

How then is habit related to virtue in the life of a developed person, and how can a morality, which is firmly rooted in habit, provide the appropriate basis for a more rational reflective type of morality? An examination of the concept of 'habit' may indicate answers to these questions which are also compatible with Kohlberg's contentions about habit formation; for it may well be the case that his contentions depend upon a limited conception of 'habit' and on the peculiarities of the facets of morality on which he has concentrated his attention.

In order to raise questions about the role of habit in morality, it is necessary to distinguish three applications of the concept of 'habit'. (See also Peters, 1963; Kazepides, 1969.) We can speak, first, in a descriptive way about a person's habits or what he does habitually. Secondly, we can use explanatory phrases such as 'out of habit', 'from force of habit', and 'a matter of sheer habit'. Thirdly, we can talk of certain things being learnt by a process of 'habituation'. Let us consider each of these applications of the concept of 'habit' in relation to the types of virtue already distinguished in section 3(a).

Habits When we use 'habit' as a descriptive term, we are making certain suggestions about behaviour. We are claiming, first, that it is something that the individual has done before and is likely to do again. It implies repetition arising from a settled disposition. Secondly, we suggest that it is the sort of thing that the individual *can* carry out more or less automatically. He does not have to reflect about it before he does it, to plan it in any way, or to decide to do it. But he may. If one of a man's habits is to get up early, it does not follow that he will not reflect about it on a particular occasion. It only suggests that he will not *have* to reflect on what he is doing on a particular occasion, that he *can* do this more or less automatically. Needless to say, also, there are many manifestations of automatic behaviour that are not usually habits – for example, automatic writing.

What forms of behaviour can be termed 'habits'? Etymologically, the word suggests forms of behaviour that one has in the way in which one has clothes. Habits, like clothes, express how a man holds himself. They thus can refer to his demeanour as well as to his clothes. Nowadays, we tend to confine the word to a person's settled dispositions which manifest themselves in behaviour which, like clothes, he can put on or take off at will. We do not, therefore, call dreaming a habit, nor do we speak in this way of stomach aches and facial tics. We thus can say that a man is in the habit of going for a walk before breakfast, that talking philosophy in the pub is one of his habits, or that he is habitually punctual and polite.

There are some forms of behaviour which may be exercises of dispositions which we do not call 'habits'. For instance, we do not talk about sympathetic or angry behaviour as 'habits'. This is because these forms of behaviour are too deeply connected with our nature; they are not the sorts of behaviour that we can put on and take off at will, like clothes. Also they are not the sorts of behaviour which, even if repeated, we tend to perform automatically. If we did, they would cease to qualify as being sympathetic or angry in a full-blooded sense.

It might be thought that there is an incompatibility between habits and intelligence or reasoning. But if there is such a clash, it is not with this application of the concept of 'habit'. Ryle (1948, pp. 42–3), for instance, sees such an incompatibility. But that is because he does not distinguish between the three applications of the concept of 'habit'.

He slides between talking descriptively of habits, which he regards as single-track dispositions, and the use of explanatory phrases such as 'out of habit'. He also seems to think that all habits are developed by a particular form of habituation, namely drill, and incorporates this mistaken empirical assumption into his concept of 'habit'. In actual fact, not all habits are single-track dispositions. Playing bridge or chess could be regarded as among a person's habits, and there is nothing single-track or unintelligent about activities of this sort. Indeed, there are writers who go to the opposite extreme. Oakeshott, for instance, regards plasticity as one of the main features of habits. To use his own words: 'Like prices in a free market, habits of moral behaviour show no revolutionary changes because they are never at rest' (Oakeshott, 1962, p. 65). Habitual forms of behaviour can involve reasoning as well as intelligence in the sense of adaptability. Indeed, we can talk about a habit of reflecting upon conduct.

Is there any reason, then, why virtues should not be described as habits, and are they of much importance in morality? Surely the importance of established habits in the moral life is manifest. Life would be very exhausting if, in moral situations, we always had to reflect, deliberate and make decisions. It would also be very difficult to conduct our social lives if we could not count on a fair stock of habits such as punctuality, politeness, honesty and the like, in other people. This applies particularly to those type (a) character traits, such as punctuality and tidiness, which are internalised social rules.

Habits, however, are not sufficient for the conduct of a person's moral life for at least three reasons. The first reason is that the different classes of virtues distinguished in section 3(a) differ in their relation to habit, and it is important to understand what underlies Kohlberg's claim that only some situation-specific types of virtue, which form part of the 'content' of morality, can be habits. Type (a) virtues, such as punctuality, tidiness and perhaps honesty, seem to be the most obvious class of virtues which can be called habits, because they are connected with specific types of acts; so there seems to be no difficulty about the condition of automaticity being sometimes fulfilled. They also lack any built-in reason for acting in the manner prescribed. They are to be contrasted with type (b) virtues, such as compassion, which are also motives for action. It seems essential to the exercise of such virtues that feelings should be aroused, that one's mind should be actively employed on bringing about specific states of affairs. The concept of 'habit' therefore cannot get a grip on virtues such as these. Nor can it get a grip on type (c), more artificial virtues, such as justice and tolerance, for a rather different reason. Being just, tolerant, or prudent involves much in the way of thought. Considerations have to be weighed and assessed. The suggestion, therefore, that acting justly might be one of a man's habits sounds strange. Finally, type (d), higher-order virtues, such as courage, integrity, perseverance and the like, would also be incongruously described as habits, because such virtues have to be exercised in the face of counter-inclinations. It is, of course, part of our understanding of what can be considered a virtue that there should be counter-inclinations which might be operative. Otherwise there would be no point in the virtue in general. But it is only essential to some virtues, namely, those that involve some kind of self-control, that counter inclinations must be present when they are exercised. Now in so far as this condition is realised, as it is in the case of virtues such as courage, it seems inappropriate to think of them as habits, for they require active attention. This would not be true, however, of all higher-order virtues – for example, consistency, which might be regarded as a habit.

The second reason for the insufficiency of habit in the moral life is that those virtues which we can call habits have an incompleteness about them because the reason for behaving in the ways which they mark out is not internal to them, which is why we do not call virtues such as thrift, punctuality and politeness motives. It is not surprising therefore, that the Hartshorne–May enquiry found that children saw being honest as a way of escaping punishment or gaining approval. These may not be particularly good reasons for acting honestly, but some reason is required; people do not act *out of* honesty, as they act out of jealousy or compassion. Honesty, in other words, is a trait of character, not a motive. Ideally, acting honestly should be connected with considerations which provide a rationale for being honest, rather than considerations which are manifestly extrinsic to this form of behaviour, such as the avoidance of punishment or the obtaining of approval. But such a rationale is beyond the understanding of young children. So it is not surprising that, in so far as they are honest, they are honest for some extrinsic reason, as Aristotle saw in his account of how virtues are acquired under instruction.

This introduces a third point about the insufficiency of habits – when people are in non-routine situations, habits, by definition, can no longer carry them through. The question then arises, with virtues such as honesty and punctuality, as to what considerations become operative. If, as in the case of the children in the Hartshorne–May enquiry, or that of the Spartans when they went abroad, the sanctions of punishment and social approval are withdrawn, they may not continue to be honest. In their case the extrinsic considerations which supported their honesty were not such that honesty seemed sensible to them when being dishonest had no manifest disadvantages and some short-term advantage. Suppose, however, that, as Aristotle put it, 'they understand the reason why of things', and connect being honest with some more general principle about human relationships – for example, respect for persons, concern for finding out what is true. They might then link particular manifestations of honesty, such as not cheating, or not lying, with further considerations falling under these principles. This would be what Kohlberg calls having a principled morality which, he claims, is the only stable sort. He usually links this with the acceptance of the principle of justice, but this is only a particular case of such a morality. What is important is that considerations deriving from such principles are reasons which always exist for various ways of being honest. Possible censure or punishment, on the other hand, do not always exist and they depend on the attitude of people generally to breaches of rules such as that of honesty. They provide reinforcements for rules rather than a rationale. If people have no rationale for rules, and only keep to them in conditions where there is positive or negative reinforcement for them, then they are ill-equipped to deal with situations of a non-routine sort where the usual reinforcements are absent. This points to the necessity for the development of reason in morals to provide a rationale for habit. Reason is a supplement to habit but not a substitute for it.

Out of Habit   It was noted that there seems to be no incompatibility between 'habit', when used as a descriptive term, and intelligence and reasoning. But there is a clash when explanatory terms such as 'out of habit' are used of behaviour; for this phrase and others, such as 'from force of habit', do suggest routine types of situations to which the concept of 'intelligence' is not applicable. The condition of automaticity, of a stereo-typed form of behaviour, seems more strongly implied. They also rule out the possibility that the individual who has done something has deliberated before he did it, has reflected or gone through any process of self-criticism or justification, or has seen what he does as a means to a further end. Of course he might, in the past, have formed this particular habit by some series of decisions involving deliberation, planning, justification and other such exercises of reason. But if we say that a man does something, for instance, calls someone 'sir' out of habit, we are denying that in this case any of the processes typically associated with reason have taken place. He might be able to give *a* reason for this if asked afterwards, but on this particular occasion he did not act with the end in view which he might specify if so pressed; it was not *his* reason.

'Out of habit' also rules out explanations of behaviour which relate to features intrinsic to the behaviour so explained. In other words, it rules out the suggestion that the individual did what he did for enjoyment, because of the satisfaction which it brought him, or for fun. It also rules out any suggestion of its being done out of a sense of duty. It claims nothing more than that this is the sort of thing that the individual tends to do because he has done it often before. To put it more technically, the explanation is in terms of the old psychological law of exercise.

In the life of any man, however rational, it is important that a great many things should be done out of habit. His mind is then set free to pay attention to things that are novel and interesting, and for which he has no established routine. Any complex skill, for instance, presupposes a number of component movements that are performed out of habit, and conversation would flag at meal times if most of our eating manœuvers were not performed out of habit. But what about the sphere of morality? Has this application of the concept of 'habit' much relevance to this sphere?

Everything that was previously said about virtues which can be called habits would apply also *a fortiori* to the suggestion that they might be exercised out of habit. The only difference would be that more might be ruled out because the condition of automaticity seems to be more strongly suggested. To say that something is a habit is to say that it is the sort of behaviour that an individual *could* perform without giving his mind to it, but to say that he performed it out of habit is to suggest that he did not give his mind to it. Obviously, therefore, type (b) virtues, which are motives, type (c) virtues, which involve much in the way of thought, and type (d) virtues, which involve self-control, would be ruled out. But even some type (a) virtues might seldom be exercised out of habit. Honesty, for instance, is exercised by means of a specific range of acts such as telling the truth, not cheating and so on. But it would not often be exercised out of habit, because people are usually honest in the face of some sort of temptation, though they might be so disciplined that they become almost oblivious of this aspect of the situation. Honesty does not *have* to be exercised in the face of some counter-inclination as does a type (d) virtue such as courage. Thus, in a particular case, a man might be honest without being troubled much by counter-inclinations, and it might be said of him that he was honest out of habit. But this explanation of behaviour is appropriate, in the main, to the more conventional virtues such as politeness, punctuality and thrift.

Habituation   Thus far I have considered only one problem raised both by Aristotle and by Kohlberg, namely, that of the relationship between virtue and habit in the moral life. We must now address ourselves to another problem, that of the development of a rational morality out of a basis provided by early habit formation. In other words, we must study the relationship between the development of virtues and various forms of habituation.

Kohlberg, like Plato, emphasises that the most important features of moral education are cognitive. The individual has to come to the grasp of principles and to connect particular rules like that of honesty with these instead of with extrinsic reinforcements such as praise and blame, reward and punishment. A grasp of principles, he maintains, cannot be directly taught; it can only develop with appropriate environmental stimulation, like the grasp of the causal principle or of the conservation of material things. This confirms Aristotle's point that children cannot, in the early stages of their lives, behave like the just man. This means two things: first, that they cannot grasp the principle of justice, which is very abstract and difficult to grasp; and secondly, that they cannot raise questions about the validity of rules, that they cannot see that principles, such as that of justice, might provide a justification for other rules. As Piaget (1932) showed, it takes quite a time in the development of children before the notion of the validity of rules makes any sense to them, before they realise that they might be otherwise, and those rules they accept should depend upon the rationale which can be provided. Thus, in their early years, they cannot accept rules in a rational way or be taught rules by processes, such as explanation and persuasion, which depend upon the ability to grasp a rationale.

What, then, is to be said about early moral education? Must children first of all become habituated to following certain rules, as Aristotle suggested, and can we conceive of a form of behaviour which is learned in this way, developing into the rational form of behaviour of Aristotle's just man or into Kohlberg's principled type of morality? We must first ask what is meant by 'habituation'. We use the term to describe a wide class of learning processes in which people learn by familiarising themselves with, or getting used to, things, and by repetition. For instance, a boy might learn not to be afraid of dogs by a process of habituation, by being constantly in their presence and getting used to their ways. This type of learning might be contrasted with being instructed or with learning by insight. Drill is another obvious example of habituation.

Ryle, as has already been mentioned, not only thinks that habits are formed by the particular process of habituation known as drill, but incorporates this belief into the meaning of 'habit'. This raises the question whether habits must be formed by *some* process of habituation, even if it is not the particular process of drill. It does not look as if this is a conceptual truth. Indeed, the *Oxford English Dictionary* explicitly states that there is no etymological ground for supposing that a habit must even be an acquired tendency. One might be led to think this because part of our understanding of 'habit' is that a form of behaviour should be repeated. We might therefore conclude that it was learned by repetition. But this is not necessarily the case. After puberty, for instance, one of a boy's habits might be to look long and lingeringly at pretty girls. He did not have to learn to do this. He just found himself doing it. The explanation would be in terms of the maturation of the sex organs and consequent sensitisation to girls, rather than in terms of any process of habituation, let alone drill.

Most habits, however, as a matter of empirical fact, are learned by some process of habituation. Not all of these are characterised by the sort of mindlessness that we associate with drill. If this was the case, the emergence of any rational type of morality out of processes of habituation would be a mystery. For instance, after reflection on the unsatisfactoriness of his daily pattern of life, a man can make a resolution to get up early; he can decide to make this one of his habits. In the early stages, when the alarm sounds, he may have to exhort himself, to rehearse his reasons for getting up early, and so on. When he has formed the habit, none of this deliberation and decision is necessary; but this is one way of forming a habit. Similarly, we can form habits intelligently in the context of an activity which has some overall end, such as a game of tennis. We may have to drill ourselves in particular movements, but we can learn also to make the movements in the context of a more widely conceived objective – for example, putting the ball where the opponent is not. Indeed, practice in situations where movements have to be varied in the light of changes in the situation is regarded by many as one of the best ways of forming habits, for this prevents too stereotyped a pattern of movements developing. Important, also, in the development of adaptable habits are the higher-order scruples connected with reason, such as having regard to whether what is done is correct, taking care, checking and thinking of objections. These scruples are learned mainly by taking part in situations where actions and performances are criticised. Gradually, through a process of role playing, the learner becomes a constant critic of his own performances.

These ways of forming habits, in which reason and intelligence are involved, can be contrasted with other processes of habituation where a habit is 'picked up' in ways which are explicable only in terms of laws of association, such as contiguity, recency and frequency. In these cases, the learner may not be trying to master anything; there may even be a suggestion of automaticity. Something is done, for instance, which is associated with something pleasant, and it is repeated as in operant conditioning. Or some constant conjunction leads the individual to expect something without any connection being consciously noted – for example, the part played by serial probability in learning to spell. Alternatively, some mannerism, or form of behaviour, is picked up by some process of imitation without any conscious modelling or copying. These principles may also be at work in cases where habits are deliberately formed, or where a person's mind is on what is being learnt. This is not being denied. For instance, in learning to spell, one can attempt to learn in a rational way by formulating rules. This can help learning; but at the same time one may also learn through 'picking up' combinations of letters which frequently occur together. The point is that there are some processes of habituation where people fall into habits in ways which are explicable purely in terms of associative principles. But not all cases of habituation are like this.

Learning the Content of Morality: Type (a) *Virtues*   What then is to be said about the role of 'habituation' in the moral sphere? Surely, it cannot refer to a process in which learning is explicable purely in terms of the principles of association. For, as in all cases of learning, one cannot apply some general theory of learning without paying careful attention to what it is that has to be learnt. And this is very complicated in the moral case, even if we take some type (a) virtue, as honesty, which is to form part of the content of morality. Learning to be honest is not like learning to swim. It could not conceivably be picked up just by practice or by imitation; for a child has to understand what honesty is in order to behave in this way, and this presupposes all sorts of other concepts such as truth and falsehood, belief and disbelief, and so on. Such understanding cannot grow just by repetition and familiarity, though they may aid it. Similarly, extrinsic reinforcements, working by principles of association, may strengthen a tendency to behave in accordance with a rule, but the child has to understand what particular feature of his behaviour is being singled out for attention. Parents often punish children for stealing, without appreciating that the child has not yet the grasp of concepts such as property, ownership, lending, giving and the like which enable him to understand that it is stealing for which he is being punished. Such extrinsic reinforcers may help to mark out the relevant features of behaviour by, as it were, underlining some aspect of it. But it is impossible to conceive how they could be sufficient to bring about understanding. Neither could understanding develop just through untutored 'learning from experience'; for 'honesty' can only be exercised in relation to socially defined acts such as cheating and lying, and these could not be understood without initiation into a whole network of social practices. There must, therefore, be some kind of teaching of rules for moral education to get started at all. The content has to be exhibited, explained, or marked out in some way which is intrinsically rather than extrinsically related to it. This is a central feature of any process that can be called a process of teaching. Moral education is inconceivable without some process of teaching, whatever additional help is provided by various processes of habituation.

Although at an early stage there is no possibility of reason in the sense of justification being operative, there is ample scope for intelligence, for learning to apply a rule like that of honesty to a variety of situations which are relevantly similar. In other words, the rule can be taught in such a way that children gradually come to see the similarity between actions like that of lying and cheating. Parents can relate rules to their point even if children do not yet grasp the idea that their validity depends upon their point. And, surely, drawing attention to the consequences of their actions will help them to understand that actions have consequences. This at least will prepare the way for the stage when they grasp that the reasons for some rules of action depends upon consequences.

Sensitisation to Principles: Type (b) *and* (c) *Virtues* Kohlberg maintains that the assessment of actions in terms of their consequences is an important feature of a developmental stage in morality that cannot be taught by any kind of direct instruction. Children, like Socrates' slave, must come to see it, which is true enough; for this is not just a matter of information, like the height of St Paul's cathedral, which simply has to be remembered rather than understood. But he also claims that 'cognitive stimulation' can aid this process of coming to understand. And what else is that, apart from presenting some kind of content in different ways until eventually the appropriate connections are made? And, in the case of rules, this is surely done by teaching them intelligently, that is, by linking rules with other rules and with consequences which will eventually come to be seen as providing some point for them. Kohlberg also argues that some features of the situation in which rules are learned, for example, parental warmth, aid cognitive development because they provide a favourable climate for it. It may also be the case that some sorts of extrinsic aids, such as punishment, may encourage a rigidity or lack of intelligence in rule following that may become compulsive. These, however, are empirical questions which are largely still a matter for speculation. All I have been trying to do is to show how it is intelligible that acquiring habits in ways that are possible at an early stage should develop into a more rational way of following rules. I have been putting the same kind of case in the sphere of morals that I previously put when discussing the general relationship between forming habits and intelligence. It is not the case that habits have to be formed by a process like that of drill. They can be formed in the context of an activity which is more widely conceived. My argument is that learning habits in an intelligent way can be regarded as providing an appropriate basis, in the moral case, for the later stage when rules are followed or rejected because of the justification that they are seen to have or lack.

The encouragement of intelligent rule following, however, in relation to what Kohlberg calls the content of morality, is not the only thing that can be done in the early stages to prepare the way for principled morality. For, although a child may not be able, early in life, to connect rules with those considerations which are picked out by principles, he can become sensitive to considerations which will later serve him as principles. Psychologists such as Piaget and Kohlberg have failed to draw attention to this because of their preoccupation with type (c) virtues such as the principle of justice, which picks out very abstract considerations that are very difficult for a small child to grasp. If, however, instead of justice, we consider the status of type (b) virtues such as concern for others, I think that we may look at moral education in a very different light. The plight of others is much easier to grasp, and concern for it develops much earlier in children. If such concern is encouraged early in children, it can come to function later on as one of the fundamental principles of morality, when the child reaches the stage of being able to grasp the connection between many rules and their effect on other people.

Can anything be done early by training to sensitise children in this respect? Habituation seems the wrong sort of term to use in this context; for the last thing we want is to habituate children to the sight of suffering. Possibly, however, by exposing them a bit to the sight of suffering in others, or rather by not shielding them from situations where they will be confronted by it in a first-hand way, their sensitivity to it may be sharpened. It might also be argued that children can be encouraged to form the habit of paying attention to people's suffering rather than just concentrating on their own projects. This habit of mind would not itself be a virtue. But it might predispose children to be influenced by compassion on specific occasions. Again, this is a matter of speculation, but this sphere of the cultivation of appropriate forms of sensitivity is certainly one of the most crucial areas in the development of a principled form of morality. It is pointless to encourage children to reflect about rules, and to link them with general considerations of harm and benefit, if these considerations do not act as powerful motives for the person who can perform such calculations.

The Development of Self-control Type (d) *Virtues* When Aristotle spoke of the importance of habituation in moral education, perhaps he had in mind the particular type (d) virtues which are intimately connected with self-control. Indeed, Von Wright (1963, Ch. VII) has explicitly suggested that *all* virtues are forms of self-control. Habituation may be very important in the development of this particular class of virtues in that it may be necessary for people to be tempted, or made fearful, by situations which appear to them in a certain light. The more familiar they become with such situations, and with the internal commotions which they occasion, the more likely people are to be led by a variety of considerations to control their immediate responses. In the case of small children, the proper reasons for self-control are not readily apparent, and they are unable to link the manner of behaviour with its proper justification. If, however, children are exposed to, for example, danger, and praised when they do not run away in terror, they may learn to control themselves for such extrinsic reasons. There is, of course, the danger that later on they will only display courage when the reinforcing conditions associated with the manner of behaviour are present. But it could be argued that familiarity with both the external features of dangerous situations and with the internal commotions, which such danger occasions in them, carries over into situations in later life when they appreciate the proper reasons for being courageous. Like Aristotle's child, who learns to be temperate by behaving temperately under instruction, they are preparing themselves, by going through the motions of self-control, for the stage when they will have a more inward understanding of the reasons for the pattern of behaviour that they are exhibiting. Habituation is important both in familiarising children with the features of such situations and in developing the relevant action patterns that will enable them to deal practically with the emotions that may be aroused instead of being overcome by them. Habituation may thus help to lay down a pattern of response that may be used in the service of more appropriate motives at a later stage.

Kohlberg nowhere deals with the development of this class of virtues which necessarily involve self-control. He might well claim, however, that even if people do learn to be courageous by some such process of habituation, there is no evidence of transfer. Like the Spartans they might display their courage only in very specific types of situations. Or people might become physically brave but moral cowards. To which it might be replied that, if moral courage is thought a desirable character trait to develop, it is difficult to conceive how it could develop without some kind of practice. Maybe there is not necessarily much transfer from situations requiring physical courage to those requiring moral courage, but some account must be given of how moral courage is developed. In this sphere the individual has to learn to accommodate himself not to dangers that threaten him in a palpable physical way, but to social threats and pressures such as ridicule, disapproval, ostracism and so on. These sorts of reactions on the part of others can be evoked by a wide range of moral stances taken up by an individual. It is therefore possible for an individual to learn to cope with typical patterns of response on the part of others on the basis of a very limited number of issues on which he may make a stand. In other words, there is a built-in type of generality about this type of moral training. The English public school system of character training, derived from Thomas Arnold, is usually associated with team spirit and moral conformism. But equally strong in this tradition is the insistence that the individual should stick up for principles connected with 'fair play' in the face of group pressure. Does Kohlberg think that an individual can in fact adhere to his favoured principle of justice, when the screws are put on him, without some such training? And does he think that generations of British administrators, who, like the Romans, were able to maintain the rule of law with a fair degree of impartiality in situations where they were comparatively isolated and subject to social pressures, bribes, flattery, etc., were quite unaffected by the type of character training to which they were subjected at school? This seems, on the face of it, a most implausible assumption, but, of course, it would be an extremely difficult one to test.

Morality and the Development of Motivation   Sticking to a principle such as justice, however, should not be represented in too negative a light, as it might be by those who are overinfluenced by the Puritan tradition. There is also strong positive aspect to it which is of great importance in considering the phenomenon of 'will'. This links with another central aspect of morality, to which Kohlberg pays too little attention, namely, the intimate connection between knowing the difference between right and wrong, and caring. It is not a logical contradiction to say that someone knows that it is wrong to cheat but has no disposition not to cheat, but it could not be the general case; for the general function of words like 'right' and 'wrong', 'good' and 'bad' is to move people to act. If there is no such disposition to act in a particular case, we would say that the person is using the term in an external sort of way, or that he is not sincere, or something similar to that. There is neither need nor time to defend such a generally accepted point about moral knowledge, though there has been no general acceptance, ever since the time that Socrates first put it forward, about the precise relationship between moral knowledge and action (see Ryle, 1958).

Now, as Hume pointed out, justice is an artificial virtue which only gets off the ground when reason gets to work in social life. Hume equated 'reason' with reasoning of the sort that goes on either in logic and mathematics or in science, and was led to think, therefore, that reason of itself provides no considerations that move people to act. On a broader view of 'reason', however, it becomes readily apparent that there are a cluster of 'passions' closely connected with it without which its operation would be unintelligible. I am referring not just to the passion for truth, but also to other passions which are intimately connected with it such as the abhorrence of the arbitrary, the hatred of inconsistency and irrelevance, the love of clarity and order, and, in the case of non-formal reasoning, the determination to look at the facts. These passions both provide point to theoretical enquiries and transform the pursuit of practical purposes.

When Kohlberg talks of the principle of justice, it is not clear whether he means the formal principle that no distinctions should be made without relevant differences or more particularised versions of this in distributive or commutative justice. But any application of this principle must involve some kind of abhorrence of arbitrariness and of inconsistency if it is to be operative in any individual's life. Also, as Kohlberg maintains that it presupposes becoming aware of some 'universal structural dimensions in the social world', some focused attention to the facts of the social world is also involved. How do such rational passions develop? What helps to foster them? Kohlberg, like Piaget, postulates some kind of intrinsic motivation which leads children to assimilate and accommodate to what is novel and to develop their latent capacities. But there is a great difference between sporadic curiosity and the passions which cluster round the concern for truth. Does not the encouragement and example of adults and older children play any part in their development? Without them a child's understanding of justice would be very external. He might know what justice is, but might not care about it overmuch. To apply the principle seriously, the child has to develop not only an abhorrence of the arbitrary, but also a more positive concern for the considerations that determine relevance. How do children come to care? This seems to me to be the most important question in moral education; but no clear answer to it can be found in Kohlberg's writings.

4   IS KOHLBERG PRESCRIBING A MORALITY?

In discussing the adequacy of Kohlberg's account of the role of habit in moral development, distinctions were made between different classes of virtues. These seemed to be of some significance in assessing his account of processes of development. But they are of even more fundamental significance if we survey Kohlberg's conception of moral development from an overall ethical standpoint; taking these distinctions seriously might lead us to reflect that Kohlberg is really prescribing one type of morality among several possibilities. 'Morality' can be used as a classificatory term by means of which a form of interpersonal behaviour can be distinguished from custom, law, religious codes and so on. But in ethics and in the practical task of bringing up children, this does not take us very far; for it would involve us in the most feeble form of the naturalistic fallacy to argue that, because we term a form of behaviour 'moral', this behaviour is one which should be pursued or encouraged. Nothing about what ought to be or to be done follows from the empirical fact that we use a word in a certain way. It might well be, for instance, that a form of behaviour, in which justice plays such a prominent part, might accord very well with our usage of 'moral'. But that is neither here nor there if anyone is troubled by the general question, 'What are there reasons for doing?' or by more particular questions about how he is to bring up his children.

Even within this principled form of morality considered thus far, there are, in fact, different emphases open. For instance, one might think that the most important things to encourage in children were sympathy, compassion, concern for others and the like. One might not be particularly concerned about consistency or about the virtue of justice, which one might think of as being a rather niggardly one. Similarly, one might think that courage, integrity, autonomy, or other such excellences ought to be encouraged without being overly concerned about the substantial rules or purposes in relation to which these higher-order traits were exercised. Finally, one might not be too impressed with the interpersonal realm. One might go along with Gauguin and say that painting pictures was the thing, or advocate some other type of worthwhile activity. This form of activity, it might be said, is so valuable that considerations of an interpersonal sort would have to be set aside. All of these are possible moral positions in the general sense that reasons could be given for behaving in the ways suggested and for bringing up one's children accordingly. Of course, an attempt might be made to introduce some kind of unity into the moral life either by attempting to show that all such considerations were derived from one type of consideration, as did the Utilitarians, or by arbitrarily demarcating the sphere of the moral, as did Kant. But prima facie it appears to be a difficult enterprise, and it is certainly not one upon which Kohlberg has embarked. His account of moral development might therefore be considered to be one-sided in that it has been erected on the features of a limited interpretation of morality.

A further point must be made, too, about any moral system in which justice is regarded as the fundamental principle: it cannot be applied without a view, deriving from considerations other than those of justice, about what is important. This point can be demonstrated only very briefly, but it is one of cardinal importance. When we talk about what is just or unjust, we are applying the formal principle of reason – that no distinctions should be made without relevant differences, either to questions of distribution, when we are concerned about the treatment which different people are to receive, or to commutative situations, when we are concerned not with comparisons but with questions of desert, as in punishment. In all such cases some criterion has to be produced by reference to which the treatment is to be based on *relevant* considerations. There must therefore be some further evaluative premise in order to determine relevance. Without such a premise, no decisions can be made about what is just on any substantive issue. In determining, for instance, what a just wage is, relevant differences must be determined by reference to what people need, to what they contribute to the community, to the risk involved, and so on. To propose any such criteria involves evaluation. This opens up obvious possibilities for alternative emphases in morality in addition to those already mentioned. But are these emphases to be put on the 'formal' or on the 'content' side of Kohlberg's account of moral development? When we begin to look at his system in this more detailed way, it must become apparent that it is either implicitly prescriptive or so formal that it is of only limited significance for those who are interested in moral education, or moral development, in a concrete way. His findings are of unquestionable importance, but there is a grave danger that they may become exalted into a general theory of moral development. Any such general theory presupposes a general ethical theory, and Kohlberg himself surely would be the first to admit that he has done little to develop the details of such a general ethical theory. Yet without such a theory the notion of 'moral development' is pretty insubstantial.

5   FREUD AND MORAL FAILURE

It would be impossible in a short space to do justice to Kohlberg's massive examination of theories deriving from Freud which explain moral development in terms of identification (Kohlberg, 1963). But one main point can be made which is in line with the general thesis of this article: Kohlberg assumes that Freudians must be in some way producing an alternative theory to his own Piagetian theory of moral development. No doubt many Freudians have thought that they were doing this, and some of Freud's speculations in this area might support such a view. But, as I have maintained elsewhere (see Peters, 1960), it is equally plausible to maintain that, in fact, Freud was attempting explanations of a rather different realm of phenomena.

Rieff (1959) makes much of what he calls Freud's ethic of honesty and of his uncompromising egoism. He suggests that Freud's 'education to reality' and his explicit advocacy of 'the primacy of the intelligence' amounted to a prudential type of morality in which self-honesty played a large part. This, as a matter of fact, is a disputable interpretation of Freud's own moral standpoint. He actually said of himself, 'I believe that in a sense of justice and consideration for others, in disliking making others suffer or taking advantage of them I can measure myself with the best people I know' (Jones, 1955, p. 464), which looks very much like the confession of a rational Utilitarian sort of code that one could find in Sidgwick – or indeed in Piaget. But what is not disputable is that Freud subscribed to some sort of rational morality, which his practice as a therapist also pre-supposed; for the aim of psycho-analysis was to strengthen the ego by making unconscious conflicts conscious and by helping people to stand on their own feet with full cognisance of the sources of their irrational promptings and precepts. But in his theory of moral development there is no explicit theory about the development of the ego, which, in Freud's rather pictorial terminology, represented a rational level of behaviour. Indeed, he was later criticised by Freudians such as Erikson, Hartmann and Rapaport for neglecting the development of the autonomous ego, the stages of which were mapped in Piaget's theory.

What, then, did Freud's theory of moral development explain? This is not at all a simple question, for Freud's theory underwent many transformations (see Flugel, 1945). One might say, for instance, that the early theory of the ego ideal was meant to explain simply how some kind of cultural *content* was passed on from parents to children by the rather mysterious process of identification. And even this limited interpretation would not be inconsistent with Kohlberg's theory in that Kohlberg is not much interested in content; from his point of view identification might be as good or as bad an explanation of the transmission of *content* as habit formation. For Kohlberg, it will be remembered, argues that it is the *form* of moral experience rather than its content which is of crucial developmental significance. But Freud was not basically concerned with a simple theory of content transmission in his theory of the ego ideal, let alone in his later speculations about the super-ego. On the one hand, he was trying to explain the fact that some children seem to develop more rigorous standards than those demanded by their parents; on the other hand, he tried to explain the fact that many people have a picture of themselves – what Adler later called a 'guiding fiction' – which is quite out of keeping with the traits which they in fact exhibit. In other words, Freud's theory of the super-ego was basically a theory of moral failure – of why people become obsessional, un-realistic and aggressively self-punitive in the moral sphere. It therefore can be seen as a supplement to Piaget's type of theory rather than as a substitute for it.

The same sort of point can be made about Freud's theory of character traits. This does not begin to look like a theory of how traits such as honesty, which were studied in the Hartshorne – May enquiry, are developed. Nor is it a theory about the development of higher-order traits such as consistency, determination and courage, to which we are usually alluding when we speak of people *having* character. Rather, it is in the tradition of characterology, which goes right back to Theophrastus, in which a type of character is portrayed. Either there is a subordination of traits to a dominant one, as in the sketch of the penurious man; or a whole range of traits are shown as being exercised in an exaggerated or distorted manner, as in the case of a pedantic person. Jones (1955, p. 331) explicitly speaks of Freud's *Character and anal erotism* as a contribution to this sort of speculation, and he notes its literary style. Freud thought that he spotted a similarity between types of character and various forms of neuroses, and assigned a common cause to both in his theory of infantile sexuality. Here again we do not have a competing explanation of the sort of phenomena in which Kohlberg is interested, namely, the determinants of a rational, principled form of morality. Rather we have an attempt to explain types of character that fall a long way short of this in some systematic way.

To discuss the status of the evidence for Freud's type of explanation, even for this realm of deviant phenomena, would require another article – and it would not be the sort that a philosopher would be expected to write. But these phenomena exist, and they certainly cannot be explained in terms of either Kohlberg's or Piaget's type of theory. Therefore, in so far as Freud and his followers have been attempting explanations, however far-fetched, of phenomena of this sort, they are providing a much needed supplement to the work of the Piaget–Kohlberg school. It is not doing justice to them to represent them as providing merely a competing theory of moral development.

REFERENCES

Aristotle, *Nichomachean Ethics*. See Thompson, J. A. K. (Ed.) (Harmondsworth: Penguin, 1955).
Flugel, J. C., *Man, Morals and Society* (London: Duckworth, 1945).
Jones, E., *Sigmund Freud, Life and Works*. Vol. II (London: Hogarth Press, 1955).
Kazepides, A. C., 'What is the Paradox of Moral Education?', *Philosophy of Education 1969*. Proceedings of the twenty-fifth annual meeting of the Philosophy of Education Society (Denver, 1969).
Kohlberg, L., 'Moral Development and Identification', in Stevenson, H. (Ed.),

Child Psychology. 62nd Yearbook Nat. Soc. Stud. Educ. (Chicago: University of Chicago Press, 1963).

Kohlberg, L., 'Development of Moral Character and Ideology', in Hoffman, M. L. (Ed.), *Review of Child Development Research.* Vol. I (New York: Russell, Sage Foundation, 1964).

Kohlberg, L. Moral Education in the Schools, *School Review,* Vol. 74, (1966) pp. 1–30.

Kohlberg, L., 'Stage and Sequence: The Cognitive–Developmental Approach to Socialisation', in Goslin, D. (Ed.), *Handbook of Socialization* (New York: Rand McNally, 1968).

Kohlberg, L. 'Early Education: A Cognitive Developmental View', *Child Development,* Vol. 39 (1968), pp. 1013–62.

Kohlberg, L., 'Education for Justice', in Sizer, N. F. and Sizer, T. R. (Eds), *Moral Education* (Cambridge, Mass.: Harvard University Press, 1970).

Kohlberg, L., 'Stages in the Development of Moral Thought and Action', unpublished manuscript.

Oakeshott, M. (Ed.), 'The Tower of Babel', in *Rationalism in Politics* (London: Methuen, 1962).

Peters, R. S. 'Freud's Theory of Moral Development in Relation to That of Piaget', *British Journal of Educational Psychology,* Vol. 30 (1960), pp.250–8.

Peters, R. S., 'Reason and Habit: The Paradox of Moral Education', in Niblett, W. R. (Ed.), *Moral Education in a Changing Society* (London: Faber, 1963).

Peters, R. S. (Ed.), *Perspectives on Plowden* (London: Routledge, 1969).

Piaget, J., *The Moral Judgment of the Child* (London: Routledge, 1932).

Rieff, P., *Freud, the Mind of the Moralist* (New York: Viking Press, 1959).

Ryle, G., *The Concept of Mind* (London: Hutchinson, 1948).

Ryle, G. 'On Forgetting the Difference Between Right and Wrong', in Melden, A. I. (Ed.), *Essays in Moral Philosophy* (Seattle: University of Washington Press, 1958).

Von Wright, G. H., *The Varieties of Goodness* (London: Routledge, 1963).

16

FREEDOM AND THE DEVELOPMENT OF THE FREE MAN[1]

INTRODUCTION

There is a presupposition implicit in the writings and practices of educators which is of interest in its own right and to educational theory generally. It is that some desirable state of mind or character-trait will be best developed by an institution whose workings reflect the principle, which is thought desirable when personalised as a character-trait. Thus Plato assumed that justice in the individual soul would flourish in society whose organisation satisfied the conditions required by this principle. The institution of punishment has been defended on similar grounds. It is claimed that it is a manifest exemplar of justice and that children who witness its operation will receive the imprint of justice on their minds. Alternatively it is assumed that if certain procedures characterise the working of an institution (e.g. rules decided by appeals to authority, by democratic discussion, etc.) corresponding attitudes of mind will be fostered amongst its members. A. S. Neill, for instance, assumes that his ideal of self-regulation or freedom of the individual will be best developed in an institution in which external regulation is at a minimum, and in which such regulation as there is does not stem from the authority of adults.

It is this type of assumption which, in my view, lies behind the intuitive plausibility of so much educational argument. A. S. Neill is actually very guarded in his claims for the long-term effects of Summerhill on its inmates. And what he does claim is based purely on selective impressions. He had conducted no surveys to find out how many of his previous pupils have succumbed to the 'fear of freedom', and ended up as members of the Communist Party, the Catholic Church or as conformists. Nevertheless, he persists with his type of school and, I suspect, would be absolutely unconvinced by negative evidence of this mundane sort. He would offer some special explanation of cases in which children of servile dispositions issue forth from an institution in which freedom, as a social principle, is 'writ large'.

There are, as far as I know, no empirical studies which can be produced to test this assumption. Yet the interesting point is that considerations can be produced to support or to cast doubt on its plausibility. By examining what is meant by 'freedom' in a social context, like that of a school, and what is meant by a 'free man', some suggestions can be made about the connection between the two. To connect them some assumptions would also have to be made about human learning. But I must not, by developing this point any further at this stage, anticipate one of the main points which I want to discuss in this paper. For it has a three-fold intention behind it. I propose to take 'freedom' as an example of the general assumption about the fit between institutions and states of mind. To develop my general thesis I will first examine the concept or concepts of 'freedom' in education and distinguish the various things that might be meant. Secondly I will explore what is involved in learning to be free, including the status of the presupposition about the influence of institutions on learning in this sphere. This will lead, finally, to a few general reflections about human learning arising from this particular case of it.

1   THE ANALYSIS OF 'FREEDOM'

In approaching these questions I shall attempt no new analysis of 'freedom'. In the main I shall rely on the distinctions already worked out by Stanley Benn[2] and William Weinstein: (a) freedom as a social principle, (b) man as a chooser, (c) autonomy, which are particularly helpful in an educational context. My use of their analysis, however, will be strictly tailored to its relevance for discussing how individuals learn to be free.

(a)   *Freedom as a Social Principle*
If we say that a man is not free to do something we are suggesting that there is something or somebody that is stopping him. We assume that there is something that he might want or choose to do and we suggest that there is some closing up of the options available to him.

The most obvious way of closing up a person's options is to restrict his bodily movements by tying him up or imprisoning him. But more usual ways are the making of laws and regulations, giving him commands, and subjecting him to a variety of social and personal pressures.

It is a common-place of political theory that the state of natural freedom is an illusion. If there are no levelling constraints like those of law and custom, men do not in fact live unconstrained lives. Those who are physically or psychologically weak are constrained by those who are strong. In spheres, therefore, in which people care what others do and in which it is possible for them to interfere with them, freedom in fact prevails only if there is a general system of regulation which safeguards these spheres against interference from others. This is an empirical generalisation derivative from certain facts about human nature and the conditions under which men live. It is not, as many enemies of freedom have argued, a conceptual truth about the meaning of 'freedom'. For 'freedom' manifestly does not mean the acceptance of constraints. It is just a general empirical fact that the acceptance of some forms of constraint by all is necessary for the avoidance of more grievous forms of constraint by some others. This so-called 'paradox of freedom' is extremely relevant to a school situation; for the constraints of the bully or the peer-group take over if the more explicit levelling constraints issuing from the staff or from the community as a whole, are withdrawn.[3] There are also more subtle forms of social pressure – e.g. those issuing from a charismatic teacher who may believe fervently in freedom – which may be more damaging to freedom in a more fundamental sense, than the straightforward exercise of authority. What, then, is this sense?

(b) *Man as a Chooser*
Presupposed by this analysis of 'freedom' as a social principle is the notion of man as a chooser who can have his options closed up in various ways by the acts of other men. We speak of various spheres of authority as being spheres where individuals are not free to do as they please. Yet there is also an important connection between 'authority' and 'consent' or 'choice' as many writers in political theory have pointed out. We often, though not always, obey a command because we accord its author a right to tell us what to do. In the case of a voluntary club or association we do actually commit ourselves to its constitution and rules when we join it and we can leave it if we so choose. And in other spheres of authority, even if we

have not explicitly committed ourselves in this way, it is open to us to reject the system as binding on us. Similarly if a person is playing football his freedom of action is limited by the rules and by the referee's decisions. But he can choose not to play football. There are difficulties, of course, about obedience to a state if there is nowhere to live that is not under the jurisdiction of some state. There are difficulties about leaving a place of employment if the alternative is the dole. But even in these dire extremities a person still remains a *chooser* even if the alternatives open to him are such that we might say that he has no choice or Hobson's choice.

In a school situation there are plenty of cases in which we would say that a student is not free to do certain things but that he still remains a chooser. For instance, he may not be free to run in the corridors, but he may, in fact, do so, knowing full well the penalty if he is caught. Indeed he may defy the whole system of rules and end up by being expelled. These situations of explicit subordination, or of refusal to be subordinated, need to be distinguished from those in which the notion of choice seems out of place. Suppose that a girl has an obsessive passion for a master. To do anything which he forbad, or of which he disapproved, would never enter her head. Indeed she might constantly look for things to do of which he approved and, if he told her to fast for a week or to steal, she would fall in with his wishes. In respect of her dealings with him she cannot really be described as a chooser; for alternatives that are presented to her are not really alternatives if they involve in any way going against his wishes. Like a person under post-hypnotic suggestion she may conjure up other alternatives and invent other reasons for doing what she is bent on doing anyway; but this is a mere shadow-play. She is really programmed to do what he wants. This kind of situation can exist in a school which has a normal authority structure; or it may exist in a progressive school that prides itself on the absence of such a structure. The lack of freedom involved is perhaps more dire than that of a situation structured by explicit regulation; for the girl is unfree in a more fundamental sense than are those who keep or break rules in a more straightforward way.

This type of case is a mild and usually short-term example of a range of cases about which we might say that an individual is no longer a chooser. They differ from the first application of 'freedom' to social situations in which what Benn calls the *objective* conditions of choice are interfered with or loaded in various ways – e.g. by threats, imposition of sanctions, etc. In this second type of case, in which we sometimes speak of 'unfreedom', men cease to be choosers, because there are various defects or interferences with the *subjective* conditions which are necessary for choice.

The forms of impairment to subjective conditions can roughly be indicated by setting out what we normally assume when people are in what I have elsewhere called a situation of practical reason, when they ask themselves the question 'Why do this rather than that?'[4] (i) We assume that there is more than one type of end which can function for them as a goal. They do not, as it were, veer towards 'this' rather than 'that' like a moth towards a light. A man who had been starved for a week would probably not satisfy this condition. He would be 'driven' towards a goal. Drug addicts and alcoholics do not satisfy this condition in relation to a whole range of their deliberations.

(ii) We assume that people are capable of weighing the pros and cons of the alternatives before them without being paralysed by indecision or going out of the field in some other way. Some hysterics would not satisfy this condition.

(iii) We assume that the weight which people attach to different alternatives can be influenced by information which is relevant to the validity of their beliefs. Paranoiacs, or people suffering from other sorts of delusions or obsessions, would not satisfy this condition. For they hold on to beliefs in the face of relevant evidence, because their beliefs cannot deviate from the lines dictated by some irrational wish or aversion.

(iv) We assume that changes in people's beliefs about 'this' or 'that' can modify their decisions. A psychopath, for whom the future has a kind of unreality and who is unmoved by the unpleasantness which he sees to be the probable consequences of his actions, and which he wishes to avoid, would not qualify in this respect.

(v) We assume that people's decisions can be translated into appropriate actions. A compulsive would fail to satisfy this condition.

(c) *Autonomy*

Our normal expectation of a person is that he is a chooser – that he can be deterred by thoughts of the consequences of his actions, that he is not paranoid or compulsive and so on. But such a person might be a time-serving, congenial conformist, or an easy-going, weak-willed opportunist. Being a chooser is a standard expected of anyone – which is related to norms of rationality or mental health;[5] it is not an ideal of conduct or of education. Certainly progressive educators, such as A. S. Neill, who equates freedom with self-regulation, have been concerned with more than this limited objective. What, then, has to be added for a chooser to develop into an ideal type of character in which being free features? To ask this is to ask for the criteria for calling a person 'autonomous'.

Authenticity Etymologically 'autonomy' suggests that a person accepts or makes rules for himself. This is clear in what it denies but not altogether clear in what it asserts. It denies that the individual's code of conduct is simply one that he has picked up from others or adopted in any second-hand way. The rules which he lives by are not just those that are laid down by custom or authority. Hence the stress on authenticity going right back to Socrates' 'care of the soul'. This asserts positively that there must be some feature of a course of conduct, which the individual regards as important, which constitutes a non-artificial reason for pursuing it as distinct from extrinsic reasons provided by praise and blame, reward and punishment, and so on, which are artificially created by the demands of others. But beyond this point it is a matter of controversy as to what is asserted by the stress on autonomy. Presumably it would be consistent with a doctrine sometimes put into the mouth of D. H. Lawrence's characters that a course of conduct should be pursued that is congenial to the 'dark god' within, namely sex, which determines the lines of individual self-assertion. For this is represented as what the individual really wants as distinct from what conformity dictates. Or it would be consistent with some existentialist doctrine of 'criterionless choice', in so far as this can be rendered intelligible.

Rational Reflection More usually, however, autonomy is positively associated with assessment and criticism, as in Stanley Benn's account in his paper on 'Conditions of Autonomy'. The individual is conceived of as being aware of rules as alterable conventions which structure his social life. He subjects them to reflection and criticism in the light of principles and gradually emerges with his own code of conduct. This is the Kantian conception of autonomy in which the 'subjective maxims' of the individual are subjected to critical examination in the light of principles such as those of impartiality and respect for persons. This does not mean that he must always reflect before he acts and ponder on the validity of a rule which he is applying; for such a man would be a moral imbecile without settled principles. It only means that he has thought about rules in this way and has a disposition to do so if he finds himself in a situation where changed circumstances intimate some adaptation of his code.

Strength of Will   It is possible for a person to have a code of conduct which he has worked out for himself but to be too weak-willed to stick to it. Usually, however, when people speak of a person being autonomous they mean that he not only has thought out his own code but that he is also capable of sticking to it in the face of counter-inclinations. Autonomy, in other words, also suggests executive virtues such as courage, integrity and determination. It is revealed not simply in the refusal to adopt second-hand beliefs or rules, but also in holding steadfast in *conduct* against counter-inclinations which also incline an individual to be heteronomous in his point of view. For the counter-inclinations, which are relevant to weakness of will, are often those springing from types of motivation that make 'authenticity' in belief difficult. The strong-willed man, like the independently minded man, sticks to his principles in the face of ridicule, ostracism, punishment and bribes. There is thus a close connection between autonomy and strength of will but the connection is probably a contingent one to be explained in terms of the group of counter-inclinations that are necessary to give application both to the notion of authenticity and to that of strength of will.

There is thus a gradation of conditions implicit in the idea of autonomy. The first basic condition is that of authenticity, of adopting a code or way of life that is one's own as distinct from one dictated by others. The second condition of rational reflection on rules is one espoused by most believers in autonomy. To discuss whether it is essential to autonomy would involve discussing the intelligibility of romantic and existentialist alternatives, which is beyond the scope of this paper. For the purpose of this paper, however, it will be assumed to be a necessary condition of autonomy. The third possible condition, that of strength of will, seems to be much more contingently associated with autonomy, and will be ignored.

2   THE DEVELOPMENT OF THE FREE MAN

So much, then, for the different ways in which 'being free' can be understood. The lynch-pin of the analysis is the notion of man as a chooser, a rational being placed in what I have called the situation of practical reason. This is a presupposition of 'freedom' as a social principle; for a man who is 'not free' is one who has his options closed up in one way or other and this presupposes a being of whom it makes sense to say that he has options, i.e. that he is a chooser. In education, however, we are usually concerned with more than just preserving the capacity for choice; we are also concerned with the ideal of personal autonomy, which is a development of some of the potentialities inherent in the notion of man as a chooser. The concept of 'freedom' has now been sufficiently analysed to permit us to say a few things about the development of free men. Manifestly, in a paper of this length, there cannot be a massive marshalling of empirical studies which throw light on the conditions under which free men emerge. There is point, however, as will later be substantiated when something is said about the role of philosophy in the study of human learning, in giving an indication of the sorts of conditions that seem obviously relevant. For when we talk about the 'development' of free men we surely have in mind some process of learning, rather than some causal process such as is involved in the development of a photograph or of a plant. What, then, could be meant by 'learning' if it is suggested that human beings learn to become choosers or autonomous human beings?

There is a general concept of 'learning' used by most psychologists to draw attention to changes of behaviour that are not the product purely of maturation. I am not concerned with this general concept but only with the more specific one in which the changes in question are the result of past experience. At the centre of learning in this specific sense is some content that a learner makes his own by various processes of assimilation. He may copy it, grasp it, imitate it, memorise it and so on, depending on the type of content that it is. And what he can make his own depends largely on the existing state of his cognitive structure, 'structure' being understood as referring not just to what he has already assimilated in the way of content but also to how the content is conceived. For instance, for most of us so-called 'instrumental conditioning' operates only because we are capable of discerning a link between doing something and being rewarded, even though the link may be one of the extrinsic type referred to in the previous section. Similarly once a child has grasped the concept of a 'thing' he can quickly learn to recognise a variety of things such as bricks and balls by being presented with instances of them and having their features pointed out to him.

Now there are some concepts, such as that of 'thing' in the latter example of learning and 'means-to-an-end' in the former example; which are of particular importance in mental development in the theories of psychologists such as Piaget and Kohlberg, who have been much influenced by Kant. For they are categoreal concepts marking stages in the development of the human mind in that they define forms of human understanding and hence set limits to what can be learnt by imposing a framework for the assimilation of content. These fundamental types of concept, they argue, cannot therefore be taught by any process of direct instruction; rather they emerge as a result of the interaction between a mind equipped with potentialities for ordering and selecting and an environment which has invariant features which are there to discover. This kind of development, however, can be aided by what Kohlberg calls 'cognitive stimulation', which he contrasts with explicit instruction (see Kohlberg, 1968, 1969).

It is, surely, the learning of forms of understanding such as these (e.g., seing something as a 'means to an end') rather than the assimilation of any particular content of experience that is crucial for the development of free men. Let me try to illustrate this contention briefly in the case of the development of the capacity for choice and in that of the achievement of autonomy.

(a) *Becoming a Chooser*
An account of becoming a chooser was sketched in section 1(a) by reference, mainly, to various forms of impairment in what were called, following Stanley Benn, 'subjective conditions'. But these themselves presuppose certain standing conditions without which they would be unintelligible. Being able to weigh up the pros and cons of alternatives and to act in the light of such deliberation presupposes that the individual can think in terms of taking means to an end. He appreciates, to a certain extent, the causal properties of things and can distinguish consequences brought about by his own agency from things that come about independently of his will. To do this he must possess the categoreal concepts of 'thinghood', 'causality', and 'means to an end'. These enable him to think 'realistically' in contradistinction to small children and paranoiacs whose consciousness is dominated by wishes and aversions. It presupposes, too, that he has a view of the world as an orderly system in which his confidence in his own powers and his expectations about the future will be confirmed. This is particularly important if his choice involves the delay of immediate gratification. Unlike the psychopath, the future is real to him and he has a steady disposition to take account of facts – both future and present. To regard himself as, to a certain extent, a determiner of his own destiny, which he must do if he is a chooser, he must have a sense of his own identity and that of others.

In developmental psychology there are two complementary approaches which throw light on these preconditions of choice. Piaget and his followers have mapped the stages at which this categoreal apparatus emerges; Freud and his followers, on the other hand, though allowing for the development of this apparatus in the doctrine of the 'ego', have concentrated more on the conditions under which it fails to emerge. They have shown the extent to which infantile, primary processes of thought persist in the mind of the adult and prevent it working rationally according to the principles dictated by this categoreal apparatus.

Piaget and Kohlberg, as has already been explained, argue that the development of this categoreal apparatus is the product, not of explicit teaching, but of cognitive stimulation. I will leave aside problematic Chomsky-type questions of the extent to which the emergence of this cognitive apparatus is innately determined; I will also leave aside the problems in the distinction made by Kohlberg between 'teaching' and 'cognitive stimulation'.[6] For, whatever allowance is made for other variables, the role of social influences which are connected with such 'stimulation' can be inferred from the fact that failure to develop such an apparatus has been shown by psychologists more interested in the Freudian type of approach, to be connected with certain types of socialisation or lack of it. Most pathological states can be described in terms of the absence of features of this apparatus and these defects can be correlated with typical conditions in early childhood. It is generally agreed, for instance, that psychopaths who live on their whims and impulses, for whom the future has little reality, and who have a way of thinking about the world rather like that of a young infant, are largely the product of homes which are rejecting towards the child and which provide a very inconsistent type of discipline.[7] Schizophrenics, whose belief-structure, especially in regard to their own identity, is deranged, are thought by some to be products of discrepant and irreconcilable attitudes towards them before they developed a secure sense of reality. They lack what Laing calls the 'ontological security' of a person who has developed the categoreal apparatus which is definitive of being a rational being or a chooser. As Laing puts it (1965, p. 39):

Such a basically ontologically secure person will encounter all the hazards of life . . . from a centrally firm sense of his own and other people's reality and identity. It is often difficult for a person with such a sense of his integral selfhood and personal identity, of the permanency of things, of the reliability of natural processes, of the substantiality of others, to transpose himself into the world of an individual whose experiences may be utterly lacking in any unquestionable self-validating certainties.

There is no need to multiply examples of failures to develop the apparatus necessary for becoming a chooser and to attempt to relate them to various types of defects in 'normal social conditions'. To do this thoroughly would necessitate writing a text-book on psychopathology. Of equal interest, however, from the point of view of educators, are cases of people who could be termed 'unreasonable' rather than 'irrational',[8] and whose way of life bears witness to the limited development of the capacities necessary for being a chooser, which again seem to be the product of a certain type of socialisation. An example of such a limited form of development is given by Josephine Klein in her book *Samples of English Culture* (1965). She singles out certain abilities which are presupposed in the account of being a chooser given in section 1(b) above. They are the ability to abstract and use generalisations, the ability to perceive the world as an ordered universe in which rational action is rewarded, the ability to plan ahead and to exercise self-control. She cites evidence from Luria and Bernstein to show that the extent to which these abilities develop depends on the prevalence of an elaborated form of language which is found in some strata of society but not in others. She also shows how the beliefs and conduct of some working-class sub-cultures are affected by the arbitrariness of their child-rearing techniques. Such happy-go-lucky people have a stunted capacity for choice because the future has only a limited relevance for them and because they are prejudiced, myopic and unreflective in their beliefs.[9]

So far examples have been given of the capacity for choice being impaired or stunted by others who, usually unwittingly, treat children in ways which bring about these results. It need hardly be added that these capacities can be neutralised, perhaps permanently impaired, by more conscious techniques which are combined together in brain-washing. The individual's categoreal apparatus can be attacked by making his environment as unpredictable as possible; his sense of time and place and of his own identity can be systematically undermined. He is gradually reduced to a state of acute anxiety, perhaps of mental breakdown, in which he is in a receptive state to being dominated by another who becomes the sole source of pleasure and security for him. He becomes suggestible and willing to accept beliefs, which, in his former life, he would have rejected out of hand. He becomes more or less a programmed man rather than a chooser. Domination by another can also take less dramatic and more temporary forms, as in some cases of being in love which in Freud's view belongs to the same family as being hypnotised. There are some people who sometimes find their way into the teaching profession, who seem to have this kind of hypnotic effect on others. These kinds of influence, which neutralise the capacity for choice, must be distinguished from others such as manipulation by bribing and threats, or feeding people with false information, which presuppose it. For these techniques rely on manipulation of the objective conditions of choice; they do not constitute an assault on the subjective conditions which are definitive of being a chooser.

It is not difficult to surmise why the most consistent finding from studies of child-rearing practices is that sensible children, who are capable of rational choice, seem to emerge from homes in which there is a warm attitude of acceptance towards children, together with a firm and consistent insistence on rules of behaviour without much in the way of punishment. An accepting attitude towards a child will tend to encourage trust in others and confidence in his own powers. A predictable social environment will provide the type of experience which is necessary for guiding behaviour by reflection on its consequences and so build up a belief in a future which is in part shaped by his own behaviour. Inconsistency in treatment, on the other hand, will encourage plumping rather than choosing and attachment to instant gratification; and a rejecting attitude will inhibit the development of the self-confidence which is necessary for being a chooser.

(b)   The Development of Autonomy

It could well be that teachers should be much more mindful than they are of the possibility that many children come to them impaired or stunted in their capacity for choice, and that they should be more mindful of providing an environment which encourages it. In particular, perhaps, they should be chary of imposing a 'self-chosen curriculum' too quickly on children from homes in which there is little encouragement for children to be choosers. The fact is, however, that when teachers talk of 'freedom' as an educational ideal they usually have in mind the development of autonomy or self-regulation which is a far more ambitious ideal.

In thinking about a child's progress towards this ideal the work of

Piaget and Kohlberg, which is confirmed by that of Peck and Havighurst, is most illuminating. There is a general consensus that children pass through various stages in their conception of rules which is independent of the content of the rules concerned. They pass from regarding conformity to rules purely as a way of avoiding punishment and obtaining rewards to a level at which rules are regarded as entities in themselves that are just 'there' and which emanate from the collective will of the group and from people in authority. They finally pass to the level of autonomy, when they appreciate that rules are alterable, that they can be criticised and should be accepted or rejected on a basis of reciprocity and fairness.[10] The emergence of rational reflection about rules, which in section 1(c) was regarded as central to the Kantian conception of autonomy, is the main feature of the final level of moral development. Kohlberg produces cross-cultural evidence to support the general claim of the Piaget school, already mentioned, that these stages of development in the conception of rules are culturally invariant. He emphasises that the explanation of this is that the levels of conceiving of rules are in a hierarchical logical order; so there could be no other order in which development occurs. Though cultures differ in the content of rules, there is thus an invariant order in the way in which rules are conceived, although, of course, in many cultures there is no emergence to the autonomous stage.[11] Kohlberg makes the same claim about the limitations of teaching in this sphere as he makes with regard to the teaching of categories for thinking about the physical world such as causality and conservation. He argues that, though the content of rules is learnt by teaching or imitation, the form of conceiving of them is the product of interaction with the environment that can be accelerated or retarded by the amount of cognitive stimulation available.

Here again there are findings which emphasise the importance of the social environment, provided that we do not enter into niceties as to what is to be called 'teaching'. Kohlberg himself stresses the difference in rate and level of development towards autonomy of those who come from middle-class homes, in which there is plenty of 'cognitive stimulation'; and those who come from working-class homes. There is, too, a series of investigations by Bruner and his associates which are more far-reaching in their implications. He conducted experiments into ideas about conservation with the Wolof, a tribe in Senegal, and found that those who had not been exposed to Western influences embodied in schooling were unable to make distinctions such as that between how things are and how the individual views them. They had not the concept of different 'points of view'. He suggests that animistic thinking, in which individuals project their own agency into external nature, is the product of cultures in which attention is paid to satisfying the whims of individual children. Also the concept of conservation is achieved much earlier by the Tiv, who are encouraged to manipulate the external world, than by the Wolof who adopt a more passive attitude towards it. Bruner and Greenfield argue that amongst the Wolof the motor competence and manipulation of the individual is not encouraged. The child's personal desires and intentions, which might differentiate him from others, are not emphasised. What matters for them is the child's conformity to the group. Thus their concept of a child is of a being who starts off full of personal desires and intentions, but who has increasingly to subordinate such desires to the group. He thus becomes less and less of an individual because he is discouraged from thinking of himself as one. In cultures such as these, therefore, there is no encouragement for the individual to explore the world 'for himself' and find out what is true. What is true is what the group or the authority figure in the group says.[12]

We are, of course, familiar with this phenomenon in a less thorough-going form; for the appeal to the authority of the leader, parent, teacher or group, and the discouragement of individual testing out, is one of the main characteristics both of the second main developmental stage in the Piaget-Kohlberg theory and of traditionalist and collectivist types of society. But this attitude towards rules need not be just the product of vague social pressures and expectations; it can also be produced and perpetuated by the conscious techniques which we now call 'indoctrination'. For 'indoctrination' involves the passing on of fixed beliefs in a way which discourages questions about their validity. Societies, like the U.S.S.R., in which indoctrination is widespread, are not necessarily societies in which reasoning is altogether discouraged. They do not aim to undermine fundamentally people's capacities as choosers. The Russians are encouraged to calculate and to plan practical projects. Indeed they are renowned for their chess-playing and for their technology. What they are discouraged from doing is to question the validity of their moral and political beliefs and to place any emphasis on the role of the individual in determining his own destiny. They thus allow plenty of scope for the attitude to rules which is characteristic of Piaget's second stage but actively discourage any movement towards the autonomous stage, which they regard as an aberration of individualistic societies.

350 PSYCHOLOGY AND ETHICAL DEVELOPMENT

In the U.S.S.R. Makarenko achieved considerable success in dealing with delinquents by reliance mainly on group projects and on identification with the collective will of the community.[13] As presumably most of these delinquents were either at the first egocentric stage or suffering from various pathological conditions, it was a distinct sign of moral advancement for these individuals to function at the second level of morality at which the individual does the done thing, which is determined either by the group or by those in authority.

If Piaget and Kohlberg are right, however, in their assumptions about the logical sequence of stages in development of autonomy, *every* individual has to go through these stages of what Kohlberg calls 'good boy' and 'authority-oriented' morality before he can attain to the autonomous level. The Public Schools, who specialised in character-training, implicitly acknowledged this; for they combined an appeal to team spirit and to authority-based rule-conformity for all, with an emphasis on independence of mind and sticking to principles for those more senior boys who were singled out to command rather than simply to obey. It is questionable whether progressive educators have been sufficiently aware of the importance of this second level of development. They have, on the one hand, been reluctant for the staff to impose the rule of law but have been embarrassed by the fact that, if this is withdrawn, bullying and peer-group pressures take its place. On the other hand, they have emphasised the importance of individual choice without paying enough attention to the developmental stage which individual children have reached. Unless a child has been through the second level of morality, at which he is made to understand what an externally imposed rule is and to have some feeling about the inviolability of rules, it is dubious whether the notion of accepting or rejecting rules for himself is very meaningful to him. Decisions which are important in the shaping of character arise out of conflict situations. And how can a child go through any kind of existentialist agony if he is not acutely aware of the force of rules between which he has to choose?

So much, then, for general issues connected with the emergence to the autonomous stage of morality in so far as this involves rational reflection on rules. Some brief comments must now be made about the other aspect of autonomy which was thought to be essential to it when the notion was introduced in section 1(c) above, namely, authenticity.

For this aspect of autonomy to be operative, namely the proclivity of the individual to be moved by considerations intrinsic to the conduct concerned rather than just by extrinsic considerations such as rewards and punishment, approval and disapproval, two conditions have to be satisfied. First, the individual has to be sensitive to considerations which are to act as principles to back rules – e.g. to the suffering of others. Secondly, he has to be able, by reasoning, to view such considerations as reasons for doing some things rather than others. How individuals develop the required sensitivity is largely a matter of speculation. Obviously identification with others who already possess it is an operative factor; perhaps, too, a degree of first-hand experience is also necessary – e.g. not shielding young people but encouraging them to take part in practical tasks where there is suffering to be relieved. This kind of development can start very early; for Piaget and Kohlberg have shown not that children are incapable of such sensitivity when they are very young but that they are incapable of appealing to it as a backing for rules. In other words it does not function for them as a principle.

What then, can be done about encouraging the development of reasoning of this sort so that rules have the backing of authentically based principles? Presumably reasons for doing things can be indicated quite early on, even though it is appreciated that the child cannot yet think in this way. For unless there is this kind of 'cognitive stimulation' in the environment it is improbable that the child will emerge to the autonomous stage. Obviously an atmosphere of discussion and criticism, especially amongst children who are a bit older, will help to stimulate this development. Language, too, which approximates to what Bernstein calls an 'elaborated code', is very important in aiding this development as well as non-arbitrary methods of teaching rules.[14] I am not saying, of course, that any sane parent or teacher will, in the early stages, make a child's acceptance of the reasons a condition for his doing what is sensible. All I am saying is that rules can be presented in a non-arbitrary way *before* children are capable of accepting them for the reasons given, to help them to get to the stage when they follow rules because of the reasons for them. But it does not follow from this that, on many occasions, parents and teachers may not have to insist on certain forms of conduct even though the children do not accept the good sense of it. Indeed this is a common feature of the 'good boy' and 'rule-conformity' stages of morality.

3 THE INFLUENCE OF INSTITUTIONS

Kohlberg claims that, though the content of the morality of a particular community can be passed on by instruction and example, its form, which is defined by the way in which rules are conceived, cannot be so passed on. It is the product of interaction between the individual and his social environment which is merely assisted by 'cognitive stimulation'. How, then, if he is right, could an educational institution such as a secondary school, contribute to such development?

Obviously much can be done with regard to the appropriate *content* by instruction, example, and on the spot correction. In this boys and girls, who are a little more advanced in development, probably exert a more effective influence than the teachers themselves, as Thomas Arnold saw when he insisted that the older boys must bear the brunt of the responsibility for ensuring that rules of conduct are known and kept. But what about the form of morality, which is characterised by the prevailing attitude to rules? What can an educational institution contribute to this? Can it do much to aid development towards the autonomous stage?

No doubt much is contributed by a general atmosphere of discussion and by providing a backing of reasons for rules as well as insisting on them. A curriculum, too, which pays proper attention to those disciplines, such as literature and history, which provide a foundation for choice, is an obvious help. But of far-reaching importance, surely, is the general control system of the school and the motivational assumptions which support it. For Piaget's and Kohlberg's stages of development are 'writ large' in these all-pervasive features of the institution. It is, surely, unlikely that autonomy will be widely encouraged by an authoritarian system of control in which anything of importance is decided by the fiat of the headmaster and in which the prevailing assumption is that the appeal to a man is the only method of determining what is correct. Similarly in the motivational sphere of authenticity students are unlikely to develop a delight in doing things for reasons intrinsic to them if rewards and punishment, meted out both by the staff and by a fierce examination system, provide the stable incentives to the discipline of learning; for the institution itself embodies an attitude to conduct which is appropriate to Piaget's first stage of development. These institutional realities are bound to structure the perceptions of the students. If an institution embodies an attitude to rules that is characteristic of an earlier stage of development, teachers who attempt to encourage a more developed attitude have an uphill task; for in their attempts at 'cognitive stimulation' they are working against the deadening directives of the institution.

The inference to be drawn from this is not that every school, which upholds an ideal of autonomy, should straightaway abolish its punishment and examination systems and introduce a school parliament which should direct the affairs of the institution in a way which is acceptable to autonomous men. Apart from the rational objections to the possibility of educational institutions being purely 'democratic'[15] it ignores the implications to be drawn from the Piaget–Kohlberg theory. For on this view children have to pass from seeing rules as connected with punishments and rewards to seeing them as ways of maintaining a gang-given or authoritatively ordained rule structure before they can adopt a more autonomous attitude towards them. Kohlberg has shown that many adolescents are still only at the first 'pre-moral' level; so the suggestion that an institution should be devised for them which is structured only in terms of the final stage is grossly inappropriate. Progressive schools, therefore, which insist *from the start* on children making their own decisions and running their own affairs, ignore the crucial role which the stage of conventional morality plays in moral development. The more enlightened ones in fact have a firm authority structure for the school which is arranged so that increasing areas of discretion and participation in decision-making are opened up for the older pupils. This attempt to arrange an institution so that its control system is not out of tune with stages of development seems eminently sensible. In fact the Public Schools, at their best, have approximated to this. They have combined a great emphasis on decency, doing the done thing, and respect for authority with a pressure on prefects to develop some degree of autonomy. The criticism of this system is that the emphasis on a second-level type of regulation was over done and that third-level type of morality was encouraged only for the few who were singled out for positions of eminence.

It might, finally, be tentatively suggested that, though there are stages in character development which are 'writ large' in systems of institutional control, the arrangement is a hierarchical one. Earlier stages are not completely superseded; rather they are, ideally speaking, caught up in and transformed by the next stage. When a system maintained purely by naked force and the dispensation of rewards gives way to a system dependent on the belief in the sanctity of rules enshrined in tradition or laid down by authority, force and rewards are not abandoned. Rather they are placed in the background as palpable supports for the authority structure, which have to be employed if the support appropriate to an authority system becomes ineffective. Similarly when, with the advent of individualism and the belief in reason, traditional systems are challenged, and fundamental questions are asked about the institution of authority itself, authority becomes rationalised, not superseded. Its structure is adapted to the reasons for having it, people are appointed to positions of authority on relevant grounds, and their spheres of competence are carefully defined.

In a similar way the autonomous man is not a person who operates only at the level of a principled morality. He is not impervious to the promise of reward and punishment; he does many things because it is the decent thing to do or because they have been laid down by authority; but he is capable both of doing the same things because he sees their point as flowing from his fundamental principles, and of challenging certain forms of conduct that are laid down and acting differently because of his own convictions. He has, in other words, a rational attitude both to tradition and to authority. My guess is, however, that much of the conduct of autonomous people is governed by a second-level type of morality. They refrain from stealing and incest, because they do not regard it as the thing to do. They pay their debts, keep their promises, and adopt the principle of first come first served when queuing for goods in short supply, without pondering much on the principles involved. Maybe they have thought about the ethics of such practices; maybe they are in part moved by considerations connected with their principles. But my guess is that they carry with them a solid precipitate from the conventional stage of morality whose motivation sustains the more mundane levels of their conduct. For unless a person has been solidly bedded down in this stage of morality he will not have the basic experience of rules as regulators of his impulses and as checks on the more calculating type of hedonism, deriving from the first level of morality. This provides a proper preparation for the autonomous stage of morality, and the attitude to rules remains with him even though the more rational attitude to rules, appropriate to the autonomous stage, is superimposed on it.

4 ASSUMPTIONS ABOUT LEARNING

Throughout this over-ambitious paper I have referred to various studies by psychologists and have indulged in what seem to be speculative sorties into the empirical which have sometimes been prefaced by remarks such as 'My guess is'. What justification has a philosopher for behaving like this, even though he is a philosopher of education and therefore necessarily has his ear closer to the ground than his less mundane colleagues in philosophy departments?

I could deploy a general thesis about the nature of philosophy to justify this procedure, in which I would try to show that the dividing line between philosophy and first-order activities, such as science and morality, is not as easy to draw as many have thought. But there is no need, in this case, to appeal to such general considerations; for the justification lies in the nature of human learning, which, as I shall try very briefly to indicate, permits observations of this quasi-empirical character to be made.

In ordinary straightforward cases of human learning, in which some content is understood, memorised, imitated or made a person's own in various other ways, there is a sense in which the concept of 'learning' is neither monolithic nor concerned with anything that requires empirical investigation. For it draws attention to a range of achievements which are diverse and whose different criteria dictate the sort of thing that must be done if learning is to take place. Suppose, for instance, that one learns, in biology, what mammals are. 'Learns' here picks out the achievement of being able to classify animals in a certain way. The achievement involves being able to relate 'mammal' to other concepts such as 'mammarian glands' and to recognise cases of mammals. The so-called processes of learning involve being put in the way of both features of what it means to grasp the concept of 'mammal'. Examples are pointed out and the features which they have in common are explained. Learning a skill is different; for this involves, in the case of bodily skills like swinging a golf-club, the co-ordination of movements in a certain pattern. But here the relevant type of mastery dictates what learning must be like; for how else could such a pattern of movements be developed except by some kind of practice in moving the body in this way? Remembering similarly must involve some content which is accurately reproduced; so learning in this sphere must involve devices by means of which accuracy in reproduction is ensured. The type of achievement determines the general form of the process of learning.

This fundamental point about the concept of learning makes clear why the philosophy is intimately concerned with it; for it is a philosopher's task to explicate in general what is meant by 'understanding', 'knowing how to do things', 'remembering', etc. Anything that is to count as 'learning' in these spheres must be related intelligibly in some way to the achievement in question. By this I mean that there must be some relationship such as that of being logically presupposed to, or conceptually connected with, the achievement in question. Of course, the philosopher may not know all the *details* of the achievement. He may be rusty on his mathematics or ignorant about golf. But the details will be supplied not by empirical psychologists but by those who know a lot about the structure of the forms of understanding or skills in question. There are, of course, important empirical questions about aids to learning such as the influence of repetition; there are empirical questions about individual differences and about conditions which militate against learning. But the central core of what we call 'learning' depends upon making explicit criteria of 'match' and intelligibility of content in the various achievements of which human beings are capable.

In this paper, however, I have not dwelt at all on the learning of the *contents* of various forms of achievement. Rather I have been concerned with the development of forms of understanding, characterising both a chooser and an autonomous person. In suggesting, for instance, that to become autonomous what is necessary is a predictable social environment, encouragement of the individual's attempts to manipulate things, and a general conviction that an individual's point of view matters, I have, in effect, been citing conditions that make the development of various components in the concept of 'choosing' intelligible. Brainwashing was explained as a process that undermines the categoreal apparatus necessary for choice by depriving the individual of a temporal framework and of a sense of his own identity. Similarly indoctrination was represented as a process that drastically discourages the fundamental questioning of the validity of rules which characterises the autonomous stage. Unreasonable people were seen to be the product of a social environment embodying arbitrariness and a language that is concrete and weak on a syntax that aids thought in terms of universals. It was suggested that it is difficult to develop autonomy in an institution that is structured in terms of appeals to authority or in which rewards and punishments are the main incentives to learning. For it is such all-pervasive procedures that determine how an individual is likely to structure his experience. In proceeding in this way I am only sketching in some of the conditions of 'cognitive stimulation', which, on Kohlberg's view, encourage development from stage to stage or other influences that fixate people at a certain stage of development.

The question must be asked, however, whether in providing this kind of social setting for Kohlberg's speculations I am doing anything for which a philosopher is specially suited. There are parts of it, surely, which are eminently the concern of the philosopher. Piaget's and Kohlberg's basic claim is that the order of development of stage concepts is culturally invariant because it is based on logical relationships between levels of conceiving. If this is correct it has manifest importance in the moral sphere. It would dictate, for instance, the rather cautious conservatism in moral education set out in section 3. For the purpose of this article I have assumed it to be a tenable view. But elsewhere[16] I have questioned it at least on the ground that Kohlberg has not clearly spelt out the logical connections.

Secondly it is a philosophical task to break down a notion like that of autonomy and to point out that some process of learning is required in relation to each aspect of the achievement of autonomy. This fits in with the general account of the philosopher's role in relation to learning set out at the beginning of this section. So does the attempt to indicate the *sort* of conditions under which forms of conception could be intelligibly learnt. For with these, as with any other concepts, one has to postulate both conditions in which they could be applied and some aids to conceptualisation, even if they take the form of 'cognitive stimulation' rather than of direct instruction. It is an empirical question, of course, to determine the conditions which actually *do* have a marked influence. For instance, in the case of learning perceptual concepts of the sort that are involved in geometry – e.g. square, round – it is a philosophical point that some kind of experience is necessary for learning the concepts; for otherwise how could the concept be *applied*, which is part of our understanding of what it means to have learnt a concept? But it may be an empirical fact that a lot of manipulatory and visual experience is a great help in learning. This may not be the case with practical concepts such as that of 'toy' or 'tool'. And with the types of concept that are crucial in the development of autonomy, the case of the Wolof, studied by Bruner and Greenfield, suggests that both exploratory experiences and social influences are very important.

There are, of course, other discoveries in the developmental sphere about which the philosopher could have little to say – e.g. the importance attached to sexual and aggressive wishes in the Freudian explanation of why people do not develop along Piagetian lines and learn ways of interpreting things that lead to various forms of irrationality which even sometimes prevent them from achieving the status of choosers (see section 1(b)). But in these types of explanation, as well as in the types of explanation which have been used to account for the influence of institutions and social conditions, there are present some all-pervasive assumptions about generalisation in learning, whose status is somewhat obscure. What is to be made, for instance, of assumptions such as:

'If human beings are exposed to a highly unpredictable environment, they will tend to lack confidence in their ability to predict and control events.'

'If children are actively discouraged from asking questions they will acquire habits of unquestioning acceptance.'

Assumptions such as these proliferate in the literature of psychology in general as well as in the particular speculations in which I have indulged in parts of this paper. All of them could be falsified in particular cases, though all of them have a kind of intuitive plausibility about them. Their plausibility derives from the fact that they all manifestly satisfy the basic condition of all human learning, namely that of an intelligible connection between what is learnt and the conditions of learning. It is not the philosopher's task to explore the extent to which these common-sense assumptions are true. But philosophical points can be made about the types of condition which must be satisfied for different types of learning to take place. Assumptions such as these manifestly satisfy such conditions. We are, I think, only at the beginning of our understanding of what is a philosophical point about learning and what is an empirical point. This distinction applies to the content of experience as well as to its form, though I have mainly been concerned with the latter in this paper. It would, however, take another paper to begin to get to grips with this central problem in the philosophy of education. I have only introduced it briefly at the end of this one in order to defend myself against the charge that, because I have referred to things that go on in the world, I am necessarily bringing the Owl of Minerva down to the level of the cuckoo in the nest.

REFERENCES

1. I wish to express my thanks to colleagues whose comments helped me to improve this paper – especially Stanley Benn and Geoffrey Mortimore of the Australian National University and Mrs P. A. White of the University of London Institute of Education.
2. Especially in Stanley Benn's paper on 'Conditions of Autonomy', which he read to a conference of the AAP in 1969 and which I discussed with him at length during my period as Visiting Fellow at the Australian National University. This paper was itself a development of ideas worked out, between Stanley Benn and W. Weinstein in their 1971 paper 'Being Free to Act, and Being a Free Man'.

3. For development of such points see Peters, 1966, Ch. VII.
4. See ibid., Chs III, IV, V, VII esp.
5. See Peters (1964, 1971a).
6. See Peters (1971b).
7. See, for instance, Peck and Havighurst (1960), pp. 109–11.
8. For distinction see Peters (1971a).
9. See Klein (1965).
10. Kohlberg actually breaks Piaget's three stages up into six stages with three levels. But it would be out of place to pursue these refinements.
11. See Kohlberg (1968, 1969).
12. See Greenfield and Bruner (1969).
13. See Lilge (1958), esp. pp. 25–6.
14. See Bernstein (1961, 1969).
15. See Hirst and Peters (1970), Ch. 7.
16. See Peters (1971b).

BIBLIOGRAPHY

Benn, S. I. and Weinstein, W., 'Being Free to Act, and Being a Free Man', *Mind*, Vol. LXXX (1971), pp. 194–211.

Bernstein, B. B., 'Social Class and Linguistic Development: a Theory of Social Learning', in Halsey, A. H., Floud, J. and Anderson, C. A., *Education, Economy and Society* (New York: Free Press, 1961).

Bernstein, B. and Henderson, D., 'Social Class Differences in the Relevance of Language to Socialisation', *Sociology*, Vol. 3 (1969).

Greenfield, P. M. and Bruner, J. S., 'Culture and Cognitive Growth', in Goslin, D. A., *Handbook of Socialisation: Theory and Research* (Chicago: Rand McNally, 1969).

Hirst, P. H. and Peters, R. S., *The Logic of Education* (Routledge & Kegan Paul, 1970).

Klein, J., *Samples of English Culture*, 2 vols (Routledge & Kegan Paul, 1965).

Kohlberg, L., 'Early Education: a Cognitive Developmental View', *Child Development*, Vol. 31 (1968).

Kohlberg, L., 'Stage and Sequence: the Cognitive Developmental Approach to Socialization', in Goslin, D. A. (Ed.), *Handbook of Socialization: Theory and Research* (Chicago: Rand McNally, 1969).

Laing, R. D., *The Divided Self* (Penguin Books, 1965).

Lilge, F., *Anton Semyonovitch Makarenko* (Berkeley and Los Angeles, University of California Press, 1958).

Peck, R. F. and Havighurst, R. J., *The Psychology of Character Development* (New York, John Wiley, 1960).

Peters, R. S., 'Mental Health as an Educational Aim', in Hollins, T. H. B. (Ed.), *Aims of Education: the Philosophical Approach* (Manchester University Press, 1964).

Peters, R. S., *Ethics and Education* (Allen & Unwin, 1966).

Peters, R. S., 'Education and Human Development', in Selleck, R. W. (Ed.), *Melbourne Studies in Education* (Melbourne University Press, 1970).

Peters, R. S., 'Reason and Passion', in Vesey, G. (Ed.), *The Proper Study*, Vol. 4, Royal Institute of Philosophy (Macmillan, 1971a).

Peters, R. S., 'Moral Development: a Plea for Pluralism', in Mischel, T. (Ed.), *Cognitive Development and Epistemology* (New York: Academic Press, 1971b).

17

MORAL DEVELOPMENT AND MORAL LEARNING*[1]

INTRODUCTION

The most obvious way in which a philosopher can contribute to work on moral education is through work in ethics. Just as work in mathematical or scientific education could not get off the ground without a determinate idea of the structure of what has to be learnt in these spheres, so too a determinate notion of 'morality' is an essential precondition for any serious approach to moral education. It might be argued, too, that it is particularly important for philosophers to do this because of the covert way in which ethical assumptions are smuggled into empirical work in this field. Any psychological account of moral development or moral education must be from a particular standpoint in ethics; for the delimitation of 'moral' is not a neutral matter. Psychologists working within Piagetian, Freudian, or social learning frameworks are too apt to work with an implicit ethical position. The job of the philosopher is, therefore, to make such ethical positions explicit and to discuss the arguments that might be given for them.

I have done some work previously along these lines[2] and do not want, in this paper, to go over that kind of ground again in any detailed way. Instead I propose to explore another range of issues which are equally appropriate for a philosopher of education. These are issues about types of learning. It might be objected straight away that these are empirical issues about which a philosopher could have little to say. But this is not true. Processes of learning and of development are processes through which a variety of abilities and achieve-

* Reprinted, with the permission of the editor, from *The Monist*, Vol. 58, No. 4 (October 1974).

ments are mastered. These are very diverse. People come to understand, to remember, to make inferences; they master skills and
develop attitudes. Learning, as distinct from maturation, involves
coming up to the mark, according to the different criteria involved in
these achievements, as a result of experience. There must therefore
be some intelligible connection between the achievements concerned and the experiences through which a person comes up to the
mark. It would be unintelligible, for instance, that a person could
attain a mastery of Euclid by just standing on his head – unless, that
is, a special story was told about the connection between adopting
this position and grasping relationships between angles, straight
lines, etc. For, if Euclid is to be understood, there must be experiences in which attention is paid to features of figures such as
triangles and squares. In a similar way it is not purely an empirical
point that practice in moving the body in certain ways is indispensable for mastering a skill like swinging a golf club. In every case of
human learning the relevant type of mastery dictates the general
character of the learning experiences. There are empirical questions
about which *particular* learning experiences, taken from a range of
possible ones, in fact tend to promote the desired achievements most
effectively. But the central core of 'learning' depends upon some kind
of match between the learning processes and the desired achievements. So analysis by philosophers of these achievements is very
important.

In breaking down particular subjects for learning, as in programmed learning for instance, the work of the specialist who knows
about the structure of what has to be learnt is much more central
than that of the empirical psychologist who knows about *general*
conditions of learning, such as the influence of repetition, rest-
pauses and incentives. The subject specialist, too, would be wise to
have a philosopher at his elbow, if he himself has not developed this
way of thinking. Otherwise a conception of a subject may be developed, as in the new mathematics, and the content carefully
structured, without adequate realisation of the presuppositions about
the nature of the subject which the programme of study embodies.
This is true of all subjects – e.g. science, art, music, history, religion,
social studies, etc., though too dimly appreciated. Unfortunately the
'philosophies of' the various subjects taught in schools, and their
relevance for how the subjects are taught, are the most undeveloped
area of the philosophy of education.

Now morality is not a subject on the curriculum of most schools –
at least in the sense in which mathematics is. And the only specialists

in its structure are moral philosophers. It is often said, too, that willy-nilly every teacher is a teacher of morals. So, whether or not programmes of moral education are introduced more explicitly into the classroom, there is an obvious case for getting a bit clearer about the achievements involved and hence the sorts of learning experiences that people must go through if they are to emerge as moral beings from their childhood. This will enable evidence produced by psychologists to be looked at with a more discriminating eye. For often evidence which is produced for confirming a particular theory in psychology does not necessarily refute another theory. For the different theories may be concerned with different aspects of moral learning or moral development, or with a different conception of what is central to morality.

It is assumed that there is a conflict between different psychological theories of moral development. Instruction-based teachers and Skinnerians are insistent on the success of their methods in moral learning as in any other form of learning. The advocates of experience and discovery are equally enthusiastic about their methods, and with encouragement from their reading of Piaget and Kohlberg, have moved into the moral sphere. And those with a more Freudian type of ancestry still stick doggedly to their belief in the role of identification and guilt. Is it possible to reconcile these seemingly discordant voices about what matters in moral education? Perhaps – but to attempt such a reconciliation I must briefly outline the standpoint about morality from which I approach these different theories of moral development. I propose to confine it to the area of morals that is concerned with interpersonal rules.

1   RATIONAL MORALITY

It is often suggested nowadays that the only alternatives open to people in the moral position that they may adopt are either the relics of some traditional code or some version of a subjectivist stance such as Existentialism or a 'situational ethic'.[3] But these, surely, are not the only alternatives open. There is a middle way between tradition and some sort of romantic protest. This middle way is closely connected with the use of reason. This enables people to adopt a critical attitude towards what has been established. They may accept it or reject it on its merits. But in so doing they need not take up a purely subjective stance. It is significant, for instance, that young people, who are very critical of what their elders do, criticise it in terms of the injustice, exploitation or suffering brought about by adult mismanagement. They are united in assuming that this line of criticism is pertinent; they do not just voice private objections to the plight of coloured people, to the selectiveness of the educational system, or to the paternalism of their teachers.

In order to make clear what is meant by the use of reason in morality it is important to make a distinction between the form and content of the moral consciousness. This distinction is similar to that which can be made in the sphere of beliefs about the world. The content of a belief might be that the earth is round. But this belief could be held in different ways. It could be believed just because it had been read in a book or proclaimed by an authority. On the other hand it could be believed because someone had examined it, had viewed it critically and looked into the evidence for it, like a scientist. Thus a belief with the same content could be held in quite different ways, which would constitute two distinct forms which the belief might have. Similarly in morals someone could believe that gambling was wrong simply because his parents had brought him up to believe it. On the other hand he might have reflected on the practice of gambling and might have decided that it was wrong because of the suffering brought about by the practice.

Holding beliefs rationally is to adopt one possible form for beliefs. It is possible, therefore, that people could share a certain content of beliefs which had a different form. An unreflective peasant and a philosopher, for instance, might both believe that it is wrong to break promises. Alternatively people might look at beliefs in the same sort of way but disagree with regard to content because they gave different weight to considerations relevant to holding them. Reflective people, for instance, after due thought, might disagree about the ethics of abortion, even though they both accepted the relevance of the considerations advanced on either side. This type of distinction is very pertinent when discussing morals or moral education. For too much weight may be given to consensus or to lack of it without considering whether the consensus relates to content or to form.

My interest, needless to say, is in the emergence of a rational form of morality, which enables a person to adopt a stance that is critical of tradition but not subjective. But this cannot be characterised purely in terms of the *ability* to reason, in the sense of making inferences, as I have argued elsewhere.[4] To start with, if this ability is to be effectively exercised, it must be supported by a group of rational passions connected with the demands for consistency, order, clarity and relevance. Secondly, if this is to be exercised in the sphere of interpersonal conduct the individual must be capable of what Piaget calls reversibility in thought. He must be able to look at rules and practices from other people's point of view. And, unless we are going to postulate a society of rational egoists, we must also assume on the part of those with a capacity for reasoning, a *concern* for the interests of others as well as for their own interests. For what sort of point could reasoning about conduct have unless there were some concern to ameliorate the human predicament, to consider people's interests? In other words I am adopting a position in morals similar to that of David Hume who argued for some kind of shared response amongst human beings, connected with sympathy, which he at times called the 'sentiment for humanity'. Perhaps neither concern for others, nor concern for oneself, can be demonstrated as necessary for the application of reasoning to interpersonal conduct. But I am assuming them as preconditions in my system of rational morality.

Other principles must also be presupposed if it is assumed that interpersonal rules of conduct are to be discussed by rational beings with a concern for people's interests. For, as one of the main features of the use of reason is the settling of issues on *relevant* grounds – i.e. the banning of arbitrariness, some kind of impartiality with regard to people's claims is also required. They cannot be ignored just because of the colour of their eyes, or ruled out of court just because of the colour of their skin. People must be treated with respect as sources of arguments and claims. Without too, the general presumption that people should tell the truth rational discussion would be impossible; for, as a general practice, systematic lying would be counter-productive in relation to any common concern to discover what ought to be done. Finally, too, there must be some presumption in favour of freedom. For without freedom of speech, the community would be hamstrung in relation to its concern to arrive at an answer; for even the most offensive or simple members might have something of importance to contribute. There must also be a presumption in favour of freedom of action; for what rational man would seriously discuss what ought to be done without also demanding freedom to do it?

These fundamental principles do not, of course, lay down in detail what ought to be done. They do not, in other words, provide any detailed *content* to the moral life. Rather they supply a *form* for the moral consciousness; they sensitise us to what is relevant when we think about what is right and wrong. But neither do the principles underlying science guarantee an agreed content for a science. In both cases all that is provided is a form of thought which structures experience. In the scientific case assumptions about the world are systematically submitted to discussion and to observational tests.

Some are discarded and others survive as the current content of scientific knowledge. Similarly in the moral case, when current codes are reflected on in the light of such principles, as happened in the seventeenth century when reflective lawyers such as Grotius tried to agree upon laws of the sea against piracy, it comes to be seen that the content of codes are not all of equal importance. There are some types of basic rules – e.g. concerning contracts, the care of the young and property – which can be seen to be necessary to any continuing form of social life in which the human condition is going to be tolerable at all, man being what he is and the conditions of life on earth being what they are.[5] But other rules are much more dependent on local economic and geographical conditions such as prohibitions on usury, birth-control and possessiveness. Stability and consensus at a basic level are quite compatible with change and experiment at other levels. And these differences in stability of content can be determined by reasons deriving from fundamental principles such as fairness and the consideration of people's interests.

Actually disagreement over content between reflective people can be greatly exaggerated. Is there widespread disagreement between reflective people over what I have called basic rules? But, from the point of view of rational morality, it is more crucial to ask whether or not, in determining any particular content, people do or do not accept as relevant more or less similar considerations, even though they give differing *weight* to them?[6] In discussing sexual matters, for instance, is not the harm done to children by being fatherless thought morally relevant, or the lack of respect for persons evident in some forms of prostitution both within and outside marriage? In considering the breaking of contracts is not the lack of truthfulness, as well as the unhappiness caused, thought to be relevant? In discussing the merits of gambling do we ever dwell approvingly or disapprovingly on the amount of greenness in the world brought about by the construction of card-tables? If we think a man wicked is it normally by virtue of his height? Maybe we do not always arrive at the same conclusion about what is right and wrong, about the content of morality. But is not the form of thought of reflective people about it structured in terms of shared principles which make considerations relevant?

2   FORM AND CONTENT IN MORAL DEVELOPMENT AND LEARNING

The distinction which I have made between form and content in presenting a thumb-nail sketch of the structure of a rational morality is also extremely relevant to accounts of moral development and moral learning. This distinction is explicitly made by Lawrence Kohlberg in his account of moral development.[7] But as he is interested only in the development of the form of experience rather than in the learning of content there is a one-sided emphasis in his theory. Kohlberg admits that the content of rules – e.g. about honesty, punctuality, tidiness – is learnt by instruction and imitation, aided by rewards and punishment, praise and blame. But he is not interested in such habit-formation; for he claims that such habits are short term and situation specific. They are of minor importance in moral development which depends on how rules are conceived rather than on cultural content. There is a transition from conceiving of rules as connected with rewards and punishments to conceiving of them as 'out there' backed by praise and blame from the peer-group and authority figures, and finally to conceiving of them as alterable conventions depending upon consent and reciprocity. Development depends not upon explicit teaching, backed by reinforcement, but upon the interaction of the child with his social environment, which is aided or retarded by the amount of 'cognitive stimulation' available to the child which helps him to conceive of the social environment in the required manner.

The relevance of Kohlberg's theory for the development of a rational form of morality is obvious enough; for that is what he is talking about. Like Piaget, whom he follows, he is a Kantian. But in contrasting the interaction with the environment, which stimulates the development of a rational form of morality, with 'teaching', which he thinks is singularly ineffective in this sphere, he makes it look too much as if the child, as it were, does it himself. This Dewey-like impression has to be corrected by a closer look at the sorts of influence that constitute 'cognitive stimulation'. But there are also, on this theory, most interesting implications for the learning of content, in which Kohlberg evinces little interest. For the form of the child's morality, defined by his conception of the rules which are constitutive of its content, on Kohlberg's theory determines both the type of content that can be assimilated and the aids which are available for this assimilation. In other words the type of 'reinforcement' used by Skinnerians can be shown to be peculiarly appropriate to learning specific types of *content* at certain stages of development. If it is important that the child should internalise a certain type of content – e.g. rules about not stealing – there may only be certain ways in which this can be done at a certain age – e.g. by being rewarded or praised for conformity. So Skinnerians may be right about the learning of content. But learning the *form* of experience may be a very different matter. And some methods of teaching content might impede the child from developing to a stage at which a different conception of rules is possible.

My argument will be, therefore, not just that Kohlberg's account of the development of a rational form of morality is compatible with a Skinnerian type of account of the learning of content in early childhood; for it is more than compatible in that it provides conceptual levels which define the types of 'reinforcement' and instruction that are possible. I shall argue, in addition, that no adequate account can be given of the development of a rational form of morality without more attention to the learning of content than Kohlberg is disposed to give. Furthermore I shall indicate that there are certain ways in which content may be learnt which actively impede the development of a rational form of morality. I will defend this thesis by considering briefly Kohlberg's thesis about stages of development with particular attention to the types of 'cognitive stimulation' that may be necessary. I will then pass to deploying my thesis about the importance of the learning of content.

In making suggestions about development and learning in these spheres I will adopt the strategy implied by my brief remarks about the relationship between the logical and psychological aspects of learning in section 1. I will indicate some of the relevant achievements as I proceed and cite empirical evidence in so far as it relates to learning experiences relevant to such achievements.

3   THE DEVELOPMENT OF A RATIONAL FORM OF MORALITY

(a)   *The Egocentric Stage*

The first significant stage in moral development, on the Piaget–Kohlberg theory, is that in which the child has an egocentric conception of rules. He does what is laid down because he wants to avoid punishment or to obtain rewards. This is not regarded as a primitive instrumental conditioning type of situation in which some response is reinforced and gradually stamped in without the individual seeing any connection between what he does and the state of affairs, whether pleasant or painful, which results. Rather the child is envisaged as seeing the means–end type of connection involved. For this stage to have been reached the child must have developed a basic cognitive and affective apparatus; he is no longer an infant beset by various forms of pre-rational wishes and aversions. He must be able to delay gratification and to plan his behaviour to a limited extent. This form of commerce with the world and with others as sources of pain or gratification presupposes the development of a primitive type of categoreal apparatus with which Piaget, following Kant, was very much concerned in his account of what he called the Copernican revolution of early childhood.[8] If the child is to think in terms of taking means to an end he must appreciate, to a certain extent, the causal properties of things and must be able to distinguish consequences brought about by his own agency from those that come about independently of his will. He must possess the categoreal concepts of 'thinghood' and 'causality' in a primitive form. He must have some kind of framework of time and space. He must be able to distinguish himself from others. These categoreal concepts define the development of what Freud called the ego, and reality thinking.[9]

What assumptions have to be made about the sorts of experiences which are likely to lead to this sort of development? Obviously, to start with, the child will have to be provided with plenty of opportunities for the manipulation of things. The more controversial issue is the role of adults and other children in bringing about this early development. Now followers of Piaget have been most active in demonstrating that this framework of concepts, necessary for rational thought and choice, cannot be imparted by specific teaching. The child has to be provided with plenty of concrete experience. He will gradually come to grasp these organising notions if he is suitably stimulated like the slave in *Meno*. And there is a sense in which these contentions *must* be true. For what is being learnt is a principle, which provides unity to a number of previously disconnected experiences. This has to be 'seen' or grasped by the individual and it cannot be grasped as a principle unless the individual is provided with experience of the items which it unifies. If information is being imparted, which has to be memorised, the teacher can instruct the learner explicitly in what has to be learnt; in learning a skill the particular movements can be demonstrated explicitly for the learner to copy or practice. But, if the teacher is trying to get the learner to grasp a principle, all he can do is to draw attention to common features of cases and hope that the penny will drop. Also once the child has grasped the principle, he knows how to go on, as Wittgenstein puts it; there is thus no limit to the number of cases that he will see as falling under the principle. There is a sense, therefore, in which the learner gets out much more than any teacher could have put in. Kohlberg's objection to *specific* teaching is therefore readily explained; for principles just are not the sorts of things that can be applied only to a specific number of items which could be imparted by a teacher.

Kohlberg, of course, is using 'teaching' in a very narrow sense to mean something like 'explicit instruction'. It is only this very narrow conception of 'teaching' which can be properly contrasted with 'cognitive stimulation'; for most people would say that Socrates was teaching the slave in *Meno* even though he was not explicitly telling him things.

The learning situation, however, can be influenced by adults in much more subtle ways. There is evidence to suggest, for instance, that these concepts develop much more slowly if the child is actively discouraged from exploring and manipulating the physical environment.[10] If the child, too, is to do what is demanded of him attention is required. Now fear of punishment for not doing what is demanded is more likely to distract attention than the prospect of a reward. All the evidence confirms this assumption; for positive reinforcement is generally accepted by psychologists as being much more conducive to learning than negative reinforcement.

There is also the negative type of evidence provided by pathological studies; for most pathological states can be described in terms of the absence of features of this categoreal structure, and these defects can often be correlated with typical conditions in early childhood. It is generally agreed, for instance, that psychopaths, who live on their whims and impulses, for whom the future has little reality, are largely the product of homes which are rejecting towards the child and which provide a very inconsistent type of discipline.[11] Similarly schizophrenics, whose belief structure in regard to their own identity, and to that of the permanence of objects and the reliability of causal processes in the physical world, is deranged, are thought by some to be products of discrepant and irreconcilable attitudes towards them before they could develop a secure sense of reality.[12]

Further evidence of the importance of such general social influences on the early development of the preconditions for a rational form of morality can be found in sociological studies of people who might be termed unreasonable rather than irrational.[13] Josephine Klein, for instance, singles out certain abilities which are important in the development of reasoning – the ability to abstract and use generalisations, the ability to perceive the world as an ordered universe in which rational action is rewarded, the ability to plan ahead and control gratification. She cites evidence from Luria and Bernstein to show that the *extent* to which these abilities develop depends upon the prevalence of an elaborated form of language which is found in some strata of society but not in others. She also shows how the belief and conduct of some working-class sub-cultures are affected by the arbitrariness of their child-rearing techniques.[14]

In brief, the empirical evidence supports the logical analysis of the learning situation. If a child has to develop a basic apparatus for conceiving of an orderly world in which concepts such as those of 'thing' and 'causality' are firmly planted, he has to be given plenty of experience of objects and processes instantiating such concepts. If he is to learn to plan and to control gratification he must also live in a social world which provides regularities for him which will enable him to predict and to enjoy satisfying consequences of his actions. And so on. It is not difficult, therefore, to surmise why the most consistent findings from studies of child-rearing practices are that sensible children, who are capable of reasoning later on, emerge from homes in which there is a warm attitude of acceptance towards children, together with a firm and consistent insistence on rules without much in the way of punishment. An accepting attitude will tend to encourage trust in others and confidence in the individual's own powers. A predictable social environment will provide the type of experience which is necessary for guiding behaviour by reflection on its consequences and so build up a belief in a future which is, in part, shaped by his own decisions. Inconsistency in treatment, on the other hand, will encourage plumping rather than reflective choice, and attachment to instant gratification. A rejecting attitude will inhibit the development of self-confidence and techniques of punishment will generate anxiety and will provide conditions which are too distracting for much learning to take place.

These social influences may be spoken of as forms of 'cognitive stimulation'. For their function is to provide conditions in which rational capacities can begin to develop. But these influences provide a type of social environment for which adults are largely responsible. A contrast should not, therefore, be made between 'cognitive stimulation' and 'teaching' of a sort that suggests that adult influence is not of central importance to both. There is a danger in soft-pedalling the role of instruction in moral development. For people often go to the other extreme and assume that children must be left alone to find it all out for themselves. But they will not develop in this way, as in discovery methods generally, unless adults provide a structured and supportive type of social environment.

(b) *Rule-following*

At the first level of development the child, as I have explained, is acquiring the general apparatus for reasoning. But his attitude is basically egocentric; he sees conformity with them basically as a way of avoiding punishment and of obtaining rewards.[15] At the next 'transcendental' stage of moral realism a rule comes to be seen as a rule and to depend for its existence on the will of the peer-group and of authority figures. This is a crucial stage in moral development; for it involves the realisation on the part of the child of what it is to follow a rule, to accept a rule as a rule binding on one's conduct. Much of what Freud wrote about the super-ego is relevant surely to this stage, though he himself was concerned more with exaggerated and distorted types of 'internalisation' rather than with the normal developmental process of coming to accept a rule as a rule.[16] At this stage of development children come to enjoy following rules and to revel in the sense of mastery that this gives them. They have as yet no notion of the validity of rules. They regard them as just there, supported by the approval of the peer-group and of authority figures. It is a period at which imitation and identification are extremely important in learning.

This stage in rule-conformity is a very important one in moral development. In the U.S.S.R. Makarenko achieved considerable success in dealing with delinquents by reliance mainly on group projects and on identification with the collective will of the community.[17] If Piaget and Kohlberg are right, however, in their assumptions about the development of autonomy, *every* individual has to go through this stage of what Kohlberg calls 'good boy' morality before he can attain the autonomous stage. It is questionable whether progressive educators have been sufficiently aware of the importance of this second stage of development.

In the history of man development beyond this stage of morality to a third or autonomous stage is probably a rare phenomenon, depending on the development of what Popper has called an 'open society'. Within our own type of society Kohlberg himself stresses the differences in rate of development beyond the second stage of those who come from middle-class as distinct from working-class homes. There is, too, a series of investigations by Bruner and his associates, to which I have already referred,[18] which are far-reaching in their implications for the importance of social influences; for they show not only how individuals pass to the second stage, but also how they are massively discouraged from passing beyond it. In cultures such as that of the Wolof in Senegal there is no encouragement for the individual to develop independence, to explore the world 'for himself'. What is true is what the group, or the authority figure in the group, says.

This lasting attitude towards rules may not be just the product of vague social pressure and expectations; it may also be produced and perpetuated by the conscious techniques which we now call 'indoctrination'. For 'indoctrination' involves the passing on of fixed beliefs in a way which discourages questions about their validity. Societies like the U.S.S.R., in which indoctrination is widespread, are not societies in which reasoning in general is discouraged. What is discouraged is the particular form of reasoning which involves the questioning of the *validity* of moral and political beliefs and the placing of any emphasis on the role of the individual in determining his own destiny. They thus allow plenty of scope for the attitude to rules which is characteristic of Piaget's second stage but actively discourage any movement towards the autonomous stage, which they regard as an aberration of individualistic societies.

(c)   *The Achievement of Autonomy*
So far I have sketched the sorts of social influences and techniques, such as indoctrination, which discourage people from passing beyond the second stage of 'good-boy' morality. What is to be said about the type of influences that encourage development? It is difficult to say much even in a brief space about this because the notion of 'autonomy', which is the dominant feature of the third stage, is itself very complex.

There is, first of all, the notion of authenticity or genuineness. The suggestion is that a person accepts rules for himself, that his responses are not simply second-hand. Negatively this suggests that he is not just motivated by approval or disapproval from the peer-group or from authority figures. More positively it suggests that there must be some feature of a course of conduct, or of a situation, which constitutes a non-artificial reason for his decision or judgement, as distinct from extrinsic associations provided by praise and blame, reward and punishment, and so on, which are artificially created by the demands of others.

Secondly there is the aspect of autonomy stressed by Kant and Piaget – the ability to stand back and reflect on rules, and to subject them to criticism from the point of view of their validity and appropriateness. On Piaget's theory this is closely connected with reversibility of thought and with the ability to adopt the standpoint of others.

Thirdly there is the suggestion of strength of will, the ability to stick to a judgement or course of conduct in the face of counter-inclinations. These counter-inclinations often derive from motivations which consolidate conformity at previous stages – e.g. fear of punishment, disapproval and ostracism.

How, then, are these different aspects of autonomy developed? A general preliminary point must be made which is that we cannot expect young people to manage on their own unless they are given concrete opportunities to do so. This thought presumably lies behind the 'Outward Bound' movement and the Public Schools system of prefects. But such opportunities must be realistically related to responsibilities which it is reasonable for people to take. If too open a situation is created we are likely to get relapses back to and embeddedness in the second stage of morality due to the fear of freedom about which Eric Fromm has written so eloquently.[19]

Authenticity   This conditional encouragement of the individual to strike out on his own is particularly important in the development of authenticity. There is a strange misconception that haunts the Socratic insistence that we should discover what we really want, which is that we can come to understand this before we actually try things out. But the truth is that we often only come to know what we genuinely want or feel *by* trying things out.

In the moral sphere 'authenticity' is closely connected with the capacity to experience compassion or concern for others in a first-hand way. For, as Hume put it, 'no action can be virtuous or morally good unless there be in human nature some motive to produce it distinct from the sense of its morality'.[20] To get beyond the second stage children must not do what is right just out of a 'sense of duty' or because it is the done thing. They must be sensitive to considerations, such as the suffering of others, in virtue of which actions are right or wrong. The findings of the Piaget school are that, at a very early age, children cannot grasp reasons for types of action in the sense that they cannot connect a practice such as that of stealing with considerations such as the harm to others brought about by such a a practice. In other words concern for others cannot serve as a *principle* for them. But this does not show that very early on they cannot genuinely feel concern for others. If they are sensitive to the suffering of others early on the hope is that, with the development of their capacity for reasoning, this will later be one of the main principles in a rational form of moral life.

How then do children come to feel concern for others? Is there an innate basis for it in sympathy? Is Money-Kyrle[21] right in arguing that the origins of what he calls the 'humanistic conscience' (Hume's 'sentiment for humanity'), which Freud neglected, are to be found in the child's early relationships with his mother? Does not this type of guilt need to be distinguished from the guilt which is the product of punishment and of internalised social disapproval? There is no answer to this type of question in the Piaget–Kohlberg theory. Yet a developmental account of concern for others is surely as important as a developmental account of reasoning and of the child's attitude to rules. In this area of moral development the findings of Piaget surely need to be supplemented by those of the Freudian and social learning schools of psychology. For there is considerable evidence to suggest that the child's capacity for sympathy and his trust in others depends very much on the pattern of his early social relationships.[22]

Reflection on Rules   What, then, in relation to the second aspect of autonomy, is to be done about the development of reasoning, so that considerations, such as concern for others, can serve as principles? Reasons for doing things can be indicated quite early on, even though it is appreciated that the child cannot yet think in this way. For without this type of 'cognitive stimulation' in the environment this reflective attitude to rules is unlikely to develop. I am not saying, of course, that any sane parent or teacher will, in the early stages, always make a child's acceptance of the reasons a condition for his doing what is sensible – e.g. refraining from playing on railway lines. This presumption is confirmed by the evidence from psychology; for the best established finding in this field is of the correlation between moral development and the use of techniques called 'induction', which cover explanation, pointing to the consequences of action, and so on.[23] There is also evidence that these techniques are ineffective until after the pre school years.[24] Language, too, which approximates to what Bernstein calls 'an elaborated code', is very important in aiding this development.[25]

Strength of Will   'Autonomy' suggests not simply reflection on rules but also following rules which have been accepted as the result of such reflection. To do this implies what psychologists call 'ego-strength' – the capacity to delay immediate gratification, or prompt-ings of approval or disapproval, in favour of some more long-term, thought-out policy. The extent to which the development of this type of motivation, once closely associated with the Puritan ethic, de-pends upon specific types of social influences has been strongly argued by Bettelheim and others.[26] It is not just a matter of 'growth'. Even less so, probably, are virtues connected with strength of will such as courage, integrity and determination. These virtues are, perhaps, too little emphasised in recent times because of their association with more traditional moralities such as that of the English Public Schools. There are few, if any, empirical studies on how they are developed. Presumably habit-training is not unimportant in their development; for the peculiarity of these virtues is that they have to be exercised in the face of counter-inclinations. Unless, therefore, a child has some training in acting in the face of fear or anxiety, it seems probable that he will be overwhelmed by them if he encounters them at a later stage when attempting to take a line of his own. This was manifestly the assumption of educators in the Public School tradition who believed in some kind of transfer of training in this sphere. They tended, however, to stress too much the negative aspect of strength of will and neglected the sensitisation to positive considerations which give authentic and long-term point to resistance to fear or temptation.

(d) *The Influence of Institutions*

So far I have been making suggestions about the ways in which individuals such as peers, parents and teachers can wittingly or unwittingly provide appropriate forms of 'cognitive stimulation' which help the development of a rational form of life. Nothing has been said about the all-pervasive influence of institutions which provide a potent source of latent learning for the growing child. Of particular significance is the general control system of the school and the motivational assumptions which support it. For Piaget's and Kohlberg's stages of development are 'writ large' in these all-pervasive features of an institution. It is unlikely that autonomy will be much encouraged by an authoritarian system of control in which anything of importance is decided by the fiat of the headmaster and in which the prevailing assumption is that the appeal to a man is the only method of determining what is correct. Similarly in the motivational sphere students are unlikely to develop a delight in doing things for reasons intrinsic to them if rewards and punishment, meted out both by the staff and by a fierce examination system, provide the stable incentives to the discipline of learning; for the institution itself embodies an attitude to conduct which is appropriate to Piaget's first stage of development. These institutional realities are bound to structure the perceptions of the students. If an institution embodies only an attitude to rules that is characteristic of an earlier stage of development, teachers who attempt to encourage a more developed attitude have an uphill task; for in their attempts at 'cognitive stimulation' they are working against the deadening directives of the institution.

The inference to be drawn from this is not that every school, which upholds an ideal of autonomy, should straightaway abolish its punishment and examination systems and introduce a school parliament which should direct the affairs of the institution in a way which is acceptable to autonomous man. Apart from the rational objections to the possibility of educational institutions being purely 'democratic'[27] it ignores the implications to be drawn from the Piaget–Kohlberg theory. For children have to pass from seeing rules as connected with punishments and rewards to seeing them as ways of maintaining a gang-given or authoritatively ordained rule-structure before they can adopt a more autonomous attitude towards them. Kohlberg has shown that many adolescents are still only at the first 'pre-moral' stage, so the suggestion that an institution should be devised for them which is structured only in terms of the final stage is grossly inappropriate. Progressive schools, therefore, which insist *from the start* on children learning only what interests them, on making their own decisions and running their own affairs, ignore the crucial role which the stage of conventional morality plays in moral development. The more enlightened ones in fact have a firm authority structure for the school which is arranged so that increasing areas of discretion and participation in decision-making are opened up for the older pupils.

4   LEARNING THE CONTENT OF MORALITY

What, then, is to be said about learning the *content* of morality? For to date I have been concerned only with the learning of its form and have been stressing the role of various social influences in promoting what Kohlberg calls 'cognitive stimulation'. There are at least three questions which demand an answer. First, is the learning of a content necessary in moral education? Could not children just develop a form of thinking which enables them to work out a content for themselves? Secondly, if it is, what should this content be? Thirdly, *how* should it be learnt if development of a rational form of morality is to be encouraged?

(a) *Why Worry about Content?*
There is a kind of abstractness and unreality about the approach to

moral education which places exclusive emphasis on the development of a rational form of morality and which considers its content unimportant, dismissing it, as Kohlberg does, as merely 'a bag of virtues'. To start with, even at an early age, children are capable of doing both themselves and others a lot of damage. Hobbes once noted a sobering feature of the human condition which is that a man can be killed by a small child while he is asleep. Also the hazards to small children in modern industrial society are innumerable. So for reasons both of social security and self-preservation, small children must be taught a basic code which, when internalised, will regulate their behaviour to a certain extent when they are not being supervised. There is also the point that a great number of people do not develop to a rational level of morality. For obvious social reasons, therefore, if the morality of such people is to be unthinking, its content is of crucial importance. If the ordinary citizen is mugged in the street, how the thief views rules about property is of academic interest to him.

But even if the focus is exclusively on the development of children rather than on these more palpable facets of social behaviour, there are logical absurdities about any cavalier disregard for content. In the first place, it is difficult to understand how a person could come to follow rules autonomously if he had not learnt, from the inside, as it were, what it is to follow a rule. And children learn this, presumably, by generalising their experience of picking up some particular 'bag of virtues'.

In the second place, how is the exercise of a principled form of morality to be conceived without reference to a determinate content? Respect for persons, for instance, as a principle is only intelligible in the context of a life in which people occupy roles, take part in activities and enjoy personal relationships. It suggests that people should not be treated just as the occupants of roles, that they should not be judged just for their competence in activities, and that, in more personal relationships they should not be used just as means to the purposes of others. Such a principle, in other words, sensitises the individual to the way in which he should conduct himself in the various areas of the moral life which constitute its content. It could not operate without such a concrete content. Indeed by calling something like respect for persons a 'principle' we mean that it embodies a consideration to which appeal is made when criticising, justifying or explaining some determinate content of behaviour or belief.

Usually a principle such as considering people's interests is appealed to in criticism or justification of a social practice such as abortion or punishment. But it can also be regarded as a τέλος immanent in roles and social practices. For parents, for instance, considering children's interests is one of the rationales underlying their role: indeed their role largely defines what this principle *means* in their dealings with their children. Most Utilitarians, too, have stressed the importance of Mill's 'secondary principles' in morality. The Utilitarian, Mill argued, has not to be constantly weighing up the effects of his action on people's interests any more than a Christian has to thumb through the Bible every time before he acts. The experience of a society with regard to the tendencies of actions in relation to people's interests lies behind its roles and rules. In a similar way concern for truth is to be conceived of as a τέλος underlying the procedures of science. If people practising activities and following rules are sensitive to such underlying principles they will adapt their behaviour sensitively to changes in circumstances. If, on the other hand, they are hide-bound traditionalists they may insist on conformity to the minutiae of a code that no longer has any point. But it is impossible to conceive of such a principled morality operating in a vacuum, divorced from a determinate content.

(b)   *What Type of Content?*
Given then the indispensability of some kind of content for moral education the second question arises about the type of content which should constitute the basis of moral education. There is, as a matter of fact, a kind of unreality about this question if it is framed in too general a way. For, willy-nilly, adults will in fact introduce children in some way or other to the type of content which seems to them important. The world which the child has to inhabit is largely a social world structured by the roles, rules, activities and relationships of his parents, which will be shot through with the morality of his parents. The question, therefore, is which elements of this content are to be *emphasised* by parents. For the child will be exposed to it *in toto* and will pick much of it up by imitation and identification whatever their more explicit child-rearing techniques.

If parents subscribe to some form of the rational morality which I am assuming in this paper they will obviously emphasise, as soon as the child is ready, those considerations which are later to function as principles in a rational morality – e.g. fairness, consideration for others. They will also emphasise what I previously termed 'basic rules' such as those to do with contracts and property which can be defended as necessary to the continuance of any tolerable form of social life. What else could they rationally contemplate doing? For they could not hold that there were strong grounds for insisting on at least this minimum content of rules, under any conditions of social life and, at the same time, decline to insist on such rules in their own home.

(c)   How To Teach Content?

The more interesting and controversial question is the third question relating to the manner rather than to the matter of early moral education. For how are they to emphasise these rudiments of morality? The obvious answer, it might be thought, is by any method which is meaningful to the child at the stage of development at which he is. In moral education, surely, as in any other form of education, parents and teachers should begin where children are. This is obvious enough; but what is implies for moral learning is not obvious without more detailed analysis of the situation.

First, there is learning and learning. A rule could just be learnt as a bit of verbalism without any real understanding of its application. But obviously, because the function of moral rules is to regulate people's behaviour rather than just to act as incantations, a child must learn them in the sense of being able to apply them to a variety of situations. This means that he must attend to the situations and to the similarities in them picked out by the rule. Now many things can be learnt just by watching others – for instance simple skills, and reactions to situations. But moral rules could not be learnt just by a mixture of trial and error and watching what others do. For a complicated network of concepts, which structure social life, have to be understood. A child could not learn what 'borrowing', as distinct from 'stealing', is without a considerable amount of instruction and explanation.

It is inconceivable, for this reason too, that a child could learn to behave morally purely by some process of conditioning in the strict sense. He could not learn not to steal simply by some process of positive reinforcement; for he has to develop the concepts necessary to grasping *what* behaviour is being reinforced. This requires instruction, explanation and other teaching methods by means of which *content* is marked out. Aids to learning, such as reinforcement, should not be confused with processes of learning.

Nevertheless, at the early stages of moral learning, aids to learning, which are developments of conditioning such as rewards and punishments, praise and blame, are extremely important. Indeed Piagetians claim, as has already been explained, that very small children can only see rules first of all as things to be done to avoid punishment or to obtain rewards, and then as forms of behaviour that are approved of or disapproved of by peers and authority figures. In the case of moral learning the importance of such extrinsic aids is not difficult to understand. For a child has not just got to learn how to apply concepts correctly; he has also to learn to behave consistently in the required way. Rules must regulate something and what they regulate are human inclinations. Children have, therefore, to start off their moral life with some kind of habit training. They may come to delight, at the second 'transcendental' stage of morality, in following rules; but often they do not do this because their counter-inclinations are strong. They want something now or they want something at other people's expense. Therefore insistence by parents or peer-groups on rules often has to be backed by extrinsic rewards and approval in order to provide positive incentives to out-weigh the pull of the child's inclinations. And so simple habits are built up, which constitute a basic 'bag of virtues'.

Parents, therefore, at these early stages have the option of supplementing example and instruction by the positive extrinsic aids of rewards or approval or by the negative ones of punishment and disapproval. There is strong evidence from psychological research which suggests that the positive aids are much more conducive to moral learning.[28] The reason for this can be related to the logic of the learning situation. If the child is going to learn, in the sense explained, he has to attend to the features of the situation, understand its point of similarity with other situations, and what his actions are likely to bring about. But, as is well known, attention is difficult to sustain under conditions of anxiety and stress or when someone is lacking confidence in his ability to understand. The hypothesis is that punitive and rejecting techniques militate against attention, and hence against learning, by producing anxiety, and undermine the child's confidence in himself. This explains, too, the lack of correlation between love-withdrawal and moral learning. For anxiety is produced by making the keeping of a mother's love contingent upon learning what 'being a good boy' consists in. Approval, on the other hand, together with parental warmth, which correlate well with moral learning, are thought to provide incentives for learning in a climate which is not fraught with anxiety.

5 TEACHING CONTENT IN RELATION TO THE DEVELOPMENT OF FORM

The use of such techniques has been considered so far on the assumption that what is being learnt is some content of morality. But an equally important way of looking at them is from the point of view of whether they aid or hinder the development of the rational form of morality. In this the validity of rules can be questioned and reasons for them discerned which fall under principles as distinct from their artificial associative connection with rewards and punishment, approval and disapproval. Obviously the use of induction is the most appropriate technique in so far as it involves, e.g. drawing attention to the consequences for others of a child's actions. But early on this type of technique makes little difference; for it is only when the child is capable of reversibility in thought and can look at actions from the point of view of others that this technique is effective. There are, understandably enough, no consistent findings relating to the effectiveness of induction in promoting moral development until after the pre-school years.[29] 'Induction', in the sense of teaching children rules, will obviously be effective. But in so far as it is concerned with trying to indicate to children the reasons for rules it will only be effective when they have reached the appropriate level of cognitive development.

These extrinsic aids to instruction and example, which have been discussed in the context of the learning of content, are also extremely relevant when the way the content is learnt is considered from the point of view of whether this learning situation is likely or not to promote a rational form of morality later on. It could well be, for instance, that many of the cases studied by psychologists of the Freudian school, of people who become fixated at an early stage of moral development with extreme irrational feelings of guilt and unworthiness about their conduct, are the victims of punitive and rejecting parental techniques. If children are to develop sensibly towards an autonomous form of morality they require a consistent pattern of rules in their early years, backed up by approval for learning. Interestingly enough, though, there is evidence to suggest that what Hoffman calls 'humanistic-flexible' individuals do emerge from homes in which parents, though relying on induction and approval, occasionally blow up and use power-assertive techniques.[30] This is quite different from the indiscriminate or systematic use of punishment. On occasions some assertion of power may be necessary for the voice of reason to be heard! Perhaps, too, there is some support for the wry advice that one should never strike a child save in anger!

Development is also likely to be stunted by complete permissiveness, whether this involves inconsistency in relation to what is expected or no determinate expectations; for the anxiety created by such inconsistency or anomie is not conducive to learning. Also under such conditions the child has little basis for predictability in his social environment which is necessary for anticipating consequences of actions. He gets little feed-back from his parents and interprets their 'liberal' policy as implying indifference to him. For children's conception of themselves, and their view of what it is possible for them to become, depends enormously on the messages about themselves that they read off from other people's expectations of them.

6   THE CHARGE OF INAUTHENTICITY

It might be objected that this willingness to use extrinsic aids such as rewards and approval is rather deplorable. It may not have disastrous consequences like the fierce use of punishment or disapproval. But will it not tend to ingrain in the individual a second-hand instrumental view of life? Will his moral life not be one of 'toil', lacking in authenticity? Would it not be better to rely on the more intrinsic motivations of delight in the mastery of rules and in the spontaneous co-operation exemplified by peer groups at play? Is not the content of morality more effectively picked up in these more spontaneous situations from older members of the peer group?

There is point in this criticism, but it represents altogether too idealistic a picture of what the situation actually is in peer-group co-operation. Certainly these intrinsic types of motivation exist, and are very important at the second stage of development. Certainly children learn much from others who are just a bit more advanced than they are – as the experiments of Turiel have shown.[31] But the pressure of social approval and disapproval is very strong in such situations. Indeed gang pressure on the individual can be much more oppressive than that of adults. Also disapproval for the unwilling or the incompetent is probably stronger than approval for the conformist. Furthermore, if an individual wishes to go his own way and to stand out against what is laid down by his peers, his situation is a parlous one unless there is some other source of approval, emanating from adults, which will support him in his strivings for independence.

The use of approval is surely on a par with the mechanisms of modelling and identification with adults which is equally important in transmitting moral content at this stage.[32] It depends on whether or not it is regarded as a transitional device. There is no evidence to suggest that these affectively charged links between the generations necessarily inhibit the development of autonomy. It depends entirely on how they are handled. The wise use of authority does not necessitate being authoritarian.

The question, too, has to be faced: what else is practicable? If children in their early years cannot acquire rules because they see the proper point of them and if, for the reasons explained, they have to start off with some 'bag of virtues', it is difficult to see what other alternatives are open. It should be stressed, however, that this early combination of 'induction' and positive 'reinforcement' does not constitute indoctrination; for 'indoctrination' picks out a special manner of instruction. It consists in getting children to accept a fixed body of rules by the use of techniques which incapacitate them from adopting a critical autonomous attitude towards them. Children are permanently fixated with a 'good boy' type of morality. They are perhaps led to associate obedience to such a fixed body of rules with loyalty to their group or to some authority figure whose disapproval they dare not incur. But not all instruction need employ such indoctrinatory techniques. Indeed it must not employ them if development towards a rational type of morality is to occur.

The crucial problem of methods in early moral education can, therefore, be stated in this way: given that it is thought desirable that children should develop an autonomous form of morality, and given that, if Piaget and Kohlberg are right, they cannot, in their early years, learn in a way that presupposes such an autonomous form, how can a basic content for morality be provided that gives them a firm basis for moral behaviour without impeding the development of a rational form of it? What non-rational methods of teaching aid, or at least do not impede, the development of rationality?

It is to this complex problem of instruction that sensitive parents and teachers should address themselves instead of withdrawing from the scene for fear of indoctrination. For by withdrawing and refusing to act as models and instructors they are equally in danger of impeding the development towards autonomy that they desire. It is indeed significant that Bronfenbrenner singles out the weakening of links between the generations, with the consequent lessening of opportunities for modelling and identification, as the main cause-factor in 'The Unmaking of the American Child'. 'Children', he says, 'used to be brought up by their parents'.[33]

REFERENCES

1. Much of the material of this paper is to be published elsewhere in books, especially in the author's Lindsay Memorial Lectures entitled *Reason and Compassion: Essays in Ethical Development* (London: Routledge & Kegan

Paul, 1973) and in a more popular paper entitled 'Form and Content in Moral Education' in the author's revised version of *Authority, Responsibility and Education* (London: Allen & Unwin, 1973).

2. See Peters, R. S., 'Freud's Theory of Moral Development in Relation to that of Piaget', *Brit. Journ. Ed. Psych.* Vol. XXX, Pt III (November 1960); and 'Moral Development: A Plea for Pluralism', in Mischel, T. (Ed.), *Cognitive Development and Epistemology* (New York: Academic Press, 1971).

3. See MacIntyre, A., *A Short History of Ethics* (London: Routledge & Kegan Paul, 1967).

4. See Peters, R. S., 'Reason and Passion', in Vesey, G. (Ed.), *The Proper Study*, Royal Institute of Philosophy Lectures, Vol. 4, 1969–70 (London: Macmillan, 1971).

5. See Hart, H. L. A., *The Concept of Law* (London: Oxford University Press, 1961), Ch. IX.

6. See Ginsberg, M., *Reason and Unreason in Society* (London: Longman, 1947), Ch. XVI; and *On the Diversity of Morals* (London: Heinemann, 1956), Ch. VII.

7. See Kohlberg, L., 'Stage and Sequence: the Cognitive–Developmental Approach to Socialisation', in Goslin, D., *Handbook of Socialisation Theory and Research* (Chicago: Rand McNally, 1969); and 'Education for Justice: A Modern Statement of the Platonic View', in Sizer, N. F. and Sizer, T. R. (Eds), *Moral Education* (Cambridge: Harvard University Press, 1970).

8. Piaget, J. *Six Psychological Studies* (London: University of London Press, 1968), pp. 8–17.

9. See Freud, S., *The Ego and the Id* (London: Hogarth Press, 1927).

10. See Greenfield, P. M. and Bruner, J. S., 'Culture and Cognitive Growth', in Goslin, D. (Ed.), *Handbook of Socialisation Theory and Research* (Chicago: Rand McNally, 1969).

11. See Peck, R. F. and Havighurst, R. J., *The Psychology of Character Development* (New York: John Wiley, 1970), pp. 109–11.

12. See Laing, R. D., *The Divided Self* (Harmondsworth: Penguin Books, 1965), p. 39.

13. For distinction see Peters, R. S. 'Reason and Passion' as in reference 4.

14. Klein, J. *Samples of Englich Culture* (London: Routledge & Kegan Paul, 1965), Vol. II.

15. Kohlberg divides this stage into two, avoidance of punishment preceding the seeking of rewards. Similarly the second stage of moral realism is subdivided into two – that of peer-group conformity and authority-based morality.

16. See Peters, R. S., 'Freud's Theory of Moral Development in Relation to that of Piaget', as in reference 2.

17. See Lilge, F., *Anton Semyonovitch Makarenko* (University of California Press, (1958), pp. 25–6).

18. Greenfield and Bruner, 'Culture and Cognitive Growth', as in reference 10.

19. Fromm, E., *The Fear of Freedom* (London: Routledge & Kegan Paul, 1942).

20. Hume D., *A Treatise of Human Nature*, Bk III, Pt II, Sec. I.

21. Money-Kyrle, R., *Psycho-analysis and Politics* (London: Duckworth, 1931).

22. See Hoffman, M. L., 'Moral Development', in Mussen, P. A., *Carmichael's Manuel of Child Psychology* (New York: Wiley, 1970), Vol. 2, pp. 329–30, 346.

23. Ibid., pp. 302–3, 325.

24. Ibid., p. 325.

25. See Bernstein, B. B., 'Social Class and Linguistic Development: a Theory of Social Learning', in Halsey, A. H., Floud, J. and Anderson, C. A., *Education, Economy and Society* (New York: Free Press, 1961).
26. See Bettelheim, B., 'Moral Education', in Sizer, N. F. and Sizer, T. R. (Eds), *Moral Education* (Cambridge: Harvard University Press, 1970), Ch. 7.
27. See Hirst, P. H. and Peters, R. S., *The Logic of Education* (London: Routledge & Kegan Paul, 1970), Ch. 7.
28. See Hoffman, op. cit., passim.
29. Ibid., p. 325.
30. Ibid., p. 340.
31. See Turiel, E. 'Developmental Processes in the Child's Moral Thinking' in Mussen, P. A., Langer, J. and Corington, M. (Eds) *Trends and Issues in Developmental Psychology* (New York: Holt, Rinehart, & Winston, 1969).
32. For summary of some of the evidence see Bronfenbrenner, U., *Two Worlds of Childhood* (London: Allen & Unwin, 1971), pp. 124–43.
33. Bronfenbrenner, op. cit., p. 95.

Part Three

EDUCATION AND HUMAN UNDERSTANDING

18

PERSONAL UNDERSTANDING AND PERSONAL RELATIONSHIPS

INTRODUCTION

It is a commonplace in the literature about understanding other people that there is a radical difference between this sort of understanding and the understanding which we have of the behaviour of things, which is connected in some way with entering into personal relationships with them of the sort that we do not and cannot enter into with things. We can, of course, know about people in the way in which we can know about things. We can know that man is six feet tall and that he will fall rapidly to the ground if pushed from the top of a cliff, just as we can know that a piece of wood is of the same height and will behave in the same way if dropped. But we also know and understand people in ways in which we do not know and understand pieces of wood. This form of knowledge is often connected with the peculiar vantage point that we occupy in relation to other people; for we ourselves are people and enter into special sorts of relationships, namely personal relationships, with the objects known. This special kind of relationship, making possible a special kind of vantage point, is the basis of the special kind of knowledge or understanding which we enjoy.

David Hamlyn's paper deals with this general type of claim and attempts to specify more precisely the ways in which personal relationships provide conditions for knowledge of other people. I do not disagree with his general thesis. Indeed I wish to take over more or less at the point at which he leaves off. I think that, in a way, his thesis is not radical enough; for he does not examine the extent to which entering into personal relationships with others is constitutive of rather than just providing conditions for knowing and understanding them. So this will be the first thought that I wish to explore in my paper. This will lead me, secondly, to try to get a bit clearer about what is meant by 'personal relationships' in this and other contexts. In my view there are distinctions here which need to be made which throw light on the understanding of ourselves and others. Thirdly, I shall advance the suggestion that there are levels of personal relationships which are connected with levels of personal understanding and personal attraction.

1   EXPLANATION AND INITIATION

The usual way for a philosopher to approach problems of personal knowledge is to set out possible conditions of 'knowledge' and to see whether knowing people can be fitted into some pattern of 'knowing how', 'knowing that', 'knowing how to', and so on. I do not propose to follow this track, partly because it has been traversed by David Hamlyn, partly because I am more interested in 'understanding' than in 'knowledge' and partly because there is another approach which is likely to be of particular pertinence in a conference between psychologists and philosophers. I refer to the sort of approach pioneered by William Dilthey who was impressed by the methodological differences between the natural sciences and human studies. He thought that the sciences of man would get nowhere if the methodological paradigm of the natural sciences was copied. His objections to the natural science approach need not detain us.[1] Indeed many of them are based on some of the misconceptions of the natural sciences which Popper tried to make explicit in *The Poverty of Historicism*. His positive conception of the epistemological basis of human studies is more important and interesting.

(a)   *The Psychology of Verstehen*
Dilthey claimed, first of all, that psychology is a descriptive science whose principles can be extracted from what is given to the individual in his inner perception. Secondly, he claimed that inner perception reveals not isolated units of mental life such as sensations, feelings or intentions but a unity of cognition, affect and conation in 'a total reaction of the whole self to a situation confronting it'.[2] This unitary reaction constitutes the ground-rhythm of mental life, and is called the 'structural system'. Psychology is an elaboration of this system which is given to us in 'lived experience'. Thirdly, our understanding of others is not, in essence, an inferential process. We are able to understand the expressions of the mental states of others because of

the psychological law that expressions have the power, under normal conditions, to evoke corresponding experiences in the minds of observers. We feel in ourselves reverberations of grief, for instance, when we see another human being in a downcast attitude, with his face marked by tears.[3]

Some of these assumptions about understanding others are shared by Michael Scriven who regards the claims of the Verstehen psychology as one example of a general type of explanation.[4] He distinguishes between two types of understanding. On the one hand there is the usual type employed by the natural sciences in which descriptions of particular events are subsumed under general laws. Secondly, there is the analysis of a structure into its components, to see how these components are related to each other as parts of a system. When, for instance, we understand how a clock works there is very little in the way of subsumption under general laws which does much explanatory work and so aids out understanding. The weight is carried by tracing the relationships between the particular springs and levers. Simple mechanics can understand how such systems work without any knowledge of the underlying physical laws. Understanding others is a particular case of this latter sort of understanding; for we extend to others the understanding which we have from our own case of the system which is our own personality. 'Now when we understand a person's behaviour in terms of his attitudes, goals, perceptions of the situation in which he finds himself, etc., in short in terms of the phenomenology of the situation – what we are doing is, so to speak, attaching the facts of the particular case to the terminals of our own response system, i.e. our own personality.'[5] We attempt to do this without crediting him with any of our own idiosyncrasies. In brief it is our own knowledge of the system constituted by our own general human characteristics that enables us to understand the behaviour of others. This is similar to the way in which we understand how other machines work if we are familiar with a machine which is like them. And general laws are not necessary for understanding in either case. The special feature of explanation in human studies is that we rely on the human model with which we are familiar through our own possession of general human characteristics.

There is much to be learned from these two versions of the psychology of Verstehen. Certainly in understanding other people we make use of concepts in which cognitive, affective and conative components have a certain structure. Certainly the notion of fitting particular forms of behaviour into a system is helpful, though it is questionable whether this means abandoning general assumptions. And certainly in relation to understanding human beings we occupy a special vantage point which we lack in our understanding of the natural world. But, in my view, neither Dilthey nor Scriven make this point in a radical enough way. Indeed the way in which they do make it results in their position being vulnerable to attacks of the sort which have been launched against views of understanding other people which gives some sort of priority to knowledge of our own case.[6] Knowledge of others is made either a matter of inference based on analogy, which is Scriven's position, or of non-inferential empathy, as in Dilthey's thesis, which can only be defended, surely, as a way of knowing a limited number of things about other people, e.g. that they are angry, afraid, or in pain.

(b)   *Understanding and Initiation*

The more radical thesis which I wish to propose is that we are indeed at a special vantage point in understanding others (or at least some others) which we do not enjoy in our understanding of the natural world. This comes about because in learning to *behave* as human beings we are, *ipso facto*, being initiated into the concepts, rules and assumptions without which we could make no sense of the life of others. Our minds, in other words, are mainly social products. In making sense, therefore, of the behaviour of others we rely on concepts, rules and assumptions which both they and we have internalized in the early years of our initiation into human life; these structure our own *behaviour* as well as our *understanding* of the behaviour of others. The level of understanding of which we are capable is largely a function of the type of social life which we have enjoyed. There is no mystery about our understanding or failure to understand others. For it depends largely on the extent to which we have been, to put the matter crudely, programmed in the same sort of way by our early social experiences. We understand people well with whom we have been in close contact from early childhood not just because we are familiar with all the particular circumstances and life history of individuals which play such an important part in understanding people as distinct from the behaviour of things, but also because we, like they, have been initiated into the same rules, concepts, and assumptions which give structure and coherence to the thought and behaviour of both of us.

This may sound rather like a crude version of Marx's aphorism that: 'It is not the consciousness of man that determines his existence – rather it is his social existence that determines his consciousness.'

Some qualification must be briefly sketched to make the thesis sound more civilised. The first type of crudity is conveyed by the image of programming. Man's consciousness cannot be solely dependent on his social existence because he differs from a machine in his capacity to understand and make something of the purposes, rules and concepts which he internalises. There are many things that can be meant by 'following a rule' which can almost be arranged in a continuum as Max Black has indicated.[7] But most of them presuppose consciousness. The Marxist thesis can be taken as a dramatic way of making the point that man's 'social existence' is constituted by various forms of learned behaviour. But most forms of learning at the human level presuppose consciousness.[8] The same sort of point can be made about language, which is the medium through which a great deal of socialisation takes place; for there is the prior problem of how the child comes to take noises as symbols. The development of thought cannot be accounted for entirely in terms of the development of language; for language has to be understood *as* language in some embryonic way from the start.

A connected difficulty for the Marxist type of thesis is that presented by the evidence relating to the development of categoreal concepts such as causality, thinghood, means-to-an-end and so on. These are the most fundamental categories of the understanding; yet, it is claimed by followers of Piaget[9] that they cannot be taught. They develop in the process of the individual's interaction with his environment. Piagetians, however, admit that development can be accelerated by what they call 'cognitive stimulation' which includes social transactions such as asking children leading questions, getting them to engage in games with other children and so on. There is evidence, too, that these concepts develop very slowly in cultures in which children are socially discouraged from manipulating the environment and finding out things for themselves.[10] A similar point could be made about the development of reasoning by means of which the range of the understanding is extended. It would, I think, be fanciful to suggest that principles like that of non-contradiction are just social products. But there is evidence to suggest that the tendency to rely on generalisations, the imagining of consequences in the distant future, and the general tendency to transcend a sense-bound, concrete, myopic sort of existence depends to a large extent on the type of language available in the home and on predictability in child-rearing practices.[11] Obviously, too, the tendency to be critical, to develop an individual viewpoint, depends enormously on the prevalence in society of a critical tradition.[12]

It would be rash, therefore, to suggest that the *form* of understanding which we employ in making sense of the behaviour of others is entirely a social product. Much more work would have to be done in answering Chomsky-like questions about the genesis of concepts such as 'purpose', and 'taking means to ends', which are the relevant categoreal concepts in this sphere. But from the point of view of my general thesis these speculations would not much matter provided they were developed to account for the fact that the categories for structuring our own behaviour and for making sense of that of others are universal, though people reach different points in culturally invariant stages of developing them. For, whatever the explanation, both our behaviour and our understanding would be programmed in terms of these universal categories. Such a cautious thesis about the *form* of our understanding would be quite consistent with a much more thorough-going thesis about social determination of its *content*. For the particular purposes and rules in terms of which we make sense of the behaviour of others are basically those into which we have been initiated and which are, therefore, constitutive of our own purposive, rule-following behaviour. We know why people arriving at a strange golf club are looking for the secretary or the steward because we too have been in the situation of looking for the recipient of a green-fee as a preliminary to playing. Reference to rules about punctuality or to motives such as ambition are obvious enough to us as explanations of behaviour because we have been initiated into a society in which time and individual self-assertion are taken for granted. But they would not be obvious explanations to members of a society which placed no value on them. The content of our understanding is certainly a social product whatever the status of its form.

Not all behaviour, however, is of this highly socialised form, and thus initiation cannot be the source of all our understanding of it. There are some emotions, for instance, such as fear and anger which have natural expressions, of which Darwin gave a biological type of explanation. There is evidence, too, that, at least amongst the higher primates, they are contagious. A snarling ape sets other apes snarling by some kind of associative mechanism. There must be some kind of mechanism, more primitive than imitation, by means of which the mother's smile activates similar expressions in the baby, together with the inner states that accompany such expression. So, at a certain level of reaction, there is probably much truth in Dilthey's contention that the expressions of the mental states of others tend to evoke corresponding experiences in the minds of observers which form the basis of empathetic understanding. We have all felt, surely, the contagion of aggression. Even the stomach responds in a queer sort of way. And does not a sudden intake of breath, quickened breathing, wide opening of the eyes, or the slight slobbering of the greedy person contemplating food convey itself insensibly to the observer and stir up a similar sort of state in him? I am not arguing, of course, that there is anything infallible in this form of understanding. Like anything of an intuitive sort it may be mistaken. I am only making the point that, at a basic, scarcely socialised level of reaction, a mechanism which is more primitive than imitation plays a crucial role. At this level, to revert to my previous crude analogy, we are not programmed with a common system of rules; we are rather wired up in a similar way.

There is, finally, another crude kind of explanation of why people, who have shared a common life together over a long period, understand each other so well that they often know just what the other is thinking even though no overt sign is given. For not only will familiarity with a person provide the common life which is constituted by the rules and purposes which render his behaviour intelligible; it will also provide a rich source of associative cues which will lead another to be right about what he is thinking or feeling without any proper basis for inference. People who have been very close to each other over a long period, and who have a fund of shared experiences, develop all sorts of common associations. X knows what Y is thinking or going to say, not because he has evidence on the basis of which he can infer it, but because similar associative tracks are activated in the two people concerned. Cues rather than clues provide the basis of understanding. X knows what Y is thinking in the sense that he is right about this and in that this is no accident.[13] But he has not really any proper grounds for his conviction. It is not like the cases when he knows, on the basis of inductive clues, that a look on the other's face will lead to a certain type of remark or behaviour. Rather exposure to similar experiences has established similar associative tracks. A particular cue activates both of them in a similar way and, because of associative tracks, they both find themselves thinking about the same thing even after quite a lapse of time, during which their thoughts have proceeded along similar lines.

My basic assumptions about understanding others can therefore be summarised as follows; I assume that, with the development of the sort of conceptual apparatus which was mapped by Piaget, children gradually come to make sense of the behaviour of others in terms of categoreal concepts such as 'purpose', 'means-to-an-end' and in terms of rule-following. Their understanding of others proceeds *pari passu* with their ability to structure their own behaviour by means of this type of conceptual apparatus. There are difficult problems about how this form of understanding is acquired, but its content, the particular rules and purpose which they attribute to others and which they exhibit in their own behaviour, is largely dependent upon the particular society in which they grow up. This way of understanding others is, however, not the only way. More primitive empathetic and associative mechanisms are also operative.

These crude epistemological assumptions give rise, of course, to a number of problems about the meaning of 'internalisation', about empathy and inference, and about the relationships between association and inference, which it is not my business to pursue in this paper. But obviously the operation of all these types of understanding is dependent upon having 'personal relationships' with people. This notion is a very cloudy one which shrouds many important distinctions embedded in the different levels at which it is possible to understand or to misunderstand others. The rest of my paper, therefore, will be concerned with trying to pin-point some of these important distinctions.

2 TYPES OF RELATIONSHIPS

The thesis that the mind of the individual mirrors the society of which he is a member is, of course, as old as Plato. Plato, however, was interested in this parallelism because of his interest in social change and social policy. He did not link it with any theory about understanding people. The distinctions which he made were therefore closely related to problems of social control and individual regulation of conduct. Not that these preoccupations are irrelevant to the understanding of people; for one of the key concepts in understanding people is that of 'motive'. And most of the motives which we ascribe to people such as envy, ambition, greed, benevolence and the like are also regarded as virtues and vices. But, in spite of Ryle's tendency to regard almost any explanatory term for human behaviour as a case of 'motive',[14] there does seem to be a radical difference between explaining what a person is doing in terms of his conscientiousness, his ambition, his interest in symbolic logic and his aims as a university teacher. How do these types of explanation differ from each other? How are they connected with social life? In what ways are personal relationships with others necessary to or constitutive of these types of explanation?

Let us begin with a very general point about the notion of having personal relationships with people. There is a sense of 'personal relationships' in which almost all explanations of human behaviour presuppose them; for most of the concepts which we use pick out various ways in which we can be related to people as distinct from to rivers, boulders, or trees. So, in this general sense, the appeal to a person's aims as a university teacher will involve reference to personal relationships just as much as speculations about his motives of benevolence or ambition. The concept can be used in this very general way, but, of course, at the expense of its doing any work; for some account must be given of the fact that we often say that a role relationship, such as that of being a teacher, is essentially an impersonal one. There is also the point that it is quite intelligible for a teacher to say that he fulfills his role as a teacher and, in addition, he shows benevolence and respect towards his pupils but has neither the time nor the inclination nor the energy to enter into personal relationships with them. Obviously some important distinctions are being made here which are connected with a more specific concept of 'personal relationships'. So I propose to try to elucidate what might lie behind this more specific concept rather than use it in a very general sort of way.

In attempting to get clearer about these types of distinctions I will concentrate on the case of a university teacher trying to make sense of the behaviour of one of his colleagues; for this is an example with which we are all familiar and which should reveal most of the basic distinctions which we need. It is, of course, possible that concentration on one type of example may bias the analysis in some respects. It may lead us to ignore distinctions which might be important if a wider range of examples was taken. And certainly, if my basic thesis is correct, distinctions will emerge that probably have no application if I were to concentrate on a simple tribe whose social structure and consciousness is far less differentiated than ours. But a start must be made somewhere and my brief is not to write a complete prolegomenon to the social sciences.

(a) *Roles and Shared Activities*
We, like policemen, may have had all sorts of idiosyncratic motives for joining our profession, and these may influence the way in which we discharge the various duties which are incumbent on us. But there are presumably some unitary aims which give coherence to our insti-

tutional lives in the same sort of way as a concern for preserving law and order gives some kind of unity to the lives of policemen. Many, like Popper, have argued that it is vain to search for essences. That may be so if we are thinking about the natural world. But in considering the social world the enterprise might not be so vain. For human institutions are constituted largely by the conceptions of men and it is possible that men might band together with some single, unambiguous aim in view, such as the preservation of the blue whale, and their institutional duties might be all clearly related to the pursuit of this aim, which would express the essence of the institution. Most institutions, however, do not present such a rational ideal. There is usually more than one aim which most members conceive themselves as forwarding, and these aims often pull them in different directions. The duties, too, which define their roles, are not always so rationally related to the aims of the institution. May be they are precipitates left by the past. May be the roles have developed a life of their own which has made them non-functional in relation to the dominant aim. And may be as most institutions have not been determinately instituted, the demand to get clear about the essence of an institution is a way of trying to rationalise an institution that has accumulated all sorts of odd traditions and practices in a period of unplanned historic growth. All sorts of qualifications of this sort have to be made if we are to talk realistically about institutions. But, nevertheless, there is something that fits the appearances in this type of analysis of institutions. As university teachers we do conceive of ourselves as concerned with the advancement of understanding and with the initiation of others into this activity. Whether we also conceive of ourselves as concerned with the more general education of students or with pressing problems of the society in which we live is much more a matter for debate. But at the moment, at any rate in Great Britain, whatever university teachers think about educating students and about 'relevance', they would at least subscribe to the first type of aim and would think that any concern for education and for 'relevance' must be understood in the context of an institution which is essentially concerned with the advancement of understanding. If this ceased to be the case, if the dominant aim became the provision of occasions for discussing what students found to be 'relevant' issues in their lives, then universities would become very different types of institutions. This type of change would affect our lives very much but would not affect the conceptual point which I am making; for the new race of university teachers would then have a whole range of their activities structured by a different type of aim.

Given, then, this dominant aim which is more or less definitive of a university as an institution, we are able to explain much of the individual's dealings with others in the light of it. In particular his dealings with his pupils will be structured in the light of his view of them as learners. This view of them provides a rationale for rights and duties which are constitutive of the teacher's role.[15] He has, for instance, the right to criticise his students' thoughts and writings, which might be resented outside a role relationship. He has, also, the duty of taking trouble over the work of students whom he does not particularly like, of meeting students whose company he would avoid if free play were given to his inclinations. Much of a university teacher's behaviour could be made sense of in terms of this over-all aim and the rights and duties that are connected with its implication. But it could only be made sense of by those who understand from the inside what 'teaching' is and who have been initiated into the concepts and rules which are constitutive of the appropriate rights and duties. Peter Winch has developed this sort of point in so much detail that it would be otiose for me to labour it any further.[16] But, to revert to my search for 'personal relationships', the point about the relationships in terms of which we give explanations at this level is that, though they hold between persons, there is an important sense in which they are impersonal. Let us call them interpersonal relationships.

'Impersonal', too, might be applied to other interpersonal relations in shared activities which have aims but not of sufficient generality to co-ordinate wide areas of life or to generate elaborate systems of duties. Examples would be activities such as gardening, singing in a choir, or playing golf. We might have a feeling of fraternity towards others who shared these activities with us of the sort that Marx hoped that the workers of the world would have for other workers; but this would be consistent with saying that the interpersonal relationship between the people concerned was rather an impersonal one.

A much stronger sense of 'impersonal' is when someone is treated, whether within or outside of an institutional context, as an object rather than as an individual who is a person in his own right, who has purposes, aspirations and a point of view of his own. He might be regarded just as somebody who could be simply used by another for his own purposes, or manipulated for the sake of forwarding some social ideal. Or he might be considered purely as an occupant of a role without any consideration for his point of view as a human being. In such situations lack of respect for persons would be shown and 'impersonal' would almost be too weak a word to do justice to the depersonalisation involved.

(b) *Interpersonal Relations and Personality*

Respect for persons introduces a whole range of interpersonal relationships which are not role relationships, but which still might not be called personal relationships in a full sense. Suppose, for instance, that a student fell down and broke his arm. It is possible that a teacher might go to his aid because he viewed this injury as likely to be detrimental to his potentiality as an essay-writer. But, more probably, he would act towards him in a way in which he would act towards any other human being, irrespective of his special role relationship. He would act out of benevolence or sympathy. And a great deal of his behaviour both towards his pupils and towards others, with whom he was not in some sort of role relationship, could be explained in terms of rules and purposes which are constitutive of relationships with people but not within the confines of any particular role or structured type of activity.

There would be, first of all, that body of internalised rules which we call 'character-traits'. Examples would be honesty, punctuality, tidiness, thrift, selfishness and so on. Such terms, like all trait terms, are primarily adverbial in significance.[17] They do not, like terms for motives such as benevolence, ambition, greed and the like, indicate the sorts of goals that give unity to a person's behaviour. Rather they draw attention to the rules which he follows, or the manner in which he pursues his goals. The connection with regulation is fundamental for distinguishing character-traits from other sorts of traits – for instance those which we connect with a person's temperament. Character-traits are regarded as virtues or as vices. There would be no point in marking them out in this way if there did not exist, in general, inclinations which they regulate or canalise. And there are some character-traits which are connected with the will, or with what we call 'having character', which *have* to be exercised in the face of counter-inclinations. Examples are courage, integrity and determination. By that I mean that virtues such as honesty and punctuality, which represent internalised social rules, would be pointless if there did not exist, in general, inclinations to say what is false or to take no account of time. To explain a person's behaviour by reference to such traits does not necessitate the existence of such inclinations in the person when he acts. But with courage or integrity the case is different. For these higher-order types of traits can only be ascribed to a person if it is thought that he is sticking to some course of action in the face of fear, temptation and the like. Most character-traits of the first sort are constituted by interpersonal rules that are internalised. This is not the case, however, with the character-traits that are connected with the will; for though very often temptations take the form of bribes or approval from others and though fear can be of social ostracism or disapproval, counter-inclinations need not be social in character. They can come from consciousness of heights or from the stomach.

There are other traits which people exhibit, which are closely connected with their interpersonal relations, which seem more indicative of their personality than of their character. (I am using 'personality' here in the way in which it seems to be used in ordinary speech, not in the omnibus way in which it is used in psychological text-books.) Examples are friendliness, cheerfulness, shyness, awkwardness, alertness and so on. We would think of such traits as developing or flowering rather than as being built up by decisions or by the internalisation of rules. They are connected much more with our perception of others and of ourselves than with codes of conduct. They are very closely connected with ways in which we impinge on others in our dealings with them. Hence their connection with our personality. For, whereas our character bears witness to the choices which we have made and suggests some sort of personal effort to make something of ourselves, our personality is very much the mask or appearance which we present to others. A man with a strong character is a man who has made efforts with himself and who exhibits virtues such as courage and integrity that are connected with the will. But we do not naturally speak of a man having a strong personality. Rather we speak of personality as being forceful, dynamic and hypnotic. These terms draw attention to his influence on others.

Underlying these character and personality traits are the wants, inclinations, motives and emotions which are constitutive of our natures. Some of these, such as hunger and thirst, which derive from deficit states, have little to do with interpersonal relations. But most motives and emotions are very closely connected with a form of social life into which we have been initiated in which we view ourselves and others in a certain light. It is only possible, for instance, to feel jealous and to recognise it in others if we are able to see another as possessing or making advances towards something or someone to which or whom we think that we have some sort of special claim. This presupposes the understanding of social concepts such as 'rights', 'claims', 'possession' and the like.[18] Some attitudes, like respect, for instance, mean different things according to the difference in the social context. Respect can be felt for someone who is superior in a social hierarchy; it can be felt for someone who is good at something, as when we speak of having a healthy respect for an opponent in debate or in a boxing ring. Respect, too, can be used in a generalised sense when we talk of respect for persons and are only viewing another as a centre of choice and of evaluation. Other emotions, such as pride, ambition, guilt and remorse imply a certain view of ourselves. They are probably not felt in cultures in which little importance is attached to individual effort and responsibility.

Fundamental to the analysis of motives and emotions are the general dimensions of liking–disliking, love–hate, pleased–displeased. Some, like Hobbes, have tried to bring this out by postulating a general tendency in human beings to move towards or away from objects. Others have tried to construct a kind of chemistry, rather than a dynamics, of the emotions in which complex emotions are represented as compounds of simple ones such as fear, anger and love. It is not my intention to discuss, or to attempt to improve on such accounts of this dimension; for this would involve a lengthy examination of the relationship between the concepts built into the cognitive components of the various emotions. My concern with it in this paper is only in the context of its relevance to questions about personal relations. And it does seem relevant in this context. For if questions were asked about a teacher's personal relations with his pupils answers would be given which revolve round this axis of his personality. By that I mean that we would not think about whether he was honest or fair in his dealings with them, or whether he was punctual, conscientious, or even unselfish, though these terms in fact pick out ways in which he deals with them as persons. We would be interested in facets of his personality rather than of his character in so far as it impinged on them. Of relevance would be whether his manner was friendly, or defensive, relaxed or stiff. Of relevance, too, would be whether he aroused feelings of insecurity or confidence in his students, whether they liked or disliked him, were afraid of him or sorry for him. We would not take account of whether they admired him for his competence as a teacher, felt respect for him as a man or even had a feeling of fraternity for him as a fellow learner. In brief the question would draw attention not to what he was like as a teacher, or as a moral agent, but to how his personality came through to them and how they reacted to it.

(c)   *Personal Relationships Proper*

Ordinary language is not very determinate in the area which is being investigated. Nevertheless it sounds perfectly meaningful to say that a teacher's personal relations with his students are very good but he does not believe in having personal relationships with them. What would he be avoiding? Immediately what comes to mind are situations in which some kind of reciprocal knowledge of private matters is built up as distinct from matters connected with the public institutionalised context in which they encounter each other. By this is meant some knowledge of the details of the private lives of the people concerned as well of their motives, attitudes and aspirations. This is surely an obvious feature of a developed personal relationship, but is it a distinguishing feature? Surely not; for examples can be produced in which we would say that a personal relationship existed without this exchange of confidences. Examples can also be produced in which a great deal of personal knowledge is exchanged but we would be disinclined to say that there was a personal relationship.

Let us consider both types of counter-example in the hope that something more fundamental will emerge. Suppose that, in the middle of a seminar, a student starts thumbing through a *Good Food Guide* during a rather boring exchange between two other members of the group. He looks up guiltily and is aware of a knowing look from the tutor who passes him a note with the name of a restaurant written on it. The student acknowledges the note with a grateful nod. Surely we would say that this exemplifies a personal relationship, though a minimal one, even though nothing further develops in the way of private disclosures. Conversely suppose that, in the course of a literature class, those participating in the discussion of a novel contribute much of their private experience to a common pool in order to arrive at a better understanding of the novel. Suppose that the tutor also reminisces about his own private life in order to illustrate a point, just as lecturers in psychology often regale their students with stories about their own children. This would not be described as entering into a personal relationship. What is present in the first example and absent in the second is a certain aspect under which the other is viewed. In the second example private matters are revealed to others but under the aspect of their role as learners. In the first example only a minimum of information is disclosed of a not very private sort, but it is not disclosed to another as a learner or in any type of role capacity.

What seems to emerge from these counter-examples is that a personal relationship involves some reciprocal response of individual to individual, which often does but need not take the form of the disclosure of private matters, but which involves a view of the other under some aspect other than that of his occupancy of a role. What is this aspect? Respect does not seem to be right; for it can be argued that one can have a personal relationship with someone whom one despises. Respect, also, can signify a rather negative attitude – just a refusal to treat another as a means to one's own ends. It need not issue in any positive sort of outgoingness which seems characteristic of entering into a personal relationship. It is too moralised, too much connected with a view of another as a subject of rights, as a chooser. Does liking, then, provide the required aspect? Surely not. Women often meet and, within minutes, are swapping notes about their confinements and maladies with great animation. They may, when they meet again, begin where they left off and build up quite a relationship. But they may not particularly like each other and yet, surely, they are not just passing the time of day. Liking is, of course, a frequent condition for people developing a personal relationship. But it is not necessary to it. Many personal relationships develop through force of circumstances. One of my previous colleagues, for instance, maintained that his personal relationships with fellow philosophers were occasioned, at one time, through meeting them so often outside rooms where committees were interviewing people for jobs. He was just left alone with people in situations which made them prone to some kind of mutual openness or outgoingness. Sympathy is suggested by this last example as the appropriate aspect. It fits also the case of the student with the *Good Food Guide*. It signifies an outgoingness issuing in responses below the level of morality, custom and institutionalised roles. It does not necessarily imply liking, either. It suggests only receptivity and outgoingness towards another at an affective level, as someone, like ourselves, who has wishes, wants and emotions, who is sensitive to pain and other such passive states. Sympathy, however, is not quite the right word; for it is usually associated with seeing another only as a sufferer. If it could be extended to cover also a responsiveness to the joys and pleasures of another, it would be the right word. This is a case, I think, where we have the concept but not just one word to make explicit what we mean. The point is that the response must be to another *simply* as an individual human being who is subject to plea-sure and pain and the usual gamut of emotions and desires. The other person must not be viewed in the context of any extraneous purpose, whether individual or shared. He must not be thought of as a means to one's ends or just as a co-operator or competitor in a common pur-

suit. Moralisation is not necessarily involved as in benevolence when
there is thought about his interests, or in respect when he is regarded
as a subject of rights. There is simply a receptiveness to him and outgoingness towards him as an individual human being. This can take
place in institutionalised situations, such as the seminar case, when
an individual steps out of his role and responds to another just as a
human being. Or it can happen in an unstructured type of situation
as when two people meet in a park.

Usually, of course, when we talk of personal relationships we
mean a development of the minimal type of relationship that I have
sketched. Receptiveness and outgoingness towards another usually
takes the form of receiving another's confidences and self-disclosures.
In this way a common world is built up which the individuals share.
This is constituted not simply by their shared experiences but by the
common stock of knowledge which has developed as a result of being
kept informed about a whole variety of private matters. When they
meet they keep each other up to date, as it were, about the details of
the private worlds that intersect on such occasions. Friendship is an
extension of such a relationship. For it requires extra conditions.[19]
First, there is the condition that the individuals concerned should
share some pattern of activities, e.g. reciprocal services, leisure-
time pursuits. Secondly, friendship requires that the individuals concerned should like each other and desire each other's company.
Thirdly, there is the requirement that this special sort of relationship
should be acknowledged. There is some sort of reciprocal commitment.

3   LEVELS OF RELATIONSHIP AND LEVELS OF UNDERSTANDING

So far I have sketchily distinguished the sorts of relationships which
people can enjoy with other people in order to get clearer about what
is distinctive of personal relationships. This analysis was necessary
because of my original suggestion of the close connection between
having personal relationships with people and understanding them.
Even at this juncture it would be possible to say a few things about
this connection which are developments of what has already been
said.

(a) *The Vantage Point of Personal Relationships*
It could be said, first, that explanations in terms of roles and general
social rules and purposes presuppose initiation into a common form

of life. So for these types of explanation the content of our understanding presupposes, in general, having entered into these sorts of
relationships with others. This applies to our explanations of our
colleagues' behaviour in terms of their conception of themselves as
university teachers, of character-traits such as punctuality and selfishness and countless other socialised purposes which structure smaller
segments of their lives. In other words, what I have called interpersonal relationships would be constitutive of the content of our
understanding. But personal relationships, in the specific sense,
would not be necessary even as an epistemological condition for
understanding particular people. For little face-to-face contact with
the particular individuals concerned would be necessary to give
explanations of this type though, of course, we might be wrong in
particular cases because of the impersonality of these explanations in
terms of generalised content. A similar point, secondly, could be
made about low-level types of explanation, grounded in expressions
of someone's personality, which give rise to judgements about his
personal relations. We can like or dislike people because they are
friendly, shy, dynamic, domineering, etc. We have to share a common
life in order to learn how to apply these descriptions; but we do not
have to enter into personal relationships with the people concerned
in order to make such judgements. We can say that we loathe a
politician because of his obsequiousness, aggressiveness, charm, or
stiffness. We can also note simple generalisations about him. But we
can do this on the basis of seeing him answer questions on television.

In both such spheres, however, it might be said that our judgements
are too quick or superficial because we do not really know enough
about him. And, indeed, we can work with a colleague for years and
make sense of countless things that he does or says in the above terms,
and yet we can say that we feel that we really do not know him. We do
not really understand what makes him tick. What is lacking is a
glimpse of the store he sets by his various roles, his underlying motives
and aspirations. Shrewd observers of people can often glean these
from observing others in their public lives. Messages can be picked
up from their frowns and hesitations, from noting the general drift
of their conduct over a period and from confrontations with them in
public situations. But personal relationships proper provide more
reliable clues. This is for three obvious reasons. First, personal relationships proper usually involve close personal contact with others,
though such contact is possible in role relationships as well. This
contact provides a context in which people reveal themselves most;
for they respond to the constant pressure on their privacy exerted by

others. Indeed many responses indicative of people's motives, aspirations, etc., are only possible if another person supplies the appropriate stimulus in such an interactive situation. As observers of other individuals we find out a great deal about them by eliciting responses from them in this way. This cannot be done with a person on a television screen if we are sitting at home. This type of interaction is likely to reveal more if the people concerned are emotionally involved with each other in ways which are characteristic of personal relationships rather than purely role relationships – in those coloured by hate as well as by love. For in role relationships there may be contiguity but each individual may, figuratively speaking, be wearing the appropriate mask. But, as was argued before, personal relationships proper, even at a minimal level, involve some outgoingness and spontaneity of response. This unguardedness suggests authenticity and an absence of role-playing in the pejorative sense, and hence indications of a person's nature.

Secondly, developed personal relationships and friendship are characterised by mutual disclosures of private matters and by the laying bare of motives, hopes, fears and aspirations. These are fundamental for discerning the main threads which determine the pattern of a man's life. Thirdly, a great deal of detailed information is necessary to understand how another person sees the world. It is necessary to know how much he knows, what he takes for granted when he faces any situation, as well as some details about his past history which predisposes him to respond in certain ways. This kind of information can only be gleaned by being with a person over a long period and in the different areas of his life – at home, at work, in his leisure-time pursuits. This sort of information is far more important for understanding another person than any generalisations about human nature suggested by psychologists. In cases of married couples, friends, etc., it often leads to the rich source of associative cues, already referred to at the end of section 1(b), which lead people to be right about what others are thinking or feeling without any proper basis for inference.

(b) *Personal Relationships as Constitutive of Understanding Others*
So far having personal relationships, in a specific sense, has only been considered as providing epistemological conditions in the sense of a favourable vantage point for understanding particular individuals. There is a question, however, about the extent to which this individualised type of understanding is itself constituted by the capacity to enter into personal relationships of the specific sort. It is interesting

to speculate about the extent to which this individualised kind of understanding of people proceeds *pari passu* with the degree of individualisation of behaviour encouraged in society.

When I spent some time in America many years ago I was puzzled by the way in which I was treated by some Americans. They behaved to me in public in a way which made me speculate about what their private thoughts and motives were behind this public display. It was pointed out to me, however, that there did not exist much differentiation between the public and the private realm. Friends could be changed as rapidly as jobs and dwelling places, and one behaved to someone in a public role almost in the same way as one behaved to him privately. Could it then be that there was actually very little extra going on behind those smiling faces? Is Behaviourism more or less an appropriate philosophy of mind in this type of culture? The Americans in question, needless to say, were not academics! But the speculation which they occasioned in me suggests one of the main sources of the superficiality of my treatment to date of the connection between personal understanding and personal relationships. I have not explored the possibility that there are levels of personal understanding which are closely tied to levels of personal relationships.

I have only space to make some speculative suggestions here which are really extrapolations of the Piaget–Kohlberg type approach to moral development. I wish to suggest that there are levels of personal relationship which correspond with levels of understanding of people and levels of affective response to them. Since my account of personal relationships has been given in terms of the aspect under which the other is viewed this should not prove surprising. I shall, therefore, be concerned not with how relationships with others are constitutive of the *content* of our understanding of people but with how they are connected with its form. This is why the Piaget–Kohlberg type of approach is relevant. For they are not concerned with the content of morality but with the form of moral understanding – in particular with how rules are viewed at different stages of development.

In using the Piaget–Kohlberg approach I do not have space to go into niceties about whether Piaget's three stages can be broken down into six. I just propose to use the rough and ready distinctions between egocentricity, realism and autonomy as indicators of very general types of difference.

The Pre-rational Level   It is worth remarking, first of all, that there is a level of experience and of reactions to others that are pre-rational. By that I mean the level of experience, in which Freud was particularly interested, which is not structured in terms of the categories of secondary processes of thought, whose emergence Piaget studied. Freud himself was more interested in vicissitudes of sexual wishes than he was in the cognitive features of this level of experience, but it has been studied by later theorists such as Arieti.[20] He noted the connection between this type of experience and a more primitive, palaeological form of thinking in which classification is purely on the basis of the similarity of predicates without any importance being attached to the identity of the object. Some primitive people, for instance, identify men, crocodiles and wild-cats because they have the common property of having an evil spirit. Very small children think in this way about people. So also do those suffering from various forms of mental disorder. Classification is based on affectively loaded similarity without regard to identity. Examples would be a paranoiac who interprets the behaviour of others indiscriminately along the dimension of threat. A less extreme case is that of a person who reacts violently to anyone in a position of authority over him. In all such cases no proper attention is paid to the identity or differentiating properties of individuals. At this level the concepts of 'personal relationships' and of 'personal relations' cannot get a grip; for there is no proper identification of individuals.

Egocentricity The main feature of this stage of moral development is that rules are seen purely as indicating things that have to be done to avoid punishment or to obtain rewards. One would expect a correspondingly instrumental view of people which would develop from a less calculating awareness of the association between a person's company and pleasure or pain. Others would be picked out and named, but would be classified mainly in terms of their frustrating or pleasure-enhancing properties. Children at this level, or adults whose thinking remains stuck more or less at this level, might be able to make quite shrewd appraisals of people in these self-referential terms. They might, too, in their dealings with others with whom they spent a lot of time, rely much on the type of empathetic cues to which reference was made in section 1. But their thinking about others would be based mainly on association steered by self-interest. They would be incapable of seeing the world from the other person's point of view, of distancing themselves and imagining what sense could be made of the behaviour of another in terms of his own purposes and plans. As others would be seen in this self-referential way the type of relationship would be basically an exploitative one. Others would be regarded as objects to be placated, manipulated, cajoled and, if necessary, eliminated or diminished if they interfered with satisfaction. Friendships could be with people whose presence and reactions enhanced the self of the individual, who, as it were, constantly massaged his ego. There would be sensitivity to personality traits such as friendliness, obsequiousness and charm, but little awareness of character.

Realism   At this stage rules are seen much more as entities 'out there' and conforming to them is seen as connected with obtaining approval and avoiding disapproval from peers and authority figures. One would expect, therefore, a much less egocentric view of others. They would be viewed much more as status holders were viewed in a traditional type of society, as global persons whose attributes were determined mainly by roles. Understanding of others would therefore tend to be in terms of typologies based upon roles – what could be expected from a father, a soldier, or a teacher. Character-traits derivative from socially approved ways of behaving would also be attributed to people and a range of emotional responses towards them would be possible that would be outside the reach of the purely egocentric man – loyalty and shame for instance. There might also be a feeling of fraternity towards others as sharing a common role or as engaged in a common pursuit. This might lead to friendships of the 'comrades in arms' type.

Autonomy   The level of autonomy is more difficult to deal with because many different but connected notions are combined. There is first of all the dawning of the notion that rules are alterable, that they can be valid or invalid, and that their content depends upon consent. Secondly, there is the notion of the individual as a chooser, as an individual who has responsibility for his actions and who can be, to a certain extent, the determiner of his own destiny. This is connected, thirdly, with the notion of authenticity or genuineness, with the individual choosing activities and codes of conduct that are based on considerations which he appreciates in a first-hand way, as distinct from on extrinsic considerations of rewards and punishments, approval and disapproval.

The individual's understanding of others now parallels the type of life of which he himself is capable. First of all he can view another as an individual existing in his own right, as it were, who has decisions to make about the roles which he is to assume and how he is to perform them. He is capable, too, of thinking about codes of conduct and trying to base his own on thought-out principles. Character-traits such as punctuality and tidiness now become superficial indicators of a person's character; for there is now a question about the individual's reason for conforming to such rules, which derive from the principles which he takes as fundamental. Account must be taken, too, of his long-term aspirations, of the way in which his activities are structured in terms of long-term concerns. Questions of motive now become much more important; for in himself and in others he becomes much more aware of the ways of viewing people and situations which make sense of a whole range of responses towards them. Understanding in depth is now possible.

This more individualised and objective view of others makes possible a different level of response and relationship. He can distinguish between an individual as a person and as an occupant of a variety of roles. He can be drawn towards him in friendship not just because of the enhanced self-feeling which he gets from his company, nor just because of fellow-feeling as a comrade or team-mate, but because he appreciates his qualities for what they are and because he is concerned about his good as a particular individual. He is capable, in other words, of love as distinct from just liking. He can, too, respect him as a person, even if he does not feel much drawn towards him.

The postulation of these different levels of response throws light on some of the theories of friendship and personal attraction that I encountered in reading through the summary of work done in this area provided by Sccord and Backman.[21] I was astonished to learn that the basic assumption is that friends are formed with those who satisfy some desire or need in the individual. The debate seems to be between those who hold that the individual's needs are best met by someone similar to himself and those who hold that preference is for someone different from himself in a complementary respect. These views can be unified by an 'exchange theory' of attraction in which it is postulated that the tendency to seek individual gratification by means of friendship works according to a kind of profit and loss estimation. If this theory were universally true of human nature Sartre, of course, would be quite right about personal relationships. The other is basically alien to us, an object whom we can only exploit, possess, or enjoy for our own ends. It suggests, perhaps, that 'liking' and not 'loving' is the only possible basis for friendship. But if my suggestion about levels of personal relationships is valid, these generalisations about the determinants of friendship would be applicable only to certain societies in which the view of others was generally an exploitative one, or of individuals in a less homogeneous form of society who were still stuck at Piaget's egocentric level of person-perception.

This type of speculation, however, raises wider questions about the concept of 'friendship', which I have only dealt with in a summary fashion, and about the logic of 'liking' and 'loving' on which a great deal more work needs to be done. But this would be a topic for another paper – perhaps even another symposium.

REFERENCES

1. See Hodges, W.A., *William Dilthey: An Introduction* (London: Kegan Paul 1944), Ch. 111.
2. Hodges, op. cit., p. 43.
3. Ibid., pp. 13–17.
4. Scriven, M., 'The Contribution of Philosophy of the Social Sciences to Educational Development', in Barnett, G., *Philosophy and Educational Development* (London: Harrap, 1966).
5. Ibid., p. 60.
6. See, for instance, Malcom, N., 'Knowledge of Other Minds', reprinted in Gustafson, D. F., *Essays in Philosophical Psychology* (New York: Doubleday–Anchor, 1964).
7. Black, M., 'Rules and Routines', in Peters, R. S. (Ed.), *The Concept of Education* (London: Routledge & Kegan Paul, 1967).
8. See, for instance, Peters, R. S., 'Reasons and Causes', Sect. 3; and Hamlyn, D. W., 'Conditioning and Behaviour', in Borger, R. T. and Cioffi, F., *Explanation in the Behavioural Sciences* (Cambridge University Press, 1970).
9. See, for instance, Kohlberg, L., 'Early Education: A Cognitive-developmental View', *Child Development*, Vol. 39 (1968).
10. See Greenfield, P. M. and Bruner, J. S., 'Culture and Cognitive Growth', in Goslin, D. A., *Handbook of Socialisation: Theory and Research* (Chicago: Rand McNally, 1969).
11. See Klein, J., *Samples from English Cultures*, Vol. 1 (London: Routledge, 1965).
12. See Popper, K. R., 'Toward a Rational Theory of Tradition', in *Conjectures and Refutations* (London: Routledge, 1963).
13. See Griffiths, A. P. (Ed.), *Knowledge and Belief* (London: Oxford University Press, 1967), pp. 12–14.
14. See Ryle, G., *The Concept of Mind* (London: Hutchinson, 1949), Ch. IV.
15. See Downie, R. S., 'Personal and Impersonal Relationships', *Proceedings of the Philosophy of Education Society of Great Britain*, Supplementary Issue, Vol. V, No. 2 (July 1971).
16. Winch, P., *The Idea of A Social Science* (London: Routledge, 1958).
17. For fuller explanation of this see Peters, R. S., 'Moral Education and the Psychology of Character', *Philosophy*, Vol. XXXVII, No. 139 (January 1962), pp. 37–56.
18. See Bedford, E., 'Emotions', *Proc. Arist. Soc.* (1956–7).
19. These suggested conditions are taken from Telfer, E., 'Friendship' *Proc. Aristot. Soc.* (1970–1).
20. Arieti, S., *The Intrapsychic Self* (New York: Basic Books, 1967), pp. 109–12.
21. See Secord, P. F. and Backman, C. W., *Social Psychology* (New York: McGraw-Hill, 1964), Ch. 7.

19

SUBJECTIVITY AND STANDARDS

INTRODUCTION

It would be possible and perhaps predictable for a philosopher to deal with this topic in the current analytical manner. A careful analysis could be made, one by one, of the rag-bag of disciplines that are grouped together under the title 'the humanities' in respect of the possibility of shared concepts, of truth-criteria and of agreement in judgements within them. The problems inherent in Lionel Knight's suggestion that literary criticism is a form of knowledge (with all that implies, epistemologically speaking) could be explored; question marks could be placed against much that John Coulson says about the status of theology; Denys Harding's claims for rigour and precision in Sherrington's work in physiology could be put alongside what might be claimed for that of Freud, Piaget, or Chomsky in psychology proper. Notorious problems about contemporary biases in interpreting history could be carefully laid out. This perhaps what would be expected of a philosopher. But to do such a job properly would require a whole volume. And, I suspect, it would be somewhat remote from the spirit and concerns of this group.

I therefore propose to attempt something more synthetic and hazardous, to revert perhaps to the older style of philosophy in trying to discern some more general attitudes to the human predicament which lie behind our approach to the humanities. I think, myself, that these are profoundly important in education. For I have the simple-minded view that education should, above all things, sensitise us to the predicaments in which we are placed as human beings, to the possibilities which it presents for joy and despair, ennui and excitement. What appals me is the sheer boredom engendered by much of our schooling. On going into classrooms I am so often struck by the looks on the children's faces. What on earth, I reflect, are we doing to these children? They, like us, have an expectation of life to say sixty-five years. This is all that they have. Why all this? What a way to spend their time! For what is it preparing them? Perhaps it is merely schooling them for a tolerance of the boredom and frustration that they will have to endure for much of their lives when they leave!

1 THE DIMENSIONS OF HUMAN LIFE

I have, therefore, as so often, a strong sympathy with Whitehead, when he says 'The essence of education is that it be religious',* but of course, without any suggestion of compulsory Religious Education or morning assemblies. He goes on to say: 'A religious education is one that inculcates duty and reverence. Duty arises from our potential control over the course of events. Where attainable knowledge could have changed the issue, ignorance has the guilt of vice. And the foundation of reverence is this perception, that the present holds within itself the complete sum of existence, backwards and forwards, that whole amplitude of time, which is eternity.'

This view of education is not incompatible with Ben Morris's conviction that education consists in the discovery of what it means to be human. For man alone of creatures is acutely aware of the dimensions within which life has to be enjoyed or endured.

Let me attempt to specify these dimensions rather more precisely. I will then pass to the location of the humanities within these dimensions and to the contrast between subjectivity and standards.

Whitehead gives clues to these fundamental dimensions of human life. The first he refers to rather too specifically as that of duty – the responsibility for actions that comes with foreknowledge. I would like to broaden and deepen this dimension. On the one hand there is the jet of human appetite. We are born into the world a bundle of insistent wishes and cravings. But, on the other hand, there is the givenness of the world. One of the most crucial steps in our early education, as Freud discerned so clearly, is our confrontation with this givenness of the world mediated through our perceptual apparatus with all that this implies for the delay of gratification.

* Whitehead, A. N., *The Aims of Education* (Williams and Norgate, 1932) p. 23.

There is also the givenness of certain human responses to the world. I would rather not use here the terminology of 'facts' because of the clouds of philosophical glory or obtuseness trailed by this term. Often, for instance, people assume some contrast between 'facts' and 'values'. But I am quite happy to talk about moral facts – for instance that avoidable pain or exploitation are evil.

(a)   *The Givenness of the World and of Human Responses*
By the 'givenness of the world' I mean such things as the phenomena co-ordinated by the law of gravitation or the indescribable stickiness of putty that has not been mixed to the right consistency, the heat of fire or the expansion of metal when subjected to it. In the face of these palpable features of our life on earth I am constantly amazed at some of the extravagances issuing from modern sorties in the sociology of knowledge. I was once, almost predictably these days, attacked by an indignant young woman in a College of Education who was accusing philosophers of conceptual imperialism in imposing categories like that of 'thing-hood' on the world. She ended up by maintaining that the planets, and presumably the earth beneath her feet, were individual or social constructions! I am also appalled by this contemporary arrogance. Bertrand Russell put his finger unerringly on what lies behind this generalised attitude when he accused the pragmatists of cosmic impiety, of thinking that what is true is what serves human purposes, be they individual or social. He was sensitive to the givenness of the world and to the appropriateness of a degree of humility in the face of it.

The Stoics used to say that a man should strive to alter what is bad and alterable in the human condition and learn to accept and live with what cannot be altered. There are limits to the assertion of will and to the fixing up of things for human benefit; for life presents predicaments as well as problems. The 'duty', to which Whitehead refers, relates to the mixture of morality and manipulation so manifest in Marxism and in the old American way of life. The Stoics had too limited a vision of what is unalterable. Ironically enough one of the first to sense the alterability of human institutions, as distinct from the alterability of nature, so clearly intimated by Francis Bacon, was Macchiavelli. Human beings, by ingenuity and foresight, he insisted, could forestall the operations of fate in principalities as well as in irrigation.

The nineteenth century witnessed the zenith of this belief in the capacity of human beings to fix things up. Utilitarianism, Marxism and the over-arching confidence in progress were symptomatic of it.

Pelagianism became a way of life for the few. Human happiness, the classless society, the superman – all such ideals seemed like attainable aspirations given human effort and ingenuity. Moreover the kingdom of heaven was not just waiting for the elect. All could be transported there along the rail-road of history given a bit more steam, solidarity and planning to speed things up.

But in the twentieth century more sombre Augustinian warnings have been sounded. Human nature, perhaps, has deeply ingrained flaws which are not just the product of institutions that crush and splinter it. Men, it is true, are morally much more sensitive than they were. But there was Belsen. And, more importantly, the social sciences have not advanced as much as was hoped. Men are not clever enough – perhaps never will be – to keep pace with their moral indignation. Economic predictions are treated with infinitely more scepticism than forecasts of the weather. And in social reform we tackle one problem, such as health, only to find equally appalling ones on our hands, like over-population and the plight of the aged. Social reform is beginning to look much more like an exercise in raising the misery threshold than a passport to human happiness.

And an even more appalling thought is beginning to seep through in countries where some, at least, have managed to surmount the obvious obstacles to human happiness. What do people do then? Are not the values of consumption really rather tasteless? The human predicament does not, as Marxists have argued, assert itself only when hunger, poverty, war and disease confront men starkly with it and occasion some comforting story about other worlds. It presents itself as well when the belly is full, the top of the promotion ladder reached and when the swimming pool has been installed in the garden. People are beginning to talk about the quality of life in prosperous countries like the U.S. and New Zealand. But what they mean by this is never clear apart from fixing up one or two more things such as new exhausts to get rid of the smog. For the point is that there are certain intractable features of the human condition that defy being fixed up. Aeschylus' sagas about human arrogance were not just directed at generals. What 'quality of life' fits these sombre parameters? If education, especially in the humanities, is not set squarely in these dimensions, it is an evasion. For education is not just, as is often said, for life. It is the search for a quality of living.

This modern Western belief in perfectibility and amelioration has recently been renewed. But it is accompanied nowadays by an emphasis on authenticity, on doing it your own way, on a state of being that lacks the staleness of second-hand role-playing. This search for a better quality of life is couched very often in the language of 'creativity' and doing your own thing. This is splendid as a counter-blast both to consumption-geared conformity and to welfare movements that, in seeking to remove injustice, impose on all the mindless conformity of a mass-meeting of shop stewards. But too often this protest borders on being a romantic luxury. It takes too little account of the givenness of social life and the unpalatable truths that have to be faced about it. It is all very well to proclaim that the police are, by definition, fascist pigs and that the police force should be disbanded. For if something is absolutely wrong, that is the end of the matter. To look at consequences would be to be guilty of what Kierkegaard called 'double-mindedness'. But the Mafia will not be converted overnight to a belief in the brotherhood of man. And they may be singularly single-minded in pursuing their aims.

This question-mark which I have placed against extreme forms of individualism is not meant in any way to down-grade its fundamental values – the importance of individual responsibility, integrity, liberty and respect for the individual and his view-point on the world. On the contrary it is meant to emphasise individual responsibility by drawing attention to the connection between duty and what Whitehead calls 'attainable knowledge' which 'could have changed the issue' – knowledge of the givenness of the human condition. Individualism, too, gives rise to another conviction of givenness – that of other people. Behind the value of respect for persons lies the conviction that others exist in their own right, that they are not to be moulded into an approved shape or just used by others for their purposes.

There is another type of obliviousness, too, which often accompanies extreme forms of individual assertiveness – an obliviousness of what I have called the givenness of human responses. By this I do not just mean the agreement in judgements about features of the world made possible by our possession of a shared perceptual apparatus. I mean also two other sorts of preconditions of human life. The first is the demands of reason which are at their most palpable in logical principles such as non-contradiction and universalisability to which we must conform if we are to string together any thoughts at all about our condition. The second is the shared response to situations such as those of danger, frustration and suffering which are features of our form of life as social animals, and which lie behind our acceptance or rejection of less deep-seated conventions demanded of us by society. Again I am often astonished at some modern subjectivist stances in their obliviousness of such features.

Do we just make ourselves by our private decisions as some Existentialists would have us believe? Do we not, for better or for worse, possess stomachs, sex organs and pain-spots? Is the lonely will of the individual all that lonely? Do not consistency and integrity presuppose shared principles constitutive of the operation of reason? The demand for authenticity itself, dates back to Socrates' insistence on the care of the soul. It is connected with the virtue of sincerity and the ancient doctrine of the lie in the soul. And when the young exhibit their authenticity by condemning the war in Vietnam, the pollution of the environment and the plight of the poor and disadvantaged, do they not do so in the name of shared principles such as those of injustice and the evil of avoidable suffering? It is often said that individuals have to 'choose' their own principles. Frankly I would feel distinctly uneasy in the presence of people who adopted this hesitant stance to principles such as fairness, avoiding suffering and telling the truth.

(b)   *The Dimensions of Time*

The other dimension of human life is that of time. There is an important sense in which, as Whitehead insists, the present is all that we have. But the present is but a precipitate left by the past and is big with potentialities for the future. And it is difficult to achieve a proper perspective on time. Marjorie Reeves has said much that is wise and illuminating about this in her paper on 'Why History?' I do not, however, detect in her account a sufficient emphasis on the reverence to which Whitehead refers. Her account stresses that human life without a collective memory is a stunted life, that the problems of present living are illuminated by their historical perspective. History, too, can become an absorbing attachment, an endless territory to travel over and explore. But there is a sense in which a people who, like the Americans, are as prepared to obliterate their past as they are to bull-dose their dwelling places, are guilty of a kind of impiety, a lack of reverence for their roots. For, as Burke stressed, we are not just men – we are also Englishmen, Americans, New Zealanders. Our past lives on in us. We take certain things for granted because our forefathers established them – perhaps died for them – when they were not taken for granted, like freedom of speech in England.

> *Vixere fortes ante Agamemnona*
> *Multi, sed omnes illacrimabiles ...*

This piety can, of course, take too extreme a form – in ancestor worship, for instance, or in the Garden of Eden view characteristic of traditionalists fixated on the past. But to lack this sense of the continuity of life is but another facet of the tendency of modern man to stride around like Lucifer – or, more probably, to drive around imperiously like Mr Toad.

A proper perspective on time is important, too, in relation to the satisfaction of our wants and choice of activities. There is, on the one hand, the progressive in search of happiness that lies always ahead. Distant goals such as the greatest happiness of the greatest number, or the classless society are the demythologised relic of the old striving for salvation. And often they involve an equally joyless, dutiful sort of toil. The present is merely the means to the future.

The reaction is the ideology of instancy. In revolt against this dreary view of life the young advance the slogan 'I want it now'. At one time this cult of the present was buttressed by arguments about the uncertainty of the future due to the threat of the bomb. But it is doubtful whether it was ever a very menacing cloud over their consciousness. What they have done is to press their parent's presuppositions to their logical conclusion. If consumer gratification is the point of life why delay it? Why not have it now? After all the elder generation, as a result of their anxious toil, seem to end up with ulcers, heart-diseases and an inability to enjoy what they have been working for. So why not have what you can get now – sex, kicks from violence and trips on drugs and in other people's fast cars?

A more rational attitude to time was enunciated by Henry Sidgwick in his axiom of prudence that: 'Hereafter as such is to be regarded neither more nor less than now.' Reasons have to be given for doing some things rather than others that include other than temporal considerations – even crude thoughts like 'If you wait you won't be able to have it at all' or 'If you wait there will be more of it'. Spinoza said that it is the hall-mark of reason to see things 'under a certain aspect of eternity'. The important thing for a man is to connect, to grasp the patterns and relationships which structure human life. It is not, therefore, the fact that the pleasure of smoking is to be had now or in five minutes time that matters; it is rather how it is conceived and its relationship to other things in life. Can smoking, like sexual activity, be conceived of not simply as a physical pleasure, but also as an expression of love? Can it be done with skill and grace like dancing? Maybe not. But perhaps it could be thought of as a symbolic gesture of peace. Poems might be written about the smoke ascending lazily upwards and linked with Heracleitus' preoccupation with fire, smoke and motion. But the full story has not yet been told; for any honest man who tries to connect must admit that it dulls the senses and is a danger to health. And, as E. M. Forster remarked: 'Yes, for we fight for more than Love or Pleasure: there is Truth. Truth counts. Truth does count.'

This more rational attitude to time is connected with what John Passmore calls 'care' – attention to the features of what is being done in relation to what has been and what will be. The values, the enjoyment, reside neither just in the past, nor in the present, nor in the future. They structure activities that extend over time. There is delight in writing a good sentence, in ploughing a straight furrow, in making a correct diagnosis, or in constructing an ingenious experiment. The delight does not derive just from a generalised love of mastery which can equally well be exhibited in playing with a yo-yo or doing an anagram. The standards that have to be attained are intimately connected with more permanent and all-pervasive concerns in human life – communication, obtaining food from the earth, the relief of suffering and the pursuit of truth. Thus the reverence, of which Whitehead speaks, is not for the passage of time in itself, but for the dimension which it provides, backwards and forwards from the present, for the concerns which constitute a quality of life. For a quality of life is intimately connected with the standards which are internally connected with these concerns. The humanities and the sciences represent the main locus of these concerns; so the scene is now set to introduce them.

2   COMMON FEATURES OF THE HUMANITIES

The dimensions of the human condition have been plotted in very general terms advisedly; for 'the humanities' include such a variety of different ventures of the human imagination that it would be difficult to describe their subject-matter in any other way. How else could much be said that is of significance for history as well as for poetry, for philosophy as well as for some of the social sciences?

In a way the term 'subject-matter' misleads from the start; for it conveys the image of some neutral material waiting to be apportioned. But not even nature, let alone man, is like that. For the world which we inherit has the imprint of mind on it from the first moment of discrimination. There is, I have stressed, its givenness. But this feature of it can only be understood against a background of attempts to impose our wills or conceptual schemes upon it. What we call 'the humanities' are the elaborations of our attempts both to understand our human world, to create and re-create it, and to take up various stances towards it. For one of the many distinguishing features of man is that he lives his life in the light of an image of himself that is not constant.

Any account of the human world which ignored some of the natural sciences would, of course, be a frivolity. For the natural world is the main locus of the givenness with which we are confronted in our attempts to construct a view of our condition. The development of the natural sciences, too, has, historically speaking, been one of the main determinants of man's changing conception of himself. The heliocentric theory of the heavens induced a degree of humility in those who had previously pictured the earth as the centre of a stage on which the drama of human salvation was being played. Belief in determinism, which accompanied the rise of the physical sciences, cut both ways. In some, like Spinoza, it induced a feeling of acceptance, almost of fatalism, in the face of the world. Others, like Bacon, Hobbes and Marx, were excited by the possibilities of power and control which were opened up – over nature and over man. It scarcely needs saying, too, that the natural sciences have exerted a profound influence on poetry, on religion and on philosophy which are 'humanities' in the narrow sense. If we say, therefore, that 'the humanities' are concerned in various ways with men rather than with nature, we must bear in mind that much of man's behaviour is only intelligible in terms of his thoughts about nature, and that the physical sciences are perhaps the finest product that yet exists of the sustained and controlled imagination of the human race.

It would not be altogether true to say, as some do, that the humanities differ from the physical sciences in their emphasis on the concrete and the particular. Psychology and sociology have, for a long time, tried to establish some generalisations about human behaviour and economics claims to have found some. A preoccupation, too, of moral philosophers has been the attempt to erect general principles of conduct. But there is something sadly lacking in these abstractions if they are regarded as being adequate to explain or justify full-blooded human behaviour. For there is always what Lewin called the individual's 'life-space'. To apply such generalisations to behaviour account must be taken of the individual's beliefs and expectations, his complex purposes and the social rules which he has internalised. Generalisations can be made, for instance, about the surroundings of human learning – about massed or spaced learning, the influence of recency and of rewards and so on; but as soon as we really get down to any concrete case so much depends on the content of the skills, beliefs or attitudes concerned. And all distinctively human learning involves this complicated sort of content.

Similarly in ethics we can formulate abstract principles like those of justice and the consideration of interests; but the crunch comes when questions are asked about how these principles are to be interpreted and applied. The point is that concepts such as wanting, taking means to ends, deciding, believing, following rules, being affected, in terms of which we have to make sense of human life, are systematically interconnected. Little is ever explained by reference to simplified abstractions as in the physical sciences. Furthermore, the content of these formal notions is highly variable from individual to individual, and from society to society. Explanations are usually much more like fitting particulars into a pattern of low-level generalisations than deduction from high-level laws.

Historians who are explicitly concerned, as Aristotle put it, with the particular – with what Alcibiades did and why, are acutely aware of this necessity of attempting to get inside another's 'life-space'. And, in so doing, they use low-level generalisations, rather than trying systematically to establish some, as do psychologists and social scientists. But the difference is one of emphasis.

Poetry and literature, too, at least according to a view of these highly complex activities that has always made some kind of sense to me, are concerned more constructively with concrete universals in human life. A particular embodiment is created which expresses something of general significance. If the author is successful this reverberates in some way in the experience of the person who appreciates it, like Tolstoy's description of Levin's feelings at seeing his new-born child for the first time in *Anna Karenina*. This sphere is enormously complicated by the highly contested category of the aesthetic. So, especially in view of Barbara Hardy's strictures on that subject, I will pass discreetly on to religion – an equally contested sphere, but not one in which I have such a fear of failure to discern what is there through lack of application in accustoming my eyes to the dark.

Most of theology, frankly, I would deal with like F. R. Tennant dealt with the doctrine of the trinity – in a footnote. But religious studies are different – and eminently worth extended exploration. Whether the attempt is made to enter imaginatively into the experiences which led the Maoris to feel awe in the presence of the forests or the Hebrews to feel it beneath the volcanoes, or whether one struggles, with Kant, to the limits of human reason and feels awe when confronted with the stark contingency of the world, here again one is traversing, with a different type of compass, many tracks from which one can get some kind of common aspect on the human condition.

And then there is finally philosophy. This has had periods when the search has been mainly for the abstract one in the many. But the emphasis now is on trying to discern the subtle accommodations of the one to its context – if there is ever just one to discern. When concepts are being considered the stress is on a rich diet of instances so that both the similarities and the differences can be digested. The notion, too, that there is just one pattern of reasoning – that of mathematics or of physical science – has been more or less abandoned. The form of thought of a lawyer in establishing a case, of a human being in understanding another, of a moral agent in a state of perplexity have all to be scrutinised. Here again, as in the other 'humanities', there is a search for concrete universals – for the forms of meaning and truth that are articulated in the various spheres of human action and belief.

The humanities, then, are a family of languages which men have developed to explain, describe and assess their behaviour, to take up stances towards the world and each other, to express how they feel and to reflect upon and try to justify what they think and do. They represent, as Ben Morris puts it, various paths that men have taken in their exploration of what it means to be human.

3 THE HUMANITIES AND THE DIMENSIONS OF HUMAN LIFE

What, then, is to be said about the relationship of these explorations to the dimensions of human life which I sketched at the start? And what is to be said about the contrast between subjectivity and standards?

The first point to stress, surely, is that in taking any of these paths we are entering a shared inheritance. Robinson Crusoe could not really have asked a scientific question, let alone made a scientific discovery. In the various branches of the humanities the concepts which we use represent centuries of effort by our ancestors. Our view of nature is never a naïve opening of the eyes; our emotional responses to it and to other people are seldom like untutored startle reactions. There may be a 'natural' basis to many of them, but they are usually overlaid with the crust of a shared inheritance.

Similarly reasoning in general, and the particular forms of it which we employ in the various 'humanities', does not represent the flowering of an inner potentiality in the individual that is simply encouraged by child-growers. It is basically a public inheritance. As such it should be employed with a certain humility and reverence – with a sense of our shared humanity. It should not be regarded merely as a tool of individual assertion or group domination. It is public not just in the sense that its vehicle is language whose concepts and rules of syntax are a public possession, but in the further sense that, even when it takes place in the individual's head, it is an internalisation of public procedures – those of criticism, the production of counter-examples and the suggestion of different points of view.

Reason, in this developed sense, of course has its origin in the primitive tendency manifest in intelligence to 'accommodate' or to change assumptions because the differences encountered in a novel situation do not permit assimilation, or the fitting of them within existing assumptions. But in reasoning proper, this caution born of the frequent experience of being in error, because of the differences between situations, becomes the principle enunciated by Francis Bacon that a search must always be made for the negative instance. Conscious, explicit attempts must be made to falsify assumptions, to find exceptions to rules; for only in this way can more reliable assumptions and rules gradually be built up. There must also be some form of public test to decide between competing assumptions. This means agreement not just about how answers are to be sought but also about the types of considerations that are to count as deciding between possible answers. Science is the supreme example of reason in action not just because of the opportunities for criticism which it provides, but also because of the agreement in judgements which it permits by means of its testing procedures. These guarantee objectivity and the escape from arbitrariness.

It is most implausible to suggest that these critical procedures develop naturally in children's minds as they grow up. History and psychology give no support to this flattering belief. In the history of man the overwhelming tendency has been for men to believe what they are told and to do what is expected of them. It is only at rare periods in history that sporadic curiosity and uneasiness about what is generally accepted have become embedded in a critical tradition. Psychologically speaking too, the general proclivity of men is to believe what they want to believe, and to accept the approved view of the group. Francis Bacon was one of the first to note what has since become a psychological platitude, that the determination to look for the negative instance, to subject assumptions to criticism, goes against a deep-seated tendency of the human mind, which

William James called 'the primacy of belief'. The determination to find out the truth, to get to the bottom of things, only tends to develop if people are brought up in contact with a critical tradition.

Thus the individual, who is accustomed to reason in this developed sense, is one who has taken a critic into his own consciousness, whose mind is structured by the procedures of a public tradition. A reasonable man is one who is prepared to discuss things, to look at a situation impartially from the point of view of others than himself, to discount his own particular biases and predilections. As G. H. Mead put it, he can adopt the point of view of the 'generalised other'. The disposition to adopt this point of view is a reflection in his consciousness of social situations in which the point of view of others has in fact been represented.

Now the humanities represent various articulations of this general tendency to reason, to criticise, to test things out. They differ from the natural sciences in that the tests are less palpable. Observations are, of course, used in history, psychology and the social sciences; but they are more overlaid with interpretation and bias than in the natural sciences. In the other humanities, such as morals, literature and religion, the basis is in shared reactions that are less uniform – e.g. sympathy for others in morals, awe in religion. These are much less predictable responses to objects and to situations than taking note of pointer readings on a dial. But they exist; they represent examples of what I previously referred to as the givenness of human responses. In the humanities, as well as in the sciences, they are transformed by reason. Just using the eyes in the satisfying of curiosity becomes in science the insistence on looking carefully at the evidence; sympathy attains a new level in respect for persons in morals, and awe felt for particular natural phenomena becomes elevated to awe felt for the contingency of the whole natural order, in religion.

What we call 'standards' represent the various demands made on us by the use of reason in its different forms, which is articulated in different ways by the concerns which underlie the various humanities. Some can be seen as implementations of the axiom of reason, that to will the end is to will the means. Efficiency of all forms comes under this – whether it be in experimental design, in organising notes, or in skills such as drawing, spelling, reading and writing.

Most of the standards in the humanities, however, cannot be conceived of simply under canons of efficiency; for their values are not just to be found in ends, to reach which means are taken. They are constitutive of a manner of travelling as well as of a destination. Indeed it is difficult to say what the destination is unless it is characterised in terms of an enhancement of the standards of travelling. In science, history, psychology and philosophy the 'goal' is truth in some fairly straightforward sense. But this is not to be interpreted either in terms of a culminating Platonic vision or in more mundane terms of amassing an endless store of true propositions. An infinite number of these could be obtained by studying a telephone directory. Rather the aim is to increase sensitivity and understanding; but this is to be interpreted in terms of values such as clarity, coherence, consistency, relevance, non-arbitrariness, humility, accuracy, precision, truthfulness, sincerity, perceptiveness and so on. These intellectual virtues are definitive of the search for truth and exert a constant pressure on our struggles for understanding and insight. As John Passmore puts it, we take care because we care.

Poetry and literature make additional demands because of their concern with the aesthetic. By that I mean that appraisals such as elegant, neat, witty, graceful and beautiful are also used. There is also that group of standards connected with what Clive Bell was feeling for when he talked about 'significant form'. But in view of my avowed nervousness with regard to the category of the aesthetic, I can only hint at what these additional demands may be. They concern the relationship between the parts which constitute them some kind of whole. The parts of a George Eliot novel express insights which ring true in themselves. The form in which they are expressed and the way in which they interlock to form a coherent whole can be *shown*. But it is difficult to pin them down with precise criteria.

The same sort of additional filling out would have to be done in the moral and religious spheres. Standards are generated by impregnation of specific responses with the general demands of reason. Sympathy becomes respect and abstract rationality the principle of justice in morals; awe becomes transformed into the sense of the sacred in religion. In the various disciplines that compose the humanities these over-arching values generate more specific sub-standards, insistence on which is the bread and butter of any valuable work with students who are new to them.

It should not be thought that submission to these standards is necessarily a cheerless grind any more than care in climbing mountains must be viewed as an irksome necessity. There is a delight in achievement, in mastery, in getting things right. If, too, the explorer is really on the inside of the activity concerned, he will also, by definition, be sensitised to its immanent standards. He will have a horror of irrelevance and obscurity, as well as a more positive love of clarity, consistency and precision.

What has this concern for standards to do with the dimensions of human life with which I started? They represent, surely, in detailed form, the pressure of the givenness of the world and of human responses which is mediated through social traditions. They represent a quality of life which takes account of the conditions under which it has to be lived. We wish for all sorts of things, are curious and are capable of all kinds of undisciplined, infantile reactions. Reason, both in its striving for order and coherence and in its mediation of the givenness of the world through its search for the negative instance, attempts to save us from constant frustration, conflict, disillusion and disappointment. It also conveys constantly to us a sense of the conditions which impose restrictions and limitations on wayward wishes and on the arbitrary assertions of will. Reason, too, elevates our sympathy for others into a conviction of their givenness, it intimates the irreverence of using them just for our own ends.

The language in which we talk about human life is shot through with demands of reason and we can make no sense of it without recourse to expressions which signify its demands. Words like 'true' and 'false' are used to appraise thoughts and utterances. We have the term 'belief' for the attitude of mind that is appropriate to what is true. Perceiving and remembering are distinguished by their built-in truth claims from merely imagining. Knowledge is similarly distinguished from opinion. Our language thus reflects our position as fallible creatures, beset by fears and wishes, in a world whose regularities have laboriously to be discovered.

In action, too, we do not just veer towards goals like moths towards a light; we are not just programmed by an instinctive equipment. We conceive of ends, deliberate about them and about the means to them. We follow rules, assess and revise them. Assessment has a toe-hold in every form of our behaviour. Words like 'right', 'good', and 'ought' reflect this constant scrutiny and monitoring of human actions. And in our interpersonal dealings impartiality and respect for persons bear witness to barriers imposed by reason on the restless sorties of the relentless ego.

Man is thus a creature who lives under the demands of reason. He can, of course, be unreasonable or irrational; but these terms are only intelligible as fallings-short in respect of reason. But men acknowledge these demands in varying degrees. Perhaps, for instance, they rely entirely on authorities or on custom; perhaps they just believe what suits them, act on whim or follow what Lawrence called 'the dark God within'. They act in a way which, in my view, is ultimately inappropriate to the situation in which we are all placed.

But those who explore science and the humanities take another course. They acknowledge the demands of reason and embark upon a systematic examination and appraisal of various aspects of life.

In doing this they pay some homage also to the dimension of time. The search for laws in science is a search for assumptions that are true of past, present and future. Works of art are possessions for ever, attempts, perhaps, to preserve in permanent form some particular insight into or expression of the human condition that is timeless. Religious studies attempt to disclose predicaments of man that are not confined to particular times and places. And in love, one of the supreme religious emotions, another is viewed as existing almost like a work of art in his own right – a whole to which assent is rendered, a sheer particular that embodies general features in a unique way. And, as I stressed before, the historian not only studies the past but should do so with a consciousness of how it both existed in its own right and also lives on in the present. Anyone working in these disciplines should experience, too, a feeling of fraternity for those who worked before him and for those who will carry on where he leaves off. He should have a sense of the universality of the values that inform their continuous creations. He should not think of himself just as 'doing his own thing'.

4   SUBJECTIVITY OR CREATIVITY?

What account, then, is to be given of subjectivity which, in some quarters, has become almost the cult of 'doing your own thing'? I have never myself been able to discern value in a purely naked ownership. Just because a wish or thought is mine I cannot see that value obviously attaches to it. Indeed, in estimating anything rationally, identity is as irrelevant as time and place. The point of view of any individual must, of course, be respected, his perspective on the world should not be disregarded, he should not be used purely as a means to the satisfaction of another's purposes or to the common interest. But this does not mean that there is any value necessarily in the *content* of his wishes, or point of view. In teaching we often have to combine a conviction that what someone says is irrelevant or false with respect for him as having a point of view and an interest in discovering what could ever have induced him to express or hold such a belief.

What lies behind this emphasis on the individual is surely values expressed by notions such as authenticity, independence of mind and creativity, in addition to sympathy, respect, or love for another individual. And the value of these is to be understood in contrast to the dreariness and cravenness of second-handedness, sentimentality and conformity. These various forms of 'bad faith' all involve going through the motions without sensing in any genuine way what the point is of the exercise. Belief, as I said before, is a state of mind appropriate to what is true. But if a person always takes his beliefs from others and never tries to find out anything for himself, he obviously cares little about truth. What he cares about is keeping in line. Similarly if people act in morals basically out of a desire to do the done thing, they must lack concern about considerations which demand that some things rather than others should be done. They are afraid of disapproval rather than sensitive to fairness and to the suffering of others. Imitativeness in art, or the elaboration of a string of clichés in an essay, indicate that the author does not care, in a first-hand way, about the values underlying the activity. Certain standards are conformed to in all such cases but mainly for approval's sake, not because the individual is on the inside of the activity and has a sense of its point.

Individuals who do begin to develop an authentic, first-hand appreciation because of their sensitivity to the values which structure such activities will, of course, be critical at times of what others say and do. But this will not be a mere contra-suggestibility which can become as much of a convention as conformity. It will be much more discriminating because it springs from a genuine sense of what is problematic in the light of underlying assumptions and values. And some will emerge who achieve new insights, who discover not just what is there to see, but what no one else has seen. They may even, like Einstein and Freud, be genuinely 'creative' in that they bring about a fundamental re-creation of the categories defining established conceptions. In poetry and literature this term has more obvious applications because such categories are less well-established and because the givenness of the world is less insistent. The products themselves are more truly 'creations' than is the case in the sciences or in philosophy. The constructiveness of reason and of the imagination is less subject to checks. The standards are more internal to the work itself than reflections of general principles, which mediate the givenness of the world and of human responses to it.

But originality such as this presupposes training in the discipline concerned, an appreciation of what has been established before and a genuine concern for the values definitive of it. Discoveries are not made by gazing naïvely at nature or at other people. How large is the sun? Does not the sun go round the earth? Answers to questions such as these do not spring from naïve observation but from a looking that is informed by a mathematical understanding of the heavens. Freud saw the importance of unconscious wishes because he noticed that a case of hysterical paralysis did not follow what he would expect from his knowledge of anatomy, but the lines of his patient's thoughts. It was his training in neuro-physiology that enabled him to see the situation as problematic and his disciplined curiosity that drove him onwards with his brilliant speculations. Individual inventiveness is always to be understood against such a background of a public inheritance.

5   EDUCATION AND THE HUMANITIES

Why, then, do we complain so much about the second-handedness of so much work in the humanities? Why do students constantly complain about 'relevance'? Partly, I suspect, because of the logic of the situation of learning and partly because of the anti-educational way in which we organise it. These are vast themes, so I can only conclude by hinting briefly at what I have in mind.

Piaget has elaborated important findings about levels of moral development. But I suspect that there are corresponding levels of motivational development as well, which are relevant to the acceptance of standards in the humanities. There is the early egocentric stage when rules are seen merely as things to be done in order to avoid punishment or to obtain rewards; there is then the stage when rules are seen as much more part of the order of the world but are connected with the desire for approval and the fear of disapproval; it is only at the final autonomous stage that rules are seen as alterable and their necessity to depend on reasons for them which are not artificially tacked on like rewards and approval. Discipline gradually becomes accepted because its relevance is seen to felt concerns and interests. It arises from the task, not from the attitudes of others to it.

Now it may well be that children are often initiated into the various disciplines of the humanities at a stage of their development when they cannot yet think of the validity of rules and standards as dependent upon some immanent purpose. They think of them as routines to be mastered because of their connection with rewards and punishments, approval and disapproval. And by our system of schooling we certainly ensure that they will think of them in this way to a large extent. For merit marks, prizes, punishments and the examination system, together with the close links between schooling and the occupational structure, provide an easily intelligible motivational pattern. The teacher may be an enthusiast sweating blood to get his students sensitive to the values immanent in what they are studying. But the institution in which he is operating may be speaking a very different and much more powerful message to them. The students may perceive their learning situation in terms of these deadening directives rather than in terms of what the teacher is trying to intimate. Their work thus becomes what Passmore calls 'toil'.

Secondly, in all branches of the humanities, as well as the sciences, there is an established body of knowledge or some collection of paradigms representing the efforts of previous generations. It is impossible to introduce a new generation to the various modes of experience underlying the humanities without reference to such achievements and artefacts. But they are too often introduced just as information to be digested and models to be copied. And, of course, learning of this sort is much easier to examine than learning which concentrates on mastery of the mode of experience. So products of the tradition may stifle the spirit which once informed its development.

Thirdly some of the humanities, though connected with shared human responses, do not come up against the givenness of the world to the extent which is characteristic of the natural sciences. As I said before their products are more truly 'creations'. But this leaves the door wider open to a certain kind of Alexandrianism, to pedantry and esoteric enthusiasms of scholars which are remote from the untutored understanding and the concerns of ordinary men. And these traditions of study may be perpetuated in teaching institutions over whose syllabuses the scholars obtain control. Their main ambition may be to turn out people like themselves rather than to open up to students a mode of experience, and to provide them with tools to explore it for themselves.

But I must not expand any more on some of the enormities that are perpetrated in the name of education. I think that I have at least intimated some of the difficulties inherent in the logic of the learning situation as well as those which we create by our institutions. The problem of the educator is rather like that of a religious leader. He may, perhaps unintentionally, be the founder of a small church; yet the logic of institutionalisation may stifle and constrain the spirit which the institution tries to perpetuate. But the spirit will not survive without some kind of institutionisation. And if, as I suggested at the beginning, 'the essence of education is that it be religious', it is not surprising that in education, as well as in religion, there are recurring attempts to free the spirit from the forms which are necessary for it to survive and develop. But they, too, whether they be Puritan or progressive movements, are likely to share the same fate of ossification. Protesters are gradually turned into Protestants. But unless they devise institutional forms the light which they shed on the human condition will be merely that of a shooting star across the firmament. This paradox represents the main problem of education. It represents too, one feature of the givenness of human life to which education itself should make us more sensitive.

20

MICHAEL OAKESHOTT'S PHILOSOPHY OF EDUCATION

'There will always remain something of a mystery about how a tradition of political behaviour is learned. . . .'   *M. Oakeshott*

INTRODUCTION

On reading much modern analytical philosophy one is often tempted to reflect that there is too much technique and too little judgement, to use one of Oakeshott's cardinal distinctions. Technical competence is shown in making distinctions, but what is often lacking is a 'nose' for the distinctions on which anything of philosophical importance depends. Oakeshott's 'style' of philosophy exemplifies the obverse combination of virtue and vice. He almost always has something to say which is interesting and important; but his impressionistic and rather literary approach to philosophical analysis often leaves what he has to say in a somewhat shadowy state. Few modern philosophers, of course, write with Oakeshott's literary skill; their articles read like work-notes rather than pieces prepared for others to read. But Oakeshott's literary virtuosity sometimes involves a systematic elusiveness when he touches upon situations covered by his key concepts.

This elusiveness applies particularly to his concept of 'tradition', on which I have had occasion to comment elsewhere.[1] It applies also to certain key concepts in his philosophy of education such as 'judgement' and 'imparting', with which I shall be concerned in this chapter. Nevertheless Oakeshott almost always raises fundamental philosophical issues in an exciting way, and stimulates others to further thought about them. This is particularly true of his philosophy of education with most of which I have great sympathy; indeed my own

views have been much influenced by his writings, though he would be
the last person to demand much in the way of acknowledgement.

1   OAKESHOTT'S GENERAL CONCEPTION OF EDUCATION

In talking about education Oakeshott always starts, as is fitting for
a philosopher of the idealist school, for whom history is of cardinal
importance, with the civilised heritage of a people, with Hegel's
'second nature' composed of 'a stock of emotions, beliefs, images,
ideas, manners of thinking, languages, skills, practices and manners
of activity'[2] out of which the 'things' which confront us in our
environment are generated. Education consists in the initiation of a
new generation into this civilised heritage. But Oakeshott never
views this initiation as a process of moulding people or of transmitting this heritage in an undiscriminating or routinised way. He usually
draws attention to the activity of the learner by using homely phrases
which avoid the jargon of 'self-realisation' and 'the development of
individual potentialities'. A typical way of putting it is as follows:

'Education I will take to be the process of learning, in circumstances
of direction and restraint, how to recognise and make something of
ourselves. Unavoidably, it is a two-fold process in which we enjoy an
initiation into what for want of a better word I will call a "civilisation", and in doing so discover our own talents and aptitudes in
relation to that civilisation and begin to cultivate and to use them.
Learning to make something of ourselves in no context in particular
is an impossibility; and the context appears not only in what is
learned but also in the conditions of direction and restraint that
belong to any education.'[3]

This civilised heritage, within which the individual has to learn to
make something of himself, Oakeshott sometimes discusses in terms
of a conversation. 'If, then, we recognise education as an initiation
into a civilisation, we may regard it as beginning to learn our way
about a material, emotional, moral and intellectual inheritance, and
as learning to recognise the varieties of human utterance and to
participate in the conversation they compose.' He uses this metaphor
in order to stress three points: first of all the fact that there are
different 'voices' – e.g. that of science, poetry, history, morals – and
secondly the necessity for communication between those who, without opportunities for cross-disciplinary conversation, are in danger
of confining their discussions to one mode of thought. He thinks that
the main function of a university, as distinct from a graduate school

or a technical college, is to provide the occasions and the facilities for a sustained conversation of this sort. This is his way of stressing the importance of what educationalists refer to in their jargon as 'developing the whole man'. He thinks, thirdly, that the metaphor of a conversation is appropriate because the relation between the voices are not those of assertion and denial 'but the conversational relationships of acknowledgement and accommodation'. By this, presumably, he means things such as that in a discussion of, for instance, a moral problem, a scientific generalisation can never of itself constitute a refutation of a moral assertion but can be relevant to it in certain ways. Arguments, or discussions, on the other hand are structured in terms of one mode of thought.

Each of these 'voices' or modes of experience has what Oakeshott calls (perhaps somewhat misleadingly) a distinctive 'language' and 'literature' of its own. The language is, for example, 'the manner of thinking of a scientist'; the 'literature' is for example, 'a text-book of geology or what may be called the current state of our geological knowledge'.[4] This distinction enables him to demarcate, in a rough and ready way, school, vocational and university education.

2 TYPES OF EDUCATION

(a) School Education

School education is concerned, in Oakeshott's view, mainly with initiation into the different literatures. After acquiring basic skills the child begins to enjoy and even to use the intellectual capital of a civilisation. Much, however, is acquired that the child does not really know how to use. It is a capital which generates something valuable on its own account. 'Learning here is borrowing raw material the possible uses of which remain concealed.'[5] Oakeshott assigns a very specific function to school education which would shock most educationalists. He regards it as

'learning to speak before one has anything significant to say; and what is taught must have the qualities of being able to be learned without necessarily being understood, and of not being positively hurtful or nonsensical when learned in this way. Or, it may be said, what is taught must be capable of being learned without any previous recognition of ignorance: we do not begin to learn the multiplication tables because it suddenly dawns upon us that we do not know the sum of nine-eights, nor the dates of the kings of England because we do not know when Edward I came to the throne: we learn these things at school because we are told to learn them. And further, school-education is without specific orientation; it is not yet concerned with individual talents and aptitudes, and if these show themselves (as they may) the design in school education is not to allow them to take charge. At school we are, quite properly, not permitted to follow our own inclinations.'[6]

So much for 'discovery' methods and following the interests of each child!

Actually Oakeshott puts his position more strongly and starkly than is really either defensible or necessary; for given that school education is all that over two-thirds of the population get at the moment, Oakeshott's view of education as consisting in 'making something of oneself' could only therefore apply to an *élite* if no account is to be taken, at the school level, of individual aptitude and talent. Also from the point of view of successful initiation some account must be taken of the inclinations of individuals and of their aptitudes; for motivation is the key to effective initiation. And though it is sheer dogma to assert that learning is only possible if what is to be learnt is closely related to the contingent concerns of the individual, it is equally dogmatic to assert that at school the individual is not allowed to follow his own inclinations, or to deny that a child may learn when Edward I came to the throne because he becomes aware of a gap in his knowledge. Perhaps all that Oakeshott means is that at the school level the content of a curriculum cannot be determined by individual interest or inclination and that at least a 'core' of our common heritage must be transmitted to all. That is reasonable enough. But within this common heritage there is plenty of room for individual aptitudes and it can only be handed on effectively if some account is taken of individual attitudes. Again though I think that Oakeshott is right, as against many modern educationalists, in insisting that at school much has to be learnt before it can be properly understood or the point of it grasped (e.g. moral rules, spelling, reading, poetry) nevertheless it does not follow that there is no place for the type of learning advocated by followers of Dewey or by adherents of 'discovery methods'. There was, after all, some point in Whitehead's polemic against 'inert ideas'.

(b) *Vocational Education*

There are two ways, according to Oakeshott, in which education can branch out after school, which he calls vocational and university education. In vocational education a literature is acquired which is relevant to the performance of some skill or to fitting a man for a specific place in a manner of living. A specific body of knowledge has to be acquired and the individual has to be able to move about within it with ease and confidence and to use it. The history of such a body of knowledge, and the errors and struggles of the past, however instructive, are of no account; what must be handed on is only the current achievement of a civilisation in respect of a skill or practice needed in the contemporary world. No provision need be made for 'teaching people how to be ignorant'.

This account of what is distinctive of technical education is acceptable in a general sort of way, though some of the details are debatable. For instance it could be argued that Oakeshott has given a delineation of technical training rather than of technical education. Education surely implies some understanding of principles, not just the amassing of information relevant to the practice of a skill or to fitting a man for a place in society. Education also implies some breadth of understanding. On his criterion we would have to say that the Spartans were professionally educated. And surely that is the last thing we would say about them; we would surely say that they were highly trained. We could, however, describe an engineer as educated if he appreciated what was intrinsic to engineering, if he had an understanding of principles and not just a mastery of information relating to engineering, and if he was also capable of appreciating aspects of life other than those intimately connected with engineering.

(c) *University Education*

A university education, according to Oakeshott, has a quite different sort of emphasis; for it is an education in 'languages' rather than in 'literatures'. 'It is concerned not merely to keep an intellectual inheritance intact, but to be continuously recovering what has been lost, restoring what has been neglected, collecting together what has been dissipated, repairing what has been corrupted, reconsidering, reshaping, reorganising, making more intelligible, reissuing and reinvesting.'[7] The direction of study is determined by academic considerations alone, not by extrinsic pressures and demands. The various modes of thought are not taught as literatures to be assimilated but as languages in which different types of exploration can be conducted. What is characteristic of a university education, however, as distinct from that of a graduate school, or a technical college, is that students are given the run of the place where these languages are being used. They do not have to assimilate a body of knowledge to apply for a practical purpose, nor do they have to engage, at the undergraduate level, in research. University teachers, therefore, are not simply frontiersmen on the boundaries of knowledge; they also have to teach from those texts which experience has shown to be most effective in conveying the 'language' of a mode of thought.

Nevertheless, Oakeshott argues, though the main function of a university is to initiate students into the 'language' of a mode of thought, this cannot be done effectively without a study of the appropriate 'literature'. Science as a way of thinking can only be acquired by studying some science; it is no substitute to study some so-called 'scientific method'. Learning to think historically is to be achieved only by observing and following an historian at work on a particular aspect of the past. A 'literature' is studied, therefore, not, as in vocational education, to use for any practical purpose but as the paradigm of a 'language'.

There is much to be said in favour of Oakeshott's account of university education, especially as a corrective to the views of those who demand that universities should become centres of the 'knowledge industry' and should be concerned mainly with providing the theory to solve the practical problems of the community. But it might be criticised in that he makes a university seem much too much like a Liberal Arts College. In countries where Liberal Arts Colleges have not been separated from Graduate Schools and Institutes of Technology, a university is surely an institution where 'conversations' and teaching are essentially conducted within the context of research. He places too little emphasis on the distinctive character given to such activities by the fact that those who provide most of the talking points are themselves exploring the frontiers of knowledge as well as teaching. On his account a good Adult Educational Settlement, where no one is actively engaged in research, and where no one is a real authority on a subject, would be indistinguishable in its essence from a university. The main difference would be that students do a three-year course – e.g. in philosophy or history – for love and without getting a degree for it. Indeed the absence of a degree would make his notion of contributing to a conversation more applicable; for the fact is that in universities there are sharp-eared men around who listen to the sallies of students and grade and assess them on criteria within one form of thought. This would be very bad form in a real conversation.

3 PROCESSES OF EDUCATION

Technical and Practical Knowledge

When Oakeshott addresses himself to the question of how the capital of a civilisation is handed on he makes the same type of distinction as that between a 'language' and a 'literature' but deploys it for a different purpose. He distinguishes *technical* knowledge which can be formulated in rules, which are, or may be, deliberately learned, remembered and put into practice, and *practical* knowledge which exists only in use and which cannot be formulated in rules. This does not mean that it is some esoteric sort of knowledge; it only means that the method by which it may be shared and becomes common knowledge is not the method of formulated doctrine. It is what we might call traditional knowledge, and is involved in every kind of activity. Oakeshott's favourite examples, which can be found both in his early article on 'Rationalism in Politics'[8] in the *Cambridge Review* and in his later 'Political Education',[9] are cookery, science and politics. There is a body of knowledge in each and recipes for proceeding with the activity; but no one supposes that the knowledge necessary for being a good cook, scientist, or politician can be written down in any book. Technique may tell a man *what* to do, but it is only practice that will tell him *how* to do it. Techniques, rules, information can be written down; instruction can be given in them; it can even be learned by correspondence. Practical knowledge, on the other hand, can only be shown. It cannot be taught or learnt; it has to be acquired or imparted. 'It exists only in practice, and the only way to acquire it is by apprenticeship to a master – not because the master can teach it (he cannot), but because it can be acquired only by continuous contact with one who is perpetually practising it.'[10]

Instructing and Imparting

In a recent lecture delivered at the University of London Institute of Education on 'Learning and Teaching',[11] Oakeshott attempts to make more explicit the distinction he has in mind between 'instructing' and 'imparting'. He argues that we carry around with us what we may be said to know in the form of countless abilities, which is an equipment which we possess in terms of what it enables us to do or understand. These abilities are of different kinds and cannot be assimilated to each other – e.g. the ability to understand and to explain cannot be assimilated to the ability to do or to make. Each of these abilities are conjunctions of 'information' and 'judgement'. 'Information' is impersonal and consists of facts that can be written down; it is the answer to the questions 'who? what? where? which? how long? how much?', etc. It may be useful or useless depending on whether the facts in question are or are not related to a particular skill or ability. Its importance depends on the extent to which it provides rules or rule-like propositions relating to abilities.

There are two ways in which such rules may be related to knowledge. Either they must be known as a condition of being able to perform (e.g. the Morse code) or they are rules for assessing performances in terms of correctness or incorrectness (e.g. grammatical rules). The latter types of rules are observed in the performance and are capable of being known; they provide the criteria for detecting an incorrect performance, but a knowledge of them is not a condition of a laudable performance. There is also a third type of rules, which may be called principles, which are propositions advanced to explain what is going on in any performance, which supply its 'underlying rationale'. These are never components of the knowledge which constitutes the performance. They belong to the performance of explaining a performance – e.g. in the case of riding a bicycle, the principles of mechanics, in the case of moral conduct Aristotle's doctrine of the mean, which are unrelated either to learning the form of behaviour in question or to a good performance.[12]

There is, then, in all knowledge an ingredient of information which may vary from an indeterminate awareness of facts to rules or rule-like propositions of the first or second sort which inform the skills and abilities in which we carry around what we may be said to know. But this ingredient of information never constitutes the whole of what we know. It must also be partnered by 'judgement'. 'Knowing *how*' must be added to 'knowing *what*'. This is not merely unspecified in propositions; it is unspecifiable in propositions. It does not and cannot appear in the form of rules. This is an ingredient of all genuine knowledge and not a separate kind of knowing specified by an ignorance of rules; for information has to be used, rules have to be applied, and it does not itself enable us to interpret it, to decide upon its relevance, to recognise what action permitted by the rule should, in the circumstances, be performed. 'For rules are always disjunctive. They specify only an act or a conclusion of a certain general kind and they never relieve us of the necessity of advice. And they never yield anything more than partial explanations: to understand anything as an example of the operation of a rule is to understand it very imperfectly.'[13]

Judgement, then, is not revealed just in skills like riding a horse or diagnosing a disease; it is involved also in the practical relationships between human beings. Maxims and interpersonal rules require interpretation; where there is a conflict between precepts it cannot be resolved by the application of other rules. Each individual has a 'style' of his own which relates to the way in which his judgement is exercised. 'Not to detect a man's style is to have missed three-quarters of the meaning of his actions and utterances, and not to have acquired a style is to have shut oneself off from the ability to convey any but the crudest meanings.'[14] In brief, unless a man has developed judgement he has acquired neither skills nor the different 'languages' characterising the modes of thought of a civilisation. A mere knowledge of the 'literature', of the information and rules, is insufficient; they may help in telling us what not to do but they provide no prescriptions for their own application.

What conclusions, then, does Oakeshott draw for teaching from this analysis of what has to be passed on? First, that the two components of knowledge ('information' and 'judgement') can both be communicated and acquired, but not separately. Secondly, that they cannot be acquired in the same manner. Indeed Oakeshott confesses that the distinction which he makes is the result of reflection upon teaching and learning rather than upon the nature of knowledge. Thus teaching consists in a two-fold activity of 'instructing' (or communicating 'information') and imparting (or communicating 'judgement') and learning is similarly a two-fold activity.

The teacher as instructor is confronted by a pupil who is familiar with the activity of acquiring information, particularly information of immediate use. His task is to introduce pupils to facts which have no immediate significance. He has therefore to decide the part of our inheritance which has to be transmitted and to make it more readily accessible by giving it an organisation in which the inertness of its component facts is modified. 'The organisation provided by an immediate application to the life of his pupil is spurious; much of the information he has to convey has no such application and would be corrupted by being turned in this direction.'[15] Dictionaries and encyclopaedias are no good either; for they are not designed for the purpose of learning. Organisation in terms of 'languages' is altogether too sophisticated. The instructor perforce must settle for more or less arbitrarily designed 'subjects', which compose a curriculum; these are convenient organisations of information, not modes of thought. But they permit facts to reveal their rule-like character as tools to be used in doing, making, or understanding and thus throw off some of their inertness. The teacher as instructor also has to decide on the order in which to present this organisation of facts and to exercise his pupils so that they recognise them in forms other than those in which they were first acquired. Accuracy is vital in this operation and readiness to recall.

In addition to acquiring information from the teacher it is hoped that the pupil is also acquiring judgement. This begins to emerge whenever the pupil perceives that information must be used and perceives the possibility of irrelevance. The organisation of information may help in this development; for the pupil begins to be able to do, make, understand, or explain in the mode of thought which underlies the information. The pupil cannot be instructed how to think in these different ways; it is a by-product of acquiring information and is imparted obliquely in the course of instruction. This can only be done if the information and maxims are constantly related to concrete situations. Also to be imparted are the intellectual virtues that go with judgement – disinterested curiosity, patience, honesty, exactness, industry, concentration and doubt. Most difficult of all for the pupil to acquire is the ability to detect the individual intelligence at work in every utterance and act, the style which each individual brings to his thought and action. 'We may listen to what a man has to say, but unless we overhear in it a mind at work and can detect the idiom of thought, we have understood nothing.'[16]

Judgement is not imparted in the abstract or separately; it is never explicitly learnt and it is known only in practice; but it may be learned in everything that is learned. 'If it is learned, it can never be forgotten, and it does not need to be recollected in order to be enjoyed. It is, indeed often enough, the residue which remains when all else is forgotten; the shadow of lost knowledge.'[17] How then is judgement imparted?

'It is implanted unobtrusively in the manner in which information is conveyed, in a tone of voice, in the gesture which accompanies instruction in asides and oblique utterances, and by example. For "teaching by example", which is sometimes dismissed as an inferior sort of teaching, generating inflexible knowledge because the rules of what is known remain concealed, is emancipating the pupil from the half-utterance of rules by making him aware of a concrete situation. And in imitating the example he acquires, not merely a model for the particular occasion, but the disposition to recognise everything as an occasion. It is a habit of listening for an individual intelligence at work in every utterance that may be acquired by imitating a teacher who has this habit. And the intellectual virtues may be imparted only by a teacher who really cares about them for their own sake and never stoops to the priggishness of mentioning them. Not the cry, but the rising of the wild duck impels the flock to follow him in flight.'[18]

The Thesis as a Conceptual Truth or as an Empirical Generalisation
Oakeshott's distinction between 'instructing' and 'imparting' is

obviously a very important one, but the details of it are not altogether clear. So it is necessary to probe a bit further into it. He seems to maintain, first, that things like judgement, taste and discernment can only be imparted; they can never be the result of mere instruction. Information and rules, on the other hand, are fit material only for instruction. Secondly, 'imparting', on Oakeshott's view, must involve the example of the teacher; things like 'judgement' can only be 'shown', and this is how they are picked up. The rule book will not do, because the rules have to be applied, and we can only learn to apply them by working with somebody who knows how to apply them.

The first part of this thesis seems to be partly a *conceptual* truth in that 'impart' rather than 'instruct' is the word which we use when we wish to indicate that something has been successfully learnt from a teacher, as well as when we wish also to suggest some sort of mystery about how this has been accomplished. 'Impart', in other words, is what Ryle calls an 'achievement' word.[19] It implies, surely, not necessarily that the teacher has been engaged in some activity additional to instructing but that he has somehow achieved success in his task. Thus, contrary to Oakeshott's thesis, information or rules can be imparted, as well as judgement and discernment. As, however, it is desirable that information should be used and rules applied, judgement would usually be regarded as a criterion of success, rather than the mere acquisition of information. The pupil should emerge with judgement and discernment rather than just be stuffed with 'inert' ideas. It is, therefore, not surprising that Oakeshott associates 'imparting' with 'judgement'; for this is the word which we use when we wish to point to the teacher's success. But it is not the case that only judgement can be imparted. It is merely a contingent fact that we do not regard the mere passing on of information as sufficiently important to grace it often with a 'success' word.

But is it also true – and this, too, might be a conceptual truth or it might be an empirical generalisation – that such successful results only occur when the teacher 'shows' or exemplifies the proper performance? Must there be some sort of mystery about the transaction which the term 'impart' also suggests? Could not, or cannot, mere instruction be sufficient? This is a much more complicated question to answer; for Oakeshott maintains that all passing on of knowledge and skill must involve the imparting of judgement if it is to be successful. But to maintain such a general thesis he uses the word 'judgement' in several different ways, at least three of which must be distinguished.

(i) There is, first of all, a general sense of 'judgement' used by

3 areas of judgement

1.

idealist philosophers such as Bradley to speak of any situation in which a concept or rule is applied to a particular case. Thus recognising something as red or as a cat or as a breach of the Highway Code involves 'judgement' in this sense, just as much as recognising someone who is in disguise or determining whether someone was driving with due care and precaution. Does 'judgement' in this very general sense have to be imparted by processes such as imitation or identification in which acts or noises are copied or attitudes, interests and wants are 'taken in' from the example of a teacher?

The answer is that, in this sense of judgement, examples are necessary for learning but not necessarily example. To be able to perceive or think is to be able to use concepts, and learning a concept involves both learning the rule which binds together the instances and learning by examples what counts as an instance. That is why a colour-blind man could not have a full concept of 'red'. But this process of producing an example to teach a concept or a rule is the most typical case of *instruction*. If we say 'cat' to a child and point to the animal in question that is a case of instruction. If we say later that 'the cat is on the mat' and again point, that again is a piece of instruction. If the instruction is successful, either in the sense that the child can go on to use the words correctly in this and in different situations, or in the sense that he remembers the piece of information, then we might say that we had taught the child a concept or imparted some knowledge to him. Judgement in its most general idealist sense would be involved; but though, at some stage, the use of examples would be necessary, the example of the teacher would not. After all, a great deal of instruction of this sort can be carried out by teaching machines. The rules, for instance, for the use of a concept like that of 'conditioning' could be roughly formulated and instances could be described in detail from the classical experiments to illustrate the use of the concept. A student could learn how to use such a concept if the relevant features of this situation were clearly made explicit by the programme of the machine. The student could then be given other examples so that he would quite quickly learn how to apply such a concept to unfamiliar situations.

Now 'judgement' of the idealist sort is involved here. But it is obviously something much more mundane than the 'judgement' of a judge, and situations can be controlled and structured in such a way that the learner can grasp the concept by instruction. He has, of course, to be brought to grasp the rules involved; but instructions can be formalised for bringing students of average intelligence to grasp such rules. Example, as distinct from examples, only becomes important when something approximating to a skill is involved. It might be argued that in the early stages of learning an embryonic sort of skill is involved; for rules and concepts at this stage are necessarily presented in unstructured and unfamiliar types of situations where the child has to discriminate between possible types of application. Even in learning 'blue', for instance, the child has to grasp that this is an information-conveying type of word rather than an order, and that it is a colour-word within the general class of information-conveying types of word. Unless he had picked up a lot about the use of language from the example of his parents he would not be in a position to benefit from instruction by examples. Once he has become a language user instruction can accomplish a lot merely by examples because he has 'picked up' the general skills involved in using language in different ways by following the example of others. This may well be true; but what it also shows is that there is a great deal of 'judgement' in the idealist sense which can be learnt by instruction once the general skill of using a language has been acquired.

(ii) The general skill of using a language may examplify a second and more specific sense of 'judgement', the paradigm case of which is the type of task performed by a judge. He is faced by a complex situation where many rules might apply to a set of facts and he has to determine which rule does apply. Judgement of a similar sort is involved in diagnosis, in tact, in deciding which golf club to use, or in dealing with non-routine types of situation in war, business and politics. This is surely the type of situation with which the term 'judgement' is usually associated. 'Judgement', in Oakeshott's thesis, is above all a term of approval. But we do not give a person a merit mark for judgement in the first sense – i.e. if he recognises an obvious breach of the Highway Code or if he straightaway follows some instructions correctly for getting to Piccadilly. If he failed in such elementary applications of rules or use of information we might think him a fool. But we certainly would not praise him particularly if he was successful or ascribe judgement to him. It may well be the case that the difference between 'judgement' in the first and second senses is a difference in degree; it may well be the case also that judgement in the first idealist sense is only possible if some skill has been mastered which once involved judgement in the second sense. But the fact is that we do not normally use the word 'judgement' for straightforward cases of applying rules or using information. We reserve it for the special cases where applying rules or interpreting information presents a problem.

Could people only learn judgement in this second value-laden sense by serving their apprenticeship under somebody who already has it? That this is the only way in which it could be learnt seems to be the burden of Oakeshott's political and educational writings, in which he usually contrasts this way of picking it up with formalised instruction or the use of manuals and guides. No doubt some kind of apprenticeship system is the most effective and the quickest way of learning judgement of this sort. But it is questionable whether it is the only way. Oakeshott has a contempt for self-made men; but though they may learn judgement the hard way, it has to be demonstrated that they cannot learn it on their own, which seems to be his thesis. Oakeshott also has a contempt for method; yet method at least provides canons laying down what should not be done; it provides boundary fences within which the learner can try out things for himself. And here we come to the core of the matter, which is insufficiently emphasised in all Oakeshott's writings: *practice*, in which the learner methodically works at some task until he has more or less mastered it and is able to rest on a solid basis of habit in tackling some novel situation. Of course what we call 'training' usually involves practice under the supervision of some skilled performer. But it is a disputable empirical thesis that this is the only way to develop skill and judgement. Who, after all, was the master whose philosophical 'judgement' rubbed off on Socrates?

Of course those who are self-taught must learn 'judgement' in the first idealist sense from others; they have to learn to speak and to apply rules in paradigm situations before they can carry on their own; they have to be familiar with a literature from which problems or incoherences arise which puzzle them. But, given such a start, practice, intelligence and method can take a man a very long way more or less on his own. Dewey's account of the development of critical thinking certainly pays too little attention to the role of the teacher as a paradigm of a form of thinking; it is *too* biased in favour of the do-it-yourself ideology of the frontier. But it would be odd if this rationalistic type of account applied to *no* cases in which people gradually learned to think for themselves and if *all* people who were more or less self-taught necessarily lacked judgement. Could it not be the case, too, that a man who was not a very good philosopher or scientist himself might be very good at initiating others in the early stages? He might have the ability to exhibit and convey to others the essentials of a form of thought in a crude but exciting way. He might lack the judgement to progress very far with it himself, to be an acknowledged master; but he might be very good at initiating others at the undergraduate level.

Oakeshott's emphasis, too, on picking up a skill by watching a master overlooks a very common learning situation that is not to be despised – that in which a learner practises a skill with a coach who is not himself particularly proficient at the skill in question. Some of the best teachers of golf or cricket, for instance, are not themselves superlative performers. What they have mastered is the art of commenting on and encouraging the performances of others. And they often do this by the reiteration of rules which are anathema to Oakeshott. They say things like 'Keep your right elbow in' or 'Don't hit from the top of the swing'. The performer gradually improves in response to such discerning instructions. There are, perhaps, many who learn much better by imitation which lacks such rule-ridden self-consciousness; but, on the other hand, others may not be particularly imitative and may learn better if coached by one who knows what a good performance looks like without himself being a superlative performer. Could it not be that Oakeshott's thesis about learning by example is merely a generalisation of his own favoured way of learning? Oakeshott produces no empirical evidence for his general thesis. But, perhaps, like Hobbes he reached it by reading in himself 'not this or that particular man; but mankind'.

Perhaps Oakeshott conflates under the general heading of 'teaching by example' two features of a situation which do not always go together. There is first of all that of the exhibition of the performance in question by the teacher and there is secondly the imparting of a skill or judgement not just by examples but by on the spot correction of the pupil's efforts towards mastery of it. It is conceivable that a learner could achieve considerable expertise in some skill like golf or shooting without reliance on *either* aspects of such an apprenticeship situation. For this would be a situation where the goal is more or less unambiguous and skill in hitting a target could be achieved by trial and error and constant practice. But in fields like that of the law or politics, where the notion of an overall 'goal' is rather out of place and where what constitutes success in a given case depends upon multiple criteria, it is almost inconceivable that a person could become proficient without one or other aspects of the apprenticeship system being present. For as Aristotle put it 'the decision lies with perception'. There may be ninety-nine ways of going wrong and only one way of going right. If judgements of this sort could be formalised in rules there would be no need to have judges for applying the rules of a legal system. A man could not, in such situations, learn 'judgement' on his own because he could never know what was constitutive of success. In shooting or golf, on the other hand, he might do this

because he would know that success consisted in hitting the bird or
getting the ball into the hole in as few shots as possible. It is only if an
activity like politics is viewed as the pursuit of an overall end such as
power that the do-it-yourself form of learning begins to look appropriate. Hence Oakeshott's strictures on books like Machiavelli's *The
Prince* and on the general conception of politics as the taking of
means to independently premeditated ends.

The upshot of this analysis would be, then, that in so far as an
activity approximates to a skill which could be said to be 'goal-
directed' in a fairly determinate way, there would be a correspondingly open possibility of do-it-yourself methods of learning, given a
preliminary period of initiation into the rudiments of the activity. In
so far, however, as 'success' in an activity is impossible to characterise
without concrete interpretations or implementations of general principles, the possibility of do-it-yourself methods would become correspondingly more remote. But though apprenticeship would be
necessary for the attainment of skill or judgement in such complex
activities it need not take the form of learning from the example of
the master; it might be sufficient for the master to correct the performances of his pupils on the spot. One of the best swimming
coaches in recent times was a man who could not swim.

(iii) Oakeshott also refers on occasions to a third sort of thing, the
'style' of the individual performer. By this he means to draw attention
not just to individual acts of judgement in the second sense but to the
individual intelligence at work in every utterance and performance. It
is necessarily the case that in so far as this can be passed on it must
involve example; for as it is, by definition, individual to the person
concerned, comprising a characteristic manner of thinking and acting, it would have to be shown to be both detected and imparted.

When talking about 'style' Oakeshott seems to conflate together
the possibility of detecting it in another and the possibility of acquiring it from another. But the two do not necessarily go together. There
are many philosophers of discernment who can detect Wittgenstein's
characteristic 'style' of philosophy; but, though their own mastery of
the 'language' might lead them to recognise the importance of many
of his insights, they might well shudder at the 'style' with which they
were delivered, Others, however, might admire the performance as
a whole and might model themselves on it – mannerisms and all. This
brings out that 'style' for Oakeshott is a term of approval which is
associated only with desirable traits. But much of a person's 'style'
may be an unnecessary and perhaps trivial or distracting adornment.
There was a time when one could almost tell where an English philoso-

pher was trained by observing the mannerisms and gestures which had been imparted to him!

Oakeshott, I feel sure, would deplore too much absorption of the 'style' of another. For that would be inconsistent with his insistence that 'making something of ourselves' is an important aspect of education. Presumably he means that it is judgement in the second sense, which is to be acquired from masters of the different languages; their individual style (including its superfluous idiosyncrasies) is to be 'detected' and admired but not slavishly copied.

When Oakeshott speaks about the imparting of judgement his own style of writing intimates somehow that we are confronted with a mystery. Indeed he perhaps chooses the word 'impart' because of its association with recondite matters. He cites no mundane empirical studies of apprenticeship and the transmission of skills; he indulges in no speculation about the psychological processes involved. Theories about roles, imitation or identification are never mentioned. He leads his readers to the uncharted region between the logical and psychological and there he leaves them. Omne ignotum pro magnifico.

There are others, however, for whom a mystery is not something that is to be hinted at and enjoyed, especially when it is alleged to pervade every situation in which a new generation is being initiated into skill, task and judgement. On the contrary it provides a splendid occasion to satisfy all those rationalistic yearnings for clarity and problem-solving that Oakeshott so deeply deplores. Any mundane fellow who is set on exploring this uncharted region will first of all have to map the concepts which criss-cross the region. He will then need a spade to dig into psychological and sociological theories in order to unearth some relevant generalisations about social learning. My guess is that he will not find himself working alone but will find that he is helping to open up a region which will prove to be one of the most fertile for the growth of educational theory during the next decade. More understanding of these apprenticeship situations may dispel the mystery a bit, but not the wonder. It may even help us to teach a bit better.

4 MORAL EDUCATION

Oakeshott's account of moral education depends largely on the distinction which he makes between the 'habit of affection and behaviour' of the person brought up in a settled tradition and the 'reflective morality' of the person brought up to pursue ideals and to implement principles. It depends, too, on the rather idiosyncratic understanding which he has of 'principles' and of the lack of connection between them and behaviour. On the one hand he argues[20] that there is (or perhaps was) a form of moral life which consists in a 'habit of affection and behaviour'. People do not reflect upon alternative courses of action and make choices determined by principles or ideals; they simply follow unreflectively the tradition in which they have been brought up. They acquire this in the way in which they learn to speak their mother tongue, by living with others who practice this morality. No doubt what they learn can be formulated in rules; but there is no need for it to be. People can learn to speak grammatically without their having also to be able to formulate rules of grammar. This sort of education, therefore, gives people the power to act appropriately without hesitation in a whole range of situations; but it does not give them the ability to explain or defend their actions as emanations of moral principles. A man has acquired what this type of education can teach him when his moral dispositions are inseparably connected with his *amour-propre*. This form of behaviour, though traditional, is not fixed; for it evolves in the way in which a living language evolves.

On the other hand there is reflective morality, which is determined not by a habit of behaviour but by the reflective application of a moral criterion. It takes the form either of the self-conscious pursuit of moral ideals or of the reflective observance of moral rules. A man must first formulate his rule of life or his ideal in words; he must also have the ability to defend these formulated aspirations against criticism. And, thirdly, he must learn to apply them in current situations in life in problem-solving behaviour. Moral education, therefore, must consist first of all in the detection and appreciation of ideals and principles. Secondly, there must be training in the art of their intellectual management and, thirdly, training in the art of their application to concrete circumstances. The danger of this form of morality is that uncertainty in action is more or less proportionate to certainty in thinking about these ideals; moral reflection may undermine moral habit. It will make people miserable because of its demand for perfection and will suffer from inelasticity and imperviousness to change.

Oakeshott realises, of course, that these two sorts of morality are really 'ideal types'. In most actual moralities there is a blend of the two. His concern is to attack a way of life in which the latter rather then the former type of morality predominates.

Before discussing the dichotomy it is necessary to clarify Oakeshott's conception of 'principles'. He regards them as 'abstracts' of practice. His frequent use of the word 'ideology' in this context is significant; for Oakeshott regards principles as being somehow spurious in relation to justification and, causally speaking, as by-products of activity. Indeed I think that it is his relativistic conviction that they cannot be justified that leads him to speak of them as 'explaining' conduct in the above passage in which he contrasts 'principles'[21] with rules of correctness implicit in conduct as well as in the grammar of a language. He exemplifies Aristotle's doctrine of the mean in the case of conduct being on a par with the principles of mechanics in the case of riding a bicycle.

There may be something rather special about the status of Aristotle's doctrine of the mean. But, whatever one makes of Aristotle's doctrine, this is really a very odd use of 'principle' in the run of the mill moral case. When speaking of principles Oakeshott always quotes something pretty abstract like 'natural rights' or 'justice', but surely, in the moral sphere, all we mean by a 'principle' is something that provides backing to a rule or which makes reasons relevant. Whether or not fundamental principles such as 'justice' or 'the minimisation of avoidable suffering' can themselves be justified is a very complicated question;[22] but certainly the relationship between rules of conduct and principles is one of justification. In a moral context a principle just *is* a higher-order rule that is appealed to when justification is required for one at a lower order. Thus if someone like Mill claims that divorce is wrong if the married couple have children, because of the probable suffering that it will cause them, then the avoidance of suffering is functioning as a principle. 'Judgement' is, of course, needed in order to apply such a principle; for what counts as suffering in a particular case and whose suffering is to be given most weight? Much of what Oakeshott says about 'judgement' is most pertinent to the application of principles. But it is his bizarre account of them that leads him to say that an appeal to them is a rationalist aberration. Indeed his own account even of 'practical' or 'traditional' knowledge is unintelligible without assuming a background of principles; for without such a background how are any reasons for action relevant? Oakeshott's account of the politician keeping the ship of state on an even keel and dealing with 'incoherences' which arise in a developing tradition presupposes not only that 'coherence' is good (whatever this amounts to in practice!) but also that considerations relating to security and stability are relevant. And if 'salus populi suprema lex' is not a 'principle' I do not know what is.

Oakeshott, too, seems to think that principles are really 'abstracts' from practices, whereas he caricatures rationalists as thinking that they are rules that are formulated as guides to practice. But why should they be either? Some principles, for instance, might be pre-suppositions of a practice. They need not be formulated beforehand by those who indulge in it, neither need they be abstracts from it. The principle, for instance, that truth matters need not be formulated beforehand by people discussing some scientific problem. It need only be appealed to if a participant in the discussion starts intro-ducing irrelevant personal remarks or disregarding some evidence. Neither is it necessarily an 'abstract' of the practice of discussion; for such a discussion would surely be unintelligible unless the partici-pants were already committed to it. For they have to conceive the situation in a certain way in order to make it a practice of this determinate sort. In a similar way the concern for health is a pre-supposition of, not an abstract from, the practice of medicine. There is therefore a sense in which Oakeshott's account of 'practices' is as inadequate as his account of 'principles'.

To probe further into the relationship between principles and practices would take us too far away from Oakeshott's philosophy of education. It must also be remarked that though Oakeshott's ideal types of morality provide two fascinating models that might have had application to classes of people within our society at some distant time in the past, they have little application to adults in modern industrial societies in the West. This is admitted by Oakeshott when he claims that nowadays the two are blended and that his main purpose is to attack a way of life which includes too much of the reflective and too little of the traditional style of behaviour.

From the point of view of moral education, however, both his dichotomy and his emphasis on tradition are instructive, as I have argued elsewhere.[23] Given that we live in a changing society with a fair degree of differentiation at a certain level in moral standards, young people are bound to be forced to reflect from time to time on where they stand. They have, therefore, to develop the elements of what Oakeshott calls a reflective morality, though his account of it, with the bizarre role accorded to principles in it, would have to be modified. But, for a variety of reasons, it is out of the question for young children to acquire such a morality until they pass out of what Piaget calls the 'transcendental stage' of moral judgement. At an early age, therefore, their morality will have to approximate to Oakeshott's 'habit of affection and behaviour'. The crucial task of moral education is to initiate them into this in such a way that they can gradually come to grasp the principles underlying what they have picked up from their parents and teachers, so that they will be able to act with understanding and adapt their practice to moral situations, make sensible choices and perhaps even challenge some practices as no longer defensible. The palace of reason has to be entered by the courtyard of habit. There are too many 'progressive' educators and parents who place too little emphasis on the enormous importance of habit and tradition in moral education. Oakeshott's brilliant sketch of traditional morality is a healthy corrective to such rationalistic excesses.

CONCLUSION

It is a recurrent theme in Oakeshott's writings that a man who is skilled at something such as cooking may not have the additional skill of being able to make explicit what he is about. Oakeshott himself provides a clear case of a person who combines both sorts of gifts. He is a gifted teacher and administrator whose unpretentious concern both for his subject and for his students is immanent in everything that he does. And I have never known a man with such a contempt for conscience discharge his duties so conscientiously. So when he reflects and writes, one feels that it is a genuine reflection of his experience and view of the world. Above all writers on politics and education today he has a style, an idiom of his own, and this is inseparable from his conduct of affairs. There is nothing second-hand or spurious about it or him. One may not agree with him – or, to put it more accurately, one agrees with him so much at first that it is particularly infuriating when he proceeds to what one thinks is the wrong conclusion! But he is there, all of a piece, to remind us perhaps of values that we are in danger of forgetting in the present gimmickry which passes for politics and in the present escalation of education, with its emphasis on quantity rather than quality.

It has not been until recently the fashion for university teachers outside education departments to write much about education. They thought they knew about it, of course; for are they not teachers themselves and have they not been to school? But their reflections about it were about as informed as a farmer's reflections about the weather. Recently, however, since it has been widely recognised that education is both an investment for the community and a means of social ascent for the individual, there have been many academics who have given forth on the subject of the organisation and distribution of education. Oakeshott, however, is one of the few who have consistently reflected and written on what the business is really about. Indeed he confesses that his views about knowledge derive from his reflections on teaching. And when he writes about education it is manifest that he knows what it is about. He knows too that matters of organisation and distribution are of secondary importance compared with the heart of the matter – the living contact between a teacher and his pupils. This article has only attempted to convey the main contours of his thought. There have, too, been criticisms and queries – mainly on points of detail. But what cannot be adequately conveyed in such an abstract of a way of thinking is the overall impression of an extremely civilised man writing with acuteness, elegance and conviction about a matter which is of no small account – the passing on of a civilisation.

REFERENCES

1. See Benn, S. I. and Peters, R. S., *Social Principles and the Democratic State* (London: Allen & Unwin, 1958), pp. 312–18.
2. Oakeshott, M., 'The Study of Politics in a University', in *Rationalism in Politics and other Essays* (London, 1962), p. 304.
3. Ibid., p. 304.
4. Ibid., p. 308.
5. Ibid., p. 305.
6. Ibid., p. 306.
7. Ibid., p. 310.
8. See 'Rationalism in Politics', reprinted in *Rationalism in Politics and other Essays*, pp. 8–11.
9. Also reprinted in *Rationalism in Politics and other Essays*, pp. 119–23.
10. *Rationalism in Politics and other Essays*, p. 11.
11. Published in Peters, R. S. (Ed.), *The Concept of Education* (London: Routledge & Kegan Paul, 1966).
12. Ibid., p. 166.
13. Ibid., p. 168.
14. Ibid., p. 169.
15. Ibid., p. 171.
16. Ibid., p. 174.
17. Ibid., p. 175.
18. Ibid.
19. See Ryle, G., *The Concept of Mind* (London: Hutchinson, 1949), pp. 149–53.
20. See 'The Tower of Babel', in *Rationalism in Politics and other Essays*, pp. 61–70.
21. See above, p. 440.
22. See Peters R. S., *Ethics in Education* (London: Allen & Unwin, 1966), Chs III–VIII.
23. See Peters, R. S., 'The Paradox of Moral Education', in Niblett, W. R. (Ed.), *Moral Education in a Changing Society* (London: Faber, 1963).

Part Four

BIOGRAPHICAL BACKGROUND

R. S. PETERS: A COMMENTARY BY PETER HOBSON

Richard Stanley Peters was born in 1919 and educated at Clifton College, Bristol, a traditional English public school, and at Oxford University which he entered just before the War, in 1938. He studied classics for his Arts degree and became very interested in religious and philosophical questions in which he also read widely while at Oxford.

When the War came he joined the Friends* Ambulance Unit in 1940, was drafted to London during the Blitz and, after a period with the Ambulance Unit, he was sent to do social relief work. This arose largely from the ambulance work because of the problem of how to look after the people in the shelters. He ran a youth centre at Toynbee Hall, Whitechapel, and then started one himself, almost from nothing, at Walthamstow.

In the meantime he had been continuing with his philosophical interests and had enrolled at Birkbeck College, University of London, to work in his spare time for a degree in philosophy. He then moved from social relief work into teaching and took a position as Classics Master at Sidcot School, Somerset, a co-educational boarding school. However, he resigned after a couple of years there to work full-time for his final examinations at the University of London and was successful in gaining a University Studentship and part-time lectureship at Birkbeck College. He later became a lecturer and reader in philosophy there, at the same time being active in adult education.

* The Society of Friends, better known as the Quakers, who organised this Unit, is dedicated to pacifism but has always been very ready to help the victims of war in whatever way it can, as well as being active in other humanitarian endeavours.

Because of his early youth centre work and his teaching experience he had maintained an interest in education, but he moved into philosophy of education in a rather unusual way. He had begun to give a number of broadcast talks on topics such as authority and responsibility, and searching around for another subject to discuss he hit upon that of the aims of education. He was prompted to this by the fact that in youth work he was continually confronted with the question of what were his aims and goals.

Peters was also attracted to philosophy of education because it draws together a number of branches of philosophy as well as psychology, in all of which he was interested. His work at Birkbeck was mainly in philosophical psychology, in particular the logical status of psychological enquiry. He wrote a book on Hobbes, who appealed to Peters because his work was a mixture of psychology, philosophy and politics. He then wrote a book examining the concept of motivation. These mixed interests, he came to find, were best satisfied in the philosophy of education where, as far as he was concerned, everything came together.

Meanwhile his broadcast talks on education and related topics were published in *The Listener* and attracted the attention of Israel Scheffler, Professor of Education and Philosophy at the Graduate School of Education of Harvard University. He invited Peters over to Harvard as Visiting Professor in 1961. Then in 1962 the Chair of Philosophy of Education at the University of London Institute of Education became vacant and Peters's application for the position was successful. This is his present position and in 1971 he became Dean of the Faculty of Education at the University of London. He is also Chairman of the Philosophy of Education Society of Great Britain and was elected to the American National Academy of Education in 1966.

Peters has travelled widely, holding various visiting positions and guest lectureships in the U.S.A., Canada, Australia and New Zealand. In so doing he has assisted the development of the discipline of philosophy of education in each of the countries visited.

Since his appointment, Peters has developed at the University of London Institute of Education the largest and probably the most influential department in philosophy of education in the world. It offers courses in the subject from Diploma right through to Doctoral level and attracts students from all parts of the English-speaking world.

In philosophical circles in Great Britain Peters is credited more or less with having established a new and respectable branch of philosophy. The Royal Institute of Philosophy organised a conference on Philosophy of Education at Exeter in September 1973, something which would have been virtually unthinkable only ten years ago when philosophy of education was still held in low repute as an academic discipline by many philosophers. Philosophers are now at last prepared to treat philosophy of education as an important and significant aspect of philosophical enquiry. At the same time the teaching profession is on the whole now ready to regard philosophy of education as an indispensable part of educational theory. Both of these achievements for the discipline have been due in large part to the work of Peters, especially since taking up the Chair of Philosophy of Education at the University of London Institute of Education in 1962.

His main hobbies are golf and gardening, which he pursues with the same fanaticism as he pursues philosophy.

22

A BOY'S VIEW OF GEORGE ORWELL

Most of you must have wondered what sort of a man it was who created those morbid and savage satires – *Animal Farm* and *1984*. Books have been written by Orwell's friends sketching his progressive disillusionment with man as a political animal and his despair for the future of human decency. I have no intention of adding to these comments on Orwell's later years. I wish purely to present to you a picture of George Orwell at the beginning of his literary career as he appeared to a boy of ten. For I knew him when he was writing his first book – *Down and Out in London and Paris*. I leave you to draw your own conclusions about the man who conjured up Big Brother, the Thought Police, and rats released at human faces.

It was in the late 1920s and we were living in Southwold on the East Coast. My father was in India and I, together with my two brothers, were proving rather a handful for my mother during our long school holidays. She therefore arranged with an Anglo-Indian friend of hers, a Mrs Blair, that her son Eric should act as holiday tutor to us. We gathered that Eric Blair, who later wrote under the name of George Orwell, was rather a strange fellow but very nice. He was very kind to his mother and helped her with the washing up; but he had given up a very good job with the Burmese Police and had chosen to do a year's trip as a tramp without any subsidy from home. He had done all sorts of dreadful things like sleeping in doss houses and acting as a bottle washer in a Paris hotel. But he had stuck it out for the full year and now he was writing a book all about it. You can imagine that we felt a bit apprehensive when the day arrived for him to take us out for our first walk.

I vividly remember the first impression of him as he came up the garden path; a tall spindly young man with a great mop of hair waving on top of a huge head, swinging along with loose, effortless strides and a knobbly stick made of some queer Scandinavian wood. He captivated us completely within five minutes. He had a slow disarming sort of smile which made us feel that he was interested in us yet amused by us in a detached impersonal sort of way. He would discuss anything with interest, yet objectively and without prejudice. We knew nothing of politics and cared less. I have only the vague impression that he thought most politicians wicked people and that making money entered into it rather a lot. But his remarks on these subjects were without rancour. He commented on the actions of politicians in the same sort of way as he commented on the behaviour of stoats, or the habits of the heron.

He was a mine of information on birds, animals and the heroes of boys' magazines. Yet he never made us *feel* that he knew our world better than we knew it ourselves. He loved H. G. Wells's scientific stories – especially the one about the school-master who got into the fourth dimension and was thus able to observe that the boys in the back row were cribbing. And it was as if he entered unobtrusively, like Wells's schoolmaster, into our world and illuminated it in a dry, discursive sort of way without in any way disturbing it. He never condescended; he never preached; he never intruded. I remember him saying that he would have sided with the Cavaliers rather than with the Roundheads because the Roundheads were such depressing people. And I can now understand what he meant. For temperamentally he was a Cavalier, lacking the fervour and fanaticism of the Puritan. Like most people who have thought out clearly where they stand, he did not make a fuss about it. He was never noisy and lacked the dogmatism of the insecure. I can only remember him getting indignant on one occasion when he told us how he thrashed a boy whom he caught blowing up a frog with a bicycle pump.

His attitude to animals and birds was rather like his attitude to children. He was at home with them. He seemed to know everything about them and found them amusing and interesting. Perhaps he thought of them like children as uncorrupted by the pursuit of power and riches, living for the moment and caring little for organised exploitation of each other. He infused interest and adventure into everything we did with him just because of his own interest in it. Walking can be just a means of getting from A to B; but with him it was like a voyage with Jules Verne beneath the ocean. He had, of course, nothing of the hearty technique of the adolescent scoutmaster or the burning mission of the enthusiast. Neither had he the attitude of the guide on a conducted tour. A walk was a mixture of energy, adventure and matter of fact. The world, we felt, was just like this. And it would have been absurd not to notice all there was to see. He even assured us, in a matter of fact sort of way, that he had seen a ghost in broad daylight in Walberswick churchyard. He saw a figure of a man in brown come up the path and thought nothing of it until it disappeared behind a derelict pillar and failed to come out on the other side. The way he spoke of this event made it as much part of the natural order as the movements of birds and boats.

These walks had often a definite purpose. Perhaps we would walk along to a nearby broad to attempt to get near a swan's nest or to find plovers' nests on the hillside that overlooked it. On another day we would walk inland to Blighburgh to look at the heronry there. Some days we went fishing in the mill-pool at Walberswick and managed to catch roach or rudd with bent pins and bread pellets. I can still remember the smell of wild peppermint or spearmint which formed a background to his exposition on the properties of marsh-gas. He also told us how he used to kill eels by firing at them with a 12-bore shot gun. But he never demonstrated this method to us. He initiated us into the delights of catching whitebait from the cross-beams of the old pier at Southwold and claimed that the beams were a very good place to have a sleep on a sunny day. We helped him, too, to dig a couple of tumuli in the search of prehistoric remains, though I think that all we found was a soldier's button. His attitude to Nature was symbolised in the prodding of his stick. There was nothing of the romantic about him. If he had met Wordsworth's leech-gatherer he would have been interested in the leeches and in how the old boy made a living.

But of all the activities which we indulged in with him, the one that stands out in my memory most is the making of bombs. We used to call him by the somewhat irreverent title of Blarry Boy and we coined a kind of war-cry which was later to make my mother and grand-mother tremble – both literally and metaphorically. 'Blarry Boy for Bolshie Bombs' would echo through the house and my poor mother would look anxiously out of the window to see which part of the garden was going to disappear next. My grandmother, I remember, nearly had a stroke when a grassy mound blew up just by the sitting-room window. George Orwell taught us a very special way of making gun-powder and he had a patent firing mechanism which involved tipping a test-tube of sulphuric acid from a distance by means of cotton on to a fuse composed, as far as I can remember, of chlorate of potash and sugar. The same energy and detached interest went to making and firing a bomb as to looking for a redshank's nest. We had to get every detail just right; we must not hurry; we must get into a really safe place before we pulled on the cotton. Nature was intriguing but predictable; we had to learn the way she worked or we would suffer.

We had another game in which he would also join with quiet nonchalance. We would stalk each other in the sand-dunes armed with small sand-bags. His calm precision was formidable. This was our world and it also seemed to be his. He was merely the boy who played the game with his head.

I suppose the nerve and quiet confidence with which he played this and other games was the quality in him which we admired most. Courage can be a dashing demonstrative business. With him it had a quality of coolness and resourcefulness which I have never since encountered. I have no doubt that it was with this calm courage that he later went to fight for the Republicans in the Spanish Civil War. The picture I shall always carry of him is of a tall lovable man striding nonchalantly across a girder about 18 inches wide on which the old disused railway bridge at Walberswick was suspended. I must confess that I was pretty frightened just jumping from sleeper to sleeper with the river swirling through the mudbanks about 30 feet below. But there was he walking as calmly as you like up to the apex of this girder miles above our heads. He told us that he had often wheeled a bicycle across. And I am sure that he had; for it was not in his nature to exaggerate or to strive to create an impression.

And was not this the core of George Orwell – a lonely, courageous figure passing with detached honesty and without rancour across the mudbanks of corruption? The tide of tyranny and double-think was rising. Human decency must have seemed to him to be in decay like the disused bridge. Children and animals, perhaps, were as yet uncorrupted. But what could they do against the organised idiocy of man? Perhaps Orwell was a man of extreme sensitivity like Rousseau who found the conventions of the city too cramping and the stupidity and power seeking of bureaucracy intolerable. Perhaps he was really *at home* only with animals and children. I cannot say, for he passed out of our life for ever. All I can say is that to us he appeared as a thoroughly lovable and exciting companion. The world, it is said, is never ready to receive its saints. Perhaps children alone can readily recognise them for what they are.

23

I WAS TWENTY THEN

In 1940 I was training with the Friends Ambulance Unit on the out-skirts of London. I remember that fantastic September day when, out for a walk in Epping Forest, the skies were filled with dog-fights and as I turned towards London a huge red glow met my eyes like a gigantic sun setting behind the forest – it was London burning. I had many questions in my head during that walk: how had we got into this plight? What did I think I should do about it? What had the future in store for people of my age? Some of these questions were going to be answered in the next ten years, though not all.

I had had two years at Oxford before starting on my National Service and was only just beginning to get interested in social and political problems. This may sound extraordinary for someone who was up at Oxford then but it was due mainly to my public school and home background. My father was in the Indian Police and politics were not discussed at home, while at school they were almost taboo. All I can remember at school is a man who gave us a lecture on what a good chap Mussolini was and another who ended an evening's entertainment by making us sing:

> 'We're all anti-Red and we're proud of it,
> We're Britons so we sing aloud of it,
> If the red, white and blue
> Isn't good enough for you,
> And you don't like the Empire – get out of it.'

At school I was an atheist and a Shavian and delighted in shocking the masters, but in my last year I became interested in St John's

Gospel and by the time I came to Oxford I was deeply preoccupied with religion; but the kind of attitude I worked out did not seem to fit any church. It was not till I came into contact with the Quakers that I found where I belonged.

All this internal struggle meant that I had not taken much account of outside affairs. I thought one had to work out one's personal attitude and standards and beliefs more or less in isolation. When I peered out from my cell of self-sufficiency I saw a struggle between sanctimonious old fools representing business interests and a lunatic who was financed by arms manufacturers. The moral defence of the war seemed to me a complete sham – otherwise we would have fought in China, Spain, Abyssinia and Czechoslovakia. I remember how people of my age seethed with fury when one of our elder statesmen came down to Oxford and told us that the ideals of British youth were an answer to the Hitler Youth Movement. I held what could be called a 'conspiracy' view of our plight. I thought that everything that happened was simply 'fixed' by cliques of unscrupulous or stupid individuals. Even later on during a heavy air-raid when I was in charge of a rest centre I remember looking above the heads of the crowd of frightened, forlorn-looking people – one, I remember, was just about to have a baby – and I saw a text on the wall: 'One command I give unto you, that you love one another', and thinking that our plight had come simply because everyone had neglected this advice.

Like most Quakers I believed that when the war came I should not serve in the armed forces but must do everything I could to relieve suffering, and do something constructive when everything was being destroyed. I joined the FAU and was sent to train and to wait for a convoy abroad. We waited and waited, kicking our heels in a quiet country hospital. I was desperately impatient to get into action; in fact several of us agitated so turbulently that we got ourselves moved and by the end of 1940 I found myself in the East End with the blitz in full swing. On my first night I was evacuating a hospital with an unexploded landmine in the middle of it.

For the next two years I was mixed up in all sorts of jobs – relief centres, shelters, advice bureaux, settlements and so on in the East End. I had to face problems far beyond my experience and my capacity. People – bombed out, bereaved, lost, cold and hungry – impinged on me in a way they never had before with problems too large and complicated and terrible to comprehend properly – I remember a night on duty in a mortuary during an air raid. And now my traditions and the attitude I had worked out for myself came into conflict. I had been brought up in a tradition of middle-class security which verged almost on snobbery. The habits and ideas I had soaked in at school put me in a particular class and put a barrier between me and other people. I desperately wanted to break through this barrier – it seemed to me wrong and artificial. I did not want to feel separation between myself and the people with whom I was working. I knew intellectually as a Christian that no such barrier existed. Yet I could not break through it; I did not know how to. Then I had a great bit of luck. I wanted a more permanent job where I could get a chance to build something up out of the mess all around, and to do it without interference and red tape. I wanted to burrow down and build up, make something. By luck I was sent to start a youth centre in the East End. Here I had to live continuously in a community and become a complete part of the lives of the people there. It was of course just what I wanted as a job but I had no idea what it would do for me.

I *think* I went there with the vague idea that my job was to do something *for* these people. I saw them, I suppose, as material – like a builder sees his bricks. But when I got to work my whole view changed. It was not a case of my being a builder and their being the bricks – they *and* I were part of the design which we were shaping together – and which was shaping us as we worked. In doing the work we shared everything – our experiences, our thought, our talk, even our razors – we *mucked in together*, the differences between us did not matter any more. And so I found the barrier between me and the others disappeared and with it the conflict in my mind. I had come to terms with people through work and to terms with my work through people. My feelings and my beliefs came together and the conflict which had started at Oxford when I was twenty worked itself out.

After the war I had to earn my living for the first time. I became a schoolmaster and then a lecturer in philosophy. I revelled in schoolmastering, it was an idyllic breathing space of construction and co-operation – a youth centre in ideal surroundings. But I missed the variety in experience and background that I got before. As a lecturer I got this but I missed the sense of community. After what I learned in the war I could not live apart. I kept feeling that I ought to take off my coat more than I could as a university lecturer with domestic responsibilities. And it was not enough just to take it off for gardening, washing-up and bathing babies.

The other thing that preoccupied me was having to work out what I really thought about the world at large. I had not given much thought to this in the war – except I had a vaguely Utopian idea that everything would be put right if we put the right people in. I remember being told by a much older and wiser man, during a spell of leave, that we were passing through a revolution and that the old order was disappearing. I felt a slight chill but I had no idea what he was talking about in social and institutional terms. Now when I came to work it out I had to abandon the easy answer I had at twenty – that our plight was due to a conspiracy of gangsters. In fact it makes me pretty impatient today when I hear people talking about the 'men in the Kremlin' and 'American pressure groups'. If we are talking about enemies it is not just individuals we are up against. I personally cannot stomach the ethics of money-grabbing with its slogans like 'Business is business' and its tendency to treat houses as investments instead of homes, and dogs as money-making machines instead of members of the family. I cannot bear canned culture which is another product of industrialism. But what I see now is that it is not just individuals who are responsible for the things I abhor – it is certain traditions and certain institutions of our system. It is very possible, I think, that the barriers I had to contend with when I was twenty were, to a large extent, the result of the changes which started when the close-knit community of Medieval England began to break up 400 years ago.

Ten years ago I couldn't have cared less about this kind of analysis. For one thing it took all my time and thought to deal with the conflict between my desire to live in the spirit of the Gospels and my traditional public school embarrassment about doing anything so eccentric. Besides, as I said, I thought one's only duty was to work out one's problems of perfectionism in isolation. The other day I bought a book on the history of Parliament to read in the train. I cannot imagine a book that would have interested me less in 1940. But now I feel intensely that it is necessary nowadays for those who believe in democracy not only to keep alive the moral principles and individual freedoms which might get lost in the maze of administrative detail and large-scale planning, but also to understand what changes are going on so that we can guide and if necessary counteract them. I do not think a slogan like 'Set the people free' is of any earthly use. The real question is in what respect 'free', and 'free' to do what?

As I came to work out this point of view I found I was advocating the sort of social policy we had tried to work out in that youth centre – to think for ourselves, make things for ourselves and share the responsibility. I found this all fitted in with my anxiety to get back into a community. I was living in a suburb then and travelling up every day to my university work, and all the time I was feeling cut off and getting back that 1940 feeling of guilt, because I could not get to the scene of action. I stuck it out for two years and then moved to a small country town and there I think I have found what I want. I want to live in a place which I can help to build. I want to know the people who live round me. And as I am coming to know them I am getting back the feeling I had in 1942 that there is something I can do which puts me into the right and satisfying relationship with them. In a small country town there is so much to do together – so much to *muck in* with. And I don't mean simply listening to travel talks in the drill hall and organising country dancing. If we are going to have central planning – and I believe we must – it seems to me we have got to have *local* initiative and make it really matter in our community – and this means a lot more than just grousing about the rates.

The religious problem of the individual soul will always be important to me: but I realise now that souls do not live in isolation and the behaviour of people and what they ought to be can only be understood and judged in a living world of people, institutions, traditions and economic forces. And now that I see this I know that a direct physical threat to our institutions would create an acute personal problem for me. What would I do *now* about another 1940 situation? I am not sure in the present situation, but I hope by lecturing in social philosophy I am playing some small part in shaping our own kind of social democracy. While by living in a community I am working out my own problem of participating – and also expiating my feeling of guilt for having an academic profession – a queer scar left on my conscience by 1940. Will this compromise satisfy me? I don't know. Since 1940 I have never planned my personal life very far ahead.

SUBJECT INDEX

Abnormality 104
Accommodation 121, 132, 138, 140, 142–4, 154, 330, 424
Achievement-motivation 91–2, 93, 94, 95, 99
Action 88–94, 104, 108, 110–12, 125–8, 146, 177–82, 189–90, 275–8, 325, 427
and movements 70, 74–5, 205–6
Activities 268, 270, 273, 276, 289, 290, 295–7, 331, 399, 419, 420, 426, 429
Aesthetics 139–40, 422, 426
Aggression 83, 86
Aims 393–9
Ambivalence 83
Anger 108, 171, 175, 176–7, 183, 191, 317, 394–5, 402
Animal spirits 53–4
Anthropology 34, 208, 255
Anthroponomy 32–3, 64
Apprenticeship 257, 272, 439, 446–9
Appropriateness 159, 160–1, 184, 205
Approval 309, 311, 312, 319, 320, 351, 372, 374, 379–83, 410, 429, 430
Arbitrariness 154, 155, 169, 170, 290–1, 329–30, 346, 356, 370, 424
Assimilation 121, 132, 138, 140, 142–4, 154, 330, 343, 366, 424
Association 33, 47, 55, 57, 58, 62–3, 72, 74, 119, 166, 204, 215, 324, 381, 395, 407, 409
Attention 310, 369, 380

Attitudes 95–6, 160–1, 245, 259–60, 310, 354, 402, 413, 422
Attraction 411
Authenticity 282, 294–5, 297, 298, 341, 342, 350–1, 372–4, 382–3, 407, 410–11, 416–18, 428–9
Authoritarianism 236, 241, 282, 301, 302, 352, 375, 383
Authority 122, 123, 134, 153, 168, 185–6, 213, 240, 256, 267, 302, 336, 338, 348, 349, 350, 353–4, 356, 363, 372, 376, 383, 409, 410, 427, 458
Autonomy 131–2, 136–8, 141, 142, 211, 216, 232, 233, 242, 249, 252, 272, 282, 292, 300, 308, 331, 340–2, 347–54, 356, 357, 371–5, 382–3, 410–11, 430
Awe 425–6

Behaviour 74–5, 90, 391–2, 421, 450
Behaviourism 31–6, 46–77, 103, 107–8, 176, 191, 195–9, 216, 219, 408
Belief 93, 95, 116, 121, 122–3, 125, 126, 129, 159–60, 168, 184–6, 340, 345, 346, 349, 363, 421–2, 424–5, 429
ethics of 127, 145–7
Blame 246, 316, 320, 322, 341, 366, 372, 379
Brain-washing 346–7, 356

469

INDEX OF PROPER NAMES

478 INDEX OF PROPER NAMES